My Life as a Mankiewicz

MY LIFE AS A MANKIEWICZ

An Insider's Journey through Hollywood

Tom Mankiewicz

and

Robert Crane

UNIVERSITY PRESS OF KENTUCKY

The University Press of Kentucky

Scholarly publisher for the Commonwealth,
serving Bellarmine University, Berea College, Centre College of Kentucky,
Eastern Kentucky University, The Filson Historical Society, Georgetown
College, Kentucky Historical Society, Kentucky State University, Morehead
State University, Murray State University, Northern Kentucky University,
Transylvania University, University of Kentucky, University of Louisville,
and Western Kentucky University.

Editorial and Sales Offices: The University Press of Kentucky
663 South Limestone Street, Lexington, Kentucky 40508-4008
www.kentuckypress.com

16 15 14 13 12   5 4 3 2 1

Library of Congress Cataloging-in-Publication Data

Mankiewicz, Tom.
  My life as a Mankiewicz : an insider's journey through Hollywood / Tom
Mankiewicz and Robert Crane.
      p. cm. — (Screen classics)
  Includes bibliographical references and index.
  ISBN 978-0-8131-3605-9 (hardcover : alk. paper) —
  ISBN 978-0-8131-3616-5 (pdf) — ISBN 978-0-8131-4057-5 (epub)
  1. Mankiewicz, Tom. 2. Motion picture producers and directors—United
States—Biography. 3. Screenwriters—United States—Biography.
4. Television producers and directors—United States—Biography.
I. Crane, Robert David. II. Title.
  PN1998.3.M3206A3 2012
  791.4302'33092—dc23
  [B]   2012008587

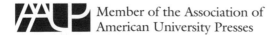 Member of the Association of
American University Presses

To Jerry Moss,
Ann Stevens,
Ron Mardigian,
and the Mankiewicz family

Contents

Preface   ix

Prologue: This Will Never Happen to You   1

1. The Family   3

2. The 1940s: Growing Up   13

3. The 1950s: Developing a Character   25

4. The 1960s: Hollywood Off-Ramp   49

5. The 1960s Gallery   101

6. The 1970s: Arrival   133

7. The 1970s Gallery   237

8. The 1980s: Calling Dr. Mankiewicz   249

9. The 1980s Gallery   301

10. The 1990s: What a Fucking Business   313

11. The Tag: Out of Film   327

Acknowledgments   341

Filmography   343

Index   349

Illustrations follow page 180

Preface

During spring 1990 I was working for actor John Candy and his company, Frostbacks Productions, in a variety of positions, including producer, publicist, and assistant. The few of us there wore multiple hats. I stuck by John's side as he filmed *Delirious,* directed by Tom Mankiewicz, in New York, Santa Barbara, and Universal City. Although John came from a working-class background in Toronto and Tom was part of the iconic Hollywood family, they hit it off immediately. Tom made references to Yale, John made references to *SCTV.* John danced with Emma Samms and romanced Mariel Hemingway, while Tom was hitting his stride directing his second feature (after the hit *Dragnet*). Doug Claybourne (*Apocalypse Now*) produced, Tom's long-time assistant Annie Stevens associate produced, and Fred Freeman and Lawrence Cohen wrote a funny script. Raymond Burr and Dylan Baker went against type and delivered comic lines, while Charlie Rocket and David Rasche were hysterical. Tom's *Hart to Hart* cohort Robert Wagner worked two days and thoroughly impressed John. The shoot turned out to be a three-month love-in.

But the best part of the ten-week experience was the end of each shooting day. John and his posse would visit Tom's trailer, or Tom and any number of cast members, producers, and crew would drop in on John's dressing room. A rum and Coke was poured for John, a Jack Daniel's for Tom. Cigarettes would be lit. The rest of us hovered and listened while the stories poured out of Tom. Brando, Sinatra, Bogart, Liz Taylor, Kubrick, Ava Gardner, Lancaster, Liza, Scorsese, Sophia, Sean Connery; 007, Superman, Detective Joe Friday; Cinecittà, Jamaica, London; the fifties, sixties, seventies; Papa Joe, Uncle Herman, Zanuck, Cohn; Nancy Sinatra, Herb Alpert, Paul McCartney. Laughs, tears, jaws dropping, heads shaking.

Damn. Tom had been everywhere and had worked with, played with, or slept with everyone in Hollywood (just females on the sleepovers). John was mesmerized. He and all of us were transported to another time, another place, when Hollywood was the entertainment capital of the world and actors, actresses, and filmmakers were the best ambassadors the United

States could offer. Before we knew it, the clock would strike midnight and in six hours the whole thing would start over again.

The distributor of *Delirious,* MGM, was in the tank financially, and the picture got a tepid release. But I made note of Tom's stories. The man was a walking Hollywood encyclopedia.

The next time I saw Tom was in 1993 when he visited John's farm north of Toronto. Tom was directing *Taking the Heat,* a low-budget Showtime film. He was miserable, though he loved his cast, of course. John made Tom laugh. It was worth the drive.

In 1994, after John Candy's death at age forty-three, I interviewed Tom at his Hollywood Hills home for an A&E Biography on John. Tom was a wonderful interviewee—funny and insightful, providing stories, quips, and observations from someone who watches and studies people. A writer-director.

During 2005–2006, while I was working on a book with actor Bruce Dern, a wonderful storyteller in his own right, I kept mentioning to my wife, Leslie, that I was going to call Tom to see what he was up to.

I didn't call Tom until 2009. I was asked to appear on yet another John Candy Biography, but I had a horrible cold and declined. I suggested Tom to the producers. He delivered another powerful anecdotal piece on his buddy. Tom's quotes appear throughout the hour, and he elevates the show above the usual surface-skimming fare.

I met with Tom and Ron Mardigian, his former agent at William Morris, at Tom's "office," table number forty, the Palm West Hollywood. We had a laugh-filled lunch full of reminiscence. Tom mentioned he had started a book years earlier with his assistant/associate producer/cohort/shrink Annie Stevens but they hadn't got beyond seventy-five pages. Maybe now was the time to share the stories with the world at large.

Tom and I started meeting four days a week at his home with the 180-degree view of downtown L.A.–Century City–Pacific Ocean. His fifth day was spent teaching film at Chapman University in Orange. At least a couple days a week ended with the meeting moving to the Palm, where Tom had his usual table among regulars such as Richard Zanuck, whose father, Darryl, ran Fox when Tom's father, Joe, directed *Cleopatra.* Full circle, indeed. The sessions were punctuated with great fare complemented by white wine for Tom and Tanqueray and tonics for me. They went on for months. They could have gone on for years.

In spring 2010 Tom suffered a physical setback. He was dropping weight, while the timbre of his voice changed and the laughs were not as constant. Pancreatic cancer. Tom assured all that everything was fine, he would get stronger, the book would continue. Except for a stay at Cedars-Sinai in Los Angeles, the writing did continue, as did his teaching.

During mid-2010, though he didn't appear to be gaining weight, Tom's voice and energy returned as before. Leslie and I attended an L.A. Zoo benefit where Tom was an emcee, and we met his best friend, Jerry Moss. Except for the pounds, it seemed Tom would kick this and return to his former self. One Tuesday in July 2010 we had a meeting at the Palm. Tom was in great form—stories abounded, laughs were had, drinks were poured. I hoped this man would live forever.

Four days later, my wife received a call from Suzy Friendly, who knew Jerry Moss and worked for his former wife, Sandra. "Tom died," announced Suzy. Leslie told me.

"Tom Munn?" I asked, referring to another friend.

"No. Tom Mankiewicz," said Leslie. I couldn't believe it. Tom was back. Stronger, more insightful, funnier than ever. His family and friends were robbed.

The Palm shut down his booth at lunch for a solid month. When I go in occasionally, I can still hear his unique voice, phrasing, terminology, reference points rise above the lunch crowd.

Robert Crane

Prologue
This Will Never Happen to You

It's 1964. I'm twenty-two years old, working on a film as an assistant-to-everyone, and am lucky enough to have been taken under the wing of the volcanically talented Gene Kelly, with whom I play tennis several times a week. Gene has invited me to dinner at his home. Among the guests is the brilliant actor Oskar Werner, who is shooting *Ship of Fools* at the time. Werner also turns out to be rather unpleasant when he's been drinking heavily. One of the others at the table finishes a story, looks at Werner, and says, "You Germans ought to understand that . . ."

"I'm not German, I'm Austrian!" snaps Werner.

There is a silence. Being a young suck-up and anxious to please, I observe: "You have to understand that calling an Austrian a German is rather like calling an Irishman an Englishman. They don't appreciate it."

"You're right!" says Werner. "How do you know that?"

"My mother was Austrian. As a matter of fact, she was an actress."

"Really? What was her name?"

"Rosa Stradner."

Werner's eyes roll back in his head, trying to find the memory: "The Josefstadt Theater, Vienna, mid-thirties?"

"Yes, she was at the Josefstadt Theater in the thirties."

He leans forward with profound sincerity: "When I first masturbated, it was to a picture of your mother."

Stunned silence at the table, punctuated by dropped silverware. Realizing he must have meant it as a compliment, I say, "Thank you."

I

The Family

The Mankiewicz family was and is a complex network of literate, competitive achievers. The majority write or have written for a living. While capable of real affection, most of us rarely show it. Rather, we caress with one-liners (usually acerbic and at someone else's expense) or shrewd (we are totally convinced) observations on film, literature, politics, or the state of the world in general.

Pop

My paternal grandfather died before I had a chance to know him. "Pop," as he was referred to by the family, was Professor Frank Mankiewicz, a German Jew who immigrated through Ellis Island with his wife, Johanna, at the turn of the twentieth century. They settled briefly in Wilkes-Barre, Pennsylvania, where my father, Joe, and his older brother, Herman, were born, then moved to New York City, where Pop taught languages at Stuyvesant High School before becoming a distinguished professor at Columbia University. Later on, I actually met two of his former students: Sheldon Leonard, an actor who for years played small-time hoods, and who wound up the successful and wealthy television producer of *The Danny Thomas Show* and *The Andy Griffith Show;* and the versatile actor Ross Martin, best known for his costarring role in *The Wild, Wild West* with Robert Conrad. They both had warm memories of Pop.

There was a darker side to Pop, though, perhaps unintentional, but crucial to the sometimes crippling insecurities in his children and some of their children—the pursuit of excellence, taken to an obsession. The original parent who, when presented by his son with an exam on which he'd scored a 96, wanted to know what happened to the other 4 percent. Both Dad and Herman were, in effect, child prodigies. Both graduated from Columbia while still in their teens. Herman had a dazzling pre-Hollywood career:

sportswriter, drama critic for the *New York World*, playwright, one of the legendary wits of the Algonquin Round Table with the likes of Robert Benchley and Dorothy Parker. His screenwriting career spanned a wide river from the Marx Brothers to the cinematically immortal *Citizen Kane*. More on Herman later. He died in his fifties, an alcoholic, compulsive gambler, unemployable and deeply in debt. To this day I'm convinced that as the eldest son, he finally cracked under Pop's impossible expectations of excellence and achievement.

At first, Dad was able to fly under that radar without missing a beat. Hell, he was nominated for an Oscar at twenty-one, writing the story for a movie called *Skippy* starring child actor Jackie Cooper. More than forty-five years later I was providing dialogue for Jackie while rewriting *Superman*, in which he played Perry White, editor of the *Daily Planet*. As Jackie said at the time, "I guess this is what they mean by 'coming full circle.'"

Pop's obsession with excellence, seemingly no less than Ahab's with Moby Dick, ran deeply through the family. I wouldn't presume to know the full effect it had on Herman's children, Don, Frank, and Josie, and their children. I do know what I believe it did to my brother Chris, and to me. I grew up in a family where to be "a Mankiewicz" really meant that you had to *be* somebody.

There was a portrait of Pop that sat on the wall directly over my father's leather chair in his study where he wrote his screenplays. It remained in that exact place through four different studies in four different homes. Pop looked to be a stern, implacable person, neither a trace of twinkle in the eye nor a tiny curve of humor at the mouth. His eyes stared straight out, never leaving you. After Dad's funeral, back at the house, various members of the family assembled in the study. Dad's then wife of some thirty years, Rosemary, asked if anyone wanted the painting. Silence. No one did. Don was the only immediate family member who wasn't able to attend the funeral. It was conveniently decided that he should have it. The last I heard, he gave it to one of his sister Josie's sons, who now has it leaning against a wall in a Santa Monica apartment. Requiescat in pace, Pop.

Johanna Mankiewicz

Pop's wife. My grandmother, the mother of Herman, Joe, and their sister, Erna. I never heard her mentioned once in any way in any story ever told by any member of the family. There was no animosity involved—she was simply a nonperson. Until I was ten or twelve, if you'd threatened to kill me unless I gave you my grandmother's first name, I'd have had to have said, "Shoot."

Dad

One of the most brilliant, complex, intensely literate, and conflicted human beings ever to inhabit the planet. Someone who began life as the kid brother and wound up the Don Corleone of his family. Every security and insecurity of his personality can be found in the characters of his best screenplays, as can many of the emotions he was somehow unable to express freely in real life.

He was both the protagonist and the victim of a long, punishing marriage to a beautiful, warm, but deeply troubled woman, Rosa Stradner, an Austrian actress. She was his second wife, and mother to me and my older brother Chris. Dad's first marriage, which lasted only a matter of months, was to a woman I would later know as Elizabeth Reynal, a Philadelphia socialite, wife of the noted publisher Eugene Reynal. She had a son by Dad, Eric, who became a successful investment banker and lives in the United Kingdom, and with whom I have a very cordial relationship.

Several years after Mother committed suicide, Dad married Rosemary Matthews, an Englishwoman who first went to work for him in Rome in the early fifties while he was directing *The Barefoot Contessa*. That's when I first met her, at age ten or eleven. They remained close friends and occasional coworkers (and almost certainly more) through the decade before Mother died, and had a daughter, Alexandra. I'm convinced that Rosemary's love and devotion to Dad added a decade or more to his life. Much more about Dad later. All about Dad.

Mother

The single most important influence in my life, although certainly not in the way she intended. She had a mental condition, a form of schizophrenia usually triggered by alcohol, and her health degenerated over the years until her untimely death in 1958. Beautiful and intelligent, a talented actress, she was haunted by a disease that made her absolutely terrifying at times, especially to a child.

She and my Austrian grandmother, whom we affectionately called "Gross" (short for *Grossmutter*), fled Austria and the Nazis in the mid-thirties. My grandfather and an uncle, Fritz, stayed behind to fight for their country. No one ever found out what happened to the old man. Fritz became an SS officer and was executed against a wall in Aachen, Germany, by Allied troops. I never knew I had an Uncle Fritz until I was about ten. Dad didn't think it was a particularly good idea to have a precocious little motormouth running around Los Angeles in the forties talking about his uncle the SS officer.

Mother was immediately signed to a contract by MGM. She performed in only two films: *The Last Gangster,* with Jimmy Stewart and Edward G. Robinson, and more famously, *The Keys of the Kingdom,* with Gregory Peck, the film that launched his stardom. He played a priest who arrives in China as a young man and stays on for the rest of his life. Mother played a nun who is his constant companion throughout the film. I'm sure (from her) she had an affair with Greg on that movie, but when I got to know him later on in life and even dropped a couple of hints, I realized he was far too classy to comment on it. Dad produced *The Keys of the Kingdom,* which was released in 1944. He and Mother had fallen in love, married in 1939, and had their first child, my brother Chris, in 1940, followed by me in 1942. But her mental problems were surfacing, and upon completion of the film, she decided to quit acting and concentrate on herself and her family.

Actresses never really quit, you know. Over the years, Mother always thought about returning to it, and she even tried once in the late forties. I remember when Natalie Wood "retired" after she gave birth to her daughter, Natasha. We would go to the movies together from time to time, and as the lights lowered in the theater and the screen lit up, I'd look over at her. It was like sitting next to a racehorse nervously prancing in the gate, waiting for it to open, but saddened by the fact that she wasn't going to be running that day. Natalie's return to the screen was inevitable. Mother was cast in a play written by Edna Ferber and directed by George S. Kaufman but was replaced out of town, for reasons still unexplained. It was a bitter blow to her.

She had been voluntarily committed to the Menninger Clinic right after I was born in 1942. For the first year or so of my life, any form of maternal care was provided by my nanny, a wonderful woman named Jeannie Smith who coincidentally shared the same birth date with me, June 1. I don't think Mother ever got over the guilt of not being there for me then. This led to a bizarre relationship in which I was on the one hand the favorite child, and on the other, the one singled out as the primary recipient of her rage and desperation. It was also deeply sexual, though never physically incestuous. She was intensely concerned about where, when, and with whom I'd lose my virginity. In the fifties we'd have long conversations in her bedroom dressing room, often with her wearing only her underwear as she put on her makeup, preparing to go out for the evening. She was so wonderfully attentive to me that when I became the principal object of her uncontrollable rage, it was doubly terrifying.

The most lasting and life-altering effect she had on me, however, was putting me on an endless quest to find her again somewhere and cure her. I developed a strange form of radar that could immediately recognize a troubled woman (almost always an actress) and elicit an instant, receptive, silent reaction from her signifying that she recognized me too. Later on, after I'd had many disastrous affairs with troubled women, Natalie Wood joked: "Mank, you could take three different women, dress them identically, have them sit motionless on separate chairs with gags over their mouths, and like a pig with truffles, you could pick out the crazy one." I was psychoanalyzed twice in my life. I knew all about my central problem but was either unwilling or unable to do anything about it. Much more about Mother later.

Uncle Herman

Several books have already been written about him: brilliantly witty, master of many forms of writing, intensely self-destructive, and hopelessly addicted to alcohol and gambling. He died penniless. Dad became the main support of his widow, Sara, and put their daughter, Johanna (Josie), through Wellesley College.

Herman was addicted to insulting studio executives, the more powerful the better. Darryl Zanuck, the absolute ruler of 20th Century Fox, had two noticeably protruding front upper teeth. Herman: "Darryl, you're the only man in the world who could eat a tomato through a tennis racket and never spill a drop." To Harry Rapf, an MGM executive with a huge nose: "Harry, you're the only guy I know who could keep a cigar lit in a shower." He once told Rapf about the brilliant new screenplay he was working on, about a little boy whose nose grew each time he told a lie. The nose became larger and larger . . . Rapf chased Herman out of his office. Harry Cohn, head of Columbia Pictures, began life in New York as a streetcar conductor. As it happened, the studio executive dining room was shaped like a train car. Whenever Herman was eating in there and Cohn entered, Herman would call out: "Ding, ding! Fares, please!" Cohn fired Herman several times, notably after he (Cohn) pronounced a certain Columbia film exactly seventeen minutes too long because "I shifted my ass in my seat seventeen minutes ago, and when I shift my ass, the movie's over."

From out of the screening room darkness came a voice: "Imagine that.

One hundred sixty million people in this country wired in to Harry Cohn's ass."

Without turning, Cohn said, "That's Mankiewicz, and he's fired."

When Herman first arrived in Hollywood, he sent a famous telegram to his friend the playwright Ben Hecht, in New York: "You must come out at once. There's millions to be made and your only competition is idiots." Hecht and his writing partner, Charles MacArthur (who later married Helen Hayes) came out immediately. One notable evening, Herman and MacArthur were invited to an elegant dinner party at the home of Arthur Hornblow Jr., a sophisticated producer with a wife named Bubbles. They arrived dead drunk and continued to drink during dinner. Suddenly, Herman vomited on the table. There was a deafening silence. Herman wiped his mouth, looked at the Hornblows and said: "I'm terribly sorry, Arthur. But don't worry, Bubbles. The white wine came up with the fish."

Years later I saw this incident immortalized in the form of an unpublished James Thurber cartoon on the wall of the office of Dave Chasen, the famous Hollywood restaurateur. Chasen's began as a chili stand in the thirties. Dave had been a "straight man" in vaudeville, moved out to Los Angeles, and changed professions. His chili was legendary. Movie people would pick some up in the morning on Beverly Boulevard (then little more than a field with a few houses), take it to the studio, and reheat it for lunch. Years later Elizabeth Taylor asked for Chasen's chili during the filming of *Cleopatra*. It was flown over by Pan Am pilots and delivered to Cinecittà Studios in Rome. When Dave decided to expand to a real restaurant, Dad was one of his original investors. As soon as I could afford it, I became a frequent patron there. Dave remembered Dad well and was welcoming. After he died, so was his widow, Maude. I always had access to the private office and was seated in the favored front section. During the sixties I attended a few Sunday-night Sinatra family dinners there. At the end of the meal, Frank was handed an envelope filled with freshly minted $100 bills. He liked the feel of new money and they simply added the amount to his check. Many of those new bills disappeared on his way out the door and the parking lot. Frank was a generous tipper.

Herman almost lived at Chasen's, drank there, and often slept it off in Dave's office when he was too drunk to drive home. On those occasions Dave would call Herman's wife, Sara, to report on his status. One morning he asked Herman, "How is Sara, by the way?"

"Sara?" Herman replied. "Don't you mean poor Sara?" The name he gave her stuck. Many of their friends referred to them afterward as "Herman and poor Sara."

The Family

Herman was a compulsive gambler. He loved to bet on the ponies. He and Dad were at Santa Anita one day, trying to dope out a race. Herman looked out at the tote board and observed: "I don't know why it says five-to-one and eight-to-one out there. Every bet is even money. Either the horse wins or it doesn't." What a brilliant rationale for a disastrous betting system.

The most poignant remark of Herman's I remember was one passed on to me by Dad. Herman was dying of multiple causes in a Los Angeles hospital. He was only in his fifties. Dad had flown out from New York (where we were living at the time) to see him. They talked for a while. There was a lapse in the conversation. Herman looked up at Dad and said: "You know what? I never had a bad steak in my life. Some were better, some were worse, but I never had a bad one."

Aunt Sara

"Poor" Sara was an absolutely delightful person, totally dedicated to Herman and her children, Don, Frank, and Josie. I saw a great deal of her when I came out in the early sixties and often had dinner at her house. She had two idiosyncratic expressions I've never forgotten. If you told her you'd run into someone she knew or was interested in, she'd say, "So tell me from hello-hello." And if you agreed to have dinner on a certain night, she'd say, "So I'm inking you in for Thursday." She had deeply adoring memories of Herman. She could talk about him for hours, and you'd never know he ever made a bet or had a drink.

Cousin Josie

My favorite family member ever, Herman's youngest child. Beautiful, devastatingly funny in a dry, smart way, and so very kind and attentive to me. We became extremely close. Dad once actually called it "an unhealthy relationship." Josie was four years older than me and as luck would have it, in the mid-fifties went to Wellesley College while I was going to Exeter, a prep school just across the New Hampshire border. She'd often have me down on weekends, when I would repeatedly "fall in love" with one of her friends, who all seemed so desirable, mature, and attractive. There's a terrible gulf between men and women at that age. The four years between sixteen and twenty might as well be forty, especially if you're the guy.

Josie graduated with honors. Dad, who'd put her through college, got her a job at *Time* magazine, working for the legendary editor Henry

Gruenwald. She eventually became the first woman to be credited as an editor in the history of the magazine. Josie wrote an acclaimed novel, *Life Signs*. She married Peter Davis, later famous for making the Oscar-winning anti-Vietnam documentary *Hearts and Minds*. They had two sons, Nick and Tim.

In the last summer of her life, she rented a house just up the road from my place in Malibu. I'd go with her to watch the kids play Little League, and we'd talk for hours on end. When she returned to New York later that year, she was walking on the street with Nick and Tim when a taxi went out of control, jumped the curb, and killed her in front of her children. I was devastated at the news. Suicide and death were invading my life like a plague at that time. This loss was totally unacceptable. I called Sara and told her I couldn't go to the funeral. I simply didn't have the strength. Sara knew how close we were and understood completely.

Aunt Erna

Pop's only female child. Pushy, forceful—I suppose it wasn't easy competing for Pop's attention while two overachievers like Herman and Dad were around—she made her presence known. Married to a doctor and living in New York, she occasionally came out to California, usually staying with Herman. Once my mother asked me (at about age six) to call over there and welcome her. She dialed and handed me the phone. Herman answered.

"Hi, Uncle Herman," I said. "Is Aunt Erna there?"

"If she was, wouldn't she have answered the phone?" he replied.

Years later, after Mother's suicide, I suppose Erna considered herself the ranking female Mankiewicz and was bitterly disappointed when Dad married Rosemary—she never liked her, and she showed it. Dad got Erna various jobs over the years and was virtually her sole financial support for the last decades of her life.

Cousins Don and Frank

Herman's sons. After serving in the army in World War II, Frank went to law school at Berkeley, ran for the California State Assembly, lost, became a successful lawyer, then quit his practice to join the Peace Corps as a worker in Peru. He soon became head of the Peace Corps for Latin America, then served as Robert Kennedy's press secretary until the tragic assassination. He later ran the Peace Corps with Sergeant Shriver, was a newspaper columnist and a TV political host, and is now vice chairman of Hill & Knowlton, a powerful Washington lobbying firm.

Don made impressive use of the Mankiewicz family writing gene. He wrote a Harper Prize novel, *See How They Run,* and the pilots for two enduring television series, *Ironside* and *Marcus Welby, M.D.* He was Oscar nominated for the screenplay of *I Want to Live,* served on the board of the Writers Guild, and like his father, remains one of the most dedicated handicappers in the history of horse racing.

Josh, Ben, and John

Frank's son Josh has had a notable career in broadcast journalism and is presently a senior correspondent on NBC's *Dateline.* Josh's younger brother, Ben, has been a sportswriter, had his own satellite radio show, took a turn as a television movie critic, and is the present host of Turner Classic Movies, as well as the CNN movie critic on weekends. Don's son, John, has been a masterful writer-producer in television, from the original *Miami Vice* to *House* and *The Mentalist.*

Pop should be beaming with pride somewhere. No matter what it cost them emotionally—no matter how badly the pursuit of excellence could screw them up—everyone was somebody.

Our Religion

Dad, the son of Jewish parents, was a confirmed atheist most of his life. Mother was a fairly observant Roman Catholic, her own mother a devout one. Her religion insisted on any children she had being brought up Catholic—not to do so meant her marriage wouldn't be recognized in the eyes of the church. Chris and I were baptized at the Church of the Good Shepherd in Beverly Hills. Dad always insisted he wouldn't have cared if we were brought up as Buddhists; he just wanted to marry the woman. But he drew the line at nuns. We were not to be taught by nuns. When Dad married Rosemary several years after Mother died, she happened to be the daughter of the Episcopal archdeacon of London. Jews, Catholics, Episcopalians, and atheists—quite an ecumenical family.

I went to church regularly as a child. The Catholic religion was uncompromising in the forties—if you ate a cheeseburger on a Friday, the clouds would part and lightning would strike you in the head. Dad always insisted that if I really had faith, he'd envy me. I never believed him. I stopped going to church after we moved to New York, except on the "big days" like Easter and Christmas. Since then I've shot filmed sequences in churches several times and entered many more, and I've always dipped my fingers in the holy water, genuflected, and made the sign of the cross every time I walked in, whether out of respect or fear I'm not sure. I never understood how the God and Jesus I knew could let such misery exist in the world, especially when suffered by innocents. I remember how chilled I felt in my early teens when I went to a performance of Archibald MacLeish's *J.B.*, a modern version of the book of Job. In the cast was a young Christopher Plummer playing the part of the Devil. At one point he leans in to the anguished Job and whispers in his ear: "If God is God, he is not good. If God is good, he is not God." That line left an impression on me. When I found myself directing Chris Plummer in *Dragnet* some thirty-five years later, I quoted the line to him—he remembered it as if it were yesterday.

Dad and Rosemary agreed they would be buried next to each other in an Episcopal cemetery in Bedford, New York. Shortly before his death, Dad was visited by the local minister, who told him how delighted he would be to have him. Dad asked, "May I be buried with a few of my favorite books?" No problem. "I've smoked a pipe my whole life—I'd like to include a few of my favorites and my tobacco." No problem. "And there, in that urn on the mantle, are the ashes of my dog, Brutus, who was my companion for many years. I'd like them buried with me too."

"I'm afraid not," came the reply. "Nothing to do with our religion, but you can't bury animal remains in a human cemetery—it's a state law. Sorry."

Dad nodded. The day of his burial he was lowered into the ground with books and pipes. Inside the tobacco pouches were the ashes of Brutus. Dad always liked to have the last word.

2

The 1940s

Growing Up

The difference between life and the movies is that scripts have to make sense and life doesn't.

—*Joseph L. Mankiewicz*

In the 1940s Beverly Hills was almost a bucolic community compared to today. A small, prosperous town with a trolley car running along Santa Monica Boulevard that could take you all the way to downtown L.A., what there was of it then. Benedict and Coldwater Canyons were paved for only a mile or so before they turned into dirt roads. Many people kept horses up there, and some preferred to ride into town on errands. Shops on Rodeo and Beverly Drives actually had the occasional hitching post to accommodate the equestrians who also used the grass median strip (still there) in the middle of Sunset Boulevard to make their turn onto the proper cross street. I remember up Benedict Canyon was the estate of Tom Mix. Tony the Wonder Horse could be spotted grazing there from time to time. Coming full circle, I spent many a night on part of that property during the past two decades in a house belonging to close friends.

I grew up in a substantial home on the corner of North Mapleton Drive and Sunset Boulevard. Tennis court, swimming pool, huge lawn, beautiful gardens—the whole nine yards. Our neighbors included Alan Ladd next door plus Harry James and Betty Grable across the street. Around the corner, on Faring Drive, lived Fanny Brice. From time to time my brother and I would walk up to the front door and ring the bell, and she would come out and do Baby Snooks for us from her famous radio show.

Because of an accident of birth, my brother Chris (born in October)

13

was destined to be two years ahead of me (born in June) in school, even though he was only a year and a half older. He was already in the first grade before I'd been to kindergarten. According to Dad, I was so upset by this and so anxious to be going to school along with Chris that he had the prop department at MGM make up a fake birth certificate showing me eligible for the first grade. The exclusive El Rodeo School in Beverly Hills accepted the document without a question. I skipped kindergarten. When Chris started the second grade I was one year behind him, in first grade. A few years later Dad confessed to his "mistake," but since I'd been doing well academically, the school agreed it would be silly to hold me back at that point. As I said, Beverly Hills was a much smaller town then.

What consistently strikes me is all the different ways I came "full circle" despite growing up mainly in New York and not really returning to Los Angeles until I'd graduated Yale in 1963. The house I grew up in was later owned by Aaron Spelling, for whom (along with Leonard Goldberg) I co-wrote and directed the two-hour television movie-pilot of the series *Hart to Hart* more than thirty years later. I remember giving Aaron a picture of myself as a kid on the diving board of what was now his swimming pool. I never knew Alan Ladd Jr. (who was somewhat older than me) while he lived next door, but I either wrote, produced, or directed three films at two different studios while he was head of production, and a damn good one too. The Fanny Brice home on Faring became the home of Jerry Moss, cofounder (with Herb Alpert) of A&M Records, for whom I wrote a musical Tijuana Brass television special in 1968. Jerry became and continues to be one of the closest friends I've ever had. Thomas Wolfe once observed, "You can't go home again." I guess he didn't know what he was talking about.

Timber

My closest pal in the forties was our dog, Timber, a magnificent German shepherd who was so smart, loving, and protective to my brother Chris and me. The school bus would let us off at the corner of Mapleton and Sunset around three thirty, and Timber would be waiting there to escort us up the street and the long, steep driveway home. To me it was magical, as if he secretly carried a watch. We'd explore the neighborhood together, poking around vacant lots, once even dislodging a grounded hornet's nest. The angry swarm pursued us all the way home, stinging us repeatedly as we ran.

When we were about to move to New York in 1951, Dad announced that Timber couldn't come with us. Chris and I were in tears. But Dad was right, of course. Timber was getting on and had been used to running free his entire life. "You can't keep him cooped up in a New York apartment and walk him around the block twice a day," Dad said. "You guys are going to have longer school hours and go to prep school, I hope. I'll be gone every day. What's he going to do? Lie around in a room twelve floors above a street full of traffic?" We gave Timber to a friend of Dad's at Fox, Otto Lang, who had a ranch in Sun Valley, Idaho. I ran into Otto much later on and he told me how happy his years with Timber were up there, and how much he loved him. So did I, pal.

The Battle for Hollywood

Before the release of *All About Eve* in 1950, and just before our family moved to New York, what my cousin Don later called "the Battle for Hollywood" took place, and Dad was directly in the eye of the storm. It was the time of the "blacklist." The country was obsessed with the red scare, the House Committee on Un-American Activities was actively investigating the motion picture community, Senator Joseph McCarthy was in full flower, and lives and careers were being destroyed wholesale by the slightest implied "pinko" association. Dad was president of the Screen Directors Guild at the time. Cecil B. DeMille, who wielded great power in Hollywood, was instrumental in getting him elected to that position. Dad had just won two Oscars for writing and directing *A Letter to Three Wives*. DeMille reasoned that a talented and popular young director would reinvigorate the Guild. Most important to DeMille, a virulent right-winger, Dad (later a lifetime liberal) was a registered Republican. While Dad and Mother were on vacation in Europe, DeMille took it on himself to announce that every director in the Guild would be required to sign a loyalty oath to the United States government in order to be able to work in Hollywood. When Dad and Mother returned on the *Queen Mary,* a gaggle of reporters met Dad on the New York docks. They asked him what he thought of the loyalty oath proposal. Dad was shocked. This was the first he'd ever heard of it, and he was president of the Guild. "I'm against it," he told them. "I think it's insulting to the membership to question their patriotism and totally unnecessary." By the time he returned to California, the Guild members had gone ballistic.

DeMille and the right wing of the Guild asked Dad to reconsider his stance. He refused. The shit hit the fan. The Hearst newspapers played it up big. They already hated the name Mankiewicz because of Herman's having written *Citizen Kane.* Hearst columnist Louella Parsons had a popular national radio show at the time. On it one night she observed, "Isn't it a pity that Joe Mankiewicz, who Hollywood has nurtured and honored, has turned out to be a 'fellow traveler.'" At school, Chris and I were called "Commies" by some of the other kids. We were a family under siege. DeMille and his cohorts sent motorcycle riders out at night to Guild members' homes, asking them to sign a petition calling for Dad's impeachment. Not to sign would be considered un-American. Dad's position seemed hopeless. At one point, he, John Huston, and George Stevens were even locked out of Guild headquarters with no one seeming to be able to find the right key to let them in.

Dad was running out of time. He placed an ad in *Variety* asking any director who agreed with him to show up that night in the back room of Chasen's restaurant. Out of several hundred Guild members, only twenty-five came. But what a twenty-five: William Wyler, George Stevens, John Huston, Elia Kazan, Billy Wilder, Otto Preminger, Fred Zinnemann, and others. Richard Brooks, who was there and at that point had directed only several minor action movies, told me later on: "I looked around that room and said to myself, shit, look at all the Oscars walking around in here. No matter what happens, all these guys are going to continue working and I'll get blacklisted."

The showdown occurred at a black-tie meeting of the Directors Guild in the ballroom of the Beverly Hills Hotel. It was not open to the public. Before anyone spoke, they had to identify themselves to the stenographer who was taking down everything that was said. At that time, only directors belonged to the Guild (no assistant directors or production managers, as is the case today) and there was only one female director, the actress Ida Lupino. This resulted, Dad remembered, in every speaker beginning with "Gentlemen, Miss Lupino . . ." DeMille spoke first, making his case: these were dangerous times; foreign infiltration into the fabric of America was a real danger. He went on to list the names of some who opposed him. Dad was appalled when, for some peculiar reason, DeMille affected a thick foreign accent while naming them: "Villy Vyler, Billy Vilder," and so on. Rouben Mamoulian (*The Mask of Zorro, Blood and Sand*) stood up. He told DeMille he'd never been ashamed of his accent before and wasn't going to start now. William Wyler rose angrily and asked DeMille what he was doing during World War II when he, Wyler, was making *The Memphis Belle* in an American bomber on missions over Germany. The meeting was spiraling out of control.

Finally, the great John Ford stood up. Dad's stomach churned. Ford's politics were to the right of Attila the Hun, but no director in the history of Hollywood had ever been held in higher esteem. Ford introduced himself to the stenographer: "My name is John Ford. I direct westerns." Nervous laughter from those assembled. Ford began: he supposed that he and Joe Mankiewicz didn't share one political opinion, that he was much closer in social philosophy to DeMille. But, he went on to say, and directly to DeMille, he didn't like DeMille personally, and especially the way he'd insulted some of his fellow directors in his speech tonight. As for himself, he'd be happy to sign a loyalty oath, but goddamnit, no one was going to force him to do it. "So what do you say?" he asked the crowd. "Why don't we all go home and give the Polack"—Dad—"back his job?"

Dad won the impeachment vote in a landslide. He never forgot Ford for what he did. DeMille left the meeting a broken man. Later on, to appease the entire Guild, especially the center right led by Frank Capra (himself an immigrant from Sicily), Dad did accept the idea of a loyalty oath, but only on a voluntary basis. He never signed himself, nor did many others. In many ways, this was Dad's finest hour. He stood up for what he believed with the odds heavily stacked against him and at great personal risk to his reputation and career. Later on he told me: "Looking back on it, I wish I hadn't been so dismissive of the oath right there on the New York docks. Maybe I could have returned to L.A. and negotiated a compromise, the kind we finally came up with. But DeMille made that impossible, and when you say what you really feel and you mean it, you have to see it through."

Shortly afterward, Dad resigned as president, but not before admitting assistant directors and production managers into the Guild. He was moving to New York and was a filmmaker, not a labor executive. He wanted Chris and me to grow up in an international city bursting with energy. The home of Broadway, the *New York Times*, the Yankees, Giants, Dodgers, and Wall Street. He wanted us to get an eastern education at the best schools in the country. He was, after all, the son of a distinguished professor. He actually believed that kids shouldn't be allowed to go to school in blue jeans. He used to say about Los Angeles only half in jest: "I don't think that people were physically meant to live here. It's an artificially inseminated desert. When the 'big one' hits, it's going to crack off and fall into the ocean. Later on, neon signs will float to the surface and the rest of the world will wonder what everyone did here."

Mother in the 1940s

Despite her illness, Mother was an extremely intelligent woman and capable of great warmth. She had a unique ear for languages and spoke English and later Italian fluently, without a trace of accent. She was of tremendous help to Dad as an in-house critic of his screenplays. He routinely solicited her opinion and acted on it. Their relationship was doubtless eroding, but I was too young to understand that. The house on Mapleton was the last time they shared a bedroom. The abortive attempt to return to the stage must have been a crushing disappointment to her. There is correspondence from both writer Edna Ferber and director George S. Kaufman commenting on what a marvelous performance she gave and how she "handled the situation with such great dignity," but no reason is given for her replacement out of town. I can only assume her mental illness must have flared up one night and it scared the hell out of them.

Dad in the 1940s

Dad was, simply put, a serial philanderer. He'd had many affairs while writing and producing at MGM, most notably with Loretta Young, Judy Garland, and Joan Crawford. Louis B. Mayer, self-appointed father to all at Metro, was extremely upset about Garland in particular because of her young age. But Dad and Judy either couldn't or wouldn't let go of each other. Their relationship included Judy becoming pregnant by him and having an abortion (I can't prove this, but I know it's true). Their affair continued well after he was married to Mother and Judy had married Vincente Minnelli. In the seventies I was best man at Liza Minnelli's wedding to Jack Haley Jr. in the same little Santa Barbara church where Judy had married Vincente. Liza and I were close at that time—she was literally bursting with humor and talent. She knew all about her mother's long affair with Dad and kidded that we could have been half brother and sister. She also told me that whenever Judy sang "Happiness Is Just a Thing Called Joe," it was silently dedicated to him. More about both Judy and Liza later.

Joan Crawford also lasted quite a while. Apparently (according to Dad), she stood over my baby crib one night, while mother was in Menninger's, looked down at me, then turned to him and said, "That should be mine."

Louis B. Mayer had always wanted to create a new Irving Thalberg for himself at MGM, and he selected Dad to fill that role. By the time he was thirty, Joseph L. Mankiewicz had already produced more than twenty films—among them, *Million Dollar Legs*, Fritz Lang's *Fury*, *Manhattan Melodrama* (John Dillinger went to see it the night he was shot leaving the theater), and *The Philadelphia Story*. He also "fixed" most of the screenplays and had been Oscar nominated for screenwriting. But Dad wanted to direct, to direct what he wrote, and Mayer refused, telling him, "You have to learn to crawl before you can walk." By letting Dad direct he would lose the most promising producer he had on the lot. Darryl F. Zanuck at 20th Century

Fox had no such limitations in mind, however. With the implicit under-standing that he would become a director, Dad moved to Fox in the mid-forties.

Major Studios in the 1940s

At that time, with a few notable exceptions (Samuel Goldwyn, David O. Selznick, etc.), virtually every actor, writer, producer, director, cameraman, and editor was under contract to a major studio. These weren't merely work centers—they were more like self-contained sovereign states. They even had their own baseball teams. The commissaries served gourmet food of all kinds, available twenty-four hours a day. The more important filmmakers had their own bungalows, often with a bedroom. There were steam rooms, barber shops, and mail delivery, and each studio had an extensive back lot with its own Western Street, Jungleland, Big City Streets, and more.

The 20th Century Fox lot sprawled over most of what is today called Century City, a major office building and condo community next to Beverly Hills. Dad had a large bungalow surrounded by fake grass and a little picket fence. When I rewrote and directed the two-hour movie-pilot of *Hart to Hart,* that bungalow was occupied by Aaron Spelling and Leonard Goldberg, then the two most powerful producers in television, with five hours on the air weekly, not counting long-form projects. The bungalow had been enlarged to accommodate both of them, but when I entered Aaron's office and saw the working brick fireplace and adjoining bedroom, waves of memories crashed in.

According to Dad, the most important man on the lot, the one you wanted on your side, was not Darryl Zanuck but Henry the Bootblack. He shined the shoes of every executive on a daily basis. They were constantly on the phone and talked freely in front of him while he worked. As a result, he knew everything that was going on at Fox: whose contract was being dropped, what project was going to get a green light or be canceled, and who was currently in or out of favor. When one of Fox's films returned to Los Angeles from African locations, the studio brought a group of Watusi warriors with them for additional shooting on the back lot. To prevent them from being culture shocked, they were housed at the studio inside the Jungle set. The commissary catered to their specific food preferences, but they still had one major complaint—no women. Henry the Bootblack was drafted to remedy the situation. He recruited a posse of downtown African American hookers who were bused to Fox several nights a week. As I said, there was absolutely nothing you couldn't get at a major studio in the forties.

Snapshots from 1940s Films

Woman of the Year (1942)

The first pairing of Spencer Tracy and Katharine Hepburn, produced by Dad and directed by George Stevens. Dad knew Hepburn well from *The Philadelphia Story*. At that time he and Spencer Tracy were great friends and habitually lunched together in the MGM commissary. Hepburn recalled she knew that and that she was about to work with Tracy even though they'd never met. One day she positioned herself in front of the commissary and "accidentally" ran into them as they were leaving. Dad made the introductions. They chatted briefly, then Tracy excused himself since he was shooting and had to get back to the stage.

Hepburn watched him leave, turned to Dad, and said, "He's rather short, isn't he."

"Don't worry," Dad replied. "He'll cut you down to size."

Dad and Tracy owned a boat together, a 104-foot schooner, the *Sartosha*. It was moored in Long Beach and was costing them a fortune to maintain, needing daily wash downs for its pristine teak decks and at least a skeleton crew on permanent salary. They tried to sail to Hawaii once, ran into a storm one day out, turned around, went home, and finally sold it. I was putting around Catalina Harbor with Robert Wagner some forty years later in a rubber Zodiac when we saw a beautiful schooner at anchor called the *Jomar*. We pulled alongside. The captain recognized R.J. and asked us aboard. It turned out he owned Martinson's Coffee (an eastern brand). Their instant coffee was called "Jomar." In the captain's cabin we looked through the ship's log. Sonofagun. It once had been called the *Sartosha*, and there were Dad's and Tracy's signatures as cocaptains. I told Dad, and he was thrilled that she was still afloat.

Dragonwyck (1946)

The great German director Ernst Lubitsch (*Ninotchka, Heaven Can Wait*) was somewhat of a mentor to Dad. Our house was always filled with the German-speaking members of Hollywood in the forties since Dad and Mother both spoke the language. Lubitsch was the original director on *Dragonwyck* but fell ill before the shooting started. Dad had written the screenplay, and Lubitsch went to bat on his behalf with Zanuck, insisting that Dad replace him as director.

While writing the screenplay, Dad once asked Lubitsch what exactly he wanted out of a certain scene. The director replied, "Give me some of those great Lubitsch touches."

They were lunching in the Fox commissary one day when a young man approached the table and stuck out his hand: "Mr. Lubitsch, I just got my first job as a director this morning and I wanted to shake your hand for luck."

"Certainly," said Lubitsch, taking it. "When do you start shooting?"

"In ten days."

He left. Lubitsch turned to Dad: "That young man is directing his first film and he has ten days to prepare. I need six months. It should be the other way around."

Dragonwyck starred Vincent Price, Gene Tierney, and Walter Huston. It was a melodramatic, gothic nineteenth-century romance in which Price played a Dutch aristocrat, "the patroon" in a huge, upstate New York manor house. Vincent later told me about the first day of shooting: "It was the most curious piece of direction I ever received. Joe, God bless him, was so psyched up on his first day. He kept reminding me how to carry myself as a nobleman. 'Erect, always erect,' he repeated endlessly. My first shot was simply to walk down a long staircase. We rolled, someone yelled 'speed,' and Joe said: 'All right then, Vincent. Nice erection!'"

Harry Morgan was also in the film. Some forty years later I was directing him in *Dragnet* with Dan Aykroyd and Tom Hanks. Harry had done the TV series with Jack Webb and was playing Danny's boss. One day he asked me, "Is this your first feature as a director?" I nodded. "How about that? I was in your father's first feature, *Dragonwyck*." As it was sinking in, Harry added: "I wouldn't make too much of that. I was in everyone's first feature."

Dad was so hyped at finally directing that one day he asked his camera-man, Artie Miller, for his viewfinder, "just because as a director I thought I should." He raised it to his eye: "I couldn't see a fucking thing." Miller took the viewfinder from him, turned it around, and handed it back. Dad had been looking through the wrong end. This mistake became a memorable moment four years later in *All About Eve* when, just before the famous party sequence, Gary Merrill says to Bette Davis, "I was just telling Eve about the time I looked through the wrong end of a viewfinder." She replies, "Remind me to tell you about the time I looked into the heart of an artichoke."

The Ghost and Mrs. Muir (1947)

The first of four films he would do with Rex Harrison. The female lead was once again Gene Tierney, whom Dad recalled as "in many ways, the most beautiful woman I ever saw." Need I say more?

The film was later made as a TV series starring my dear friend Hope Lange. Mrs. Muir's little daughter in the film was played by a very young Natalie Wood, later to become one of the best friends I ever had. Natalie's Russian mother (we called her "Mud") was fiercely ambitious for her daughter. The first day Natalie was to work, Dad was behind schedule and couldn't get to her. He called her and "Mud" over and told them she'd work tomorrow, then gave Natalie an overnight assignment to keep her busy. "Learn how to spell Mankiewicz," he said. "Once you can spell Mankiewicz, you can go to work."

The next morning, an eager little Natalie arrived. "Mud" ushered her up to Dad. Natalie took a deep breath and said, "M-A-N-K-I-E-W-I-T-Z."

"Almost," Dad replied. "You only got one letter wrong."

Natalie turned bright red. Her mother scowled at her. Dad remembered: "I suddenly realized that it wasn't Natalie's fault, that this horrible woman had drummed the wrong spelling into her and was now blaming the child."

Years later Dad flew to L.A. from New York to visit his longtime agent, Burt Allenberg, who was dying in the hospital. As he walked down the hospital corridor, a voice suddenly spoke up from behind him: "M-A-N-K-I-E-W-I-C-Z." It was Natalie. He hadn't seen her since the film. She winked. Years later, no matter where we were, I could turn to Natalie and say, "Spell Mankiewicz," and she would rattle it off as if it were indelibly imprinted in her brain, which it was.

All About Eve (1950)

A classic film. Dad's high water mark. Among its many virtues was a wonderful supporting performance from a young Marilyn Monroe. Dad told me this story about her, which I've never forgotten: Right after the film had wrapped, Dad was browsing at the magazine stand outside Martindale's Book Store in Beverly Hills. Exiting the store came Marilyn, carrying a paper bag with what she'd bought. He was surprised to see her leaving a bookstore, which he hardly thought would be her natural habitat. They hugged. Pointing at the bag, Dad said, "What've you got there, Marilyn?"

She pulled out the book. It was a volume of nineteenth-century poetry by Heinrich Heine.

Dad was shocked. "You're a fan of Heine?"

"I don't know who he is," she said. "Sometimes I come in here to look around and I try to find a book that seems lonely, like no one's ever going to buy it, and I take it home with me." I've always found that story so touching and so indicative of what I imagine to have been her real personality.

Certainly, the towering performance in the film was given by Bette Davis as Margo Channing. Some forty years later I was having dinner with her at Robert Wagner's house. I asked her who her favorite director had been. She replied: "My favorite was my dear Willy Wyler, what a charming, wonderful man. The most talented director I ever worked with was your father, but of course, he was a prick."

I called Dad to tell him what she'd said, and he roared with laughter. "I'd have expected nothing less from her," he said.

There was a hit Broadway musical based on the film called *Applause*. It opened decades later and starred Lauren Bacall as Margo. Weeks before the opening, Bacall ("Betty") called Dad and asked him to please attend on opening night. She wanted to bring him out onstage during her solo curtain call. Dad had been friends with Betty (and Bogart) for years. He told her how flattered he was by the gesture, then said: "I wish you all kinds of luck, Betty, but I'm never going to see it. I think it was a pretty good film and I'll never understand why anybody thought it was a good idea to stop it a dozen times for songs." The show was a hit. Betty won the Tony. Dad never saw it.

3

The 1950s

Developing a Character

In movies today, if you steal a scene from another writer, line for line, it's still called plagiarism. If you steal a scene from another director, shot for shot, it's called an homage.

—*Joseph L. Mankiewicz*

New York City

Needless to say, moving from laid-back southern California (the late comedian Fred Allen called it "a great place to live if you're an orange") to the cacophony of taxi horns and bustling pedestrians that was and still is New York City was a culture shock to a nine-year-old. Everyone on the street seemed to walk with a sense of purpose, as if he or she had a mission to accomplish, and right now.

We moved into a large apartment (the entire ninth floor) at 730 Park Avenue, on the corner of Seventy-First Street. It wasn't easy getting in. First, the family had to pass muster with the Admissions Board of the building. Luckily for us, Dad had won four Oscars in the last two years, and both the great composer Richard Rodgers (who lived on the floor below) and the celebrated novelist Edna Ferber were residents who were happy to vouch for us. Also on the board was John Loeb, cofounder of the noted brokerage house of Loeb, Rhoades, later to become Shearson Loeb Rhoades. He was apparently so picky that he'd denied occupancy to V. K. Krishna Menon, India's ambassador to the United Nations and later its foreign minister, on the grounds that he didn't want people wearing turbans going up and down in the elevator.

The only problem we ever had with a neighbor was after Chris and I got a miniature pool table in our bedroom. The pool balls themselves were normal size and weight. We used to try all sorts of trick shots—the balls constantly hit the floor. One day a visibly troubled Richard Rodgers rang our bell. It seemed our bedroom was directly over the office where he wrote his music. At that time he was composing his famous symphonic poem *Victory at Sea*. When the series named after it subsequently aired on television, every time the cymbals clashed, signifying the pounding waves, Chris and I fantasized that it was our contribution, clearly one of the pool balls hitting the floor. I got to know Dick a little in later life. He finally found it funny.

Dad and Mother had separate bedrooms for the first time. Hers was at the end of the hallway, directly opposite the bedroom occupied by me and Chris. The kitchen, pantry, formal dining room, and living room were spacious and comfortable. Life should have been good. Unfortunately, Mother's illness was recurring more frequently and with greater intensity. She would actually become a completely different person, one full of anger, even rage, and her frequent nighttime visits to our bedroom to yell were a source of dread—especially to me, since I was her favorite target. I would pretend to be asleep, but to no avail. I'd already developed pronounced asthma, and the attacks were getting worse. After she'd finished her outburst and left, my wheezing would keep Chris awake. I would go into our bathroom, close the door, and lie there, fighting for air, staring at myself in the full-length mirror until I finally fell asleep.

Dad and Mother thought it best if Chris and I went to different schools. Chris was enrolled at Collegiate, and I attended St. Bernard's School for Boys, a posh grade school on Ninety-Eighth Street between Fifth and Madison Avenues. I had a little cap with the school shield on it that I wore every day taking the Madison Avenue bus up and back. I'm sure these days no one would let their ten-year-old child take the bus alone that far on a daily basis, but New York City in 1951 presented no such problem. The fare was a dime. The work was hard, but I relished it. To this day, more than half a century later, I still get my yearly invitation to "The Old Boys Dinner."

Full Circle with Willie

Dad knew Leo Durocher, who was then the manager of the New York Giants baseball team. I thought he was a cool guy and became an immediate Giants fan. It was 1951, the year of Bobby Thompson's "miracle" home run, which beat the Dodgers and won the pennant. That year was also the rookie season of my all-time baseball hero, Willie Mays. Even Vin Scully, the legendary Dodger announcer, told me one night Mays was the best all-around player he'd ever seen. Half a century later I was having a drink in L.A. at the bar of the Palm restaurant (I'm a regular) chatting with a friend when a waiter who knew me came up and said, "You'll never guess who just walked past you—Willie Mays."

My head snapped around. There he was, about to sit down at a table. I have never, ever, approached a celebrity in my life, but I made an immediate beeline for him.

"Mr. Mays?" He turned. "My name is Tom Mankiewicz, my first year in New York was your rookie year, and I have a framed, autographed uniform of yours on the wall of my office, right next to my desk."

Mays smiled. It's funny what happens when you meet a childhood hero. I'd worked with John Wayne, Frank Sinatra, and Marlon Brando, but for the first time in my life my knees started to wobble as I quickly regressed to nine years old.

"I . . . just wanted to say there's only one best player who ever lived, and you're it."

"Hey, thanks a lot," Willie replied. "But there's a guy right behind you who might disagree."

I turned. It was Frank Robinson. They were eating together. When they finished and started to walk out, the entire restaurant gave them a standing ovation.

Meanwhile, at Home

At home there were frequent fights between Mother and Dad now, all of them at night, complete with yelling and slamming doors. And then, the next morning, the skies cleared and no one mentioned a thing. It was like living simultaneously in two parallel universes, and it instilled in me a grim determination to one day be independent from all of it, to have my own, private safe place, which I would create for myself. But there was worse yet to come. Much worse.

The Barefoot Contessa

(Nights of terror, a drink from Bogie, I meet a killer and take Ava Gardner to the movies)

Dad made *The Barefoot Contessa* in Italy in 1953, directing his own screenplay. It was the first film he made for his recently formed independent production company (Figaro) and starred Humphrey Bogart and Ava Gardner. Dad was nominated for his writing. Edmond O'Brien won the Oscar for

Best Supporting Actor. Dad and Mother had decided to take me to Rome with them. I was going on twelve. Chris was almost fourteen and would go to Lawrenceville prep school, which had an eighth-grade year. He would join us on vacations.

We moved into a beautiful apartment on the Via Bruxelles. I was tutored by an American teacher every day, keeping up with the academic requirements of St. Bernard's, and had plenty of time to explore the wonders and beauty of Rome, a city with which I fell in love. Little did I know then that I would return to shoot films there twice in my life. Many of my childhood excursions were taken inside a tiny Fiat "Topolino" (Italian for Mickey Mouse) driven by Rosemary Matthews, a young Englishwoman in her twenties who had signed on to the movie as an English coach for Rossano Brazzi. The Italian actor was making one of his first appearances in an American film. Rosemary was smart, fun, spoke fluent Italian, and proved invaluable to Dad on the film as her responsibilities increased. If you'd told me then she'd later be married to him for more than thirty years, I'd have thought you were nuts. Looking back now, I'm sure they must have had an affair during that time, but neither one was forthcoming about it during their lives, and I never asked.

The city and apartment had changed, but not the relationship between my parents. There were the same screaming fights at night, not every night but too many nights. This time, Dad was actually shooting a film, working fourteen hours-plus a day. Sometimes he took off in the middle of the night for somewhere unknown to get some sleep. But, thank goodness, I wasn't alone. Mother's mother ("Gross") had come down from Austria to stay with us and proved a godsend for me as my protector whenever Mother made an unscheduled visit to my room late at night. Gross was devoutly Catholic. She was terrified by and heartbroken at her daughter's condition, but she was a staunch defender of mine, yelling back at Mother every time she castigated me. Those nights were scenes from a true horror movie. Mother yelling, Gross yelling back, then dropping to her knees, making the sign of the cross and praying loudly in German to God and Jesus while I put an oxygen mask over my mouth from a tank that sat at my bedside. One night I had desperate trouble breathing. Dad called a doctor, who came around and gave me a shot of adrenalin directly over my heart. Decades later, while shooting a film in Europe, I drove to Bad Gastein, Austria, where Gross lived. She was quite elderly but thrilled to see me. We both cried when we hugged. I took her to lunch, and she knew the names of the films I'd done. Someone must have given them to her—I couldn't imagine Gross was much of a James Bond fan—but she was so proud of me.

The nights of terror weren't every night, and believe it or not, there were wonderful times too. The "good" Mother was warm, intelligent, and caring. Her incredible ear for languages enabled her to speak nearly fluent Italian in record time, without a trace of accent. She took me everywhere around Rome and out to Tivoli and Ostia, with many walks in the Villa Borghese thrown in as well.

Dad was keenly aware of my situation and took me on location with him as much as he could. After sessions with my tutor I'd habitually be dropped off wherever Dad was shooting and eventually drive home with him. During these trips I'd sop up as much about filmmaking as I could. Movies were the kinds of fantasies I desperately sought out then, and Dad seemed to know that. He also seemed genuinely enthusiastic about the prospect of my getting involved in "the business" one day.

I remember one cold, cold night when the film was shooting in a cemetery. I'd been dressed for the day in shirt sleeves, and the wardrobe man got me a jacket. I was still shivering. Humphrey Bogart walked by and noticed: "Are you cold, Tommy?"

"I sure am."

"Here, try some of this." Bogart pulled out a flask, took off the top, and filled it with a thimbleful of scotch.

I'd never had a drink of hard liquor in my life, only an occasional sip of wine at home. But what the hell, he was Humphrey Bogart. I downed it, just like they do in the movies. My throat started burning. I coughed. And then, son of a bitch, my chest did feel warmer. Bogart grinned.

In a half hour he passed by again. "Still cold?"

"A little bit."

He filled the top again. I drank.

Later on Dad came by to take me home. "Ready?"

I looked up at him with a stupid smile. "Yesss . . ." The smile remained plastered on my face.

Dad looked around, zeroing in on Bogart. "He's drunk. It has to be you, you prick."

"Christ, Joe, the kid was cold. I was just trying to help out."

To this day I have the singular honor of having received my first real drink from Humphrey Bogart.

On another late afternoon I found myself sitting near the set with Ava Gardner and several cast and crew members. Ava was described in the film as "The World's Most Beautiful Animal." She was certainly all of that at the time. A huge celebrity, constantly pursued by a gaggle of paparazzi, she had recently divorced Frank Sinatra and was currently keeping company with

Luis Miguel Dominguin, the most charismatic matador of his day. Part artist in the bull ring, part rock star, he was impossibly handsome with zero body fat and a thin scar running down the side of his face. Sinatra had come to Rome in an attempt to get Ava back, but left empty handed.

During this particular week, Dominguin was fighting in Spain and Ava had time on her hands after shooting. "I want to go to the movies tonight," she announced. "What's at the Fiametta?" (The Fiametta was a little theater that ran American films in English, the only cinema in Rome to do so.) "Who wants to take me to the movies?"

She looked around. Silence. "Anybody?" Silence. Clearly, the prospect of escorting a publicity magnet to a public venue was too intimidating to those sitting there.

"Tommy, how about you? Want to take me to the movies tonight?"

"Sure," I said.

She grinned. "Great. It's a date. I'll send my car to pick you up at Joe's." She smiled at me and walked off.

A while later Dad had wrapped and was ready to take me home. "Guess what, Dad? I'm taking Ava Gardner to the movies tonight."

His face darkened. "Like hell you are."

"Why not? She asked me to."

"Because I'm not going to have my twelve-year-old son's picture in a hundred magazines escorting Ava Gardner in Rome for the evening. When you're older you'll understand how truly bizarre that's going to look."

My eyes misted over. I was about to cry. Dad noticed, softening. As usual, he solved the problem. That night, the public relations man on the film escorted Ava to the movies. I went with them. It was fine with me since secretly I knew I was the one who was really taking her.

Just a note, though it doesn't really apply to a twelve-year-old and Ava Gardner. Actresses, especially beautiful or publicly famous ones, are quite intimidating to most men. At the end of a marriage or a publicized affair, you'd be surprised how often their phone doesn't ring. Many guys are too scared to call. "Oh, she'd never go out with me. I'm not rich enough, good looking enough, famous enough, etc." The truth is that most actresses are simply women with a fragile public occupation. They're just as insecure and sometimes more so than anyone else. There is, after all, a certain pressure on them to be seen as publicly desirable, which sometimes forces them to make terrible personal choices in their lives. I've known several who got married just because they thought it looked good and relieved them of the need to date men in order to stay in the news. God knows, I've had relationships of all kinds with dozens of actresses over the years. Some are wonderful people, some are not, some are smart, some are not, some are great lays, some are not, just like the rest of us.

I remember going to Disneyland in the late seventies with Kate Jackson and her little niece. She'd been somewhat known for a TV series called *The Rookies*, but now was one of Charlie's Angels, which made her as instantly recognizable as anyone in show business. The three girls had made the cover of *Time* magazine, for God's sake. Suddenly, restaurants you couldn't get into before are holding their best table for you. Going to be a little late? Don't worry about it. Disneyland called out security to escort us, no waiting in line, as hundreds of fans screamed at and for her. Kate, a very private person, seemed almost scared. "You know, Mank," she said, "I'm still little Skater (her father's nickname for her) Jackson from Alabama. I haven't changed. Everyone else has."

I never knew where Dad went those nights he left our Rome apartment. All he would offer by way of explanation was: "Somewhere down by the train station where I can sleep." A few weeks before the end of shooting, Bogie and Betty Bacall invited me to have Sunday brunch with them in their suite at the luxurious Excelsior Hotel on the Via Veneto. I arrived at the appointed time, picked up the house phone in the lobby, and asked for Mr. Bogart.

He answered. "We're in 675, you know, just a couple of doors down from where Joe keeps his suite."

I could hear Betty's voice in the background, warning him: "Bogie . . ."

"Come on up," he said quickly.

It was a wonderful brunch. They were both so kind to me and such fun. When Betty wrote her autobiography *By Myself,* she inscribed a copy to me: "Tom. Remember Rome . . . Love, Betty." By the way, the Excelsior Hotel is kind of near the train station. Say . . . two miles away.

Meeting a Killer

During the shooting, Dad had an important meeting in Paris on a weekend and took me with him. We stayed at the Georges V on the Champs-Elysées. I toured the city while he took care of his business. The next morning we were in the lobby about to check out when a voice made Dad turn: "Joe? Joe!" It was a shortish, distinguished-looking elderly man with long gray hair, wearing a fur coat.

"Hello, Felix!" Dad replied. They exchanged a hug. I was introduced. Felix wanted us to have dinner with him that night, but Dad explained we were on our way back to Rome.

As Felix started to walk away, Dad suddenly took my wrist and squeezed it tightly. "He's going to turn around. Remember his face." I nodded. "Felix!" Dad called out. The man turned. "So good to see you again!"

Felix smiled and walked off. Dad looked down at me. "That was Prince Felix Yusupov. The man who killed Rasputin."

I later learned about Rasputin, the "Mad Monk," while reading about the Russian Revolution. Dad had met and known Yusupov in Hollywood at MGM in the thirties when the film *Rasputin* was made, starring John Barrymore. What better technical advisor could there have been on the film than the man who engineered his death?

Full Circle with David Lean

On another occasion (I believe Chris may have been with us, on vacation), we drove to Venice, which Dad wanted us to see. He also wanted to say hello to his friend David Lean, who was directing a film there starring another friend, Katharine Hepburn. It was called *Summertime*. I remember watching the shooting near the Grand Canal. When they wrapped for the morning, we all had lunch at the legendary Harry's Bar.

More than thirty years later I had a house in Kenya, having been lured there by Stefanie Powers, who knew it well through her relationship with William Holden (more about Bill later). She had and still has a beautiful home on the Mount Kenya Game Ranch, which Bill founded with his partner, Don Hunt. Inside the ranch's property sat the world-famous Mount Kenya Safari Club, also founded by Bill and several others. The superb British actor John Hurt had purchased a house there as well. It was during the Christmas holidays. Stefanie, Don and Iris Hunt, John and Donna Hurt, and I were about to leave by four-wheel drive for a game camp in the Northern Frontier District. The night before we left, David Lean showed up at Don's house, having just been married, at eighty-four, for the sixth time. He was going to take his new wife on an aerial tour of Kenya with his favorite female bush pilot, All-Weather Heather. We started talking at Don's bar. David wanted to know all about Dad, who was also eighty-four at the time. He had a quick smile, a sharp mind, and a gruffness about him that I later found out was at least partially put on. I took him to task politely for using the credit "A Film by David Lean" when he hadn't written the screenplay. Surely Robert Bolt's writing in *Lawrence of Arabia* was one of the principal virtues of that magnificent film.

"But don't you see, my dear Tom, that by the time I've finished fussing and tweaking the script, the camera, and the actors, it is a film by David Lean." Case closed.

Stefanie and John Hurt were sitting a few feet away while we talked, listening with elephant ears and joining in the conversation from time to time. David feigned irritation. He was publicly famous for his supposed contempt for actors, although he certainly cast wonderful ones. At one point he turned to John Hurt and said, "You know, with all the money we pay you people, the least you could do is shut up once in a while." Wow. He turned back to me: "You know, that's why I loved Bill Holden so. You could talk to him for hours and never get the slightest indication that he was an actor."

David's current passion was to make a film of Joseph Conrad's *Heart of Darkness*. Warner Brothers had only agreed to put up half the money. My little production company had a bungalow at Warners then. He asked me about the executives there. Why only half the money? I said: "My guess would be that it's going to be a very expensive film and at your age they're wondering whether or not you've lost it. If the film's a flop, their exposure will be cut in half, and if it's a hit, they'll say they always knew it would be and that's why they were the first to put up money for the legendary David Lean."

David grinned: "You do know this business, don't you." Then he said something quite touching. "When you get back to the States and see Joe, tell him that at our age we should direct a film together. I'll do all the wide bits and he can do those little sophisticated things he does so well."

I told Dad. He smiled and said, "Actually, that's not such a bad idea."

Two postscripts on David Lean. First, my assistant at the time (and for twenty-five years) was Ann Ford Stevens, née Ann Ford, daughter of Cecil Ford, a legendary British production manager who did *Bridge on the River Kwai* with Lean. When I told David, he grew instantly nostalgic. "Annie? Dear little Annie . . . is now your . . . my goodness . . ."

"Write her a note," I said. "She'd be so thrilled."

"Oh, no, dear boy, I simply don't do that sort of thing."

During our long conversation I asked him several times again. Just jot down a greeting to her. No luck. The next day our group took off on Christmas safari. When I returned after New Year's, there was a handwritten note waiting for me at my house. It was from David Lean, addressed to Annie Stevens. She still has it.

I still had my bungalow at Warners in the early eighties. Steven Spielberg had one nearby. I was helping him out with the script of *Gremlins,* a film he was executive producing for his company. One day he came into my office and told me he was going to present the Best Director award at the Oscars. I was surprised, since the Academy (in my opinion) had treated him rather shabbily up to that point. In spite of his great films, he was still regarded by some as an upstart. How could, for example, *The Color Purple* be nominated for Best Picture, Best Actress, Best Screenplay, and two Best Supporting Actresses, and Steven not be nominated? If it was such a good film, surely the director must have had something to do with it. Steven explained: "David Lean is nominated for *A Passage to India*. At his age he may never make another film. In case he wins, I want to be the one who hands him the Oscar." That's the kind of reverence in which Lean was properly held by every generation of filmmakers.

The Far-from-Reclusive Mr. Hughes

The Barefoot Contessa received four Oscar nominations, including the statuette awarded to Edmond O'Brien for Best Supporting Actor. Dad called it his "best bad movie." It was about a megalomaniac millionaire/tycoon/film producer, based on the real-life character of Howard Hughes. Ava Gardner was an actress who rises from obscurity to stardom, and Bogart was her washed-up director who'd seen better days. O'Brien played Oscar Muldoon, the press agent, a crude version of George Sanders's Addison DeWitt in *All About Eve*. Roles like these usually delivered the bulk of Dad's acerbic cynicism, especially about show business, and in both cases delivered Oscars to the actors as well.

The Howard Hughes character in the film was unmistakable. At the time, Hughes kept different women waiting for him in different places on a nightly basis in case he wanted to join them, all conveniently "under contract." When the Italian actress Gina Lollobrigida seemed destined to become a star, Hughes brought her to California, offering a fat contract, and reportedly kept her a virtual prisoner in a rented house for days. When he finally showed up, she bashed him in the head with a vase and left. This incident is reenacted in the film when Ava Gardner bops Warren Stevens under the same circumstances. (It was further repeated much later in *The Aviator*, Martin Scorsese's film about Hughes.)

Dad knew Howard Hughes well in the thirties. After all, Hughes had bought the rights to *The Philadelphia Story* for his then paramour Katharine Hepburn. He was far from reclusive at the time, having affairs with many actresses and being conspicuously visible about town. By the early fifties he'd changed, leading a much more secretive life. Dad and Mother were in L.A. shortly before *Contessa* started shooting. As usual, Dad hadn't let his script be widely circulated. Only a chosen few had read it. One night, he got a phone call. It was Howard Hughes. He wanted to see Dad and would send over a car and driver to get him. Dad figured out that somehow

Hughes had read or gotten wind of the script. He was privately furious, but agreed to meet him. Mother was terrified. Who knew what Hughes would do? He was a crazy man. Why did Dad have to go, why didn't Hughes come over to see him? Dad told her to calm down: "Howard's not going to kill me, I promise you."

The limousine arrived. It took Dad to an unfinished section of a freeway past red warning cones that had been pushed over to the side. The limo stopped. Another limo arrived and flashed its lights. Dad left his car and joined Hughes, who immediately came to the point. He wanted Dad to drastically revise the character of the producer and totally eliminate the scene where he was hit in the head with the vase.

"I'll do what I can, Howard," Dad said.

"That's all I'm asking for," Hughes replied.

Dad exited the car and was driven home. He never changed a word of the script and never heard from Hughes again.

There's one line in the film that I always thought succinctly summed up Dad's attitude toward the motion picture industry. It's in a scene where Bogart has just screened Gardner's first film for a group of movie exhibitors. Their names are Mr. Black, Mr. Brown, Mr. Green, Mr. White, and so on. They like the film and agree to show it. "Gentlemen," says Bogart, "it's a wonderful art we're doing business in."

Back in New York

After we returned to New York from Rome, it was clear that Mother's situation wasn't improving. She was under the care of an eminent psychiatrist, but at that time there seemed to be no proper drugs available to alleviate her condition. I finally gathered the courage to ask Dad the question that Chris and I had been asking ourselves for so long: Why didn't they simply get a divorce? Why torture each other on an almost nightly basis with no end in sight? Dad explained as much as he had to, without any visible emotion. A divorce would mean she'd get automatic custody (especially in those days) of Chris and me, and he couldn't permit us to live in a household with someone that unstable, mother or not. He could go to court to have her declared mentally incompetent, but that would be a crushing public humiliation that he was unwilling to put her through. Obviously, it would have been almost equally uncomfortable for him, but he didn't go into that. For his entire life, if Dad didn't want to discuss something, it simply wasn't discussed. There was an impenetrable locked door in the man that would open only as far as he wanted to let it.

La Bohème

Mother was a huge opera fan. Some nights after a few drinks she would listen to one at top volume, usually a romantic tragedy such as *Tosca*, and preferably with an emotional star turn by a diva such as Maria Callas. She and Dad traveled in all strata of New York society and had made the acquaintance of the great Metropolitan Opera impresario Rudolf Bing. The family would go to the Met from time to time, eventually sitting in Bing's private box. All of a sudden, the project was on: Dad would direct a new production of *La Bohème*. It would be in English; Bing wanted to broaden opera's appeal, and Dad agreed. He'd always been obsessed with the idea of writing and directing for the theater, as evidenced by *All About Eve*. Staging an opera at the Met would be personally important for him, bring the right kind of notoriety and respect, and show that no matter how good his films were, he was more than just a movie guy.

The first problem he faced was that he didn't read music. So that Dad could familiarize himself with *La Bohème*, the opera boomed throughout our apartment on a daily basis until everyone in the family knew it by heart. To this day you can drop a needle at any point during the four acts and I'll start to sing along without missing a beat. Dad was now free to concentrate entirely on directing since the piece was totally familiar to him.

Opening night was a genuine success. The English lyrics by songwriter Howard Dietz were solid and easily flowing with only a few forced, wince-inducing rhymes. The cast was superb. It included the great tenor Richard Tucker, the popular and beautiful coloratura Patrice Munsel, and Robert Merrill, the reigning lyric baritone of his day, forever famous in New York for his full-throated version of the National Anthem at Yankee Stadium. All forms of theater have their own particular conventions, as Dad quickly found out when he was led onto the stage and joined the cast for a standing ovation. He looked down into the orchestra pit and gestured for the conductor, Alberto Erede, to join them.

"Alberto!" he called out. "Come up, Alberto!" Erede didn't budge.

Merrill leaned in and yelled into Dad's ear: "He answers to Maestro!"

Dad yelled, "Maestro!" gesturing again. Erede came up at once.

Dad's production of *La Bohème* lasted for more than a decade at the Met. It had wonderful, modern, and inventive directorial touches. Merrill tried to get him to direct a production of *Otello* in which he was to play Iago, but Dad decided to quit opera while he was ahead. Next stop, Broadway? It never happened. Despite his near worship for the theater, only a few faint attempts materialized. According to Moss Hart, when he visited his dear friend and coplaywright George S. Kaufman, who was terminally ill in the hospital, Kaufman looked at him and said, "Don't worry, I'm not going to die until Joe Mankiewicz writes his first play."

When Moss Hart was directing the classic musical *My Fair Lady,* he gave a young actress what I consider to be the ultimate piece of direction. She played one of the maids who greeted Julie Andrews when she returned triumphantly from the ball and sang "I Could Have Danced All Night." They were out of town, putting the number on its feet for the first time. Moss told the maids, "You can fuss about her as the music begins, then gradually make your way out through the side doors, leaving Julie alone to sing."

One of the maids was a through-and-through Method actress, the Actors Studio being all the rage then. "But I wouldn't leave," she told Moss. "I'd want to hear all about it. I'd have no motivation to go."

Moss said he understood her point, but Miss Andrews was going to be alone onstage for the number, so she'd better find her motivation.

"I don't think I can," the actress replied.

"I forget," said Moss. "How much are we paying you a week?"

"One hundred fifty dollars," came the reply.

"Ahhhh," he said. "There's your motivation!"

Prep School

Chris was already attending Lawrenceville. My grades at St. Bernard's were excellent and the school's reputation as a prep school feeder immaculate, so I pretty much had my pick and settled on Philip's Exeter Academy. It was the classic New England prep school nestled in a small New Hampshire town. Unlike some young teens who are apprehensive leaving home, I welcomed the prospect eagerly, with a real sense of relief. Exeter became my safe place where I could make new friends and develop myself in private, at my own speed.

Exeter was a happy, creative, and constructive time for me. As I mentioned earlier, my cousin Josie was attending Wellesley College and I could go down to Boston (it was only one hour by train) to see her. The work was challenging enough to make it interesting. I sucked at math or any kind of science but was a star in English, French, Latin, and History. I joined the school Dramatic Club and costarred in a production of Gore Vidal's *Visit to a Small Planet.* Gore, himself an Exeter graduate, actually came up to see the production and was quite complimentary to me. He couldn't have known at the time, but he would be adapting Tennessee Williams's *Suddenly, Last Summer* for Dad in a few years, and I would be the "production associate" (glorified gofer) on his screen version of his hit Broadway play *The Best*

Man in 1963. It was the first film I worked on after college. I also wrote for *The Pean,* the school yearbook. The editor was Peter Benchley (who wrote *Jaws*), then a couple of years ahead of me. I came full circle with Peter while doing a major rewrite on the screenplay of his second novel, *The Deep,* filmed some twenty years later in the Caribbean.

Mother rarely came up, so I was surprised when she called one day and said she was coming to Boston to spend the weekend with me. We went to the theater on Saturday night. It was a play heading for Broadway, starring Louis Jourdan (of *Gigi*). After the performance, the three of us had dinner. I didn't know she even knew him. Then we went up to his suite. After some strained small talk, the situation seemed pretty clear to me: they were interested in each other. I excused myself politely and went to my room. On Sunday, Mother and I saw the sights in Boston and she put me on the train back to Exeter. No mention of Louis. Looking back on it now and considering Dad's record of serial infidelity, I suppose a little turnabout was fair play.

Westchester

We started renting a house out of town every summer. Once in Long Island, then repeatedly in Westchester County, where Dad was eventually to spend the final decades of his life. Our favorite place was Mount Kisco. Our best friends up there were Bennett Cerf (Random House publisher and permanent panelist on *What's My Line*), his wife, Phyllis (later married to New York mayor Robert Wagner), and their son, Chris, who was my age. The area was and continues to be (along with Bedford, Katonah, and Pound Ridge) a rustic haven catering to the wealthy.

Mother wasn't doing well. She took a great many prescription pills, sedatives mainly, in an attempt to control her illness. I met my first steady girlfriend in Mount Kisco. Her name was Freddy Espy. It was puppy love run amok. Endless teenage necking without consummation. She was a talented artist and sent me countless letters at school filled with hearts of all sizes and idealized depictions of herself as a love-smitten pixie. Freddy would later marry the celebrated George Plimpton Jr. (author of *Paper Lion*), the editor of the *Paris Review* and a wonderfully literate and amusing man with whom I would later spend delightful evenings in New York and L.A.

One Bad Fall Day

I was already back in school for the fall term. The family's lease on the Mount Kisco house didn't expire until later. One Saturday night I was having dinner with a couple of classmates at a diner in the tiny town of Exeter. I remember it was very cold outside. I was also smoking a cigarette, which was absolutely verboten at the school. There was a rap at the diner window. I turned and saw the dean staring in straight at me. Shit, I thought. I'm going to get thrown out. The dean gestured for me to join him outside. I started for the door, trying to think of an excuse, any excuse. Once outside: "Dean Kessler, I know this looks . . ."

"Your mother is dead," he interrupted. I blinked. "I know it may seem cruel to just say it like that, but I've been through this before and I've found it to be the best way."

My head started to swim. A reservation had been made for me on the next train to Boston. I would be met at the station by a female psychiatrist who would then accompany me on a plane to New York. Did I need company on the train? It could be easily arranged. I shook my head.

The next days were and are a blur to me now. I remember what seemed like an endless reception of the great and the near great coming by the apartment to pay their respects. Mother's psychiatrist, the eminent Dr. Lawrence Kubie, was there. Did I want to talk to him, get things off my chest? No, that's okay. Don't worry about it, I'll be all right. I barely remember her funeral. It was at Kensico Cemetery in Westchester. I couldn't even tell you who attended.

How did Mother die? This was the initial story I was told, tragic, but fit for public consumption: Dad and Bennett Cerf had been out to dinner. Mother wasn't feeling well. When they returned, they found her dead, an empty bottle of pills on her bedside table. She had clearly forgotten she'd already taken a few and in her altered state accidentally took some more—a terrible accident. That's what was printed in the newspapers, so it had to be true. Here's what I found out later, piece by piece: Dad and Mother had a whopper of a fight. He drove back to New York. Later on he called her repeatedly with no answer. Fearing the worst, he called my cousin Josie and asked her to drive up to Mount Kisco with him for the night. Mother would be so delighted to see her. When they came into the house, they called out to her. Silence. Dad said he'd look around downstairs and asked Josie to check the bedroom. Josie found her, dead. Bennett Cerf, a kind and distinguished man who clearly knew the truth, was in no way involved. I always felt sorry that Bennett felt he had to help Dad make the discovery more publicly palatable by saying he was there. It was a true act of friendship, but it was a lie. Mother apparently left a suicide note (that's what the Mount Kisco police said at first), but after a reported phone call from Dad's friend, Governor Averill Harriman, the note miraculously disappeared. The local authorities said they must have made a mistake. I never read the note or found out what was in it. Be that as it may, my overwhelming feeling at the time was truly one of relief for Mother. She led such a tortured life. Thank God she was finally at peace. That's why, at the time, I never cried. I tried to, but I couldn't.

More than a decade later I was asleep in my house in Malibu. It was early, early in the morning. I'd fallen asleep with the television on. I heard something that half woke me. My head started to pulsate. My eyes popped open. The sound I heard was Mother's voice. I was suddenly staring straight into her face on the screen, which was televising *The Keys of the Kingdom*. I was transfixed, stunned. Then tears began to roll down my cheeks. I must have cried for more than half an hour. It felt good to finally get it all out. It was the very least I owed her and myself.

Mother's suicide happened at the start of my senior year at Exeter. Fortunately, I had already been given an A rating by Yale University in my junior year, which basically meant that if you didn't really screw up before graduation, you were in. On my Preliminary SAT achievement tests I had scored an 800 in English, which was the highest score one could get. I sent a letter to Dad, who was shooting *Suddenly, Last Summer* in England, and told him. He cabled me back: "Ain't you lucky they didn't ask you to spell achievement?" I had misspelled it in my letter. Dad always liked to have the last word.

As the 1950s ended, I entered Yale. Dad told me how proud "Pop" would have been of me and that being educated at schools like St. Bernard's, Exeter, and Yale was everything he envisioned for me when we left California. But there was still one thing I wanted to do more than get a first-class education, and I begged him to help me. I wanted to work, in any capacity, on a movie. Dad agreed to do it, with the following caveat: He'd get me on a film made by people he'd never worked with. There would be no past relationships for me to fall back on if things went wrong. He also (correctly) told me that there would be some on the film who'd be hoping I screwed up, who'd say the only reason I was working on it was because I was Joe Mankiewicz's kid. He wrote a letter to Doc Merman at Fox, head of the physical production department at the time. Dad was an independent company with no ties to Fox anymore, but he knew and liked Doc. I still have the letter he sent. As luck would have it, Fox was shooting a western called *The Comancheros* at the start of the summer. It was starring John Wayne, would be directed by the legendary Michael Curtiz, and would be shot almost entirely on location near Moab, Utah.

Snapshots from 1950s Films

No Way Out (1950)

An extraordinary film for its time, dealing brutally with race. The first film ever made by a major studio in which contemporary black people were seen in their own apartments and homes, sitting down to meals, leading lives as ordinary and complex as their white counterparts. It was Sidney Poitier's first part—the leading role. There were no black leading men at the time in Hollywood, only "specialty" stars such as Paul Robeson or Bill "Bojangles" Robinson, singers and dancers. Hattie McDaniel had won a supporting actress Oscar for *Gone with the Wind,* but she played a slave and had to sit in the back of the auditorium. Sidney was washing dishes in New York at the time. He had, I believe, briefly appeared in off-off-Broadway theater, but dishwashing was how he earned a living. He was one in a group of young black actors who read for the part, and Dad cast him immediately. During his Lifetime Achievement acceptance speech at the Academy Awards decades later, Sidney remarked on the oddity of his straight away playing the lead in a major Hollywood film: "I arrived in Hollywood at twenty-two in a time different than today's, a time in which the odds against my standing here tonight would not have fallen in my favor. Back then, no route had been established for where I wanted to go, no pathway left in evidence for me to trace, no custom for me to follow."

Darryl Zanuck was quite socially committed for a major studio head. Fox had made *Gentleman's Agreement* about anti-Semitism and *Pinky* about a black girl "passing," but the latter part was played by the super-white Jeanne Crain. Casting a black actress in that role would have been out of the question at the time. Racism was the elephant in the room for Hollywood. This was a time when the few black baseball players who existed had to stay at separate hotels from their white teammates, when Sammy Davis Jr. could sell out the Copacabana in New York but blacks weren't allowed to sit at the tables. Explicit racial slurs were frequent in the script, which Dad cowrote with Lesser Samuels. "Coon," "Sambo," "jig," and "Niggertown" were just a few. Sidney plays a young black doctor in a hospital prison ward who treats a viciously racist Richard Widmark and his brother. The brother dies, and Widmark erroneously blames Sidney for his death. Widmark later told me that his dialogue was so raw and evil that he actually felt compelled to apologize to Sidney after many scenes: "I'd played bad guys before, but this was the biggest lowlife creep I'd ever seen."

There's a race riot in the film, something unthinkable to have put on the screen at the time and something the moviegoing public wasn't prepared to look at. Both Dad and Zanuck realized the film wouldn't be shown in many states—indeed, it was never exhibited south of the Mason-Dixon Line—but they went ahead and made it. Right-wing publications damned it as hysterical "Commie" propaganda, but *Ebony* magazine, the most influential black publication in the country, praised it as the first honest film ever made about contemporary black life. Ossie Davis was also in the cast and gave a wonderful performance. His wife, the hugely talented Ruby Dee, joined Sidney in making her screen debut.

After the film finished shooting, Dad asked to see Sidney. He gave him an office address in New York and told him to go there and say he was sent by Joe Mankiewicz. The office belonged to Zoltan Korda of the famous British film family. Dad knew Korda was about to make *Cry, the Beloved Country* and thought Sidney would be perfect for the lead role. He asked him to fly Sidney to London and test him. He was confident he'd get the part. Korda did exactly that. Sidney starred in the film, which was wonderfully received internationally, and the rest, as they say, is history. I recently sat on a panel at the Motion Picture Academy with Sidney, Martin Landau, and others, celebrating a new print of Dad's film *Suddenly, Last Summer.* When Sidney was introduced, he got a standing ovation from a packed house in the main theater. He thanked the audience, then noted: "Were it not for Joe Mankiewicz, there's a good chance I wouldn't even be on this stage tonight." *No Way Out* represented the best that was inside Dad, the kind of courage he showed fighting against the loyalty oath at the Directors Guild. At times like that, I was so proud to be his son.

At the end of *No Way Out,* Widmark lures Sidney to a house to kill him, but is himself accidentally shot in the dark. His leg is gashed wide open, the blood flowing freely. Sidney applies a tourniquet and delivers the last line of the film: "Don't cry, white boy. You're going to live." Thirty years after the film's release, I attended a wake for William Holden at Stefanie Powers's house. Sidney and Widmark were both there, fast friends, having made at least one other film together. The three of us were talking at the bar. Widmark took a handful of peanuts and tossed them down his throat. He gagged, horribly. They'd gone down the wrong way. He coughed violently as Sidney pounded him on the back. His eyes glassed over. Suddenly, the obstruction cleared. Sidney smiled and said: "Don't cry, white boy. You're going to live."

Julius Caesar (1953)

Generally regarded as one of the best adaptations of Shakespeare ever put on the screen. Marlon Brando played Mark Antony. He had never performed Shakespeare before, not even in acting class. This daring piece of casting resulted in an Oscar nomination and his actually winning the British Academy Award. Dad was particularly proud of that, since in his opinion the Brits would rather have committed mass suicide than given an American actor their Oscar for performing Shakespeare in the 1950s. Almost thirty years later I was having lunch with Marlon in London while we were doing *Superman*. I asked him how different things were making films now than earlier in his career. "In those days you knew whose set you were on," he replied. "It was Kazan's set, your father's set. Today, sometimes I work with directors who actually ask me if I think they're doing a good job."

It's crucial, as I found out later, for a director to be able to control his or her set, especially when things start to get out of control, as they often do. Marlon told me about the day they were filming Caesar's entrance into the Colosseum, when he meets the soothsayer who gives him a warning. Dad was up on a crane, shooting down at the actors. The problem was that they were all waiting for a "day player" who had two lines. He'd ducked out to relieve himself and hadn't come back yet. Marlon: "This was a pretty amazing cast standing there, waiting: James Mason, John Gielgud, me, Deborah Kerr, Greer Garson, Louis Calhern, and Edmond O'Brien. Being actors with nothing to do, we started kidding around, making pee jokes. Gielgud 'confessed' that he'd peed in his pants twenty minutes ago, sacrificing himself for his art. I asked Deborah when she peed, did she have to take off her whole fucking toga? It started getting boisterous. Joe was looking down from the crane, the ever-present pipe in his mouth, silently fuming. Suddenly, the guy came running back onto the set, totally out of breath. He looked up at Joe apologetically: 'I am so sorry, Mr. Mankiewicz. No one told me they'd be ready this soon.' Joe nodded. The guy took his place. We were still stifling laughs about pissing when the buzzer sounded. Everyone put on their game face. 'Rolling!' 'Speed!' It was totally quiet. Joe took the pipe out of his mouth and stared down at the guy: 'You don't have nearly the talent, young man, to keep this company waiting twenty minutes.' We all snapped to, straightened up like a bunch of schoolkids. We were doing Shakespeare. It was an important scene. Joe had just taken his set back."

Guys and Dolls (1955)

The only film Dad ever made that was the top grosser of the year. He always said, "I'm so happy I worked when I did, because every film I'm best known for would never get a green light today." He loved that musical—it lived and breathed New York to him. Another daring piece of casting with

Marlon. Dad cabled him in Europe: "How'd you like to play Sky Masterson in *Guys and Dolls?*" Marlon cabled back: "Very nervous. Have never done a musical before." Dad cabled back: "Don't worry about it. Neither have I." Frank Sinatra was cast as Nathan Detroit. Jean Simmons as Sister Sarah. Dad retained many players from the stage version, notably Vivian Blaine and Stubby Kaye.

It was a wonderful concept for a film. There were no exterior scenes. Everything happened in stylized interiors. Dad thought of it as a fable and shot it that way. The choreography by Michael Kidd was brilliant. Dad wanted the actors to sing for themselves. He hated the usual practice of dubbing in other voices when they burst into song. This was obviously no problem for Sinatra, and Jean Simmons turned out to have a lovely voice. Brando did the best he could, his singing usually pieced together from multiple recording takes, sometimes line by line. He was fine with the ballads but suffered more in the driving "Luck Be a Lady." Sinatra had desperately wanted to play Sky Masterson. In Las Vegas, where he performed many nights, commuting by private plane from the set, he was Sky Masterson and made a point of including "Luck Be a Lady" in his act. I was on the set often during summer vacation. I still have a picture of me behind the camera, squinting through the barrel, with Dad's inscription: "Son, didn't I tell you you peaked too soon? With my love, Dad."

Enchanting in the movie, enchanting in real life, at the time of *Guys and Dolls*, Jean Simmons was married to Stewart Granger, the swashbuckling star of *Scaramouche* and *King Solomon's Mines*. He was devastatingly handsome but somewhat of a prick and treated her badly. I was to run into him later in life. Jean and Dad had a huge affair during the shooting of the film. Granger must have known but thought, what the hell, I'm not working that much anymore and she always comes home to me. Twenty years later I found myself a frequent guest at Jean's home. Divorced from Granger, she had married the writer-director Richard Brooks (*Blackboard Jungle, In Cold Blood*) after costarring with Burt Lancaster in his film version of *Elmer Gantry*. Richard was a tough, no-nonsense guy, extremely talented and prickly. I was introduced to him by Gene Kelly, who was a good friend of his and a sort of self-appointed godfather to me. The mutual attraction was tennis. Gene and I played all the time. I wound up playing at the Brookses' house on a regular basis and was often invited to watch movies in their screening room at night.

I was totally besotted with Jean. She was so beautiful, sweet, and caring. I winced privately when Richard barked at her every time she made a mistake on the tennis court while playing doubles. She wasn't that good, but she was doing the best she could. She seemed to have an affinity for men who didn't treat her well, although Richard was a big improvement over Granger in intellect and talent.

One night when Richard was shooting on location, Jean asked me up to the house for a screening. After the film ended and the guests were leaving, she silently signaled me to stay behind. I did. She made me a drink and then gently placed her hand on my crotch. I turned scarlet. She looked into my eyes: "Oh, dear. I'm asking you to do something you don't want to." Didn't want to? I was terrified. For Christ's sake, this was Jean Simmons and the wife of Richard Brooks. We had a drink and I left. I sensed a real loneliness in her and couldn't understand why. She was so enchanting in every way. Perhaps it was because of the reciprocal radar I had with troubled or unhappy women (especially actresses), but one thing eventually did lead to another.

One night later she asked me to escort her to a formal dinner for Princess Margaret of England who was making a state visit and stopping in Los Angeles. It was almost a command performance for every celebrated Brit in Hollywood. Richard was still on location. I rented white tie and tails and escorted her. We sat at a table with people I knew: Leslie and Evie Bricusse, Tony Newley and Joan Collins, Michael Caine, and others. During the meal I got up to go to the men's room. As I was about to enter, I saw Gene Kelly following me.

"Cut it out, Tom," came the warning.

"Cut what out?"

"You know what I'm talking about."

"Gene, you don't think that Jean and I . . ."

"Yes, I do."

"Gene, if there was anything going on, do you think I'd be dumb enough to bring her to a public event like this?"

"You bet. Dumb enough and young enough. So cut it out before you get in over your head, if you're not there already."

Gene was right, God bless him. Everything out of bounds with Jean ended that night. She died recently at eighty. I never would have included any of this in a public memoir were she still alive. But she was the most ethereal, vulnerable woman I ever met. My feelings for her ran very deep. I felt I needed to mention her.

Suddenly, Last Summer (1959)

One of the few pictures Dad made when he did not write the screenplay. Gore Vidal adapted the script from the Tennessee Williams play. It starred

Elizabeth Taylor, Katharine Hepburn, and Montgomery Clift, and dealt with, among other things, mental illness, homosexuality, pedophilia, and cannibalism. The producer was Sam Spiegel (*The African Queen, On the Waterfront, Lawrence of Arabia*), who liked to pop up occasionally on the set without warning. Dad called him "Suddenly Sam Spiegel."

Dad had never worked with Elizabeth Taylor before and was apprehensive since he'd been told she was quite a handful. Kate Hepburn was an old friend. Montgomery Clift wasn't Dad's first choice to play the psychoanalyst. Clift was slowly disintegrating at the time, following a tragic car accident. It had happened after he left a party at Elizabeth's house. She and Clift were close friends, and she lobbied hard for him. He was still a wonderful actor, but the booze and drugs were taking their toll on him, resulting in a somewhat jerky and halting performance.

The interiors were shot at Pinewood Studios, outside of London. The exteriors were shot in Spain. The first day at Pinewood there was a 9:00 A.M. shooting call. Dad was on the stage earlier, planning the day's work with the cameraman. An assistant told him they'd just received a phone call from London: Miss Taylor was just now leaving her house. Dad looked at his watch: it was 8:15. Pinewood was more than an hour away from London. That would put Elizabeth in the studio at about 9:30, assuming she really had left. Add an hour and a half minimum for hair and makeup—she wouldn't be on the set until well after 11:00. He thought, Christ, is this going to be a daily experience? Elizabeth arrived on the stage around 11:30. It was empty. There was a note left for her, taped to the camera, reading: "Dear Elizabeth. We were all here at nine. So sorry to have missed you. Love, Joe." Dad waited all day for an angry phone call, but never heard from her. The next morning he arrived on the stage around 8:00 to set up the first shot. Already sitting in the corner in full hair and makeup was Elizabeth. She raised her wrist and tapped her watch, silently scolding him for being late.

They got along like a house afire after that. Elizabeth was nobody's fool. She was direct, smart, warm, and as I found out later for myself, extremely funny. She arguably gave her finest performance ever in that film. She and Hepburn were both nominated for Oscars. They "knocked each other off." Dad and Elizabeth were in constant contact after the film, signaling to me that they'd almost certainly had an affair. The same harmony did not exist with Hepburn, however. Rightly or not, he thought she'd become a truly mannered actress over the years who was starting to give the same performance over and over again. In an interview, he described her as "the most talented amateur actress I've ever worked with." That didn't help matters any. After her last shot, she reportedly spat at him. Years later I spent some time with Hepburn. She had only warm memories of Dad, at least for social publication. I found her to be one classy broad.

A footnote about Elizabeth (before we eventually get into *Cleopatra*): She'd been famously married to Mike Todd, the showman-producer who made *Around the World in Eighty Days*. A year or so before *Suddenly, Last Summer* Dad had been meeting with Todd about writing and directing a screen version of *Don Quixote*. Danny Kaye would play the title role, and the Mexican star Cantinflas would play Sancho Panza. Todd was going to fly across the country in his private plane, the *Lucky Liz*. Dad agreed to go with him to discuss the intended production. At the last minute he had to get back to New York on business and took the red-eye out of L.A. Chris and I drove out to Idyllwild Airport (now Kennedy) to meet him just as the news broke in headlines across the country: Mike Todd's plane had crashed, killing him. There was another dead man found as well. Since Dad's name was on the passenger manifest, some newspapers first assumed it was him. His death was announced in print directly under Todd's on the front page of the *New York Daily News*. It turned out that the other unfortunate human being was a writer, Art Cohn, who was doing a biography of Todd. Dad always kept the newspaper announcement in his files, however, as a reminder that from now on, he was living on borrowed time.

4

The 1960s

Hollywood Off-Ramp

> If my toilet's stopped up and the repairman shows me a card from the plumber's union, I have a reasonable expectation he can fix it. If someone shows me their Writers Guild card, I have no idea whether or not they can write.
>
> —*Joseph L. Mankiewicz*

The Comancheros

(I work with the "Duke," dance with the Navajos, get fired by Michael Curtiz, and lose my virginity)

I'm kind of a "third" assistant director on the film. Today's equivalent on a crew would be called a "trainee." My first task is to go to the Burbank airport where the film company will take off in a chartered plane for Moab, Utah. I am to check everyone onto the flight. The night before I'm so keyed up I can't sleep, at least until about 3:00 A.M., when I finally do fall asleep, sleep through my alarm, and miss the flight. Hardly an auspicious start to a show business career. I drive to Fox to take my medicine from Doc Merman. He sees how horribly shaken I am and, thank God, doesn't rub it in. I'm put on a tiny, single-engine Cessna that day, flying to Moab with the raw film stock for the movie. The flight is interminable and bumpy. I think it will never end.

My boss is the first assistant director, Jack Berne. I'm working doubly hard to make up for my disastrous start, and thank goodness everyone seems terribly helpful in breaking me in. I bury myself in crew lists, schedules, and budgets and familiarize myself with all the local desert locations.

I start with the easiest of jobs. The first morning of shooting I'm to take a car driven by a teamster and pick up John Wayne at 6:00 A.M. at the house he's renting nearby. By 5:00 A.M. I'm already in the coffee shop of the Apache Motel, where most of the company is staying. I have about eleven cups of coffee, then check my watch: it's 5:40. I'd better get going. Suddenly, I hear a sound behind me: "clink, clink, clink . . ." I turn and look up into the iconic face of John Wayne, who is peering down at me. He's already dressed in his film wardrobe. His gun belt is on, boots, spurs, Texas Ranger's badge, the whole nine yards. From my position on the stool he seems nine feet tall and three feet wide.

"Are you the fella who's supposed to pick me up?"

"Yes, sir, Mr. Wayne."

"Well, I like to drive myself with my wardrobe and makeup guys. I know this valley pretty well by now. I'll get there."

"Yes, sir, Mr. Wayne, whatever you say."

He nods, looks down at me, and notices a "Kennedy for President" button on my shirt lapel. "I'd take that button off if I were you. We don't advertise socialists on my set."

I blush. He suddenly gives me that great, big, wide, wonderful John Wayne grin. I think he's trying to tell me he's kidding, but the Kennedy button never reappears for the duration of the film.

The picture starts shooting in the desert, and I drink in every minute of it. It's a wonderful experience to be out there with Wayne and his legendary stunt men from the John Ford stock company. This is, I am convinced, what making movies is all about. Wayne is the leader, there is no doubt. He's giving and kind to everyone, although he can be gruff and single-minded at times. His loyalties run deep, and it sometimes seems that many people working on the movie have done at least a dozen films with him. Anyone who's worked with Wayne before and been asked back can call him "Duke." Until he lets you know, if he lets you know, it's "Mr. Wayne." This stems from his days with John Ford. Everyone—I mean everyone—called him "Mr. Ford." In the eighties, when I had dinner with Maureen O'Hara, who'd starred in five or six pictures for him, she still referred to him as "Mr. Ford." John Wayne called him "Pappy." He was the only one allowed to do that. If you tried to call Ford "Pappy," you'd get a knuckle sandwich before he fired you.

A few weeks into shooting I came up to Wayne sitting in his chair on the set. "They're ready for you, Mr. Wayne." He nodded and got up. As he started off for the camera, he turned and said: "Oh. By the way. Call me Duke." My answering grin must have been a yard wide. When we wrapped in the hot desert afternoon, sometimes Duke would stay behind, break out a bottle of Cuervo Gold tequila, and swap stories with the stuntmen, wranglers, and some of the crew. I listened, laughed, drank, and thought: can life be any better than this?

A note or two about John Ford: He was obviously the seminal American director and a total autocrat on his films. Robert Wagner told me that when he was a young actor just starting out, he got a small part in *What Price Glory*, directed by Ford. They had wrapped locations and were back at the studio. R.J. was standing by his mentor, Spencer Tracy, as they listened to Ford talking to his cameraman on the back lot: "Shit, we took him out of frame in Utah going left to right, so he's got to come in right to left, and that fucking telephone pole is sitting there—"

R.J., being an eager young suck-up at the time, interrupted: "I've got an idea, Mr. Ford!"

Without even looking, Ford whacked him in the side of the head, knocking him down, then spoke to the cameraman again. "Anyway, he exited left to right . . ."

No director could get away with that kind of behavior today. But that was then, and the director was John Ford. Henry Fonda told me that when he and Leland Hayward were making the film version of their Broadway hit *Mister Roberts*, they first hired John Ford to direct. His directorial style rubbed the entire crew the wrong way. He would chew out people mercilessly, and that sort of behavior was becoming out of date. After only a few days, several crew members were threatening to quit. Hank asked to see Ford in his motor home. He was the star and coproducer of the film. Hank said: "I told him, 'Jack, you've got to ease up a little, you've just got to, they won't put up with it.' His face got red and he tried to punch me. I paused for a moment, then said what I had to: 'I'm sorry, Jack. You're fired.' Ford stormed out. This was the man I owed my career to, the man who directed me in *Grapes of Wrath*, *Young Mr. Lincoln*, and *My Darling Clementine*. My eyes misted over. It was the toughest thing I ever had to do in my professional life." Hank and Hayward hired their friend Josh Logan, who'd directed the play on Broadway.

Speaking of autocrats, Michael Curtiz is the renowned director of *Captain Blood*, *Robin Hood*, and the immortal *Casablanca*. *The Comancheros* is to be his last film. In his seventies, he's been diagnosed with cancer and is slowly dying. Wayne heard about it and decided to give him the job because no one seemed to want him anymore and he needed a payday. Curtiz has a reputation for being a somewhat objectionable human being. From what I can see, he certainly deserves it. He is rude to everyone, an arrogant prick with a thick Hungarian accent. Two days before filming, we have lunch with the mayor of Moab. Curtiz has to sneeze, and he does so into our table-cloth. I swear. He sunbathes nude at the tiny pool of the Apache Motel, not a pleasant sight, and outrages other guests, some of whom have children. The manager threatens to evict him. He stops.

Wayne doesn't seem to like Curtiz personally, and Curtiz definitely doesn't like the fact that Duke controls the production, but at his advanced age, feeble and sick, there's little he can do. In Moab during the summer, temperatures can reach 110 degrees. Curtiz usually falls asleep in his chair by early afternoon. We protect him with umbrellas to keep the sun off and put chamois cloths filled with ice around his neck. We all take salt pills. Once Curtiz is asleep, the picture is directed by Wayne. With seasoned actors such as Lee Marvin and Stuart Whitman, and the veteran Bill Clothier behind the camera, it all gets done effectively.

Toward the end of one particularly hot day, the late afternoon sun burns like a laser beam on the horizon. We have adjusted the umbrella behind Curtiz to shield him. Wayne is doing a scene with Lee Marvin. We've done the "over the shoulder" favoring Lee. I look over at Curtiz and ask, "Turn around on Mr. Wayne now, Mr. Curtiz?"

"Yes," he mumbles. "Just don't turn me around."

One hundred Navajo Indians are transported up from Arizona. They have worked in previous John Wayne westerns, and he is particularly fond of them. Indians are not allowed to drink in Utah, and no motel would give them rooms, so a tent village is set up out of town. I'm to pick up the Indians in the morning, put them on buses, and at night pay them each five dollars for their day's work. At the end of the first day I sit behind a table in the village with one hundred five-dollar bills and a list of names in front of me. The Indians get into line. The names are strikingly similar: Wolf That Smiles, Bear That Stands, Horse That Runs, and so on. I check them off as they give me their names. I dole out the hundred five-dollar bills and look up: there's still about twenty people in line. They start to argue with me: "No, no, you gave five dollars to Bear That Stands, I am Bear That Growls," and so on. I realize I've been taken. I turn to the chief. "Listen, tomorrow morning I'm giving everyone a number from one to a hundred. At night they hand in their numbered slip and get their five dollars."

The next morning the Indians get on the bus. I give them each a num-ber, but at 98, there are no Indians left to board. "Chief, what's the deal? Where're the other two guys?" He tells me they were arrested in Moab last night, for drinking. I take a chance and swing the buses by the jail. The sheriff comes out.

"Sheriff, do you have two of our Indians?"

"Sure do."

I say, "I realize this is asking a lot, but we need them. Do you think they could work on the movie during the day, and at night I'll swing by and return them to you?"

The sheriff says, "That's great with me. The other prisoners don't like Indians, and it'll save me a couple of lunches."

That night, we go by the jail. Two Indians get up, but I can see right away they're not the same two who were arrested. The sheriff is in front as they get off.

"Sheriff, I have to warn you, those are not the Indians you arrested."

He says, "Makes no difference to me. I arrested two Indians, I just need two Indians." For the rest of the film, two different Indians get off each night.

The female lead is played by Ina Balin, a young stage actress doing her first big part in a film. She arrives two weeks into shooting and is driven out to the desert to start work. It's a small scene with Wayne. She says something like, "Ranger Jake, Ranger Jake, they've got my father!" Duke says, "Let's go!" That's the whole scene. Curtiz is asleep in his chair, but we're lit and ready to go. Duke says, "Let's shoot it."

Ina says, "Excuse me, aren't we going to rehearse first?"

"What's to rehearse? You say, 'They've got my father,' and I say, 'Let's go.'"

"Well, I don't know, maybe it's because I'm from the stage and I'm used to rehearsals."

"Let me tell you something, little lady: I've worked with stage people before. I've worked with Miss Geraldine Page of the New York stage, best goddamn part she ever had—*Hondo*." He turns to Jack Berne. "Shoot the rehearsal."

We roll. Ina runs into the shot: "Ranger Jake, Ranger Jake, they've got my father!" Duke says, "Let's go!" They run out of the shot. Jack Berne says, "Cut it." Wayne says, "Print it."

He turns to Ina. "See how easy this is?"

There's a frequent poker game during shooting usually attended by stuntmen and other members of the crew. I've been in the game twice and both times lost my weekly paycheck. I'm so thrilled to be playing poker with these guys that I don't care. The actor Jack Elam plays one night; he's one of the villains in the film. Elam is known for his crazed look and cocked eye. (He later becomes a favorite in Sergio Leone's westerns.) He's also nuts. The next day we're going to shoot a scene in which Wayne and Stuart Whitman are staked out on the ground with two vultures in a tree looking down. The birds have been brought up from L.A. along with their wrangler, the person who trains and owns them. The "Vulture Man" plays in the poker game. It's table stakes. On one particular hand that he's sure he's a lock to win, he puts up his vultures as collateral. He loses them to Elam.

The next day on set we're prepping the first shot. It's already about a hundred degrees. Stand-ins have been staked out to represent Whitman and Wayne. I see the Vulture Man nearby and say, "It's time to put the birds in the tree."

He looks at me sadly: "They belong to Elam now. They're in his trailer. Better talk to him."

I knock on Elam's trailer door. He opens it. I can see both vultures behind him, eating some God-awful-looking food from a large bowl. "Jack, we've got to get those guys in the tree."

Elam: "How much do my birds get?"

"Geez, Jack, I don't know. We don't have a budget out here."

"Find out how much the birds get."

I go to Jack Berne and explain the situation. This gives him Excedrin Headache #70. We use a mobile phone to call the production office in Moab. I return to Jack's trailer. "Jack, they get a hundred dollars a day, each."

He grins: "My birds don't work for less than two hundred fifty."

Suddenly, a station wagon pulls up and Duke gets out, dressed for action. "Christ, it's hot. We ready to go?"

"Duke, we're waiting for the vultures."

"What the hell's wrong with the vultures?"

I explain. Duke strides over to Elam's trailer and bangs on the door. Jack opens it. "You get those goddamn birds up in that tree right now or one of their heads is gonna be sticking out of your mouth and the other head out of your asshole!"

Elam: "Putting them in the tree right now, Duke; they're moving even as we speak."

One day the principals wrap in the morning. We're going to shoot second unit in the afternoon. A minor cattle stampede. A couple hundred of

Wayne's own Texas longhorns have been shipped up for the scene. The second unit director is Cliff Lyons, a veteran of many Wayne and John Ford westerns. Curtiz tells him he wants the cattle to be driven into a nearby draw with about a five-foot drop. They'll have to scramble up the other side. Cliff tells him that some of the cattle will break their legs going in and others might break their legs trying to climb over them and up the other side. Curtiz snaps, "Don't argue with me, just do it!" He walks off.

I say to Cliff, "You can't possibly shoot this, right? They're Duke's cattle."

"Fuck it. He's the director. If he wants to commit suicide, that's up to him."

I go over to Curtiz. "Mr. Curtiz, don't you think we should call Mr. Wayne in Moab first, since these are his cattle?"

He turns around with a look of fury, suddenly grabs a gun from an extra's holster, and fires a blank at me! "You're fired! Get out of here!"

I drive back to Moab. I'm up in my room, packing, wondering how I'll ever explain this to Dad. The phone rings. Miracle of all miracles—it's Duke. "I heard what you did out there. Thanks. I'm going out to see what that Hungarian piece of shit's doing with my cattle. See you in the morning."

"I don't think so, Duke. He fired me."

"Hell, by the time I'm through with him, he won't even remember that. See you tomorrow."

The next day I go back to work. Perhaps Curtiz does remember, but he doesn't say a word about it for the rest of the film.

I'm eighteen years old and still a virgin. There's a very attractive actress in the cast named Joan O'Brien. She worked with Wayne in his previous film, *The Alamo*, which he directed. She and some children are the only survivors at the end of the movie. For some reason she seems to take a keen interest in me. I'm very flattered. We have dinner one night, following which she asks me to come up to her room. It's an amazing evening. I'm "all thumbs" at what I'm trying to do for the first time, and she is wonderfully helpful, understanding, and kind. Our "relationship" continues for the last few weeks of filming. It seems there are no secrets on location, something I found to be totally accurate years later. The stuntmen dub me "Wrangler Tom." When I come on the set wearing one of my brother's shirts, which I mistakenly packed and which is much too large for me, they marvel at how much weight I've lost since I met Joannie. I'm still deeply grateful to Joan O'Brien. I couldn't have had a warmer, more attractive, and understanding teacher.

Boola Boola

Thinking of my time at Yale (1959–1963) reawakens so many rich memories: professors who opened cultural, political, and ethical doors for me; classmates from every conceivable background—half the student body was there on scholarship. New Haven was also within inhaling distance of New York, so I could go home on weekends whenever I felt like it. After Mother's death, we'd moved to a four-story townhouse on Seventy-First Street between Park and Lexington Avenues. It had its own elevator and a little garden. Chris was attending Columbia University and living uptown. We were a family of three guys now: Dad, Chris, and me. Adelaide Wallace, Dad's secretary for more than thirty years, occupied a small office on the ground floor. She was, in effect, the female component of the family. Addie was sharp, funny, loyal, and helpful. Everyone loved her. Things finally seemed to be calming down for me at last. But not for long.

Bridget Hayward

Bridget Hayward was the younger daughter of Leland Hayward and Margaret Sullavan—blond, emotionally fragile, and attractive to the point of being ethereal. I fell desperately in love with her. She was in her early twenties.

I was a smitten eighteen-year-old college sophomore staring at an age gulf that effectively made her unattainable. Because of that, I loved her more. To me she was as magical as a character in *A Midsummer Night's Dream*. Bridget was troubled enough to have earlier been committed to the Austen Riggs Center, something I either wasn't aware of or ignored.

Her older sister, Brooke, also became a friend. Unlike Bridget, Brooke was knockout glamorous, outgoing, and a sought-after photographic fashion model with acting aspirations. She has remained a good friend of mine over many years, especially in California after I moved back and she'd married Dennis Hopper. My obsession with Bridget was well documented by Brooke in her best-selling family autobiography, *Haywire,* which also became a highly rated TV miniseries. It's a wonderful read, beautifully written, and if anyone thought the Mankiewicz family had its emotional problems, we were pikers compared to the Haywards. Leland, a legendary agent and producer, was Brooke and Bridget's father. Their mother, Maggie Sullavan, had committed suicide. There was a younger brother, Bill. He too had once been committed to Riggs. He tried to straighten himself out by doing a stint as a paratrooper, then had a brief romance with the movies, attaching himself to Dennis Hopper and Peter Fonda on *Easy Rider*. In 2008 he put a bullet in his head and killed himself.

As fate would have it, Bridget struck up a relationship with a young director named Bill Francisco who taught at the Yale drama school and staged productions at the Williamstown Summer Theater in Massachusetts. I took courses in the drama school as an undergraduate, and Bill invited me up to Williamstown one summer as his assistant. Bridget came up as well, working as an apprentice. Bill was smart and talented, but he was also clearly gay, so I felt free to continue my fantasies about her. Bridget took her job seriously and worked hard, seemingly trouble free until one night at a cast party in a Williams College fraternity house. It was late, she'd had a little to drink. We were sitting together at the top of a staircase when suddenly, in mid-sentence, her eyes rolled back into her head. She called out for her mother, then collapsed and pitched forward down the stairs, unconscious, the victim of what looked like some sort of catatonic fit. A doctor was called. Bridget was taken back to her room and medicated. I sat on the carpet outside her door all night.

Later, back in New York, Brooke and I visited Bridget in her apartment one day. The two of them began negotiating over some belongings that Maggie had left them in her will. I remember Brooke asking Bridget what she wanted in trade for two small paintings she had. "The only way you're going to get these paintings is when I die," Bridget said. A few weeks later I returned to my room at Yale after having dinner. My roommate had left a note on the table in big letters: "Call your father, Brooke Hayward, and your cousin Josie. Very important!" A sense of dread instantly shot through me. That combination of messages could only mean one thing. I decided to call Josie first: "Hi, it's me."

"Bridget's dead, kid. I'm so sorry." Another suicide. But this time I felt no sense of relief as I had after Mother died. Only a huge hole in my heart, a loss from which I thought I'd never recover.

The funeral was held at a Park Avenue cathedral. I went to it with Dad and sat on the aisle. I remember some of the speakers: Hank Fonda, Josh Logan—the entire eastern show business clique was fully represented. I kept my head lowered during the entire ceremony. My tears were flowing so freely they made a small puddle on the floor. Then it was over. The immediate family left first. As they passed by, I remember—I'll always remember—Leland stopping, looking down at me, then placing his hand on my shoulder and giving it a gentle squeeze. It was such a kind gesture. I'll never forget him for it.

Williamstown

The Williamstown Summer Theater was a wonderful experience for me. A new production opened every week featuring first-rate talent on and off the stage. It was so celebrated in those days that a correspondent would broadcast live from in front of the theater on *The Today Show*. I worked with so many young and gifted talents there, some of whom remain friends even now. John Badham (director of *Saturday Night Fever, War Games,* and *Stakeout*) was building sets. Peter Hunt (Tony Award winner for directing *1776* on Broadway) was the lighting designer. Arthur Rubenstein (composer of many fine film scores) led the orchestra in the pit when we did a musical. Add to them a young Dick Cavett, his talented wife, Carrie Nye, the future actor/director/playwright Austin Pendleton, Sam Waterston, and the guest stars who came up from New York and you had a totally enjoyable creative cocktail.

A young actress named Suzanne Pleshette was making her name on Broadway and came up to play the lead in *Two for the Seesaw.* She was being flown to the tiny airport in Bennington, Vermont, just across the border. I was deputized to pick her up. I borrowed Peter Hunt's little white Triumph convertible. Her single-engine prop plane landed with a bit of trouble. It was extremely windy that day, and I soon gathered Suzy had been bouncing around like that all the way up from New York. The plane door opened. Suzy walked unsteadily down the steps looking slightly green. I introduced myself. She gestured off at the pilot, who was still inside the cockpit. "That cocksucker hit every goddamn air pocket for two fucking hours. Jesus Christ, I couldn't even take a fucking piss, there's no goddamn toilet in there!" My eyes popped open. I'd actually never heard a woman talk like that. She kept it up all the way back to Williamstown. Suzy was a terrific actress, a warm woman with a God-given earthy sense of humor. In the decades to come, I'd run into her often. I'd always smile and whisper, "How the fuck are you, bitch?" She'd grin: "Still a prick, huh? Jesus fucking Christ." She wound up married to Tom Poston, a delightful, talented man. What great laughs the two of them must have had together. Suzy died at much too young an age.

Dad and Moss Hart came up to visit Williamstown one night. For all of those eying a future on the stage or screen, it was quite a big deal. I had a small part in the production that was playing, and I tried extra hard with the few lines I had. I thought I was a pretty good actor. I even had the occasional youthful fantasy of making a career out of it. That is, until I asked Dad what he thought of my performance: "Tom, I've always told you to be anything you want to be, a dentist, a cab driver, whatever. But I'm begging you. Eat with them, sleep with them, laugh with them, marry them, divorce them, but for God's sake, don't be one. With your personality I can't imagine what would be worse, if you were a big success or a total flop."

Years later I was having a terrible time revising a screenplay of mine. I said to him, only half joking: "And you talked me out of acting."

"No, I didn't. If you'd have really wanted to be an actor, you'd have told me nicely to go fuck myself and gone ahead with it. There's so much painful rejection involved with that profession. If you don't really want it, if you're not convinced you can't live without it, stay away."

Back to Yale

Going to Yale had a certain cachet in those days. The "Big Three" were Harvard, Yale, and Princeton. It was hard not to feel a tiny bit of snobbish entitlement as a "Yalie." In my junior year President John F. Kennedy was the speaker at graduation. After receiving academic honors he rose and said: "It might be said now that I have the best of both worlds: a Harvard education and a Yale degree." What a charmer. And what a hero to my generation.

My social life was blossoming. I fell in love often, which led me to commit one of the most ham-handed, pretentious teenage mistakes of my life. I'm still embarrassed by it. I had the hots for a beautiful girl at Bennett Junior College, and the feeling seemed to be reciprocal. I knew Dad was going to be out of town for Saturday night on one particular weekend. I arranged for her to meet me at our house in the city. I had money saved up from my allowance. Where could I take her to dinner? Question: Where did Dad go to dinner? Answer: The 21 Club, one of the most exclusive restaurants for the New York power elite at the time.

God help me, I called 21: "This is Mr. Mankiewicz. I'd like a table tomorrow night."

"Our pleasure, Mr. Mankiewicz. What time?"

The next night, we arrived at 21. It was packed. One booth against the wall was conspicuously empty. I identified myself to the maître d', who looked puzzled, then reluctantly seated us. The dinner was fabulous. I paid cash. We made wonderful love back at the house. Any and all physical love was wonderful then. She left to go back to Bennett early Sunday morning. I stayed behind. Dad walked into the house late that afternoon and headed for his study. I joined him. "Hi, Dad, welcome back."

"Thanks. Oh, by the way, Tom, did you by any chance have dinner at 21 last night?"

Fuck! How did he know? I turned beet red and became instantly defensive. "It was money I saved from my allowance. Okay, okay, I guess I knew when I said Mr. Mankiewicz they'd think . . . I mean, I've never even eaten at 21."

"Nineteen years old and you've never eaten at 21? That's amazing. Don't worry, I'm not mad."

"You're not?"

"No, I just have one question because I'm worried about your future."

"What is it?"

"Where are you going to eat when you're successful?"

Cleopatra

In some ways the most pivotal film Dad ever made—it changed his professional life, and not necessarily for the better. It became a burr under his creative saddle and an unpleasant memory from which he never really recovered.

First things first: Elizabeth Taylor had received the highest amount of money any actor, male or female, had ever been paid for a film—$1 million. At the time *Cleopatra* started shooting, Dad was working on an adaptation of Lawrence Durrell's *Alexandria Quartet*. He intended to write and direct a single movie using all four books. *Cleopatra*'s original director was Rouben Mamoulian, an older man, competent and respected, but perhaps not the sort to get your creative blood pounding. Peter Finch was playing Julius Caesar. Stephen Boyd (Messala in *Ben-Hur*) was Mark Antony. Shooting had begun in London with almost immediate critical creative problems. Depending on who you talked to it was either that Mamoulian couldn't handle Elizabeth or a production of that size, or that the script was never really right, take your pick. After approximately twenty minutes of film was already in the can, shooting shut down when Mamoulian quit or was fired, probably a combination of both. What Fox apparently didn't realize at the time was that in addition to her unprecedented salary, Elizabeth had director approval. She approved only two: Dad and George Stevens, who'd directed her in *A Place in the Sun* and *Giant*. If Fox didn't get one of them, they'd have to shut down permanently. George Stevens had a problem: he was about to start production on a little film called *The Greatest Story Ever Told*. That train was already headed down the track and couldn't be stopped. That left Dad. Fox was over a barrel.

Elizabeth and Dad had stayed in touch since *Suddenly, Last Summer*. He adored her. She felt she'd given her finest performance in that film.

Somehow, a deal had to be made. *Cleopatra* was the antithesis of a Joseph L. Mankiewicz film. A sprawling historical epic with no biting social commentary exchanged in small, sophisticated living rooms. He asked Fox if they would shut down until someone (at first, not him) revised the screenplay. No, they wanted to shoot right away. They were cast, huge sets had been built in England—all systems were go. Dad was tempted. He wanted to work with Elizabeth again and realized that her right of director approval might result in his getting a huge deal. Still, it was the wrong kind of film for him to make. He'd always trusted Mother's opinion on career matters. I'm convinced if she'd still been alive, he wouldn't have done it.

Fox finally made Dad an offer he couldn't refuse. They'd buy his independent company (Figaro) from him. This would pay for his services and give them ownership of *The Barefoot Contessa* and *I Want to Live,* a successful film starring Susan Hayward (she won an Oscar) that Robert Wise had directed for the company. Dad and NBC were fifty-fifty partners in Figaro. The offer was for $2.5 million. Dad would get half. After paying capital gains taxes, he would net over $1 million, which actually meant he'd be getting more than Elizabeth. No director had ever been paid that much before. The idea of taking on *Cleopatra* was getting more irresistible every day.

I remember seeing the twenty minutes or so of film Mamoulian shot with Dad in a New York screening room. He was a big fan of Peter Finch and intended to keep him. A close-up of Stephen Boyd flashed onto the screen. "Who's that?" Dad asked.

"That's Stephen Boyd. He's playing Mark Antony."

"No he's not," came Dad's reply.

Before shooting could begin, Elizabeth became desperately ill. A tracheotomy was performed on her neck to assist in her breathing. It would take her months to recover. There was no getting around it: now they had to shut down. The entire cast (except Elizabeth) was suspended or let go. Dad told Peter Finch that if he were available, he'd love to have him play Caesar when they started up again. Stephen Boyd was history. Brando was Dad's first choice for Antony. Marlon had just started shooting *Mutiny on the Bounty* in the South Pacific, another film that had replaced its director and looked as if it would never end. Richard Burton was bought out of the Broadway musical *Camelot,* in which he was playing King Arthur. Peter Finch was just about to shoot the title role in *The Trials of Oscar Wilde* and was unavailable. Rex Harrison came aboard to do his third film for Dad, playing Julius Caesar.

It was nonsensical to shoot in England. Dad was astounded that huge Roman and Egyptian exterior sets had been constructed in a country where it could rain for months before even colder and wetter winters. He moved the production to Rome, to Cinecittà, where he'd shot *The Barefoot Contessa*. *Cleopatra* took over virtually all the space the large studio had to offer. Dad had tried to avoid taking over the screenplay, but after several false starts, he finally did so. Whether or not he was kidding himself, he'd become convinced that if George Bernard Shaw could write *Caesar and Cleopatra* and Shakespeare could write *Antony and Cleopatra*, there was real buried treasure in the project waiting to be unearthed. He planned on making two separate films, one to be released directly after the other. It was a laudable ambition he could never achieve. When Elizabeth was ready to shoot again, he'd barely scratched the surface of the films he wanted to make. But they had to shoot, and shoot they did, endlessly. Dad stayed up nights writing, trying to keep far enough ahead of what he was directing during the day. There wasn't anything like a final completed draft until the film had been in production for many months.

Dad wanted the family with him. Chris had just graduated from Columbia. Dad gave him a job as a second assistant director on the film. I was still at Yale and could come over only on vacations. Fortunately for me, the film shot so interminably this meant two summer breaks and the intervening Christmas and Easter holidays. There have been countless documentaries and accounts of *Cleopatra* aired and published over the years. I have my own private memories.

The Production

The production was massive, on a scale never seen before. At times there were as many as five separate units either prepping or shooting simultaneously. The port of Alexandria was constructed near Anzio on the Mediterranean coast. While clearing the land, bulldozers struck buried, still-active land mines left over from the famous World War II landing. One worker was killed and several others wounded. The sheer size of the film alone would have been enough to generate worldwide publicity, but suddenly the ultimate wild card fell out of the deck: Richard Burton and Elizabeth Taylor had fallen in love. It was, at the time, the most internationally celebrated romance since Edward VIII abdicated the British throne for Mrs. Simpson. Both Elizabeth and Richard were already married to other people. Their affair was publicly condemned by the Vatican. In Washington, D.C., a member of Congress took the floor to demand that Elizabeth (born in England) relinquish her American passport. There was virtually no publication of any kind anywhere that didn't feature the story on its cover, and more than once. Flocks of the press descended on Rome from all over the world. Art Buchwald announced in the *Washington Post* and *Paris Tribune:* "It used to be that one couldn't leave Rome without having seen the Colosseum and the Roman forum. Now you can add having been on the set of *Cleopatra.*" Foreign dignitaries, even heads of state, were not uncommon. I remember President Sukarno of Indonesia, among others.

Walter Wanger was the nominal producer on the film. I say "nominal" because he had no real power and found it easier to ignore the mounting production problems, preferring to socialize with Italian society on the Via Veneto. Dad liked Walter. He'd produced *I Want to Live* for Figaro and was a warm, gutsy man. During World War I he'd volunteered for the brand new American Air Force, but after crashing five training planes was asked politely to find employment elsewhere in the military. He was given an enemy air medal and dubbed "the Italian Ace." In the 1950s his wife, the actress Joan Bennett, was having an affair with her agent, Jennings Lang, later the executive vice president of Universal Pictures. Walter shot him in the balls. He did a short stint in prison, then resumed his marital life and career.

The original production manager on the film was Johnny Johnston, someone who'd worked with Dad before and in whom he had absolute confidence. Johnny had been working in Spain for Samuel Bronston. His right-hand assistant was Rosemary Matthews (remember *The Barefoot Contessa?*). She'd also just worked for Dad on *The Quiet American,* which he'd shot in Vietnam and Rome. They'd grown closer over the years, to say the very least. Shortly after arriving on *Cleopatra,* Johnny tragically died of a heart attack. His talented and experienced replacement was C. O. "Doc" Erickson, who later continued to work with Dad on several more films. Needless to say, Rosemary stayed in place. Her presence was essential to Dad's maintaining his health and sanity. The roots of their future marriage were starting to take hold.

Freddy Simpson was the first assistant director. Gruff, funny, no-nonsense, he'd started as a prop man for Dad many years earlier. The myriad of production problems soon began to overwhelm him. Among them: Elizabeth's unprecedented contract allowed her two days off for every menstrual period. One day she notified the production that she was having it and wouldn't be available to shoot. The only problem was she'd claimed the same thing just two weeks earlier. Freddy was beside himself: "Two periods in less than three weeks? When this broad dies they should send her body to the Harvard Medical School." He was going to have a doctor go over to her villa to verify her condition, but Dad called it off: "The problem, Freddy, is that she's smarter than you are. This time it is her period. I know her too well. You're going to have egg all over your face."

Rex Harrison wore leather leggings as Julius Caesar, principally because his own legs were so skinny they didn't seem to belong to the then conqueror of the known world. His nickname among the crew was "Birdlegs." One day Freddy was barking out orders on the set and yelled to someone, "We're ready. Get Birdlegs in here!" He turned and suddenly found himself face to face with Rex. Freddy managed a weak smile. "Should I just take a cab to the airport now, or . . . ?" Rex shook his head in disgust and walked past him.

Richard Burton

Richard Burton was that rare and enviable male who is the consummate ladies' man and man's man. He could be a boisterous drunkard as well as a thoughtful intellectual. His capacity for booze was enormous. I once saw him consume more than a bottle of vodka before lunch while working. In makeup at five thirty or six in the morning he could toss back a triple brandy followed by a cheery "Good morning, all!" One day when a rainstorm interrupted filming on the island of Ischia, the cast and crew ducked into a bar. I remember Richard had at least five vodkas in the half-hour period before the rain stopped.

Richard possessed a wonderful intellect and the curiosity to go with it. He had a deep background in classical theater, having been the resident leading man at the Old Vic, where he was once described as "the first Hamlet with balls." Over dinner he would love to make a statement like "No German has ever had an original thought" and then defend his proposition against all comers. I always suspected that some of these intellectual exercises were setups to show off his knowledge, but in the German example I remember he could successfully show you that the thoughts of Hegel, Marx, Goethe, and so on, were far from original.

Richard could be moody. He had quick flashes of anger, especially when drunk. He turned his magnetism on and off like a stereo. When he decided to charm you, he enthralled you. I never saw it fail with anyone. And when he misbehaved, he got forgiveness from everyone as if they were excusing a brilliantly talented "bad boy."

The timber of his voice was legendary. A deep Welsh baritone heavily seasoned by years of incessant smoking and drinking. He had an almost unbelievable ability to project his voice, which he said came from his stepfather, Phillip Burton. When Richard was young, the two of them would stand on opposite sides of a chasm between two cliffs in Wales. The wind noisily whipped through the gap, and Phillip made Richard project his voice over the racket until he could be heard clearly. It seemed a fanciful story, but Richard insisted it was true. He played his voice like a virtuoso plays a musical instrument. When I saw him on Broadway in *Camelot,* he received a standing ovation not only at the end, but at the close of the first act as well. And that was at a time when standing ovations actually meant something. An actor's ability to "take stage" in a role can completely distort your perception of the play. I remember seeing *Equus* in London when it opened at the National Theatre. It starred Colin Blakely as the psychiatrist and Peter Firth as the troubled young boy. It was clearly a two-handed piece, and the balance between both roles made the play. Later, in New York, Anthony Perkins played it with Peter Firth. I went to see it and was surprised to discover that the play now belonged to Peter Firth. It wasn't that Tony was bad. He simply didn't "take stage" to the degree that Firth did. The balance of the piece had changed. Even later, when Richard agreed to do *Equus* on Broadway for a limited run, I went to see him. The play had changed once again. This time it belonged to Richard, and it was more than simply because of the star power he carried with him. It was the force of his performance. Peter Firth had been reduced to playing a wonderful supporting role.

Coming onto *Cleopatra,* Richard was famous for supposedly having slept with every leading lady he ever worked with. This time it would be with a very much married Elizabeth Taylor, but from the moment the picture began there seemed to be an inevitability about it. Everyone watched the two of them circling each other, these two volatile, ignitable personalities. The day they consummated their relationship, everyone seemed to know it. Richard had apparently intended to do a hit-and-run, to make a conquest and then go back to his wife, Sybil, as he'd done countless times before. Elizabeth was having none of it. You didn't hit-and-run with Elizabeth Taylor. The affair continued, grew deeper, and the rest, as they say, was history. I remember Dad telling me at the time: "You know, when you see one of these marriages, the kind Richard and Sybil have, it's taken for granted that every time he misbehaves he'll come home and be forgiven because that's where the real love is. The only problem with a relationship like that is the near inevitability that one day he'll find his real love somewhere else."

Elizabeth Taylor

The first thing you noticed when you met Elizabeth Taylor was that she was small in stature, almost tiny compared with the way she photographed onscreen. She had a full, almost lush body and was so beautiful it made my hair hurt. She was also the biggest celebrity of her day, even before the affair with Richard. When she arrived in Rome, she briefly stayed at the Grand Hotel until moving to her villa on the Appia Antica outside the city. While she was at the Grand, hundreds of people congregated in front of the hotel day and night behind police barricades, hoping for just a glimpse of her. On her thirtieth birthday there was a small party upstairs at Bricktop's, a famous nightclub on the Via Veneto. When word got out that she was there, the boulevard outside suddenly became packed wall to wall with people waiting to see her leave. The police had to escort us down a back staircase into an alley, where cars whisked everyone away. Even Richard was astonished. "I'd no idea she was that famous," I remember him saying.

The second thing one immediately noticed about Elizabeth was her sense of humor. It was earthy, even bawdy; she loved to have fun. When I told her the crew's nickname for Rex was Birdlegs, she roared with laughter, then asked, "And what's their nickname for me, 'Cooseburger'?" She was a wonderful and inquisitive gossip. Wanted to know everything that was going on with everybody. One day she, Dad, and I were talking on the set. Dad told her that he'd always reminded me it was just as easy to marry a rich woman as it was a poor one. She laughed. Two days later I received a beautiful photograph of her taken by Roddy McDowall with the inscription, "Dear Tom. What happens if I'm broke? Love, Elizabeth."

One afternoon she asked me if I'd like to have dinner with her and Eddie Fisher (her then husband) at their villa. Just the three of us. Would this twenty-year-old like to have dinner with Elizabeth Taylor? How about yes, devastated, thrilled, couldn't wait. Her driver picked me up. As I got out in front of the villa it was suddenly illuminated by dozens of flashbulbs. The paparazzi were up in the trees of the adjacent gardens, keeping track of whoever entered or left her house. I don't know if there's ever been a human in a fishbowl quite like that, before or since.

Once I was inside, Elizabeth and I had a drink and then went into the dining room for dinner. As we sat down I saw the table was only set for two. She told me that Eddie sent his regrets. He wasn't feeling well and was in bed upstairs. The affair with Richard had begun and must have been taking a terrible toll on Eddie. In spite of being a celebrity himself, a famous and popular singer, he seemed to be at loose ends all the time since he wasn't performing. He had vague aspirations of becoming a producer and would visit the studio too often, finally becoming something of a pest. I'm not sure, given the circumstances, what other options he had. He was a very nice man, but clearly unsure how to handle the situation he found himself in. Dad put it succinctly at the time: "Poor Eddie. Richard and Elizabeth are world-class killers, and he's basically a singing waiter from Grossinger's." (I should add that Dad had great affection for both Elizabeth and Richard. He meant "world-class killers" as a compliment.) The affair took a terrible toll on all the participants. None of them was even remotely frivolous about it. Elizabeth was constantly ill on the picture and later even underwent what certainly looked like a suicide attempt. Richard's life with Sybil was torn apart. At one point, his half brother Ivor came down to Rome from Wales to support Sybil and punched Richard in the eye. Eddie eventually went back to New York where, ironically enough, as the "victim," he became a more popular performer than ever.

Meanwhile, back at the villa: My dinner with Elizabeth was over. We retired to the living room for an after-dinner drink and coffee. Suddenly, the back door opened. Richard appeared: "Hello, luv," he said to me. "Mind if I join you?" He and Elizabeth embraced. I realized that in some strange way I was meant to be a "beard" for them so that Richard wouldn't be alone with her in Eddie's house. The drinking started fast and furious as it always did when Richard appeared. Elizabeth did her best to keep up with him. Richard was in his devastatingly charming mode, telling stories and making us laugh. There was a noise from the staircase. We turned. There was Eddie, looking down into the living room, dressed in a bathrobe and slippers. It became very quiet.

Eddie said in a calm voice: "It's late, Richard. Elizabeth has to shoot in the morning."

Richard answered cheerfully, "I just came by to see my girl."

Eddie looked back evenly: "You already have a girl, Richard. You have Sybil."

Another silence. Richard: "They're both my girls."

Eddie paused, then walked back upstairs. I was so embarrassed, if I could have dug a hole, jumped in, and put the dirt back over my head, I would have. Instead I said, "Thanks for the lovely dinner, Elizabeth. I guess I've got to get back home."

Egypt

The interminable shooting finally ended on location in Egypt. In the beginning, the Nasser government had refused entrance to Elizabeth on the grounds that she was Jewish. But faced with the potential loss of millions of American dollars, they finally relented, rationalizing that she'd "converted" and therefore wasn't really a Jew. Nevertheless, she remained in Italy while the rest of us made the trip.

Egypt was fascinating, two countries in one. If you stayed at the Nile Hilton and had a car and driver, Cairo was elegant, even European. If you looked behind the curtain, the poverty was blinding. We shot in the desert, outside a little town called Edku, near Alexandria. Most of the sequences involved the Roman army. Studios usually co-opted actual troops from the country they were shooting in, but Nasser was keeping a wary eye on Israel, so this was impossible. Many hundreds of extras were needed, extras who could march in step with one another. The people of Edku had rehearsed for weeks and promised they could do it. They were desperate for the dollar-a-day salary. A few weeks' employment could mean a year's pay for some of them. Unfortunately, they were hopeless at marching, and we started hiring young students from the University of Alexandria who were up to the task.

One morning, hundreds of townspeople showed up at our location, led by the mayor of Edku. They demanded employment and were clearly ready to riot if they weren't going to be hired. Everyone on the crew was terrified. We were in the middle of nowhere. Our only protection was four uniformed members of the Egyptian Camel Corps, each one riding a camel and carrying an automatic weapon. Nasser's son-in-law, also in uniform, had been visiting our location for several days. He heard the ruckus, exited a tent, faced the multitude, and screamed at them, ordering them to line up in rows. This was my first and only personal lesson in seeing just how effectively Fascism could work at times. I couldn't believe it. The mass of belligerent villagers suddenly started to tremble as Nasser's son-in-law identified himself and continued yelling. The four Camel Corpsmen fanned out behind him, weapons cocked and ready. Nasser's son-in-law demanded that the mayor step forward. He did so. The young man pulled out a leather quirt and whacked the mayor in the side of the face, opening up his cheek. The villagers turned and headed back for Edku. I was stunned. I'd never seen anything like it. The fear of the state was so powerful it trumped everything.

Dad was literally on his last legs by then. For months he'd been taking injections to keep going during the day, then sedatives at night to get some sleep. He'd developed a drug dependency that took him years to get rid of. A nurse, looking for a new injection site, had accidentally hit his sciatic nerve with a needle. He could walk properly on only one leg. They put his chair right next to the camera so he didn't have to get up, but when it came to Richard Burton's last shot, he insisted on it. He limped in front of the lens and changed the scene number on the slate while Richard held him steady. The slate now read: "This prick is through." They both grinned as the camera rolled. For all I know, the scene is still listed that way in the editor's log.

Cleopatra Shuts Down Fox

The $42 million *Cleopatra* had bankrupted Fox. The California studio was shut down for the first time in its history. Normally, when you make a film for a major studio, the budget of your picture contains an "overhead" fee, usually 10 or 15 percent. Spread out across the multiple yearly productions, this overhead cost plus the distribution fees pays for the actual operations of the studio. Since Fox was shooting only *Cleopatra* and nothing else, the entire worldwide expense of running the company was added to the film's budget. If two Fox employees went out to lunch in, say, Paris, the cost of that meal was charged to *Cleopatra*. This meant that the announced budget was perceived as not only unforgivably profligate, but obscene.

Darryl Zanuck had taken the studio back from its former head, the dotty, incompetent Spyro Skouras. He began his own Night of the Long Knives. In a totally meaningless gesture, he fired Walter Wanger. Dad ran the rough cut of the film in Paris. It lasted more than seven hours. When the lights came up there was a silence, following which Zanuck said, "That Antony's a weak man."

"Yes, he is, Darryl," came Dad's reply.

"If any woman did that to me, I'd kick her right in the balls."

"The picture's not about you, Darryl."

Even though they'd made Oscar-winning films together in the past, the irresistible force was now meeting the immovable object. Zanuck insisted on one film, and at less than four hours. Dad refused. He wasn't about to leave all that hard work and sweat on the cutting room floor, especially since he knew it contained all of the best character scenes that truly fleshed out the principal roles. What Zanuck wanted would now be an exercise in simply stringing together an abbreviated story so it made sense to the audience. Dad would have none of it. Zanuck fired him. Dad was stunned. There were a few additional scenes that had to be shot for the shortened film to make narrative sense. Zanuck would get another director. When news of the situation leaked out, the Fox Board of Directors, led by William Wyler, threatened to resign unless Dad was allowed to finish his film. The principal actors suddenly "weren't sure" they'd be available to return. Dad was rehired. He'd decided that if someone was going to mutilate his film, it might as well be him.

From his point of view, Zanuck had a logical point to make by insisting on one film instead of two. The real potential box office gold lay in the Taylor-Burton relationship. The whole world was waiting to see them on the screen together. Richard appeared for only approximately ten minutes in the first half. If they released a *Caesar and Cleopatra* first, what would happen if Richard and Elizabeth broke up before *Antony and Cleopatra* came out? What if they went back to their respective spouses? Who'd want to see them then? Fox would suffer a tremendous financial loss from which it might never recover. What was that line from *The Barefoot Contessa* again? "Gentlemen, it's a wonderful art we're doing business in."

The opening of *Cleopatra* in New York was broadcast on *The Tonight Show*. Johnny Carson was in his studio. Bert Parks interviewed the celebrities as they poured in. Dad arrived, suffering in silence. He knew that because of the notoriety of everything that had gone on, most critics had already written their reviews. Bert Parks intercepted him: "And here's Joseph L. Mankiewicz, the multiple Oscar-winning director. Mr. Mankiewicz, I hear we're in for a truly magnificent film tonight."

Dad stared, then said, "You must know something I don't."

Parks blinked. "Ah . . . exactly how long did it take you to make this film?"

Dad: "I can't remember ever having been on anything else."

He walked past a totally nonplussed Parks. Carson and the studio audience exploded with laughter. Johnny told me later it was one of his favorite moments ever in the decades he did *The Tonight Show*. He always included it on his anniversary broadcasts.

The film received mixed reviews, though oddly enough, a total rave from Bosley Crowther in the *New York Times*. Years later, it finally broke even on the books as a result of television sales. In the nineties, Roddy McDowall, Martin Landau, and I went to see Bill Mechanic, then president of the studio, in a vain attempt to have the remaining footage reassembled and released in the form Dad intended. Mechanic was in favor of it, but the missing footage was spread out all over the world, some of it without sound. The largest batch was in the possession of two projectionists in London who'd stolen it from the lab at the time it had been processed. They were willing to sell it but wouldn't show it first, and Mechanic was adamant about Fox not paying a ransom for stolen material. For the rest of his life, Dad had a framed *New Yorker* cartoon hanging in his bathroom. It depicts two suburban women commuters at a train station, staring at a *Cleopatra* billboard featuring Elizabeth and Richard in a sexy pose. One woman is saying to the other, "What really annoys me is I know I'm going to see it."

There were important consequences to the film in terms of our family. Dad would soon marry Rosemary and move to a beautiful, peaceful Pound Ridge estate in Westchester County. My brother Chris fell in love with one of Cleopatra's handmaidens on the film. Her name was Bruna Caruso. They went back to New York, where they were married and she became a top model. Before their divorce, they had a son, my nephew, Jason. As for me, Yale was over. Now it was time to go to work.

The Best Man

After graduating from Yale, I headed to Los Angeles. I suppose if Dad were still living there I'd have probably gone to New York. I needed the space to try to do things on my own. I'd met two young producers, Stuart Millar and Larry Turman, through my aunt Sara, who knew Stuart's family. They were about to make a film of Gore Vidal's hit play *The Best Man* and were looking for an assistant who could help out in multiple areas. My previous work on film crews and experience in summer stock sufficed to qualify me, and I was hired. I got $125 a week. I took a room at the Montecito Hotel on Franklin Avenue—at the time, the poor man's Chateau Marmont. So poor, in fact, that they didn't have the money to fill the hotel pool, which remained empty all year. Sometimes the residents held improvised cocktail parties on the dry cement after climbing down the ladder. The hotel was filled with up-and-coming (they hoped) actors from New York who were playing one- or two-day parts in television shows. No room service, but there was a kitchenette area and a Hughes market on the corner. I spent a lot of time defrosting frozen meals. A housekeeper went over your carpet with a vacuum cleaner on a daily basis.

The Best Man shot at Columbia Studios, which was then on nearby Gower Street. What a heady experience it was, and what talented people to work with. The cast included Henry Fonda, Cliff Robertson, Margaret Leighton, Kevin McCarthy, Shelley Berman, Edie Adams, and Lee Tracy, who received an Oscar nomination for playing Vidal's version of Harry Truman. Larry Turman would go on to produce many successful films, including *The Graduate*. The director was Franklin Schaffner, an Emmy winner from television, making his second film (*The Stripper* was his first). He went on to make *Patton, The Planet of the Apes, Nicholas and Alexandra*, and more. The cameraman was a young Haskell Wexler, later to photograph *The Loved One* and *In the Heat of the Night* and win an Oscar for *Who's Afraid of Virginia Woolf?* The assistant editor to Bob Swink was Hal Ashby. Endlessly cheerful, he was determined to direct one day. I sympathized, but wasn't sure he had much of a chance. Later on, after seeing *Harold and Maude, The Last Detail, Shampoo, Coming Home*, and *Being There*, I decided I was wrong. In 1976 Hal directed *Bound for Glory* and Haskell Wexler won yet another Oscar for photographing it. What a talented group to start a creative learning curve with.

Gore Vidal came to L.A. for the shoot. He was already a celebrated novelist, playwright, and screenwriter. He had script approval. Nothing could be changed without his okay. I remember one day when we were shooting at the Ambassador Hotel. The film was behind schedule. Stuart, Larry, and Frank were trying to find ways to catch up. It was decided that a short two-page scene featuring Ann Southern was unnecessary, but we needed Gore's approval. I was deputized to go to the Beverly Hills Hotel to get it personally. I found Gore lying by the pool, caked in suntan lotion. I explained the situation. The scene was fun, but incidental to the plot and perhaps expendable. Gore raised his wrist: "You see this watch, Tom? It's a Patek Phillipe, the most expensive timepiece in the world. What do you say we open the back of it and remove the smallest little thing we can find, something that looks totally unnecessary. You know what then? I might as well be wearing a turd on my wrist." I went back downtown and reported: the answer was no.

I made friends easily, and Columbia was a fertile place to find them in 1963. Alan Pakula and Bob Mulligan had just made *To Kill a Mockingbird* and were on the lot, working with Steve McQueen and Lee Remick. Screen Gems had big hits on television. Stanley Kramer was starting *Ship of Fools* with an all-star cast on the stage next door. In my spare time I wrote an original screenplay. It was about the suicide of a young actress. The script dealt with the last ninety minutes of her life, between the time she takes the pills and the time she dies, with flashbacks (every writing Mankiewicz loves flashbacks). The original title was rather unwieldy: *Everything the Traffic Will Allow.* I later shortened it to *Please.* It was optioned five separate times, and never made, but the dialogue apparently was impressive enough to get me hired as a writer.

My First Paid Writing Job

By the mid-sixties, the last dramatic hour anthology show left on television was *Bob Hope Presents the Chrysler Theatre.* It was produced by Dick Berg, the father of Scott, the author, and Jeff, later chairman of the powerful ICM (International Creative Management) talent agency, and was shot at Universal Studios. Universal had optioned my original screenplay. A young associate producer named Ron Roth had read it. He loved the dialogue. Emmy-winning television director Stuart Rosenberg (later to make *Cool Hand Luke, The Amityville Horror,* and *The Pope of Greenwich Village*) was desperate for a rewrite on the show, which was about to start shooting. Ron gave Stuart my script, and suddenly I was hired. The pay was only $500, but at this stage of a nonexistent career, why quibble? The sponsor of the show was almost totally in control of content in those days. A representative of Chrysler came to a script meeting with notes. I was asked to change the line "You've been avoiding me" to "You've been dodging me" because they made the Dodge automobile. I remember observing out loud that I supposed no one was ever going to "ford" a stream on that show. The man from Chrysler didn't smile.

The hour teleplay was titled *Runaway Boy*. It starred Robert Wagner and Carol Lynley. Carol and I went out a lot during the sixties. We were somewhat of an "item." One day I walked into a casting session. Surprise, surprise, the assistant to the casting director was John Badham, my friend from Williamstown. Shortly afterward, John started directing television at Universal, and then his first feature, *The Bingo Long Traveling All-Stars and Motor Kings*, with Richard Pryor, James Earl Jones, and Billy Dee Williams. It was the first of many terrific films to come.

I was still rewriting while the show was shooting. I remember one day at Paradise Cove, north of Malibu. I sat in the back of a limousine on the pier, my typewriter perched on a folded jump seat. I banged out new dialogue for the scenes and handed the pages out the window to the assistant director. Geez Louise, I thought, this was a tough job. But boy, what a lot of fun. When I got home at night, it felt great to know I'd finally made a real contribution to a piece of film. There's a wonderful sense of achievement in writing if you're the child of a famous parent. Someone may give you a job as their assistant to curry favor, or even make you an associate producer, but *no one* shoots a script they don't think is good enough to make. No one in the movie business is willing to commit financial suicide, it's that simple.

The night the show aired I watched it alone. I'd written so much of it I'd received cowriting credit. Dad was always billed onscreen as "Joseph L. Mankiewicz"; his brother as "Herman J. Mankiewicz." So there I was: "Thomas F. Mankiewicz." But it looked so incredibly pretentious to me, the "Thomas" and the middle initial. That was the first and last time I would see it. On the literally hundreds of onscreen credits I've received since then, a simple "Tom Mankiewicz" did very nicely, thank you.

Malibu in the 1960s

I was at a party in 1964. Roddy McDowall was there and announced that he was leaving for England to do a film and would be gone for some time.

He'd rented a house in the Malibu Colony on the beach for $500 a month (that's right, $500) and still had six months left on his lease. Did anyone want to take it over from him? Being a month-to-month renter, I jumped at the chance. Malibu in the sixties was a starkly different community than it is now, more like a small town than a chic extension of L.A. Today, the Pacific Coast Highway across from the Colony and the Old Malibu Road features shopping centers, "in" restaurants, movie theaters, and Pepperdine University. Then, there was nothing on the other side of the road. Zero. If you needed something, there was one of everything. If your kitchen sink was clogged, you didn't call a plumber. You called *the* plumber. There was one market (the Colony), one pharmacy, one gas station, and one vet for your ailing dog or cat. You had to dial the operator to call Beverly Hills. Because of their circumstances, the year-round residents developed a small-town camaraderie. If you didn't have enough cash to cover your groceries at the market, it was a case of "We'll get you next time, Mank." Most people had dogs of various shapes and sizes. When I wrote on my patio, I always kept treats for them for when they'd climb up my steps for their daily visits: Bo, the black lab, carrying in his mouth his Frisbee, which you had to throw for him, preferably out into the ocean so he could swim out to retrieve it. Homer, the bassett hound, who always left two rivets in the sand when he passed by from his oversized ears. You could ride on the beach back then. A little horse shit didn't bother anybody. I bought a cheap but beautiful quarter horse, boarded her on a ranch across the highway, and rode her several times a week.

In the summers, many of the residents rented out their houses for hefty sums. I never did (not that a house with minimal furniture and no heat would fetch a big price). But in the years I lived there, passing through were the eclectic likes of Jane Fonda and Roger Vadim, Tuesday Weld, Terry Southern, Larry Hagman, Rod Steiger, Herb Alpert, Jerry Moss, Jack Warden, Norman Jewison, Christian Marquand, John Frankenheimer, Deborah Kerr and Peter Viertel, Merle Oberon, the Mamas and the Papas, Angela Lansbury, and the Byrds. You could have dinner at the home of Paul Ziffren, powerful attorney, Democratic National Committee member, and chairman of the L.A. Olympics, and eat with the likes of Henry Kissinger, Lew Wasserman, and Norton Simon. Or you could walk through the sand with Larry Hagman, who would be dressed in a caftan and carrying a Hopi Indian flag, and share a truly fine joint. Larry never spoke on Sundays. When a prominent geologist at UCLA predicted the arrival of the "big one" on a specific day at a specific time, a group of us dressed up in black tie and gowns, sipped champagne, and sat on the beach waiting to be cracked off into the ocean. There were many famous and infamous residents of Malibu, but the most important one to me then was Tuesday Weld.

Tuesday Weld

The enfant terrible of Hollywood. Impudent, funny, devastatingly attractive, wildly talented, and totally nuts. I was instantly fixated on her. Tuesday was (and is) uncommonly bright in spite of not having any formal education. She could trade one-liners with anyone but was incapable of finding north on a map. She was also the only actress I've met in fifty years who desperately tried to avoid becoming a star. I mean it. When Samantha Eggar was fired (she was later rehired) on *The Collector,* Tuesday was William Wyler's choice to replace her. But after a long meeting during which she disagreed with the legendary director on absolutely everything, he decided to look elsewhere. She turned down the part of Bonnie in *Bonnie and Clyde* on the grounds that she'd just had a child and didn't want to go to Texas. When Joshua Logan offered her the female lead in *Paint Your Wagon* opposite Clint Eastwood and Lee Marvin, Tuesday asked him when shooting would begin. He told her September. "Oh, damn, I can't do it," she told him. "September and October are the two best months of the year at the beach."

Josh knew that we were close and called me: "What is she, fucking nuts?"

"No comment, Josh."

One night several of us were sitting around her house. Carol Lynley had costarred in *The Cardinal* for Otto Preminger. It had just opened, and she was prominently billed on the marquee of the Fox Wilshire Theater. I told her it must feel great to drive by and see your name in lights. She agreed.

"That's the only thing I hate," said Tuesday. "I love to work, but I hate to see my name."

Tuesday lived alone when I met her. Her only companion was her dachshund, Luther, the last remaining Nazi in the world. Luther had a black spot on the top of his head from where she'd accidentally dropped hot bacon grease on him. It looked exactly like a yarmulke. If you didn't pay enough attention to Luther when he wanted you to, he would pretend to be blind, bump into the couch, fall over, and wait for you to come over and pet him. He and Tuesday were a perfectly suited pair.

She was eager to sop up the formal knowledge she'd missed out on growing up as a child actress. She started learning one new, unusual word a day. She'd find it in the dictionary and then use it constantly until it was printed inside her as part of her vocabulary. One day she said to me, "I bet you don't know what an atavism is."

I did. "It's a throwback. Right now you could call Barry Goldwater an atavistic politician."

That night we went to a dinner party at Larry Turman's house. Gore Vidal was among the guests. I introduced them. Tuesday opened with: "You, Mr. Vidal, are an atavism."

Gore smiled. "I hope, Miss Weld, you don't mean that in its pejorative sense, the difference between us being that I know what pejorative means." Tuesday roared with laughter. Gore never left her for the rest of the evening.

There was a party at Tuesday's house one night. It grew larger as crashers arrived, having heard about it on the Malibu grapevine. Around midnight she said to me, "Get all these people out of here, okay?"

"Jesus, there's got to be eighty people here. How the hell do I do that?"

She turned, walked upstairs, then reappeared at the top of the landing, holding a gun. "Hey!" she yelled. Everyone looked up. There she was, an angry Tuesday Weld with a loaded revolver in her hand. Your worst nightmare. "Get out!!" Eighty people immediately rocketed for a three-foot-wide doorway, elbowing each other out of the way. It was a perfect Tuesday solution.

Tragedy struck in 1965. She was shooting *The Cincinnati Kid* for director Norman Jewison and had been invited onto producer Martin Ransohoff's yacht off Catalina for the weekend. A huge fire started just over the brush-clogged hills leading to Malibu and rapidly rolled down toward the coast. It was darkness at noon. The smoke completely blocked out the sun. Truly terrifying. In those days there was no such thing as a helicopter water drop. There was nothing in front of the raging fire except for the brave fire fighters who clustered around their engines, trying to make a stand on the highway. The sparks and embers jumped the road, picking off individual houses, sparing others. After several interminable hours, it died down as the flames met the ocean, and the fire fighters tried to mop up. The Colony was largely spared. Not so the Old Malibu Road, where Tuesday lived. I drove up to take a look. Her house had totally burned to the ground. Ironically, the two houses on either side were largely intact. My heart sank. I drove back to my house and called her in Catalina: "There's been a terrible fire going on here. I'd get back right away." Her daughter, Natasha (from a brief marriage to a writer, Claude Harz), was in school. Arrangements were made for her to stay with someone until Tuesday could pick her up the next day. I couldn't bring myself to tell her what had happened. Not right then. She'd find out soon enough.

76

The next morning I parked in front of what used to be her house. It was still faintly smoking. After two hours she still hadn't showed, so I reluctantly drove back to my place. When I entered, there she was, sitting in my living room with an overnight bag on the couch next to her. That was all she had left now. "It's all gone, isn't it."

"Yes, how do you know?"

"The sheriffs told me at the roadblock on the highway. Can Tasha and I stay with you for a while?"

"Sure."

"Thanks. Okay, I'd better go over to the pharmacy and get some stuff. Oh, can I go through your phone book and copy some numbers? I left my book at home."

I couldn't believe her attitude, facing such a devastating loss. Here was a young woman who'd made her first suicide attempt at twelve. She'd try again later. But at this particular time she was such a determined pillar of strength for herself and her daughter. Tuesday never knew her father. She had a treasured portrait of him on the wall of her living room. It went up in flames along with the rest.

Tuesday didn't rebuild. I suppose the memory was too bitter. Later on she lived in an apartment just below the Sunset Strip where she attempted suicide. She would have died had Luther not howled incessantly behind the door, causing the building "super" to open it and discover her with no time to spare. Most child actresses have one unfortunate thing in common: a determined, sometimes ruthless mother who pushes and drives them mercilessly so she can live in her daughter's reflected glory. I've met at least half a dozen, but far and away the most unpleasant example was Tuesday's mother. I'd come to visit her in the hospital the day after her suicide attempt. She was lying in bed with various tubes stuck in her. They'd pumped her stomach. She'd been sedated and spoke softly, haltingly. The door opened behind us. Mrs. Weld entered, holding some papers in her hand.

"Hey, Ma," Tuesday mumbled. I don't think I've ever heard anyone else call their mother "Ma."

Mrs. Weld crossed to the bed, raising the papers: "Listen, your business manager says they won't pay these bills without your okay. I told them you couldn't talk right now, so just sign them."

Tuesday blinked. "Oh, Ma . . ."

"This is important. I've got to get these paid, understand?"

I couldn't believe it. "Mrs. Weld, why don't you get the hell out of here?"

She suddenly exploded, pointing her finger at me. "You're next, you know! You're the next one she'll betray! Don't worry, you'll see!"

I've never hit a woman in my life, but I swear I was fully capable of it at that moment. With every mother-child star relationship there comes a moment when the girl becomes a woman and the balance of power changes forever. And boy, can it get ugly.

But it's the upbeat Tuesday I remember best, the one who made you grin and shake your head in disbelief. We had lunch in town one day. She was shooting a film called *I'll Take Sweden,* starring Bob Hope. She was running late and sped back to Goldwyn Studios in her little red Porsche convertible. She tore down Formosa Avenue, heading for Goldwyn, when a motorcycle cop pulled her over. The conversation went this way:

"I'm sorry, Officer, was I speeding?"

"Yeah, about forty miles an hour over the limit. License and registration?"

"Listen, I don't have time, I'm late for shooting, the studio's right across the street, I have to go, so just write out whatever you want and I'll sign it, okay?"

"It's not that easy. You don't have any license plates on your car."

"Oh, right, they're still in the glove compartment. Here, look, here they are, and here's my license, so just add that on too and I'll sign it. I have to go back to work."

"Miss Weld, this driver's license has expired."

"Like I said, add it on, I have to leave."

"You're not going anywhere."

"I have to, I'm late."

"I don't want to take you in for resisting arrest, but . . ."

"You can't take me in for resisting arrest because I won't go with you." Tuesday started her car and crossed Santa Monica Boulevard. The dazed motorcycle officer followed, red lights flashing, siren wailing. Tuesday rolled past the studio gate guards, pointing behind her: "Don't let him in." Good luck with that. The officer followed her all the way onto the sound stage, where Tuesday ran inside her trailer, locked the door, and called me. As we talked, the motorcycle officer outside was intercepted by none other than Bob Hope. The situation was explained to him. Hope told the officer Tuesday had been under enormous strain lately. He'd personally make sure her plates got on her car and her license was renewed. He'd also take it as a personal favor if they could just forget about the whole thing. I can't explain adequately today the unbelievable respect with which Bob Hope was held at that time by anyone wearing any kind of uniform. The officer agreed and left, but not before getting an autographed photo. As for Tuesday: "You can't take me in for resisting arrest because I won't go with you"? Try *that* on a cop someday and see how far you get.

My favorite recollection involving Tuesday actually came from my father. In the mid-sixties he phoned me from New York one day, early in the morning. He rambled on for a while, then came to the real reason for his call. "Listen, Tom. There's an item in Dorothy Kilgallen's column back here saying that you and Tuesday Weld are getting married. Is that true?"

"Oh, Dad, *you're* the one who always tells me not to believe what you read in the papers. It's absolutely not true."

Brief silence. "Okay, okay, but let me just leave you with a two-word question: Tuesday Mankiewicz?"

Tuesday later married the wildly talented Dudley Moore. They had a child, Patrick. Dudley introduced me to his ex-wife, the British actress Suzy Kendall. Suzy and I had a brief but wonderful relationship both in L.A. and in London. For a while there, it was change partners and dance. After Dudley, Tuesday improbably married the brilliant viola and violin virtuoso Pinchas Zukerman. They divorced some years later. She lives in Colorado now, near her daughter, Natasha. Her talent lives on. Every year there are Tuesday Weld film festivals, notably in New York, where her wonderful performances in *Pretty Poison, Lord Love a Duck, Play It As It Lays, Looking for Mr. Goodbar* (Oscar nominated), and others, are shown. We still talk from time to time. A few years ago she told me, "I don't want to live in a world where Tuesday Weld is sixty." Thank goodness she still does.

Jack Haley Jr.

One of the best friends I ever had and the director of my first professional collaboration. The son of Jack Haley, the iconic Tin Man in *The Wizard of Oz*. When I met him, he was working for David L. Wolper, whose production company made the great documentaries *The Race for Space, The Making of the President,* and the Jacques Cousteau specials. Jack was in charge of the entertainment division, producing and directing a TV series called *Hollywood and the Stars*. Everyone knew Jack. His house, overlooking the Sunset Strip, was constantly filled with everybody who was anybody, especially in the younger generation. It seemed each night was a different party. I first met Richard Donner with Jack. Dick was a close friend of his and soon of mine. I would later write *Superman, Superman II,* and *Ladyhawke* for Dick. Jack's personality and mine meshed perfectly. Shortly after meeting each other we became almost inseparable.

Jack was hugely talented and wanted to expand his horizons. Nancy Sinatra was a major singing star at the time ("These Boots Are Made for Walking," "Sugartown") and Jack had come up with a different notion of what a TV musical variety show should be. He pictured a filmed hour starring Nancy with nonstop musical numbers performed on exterior locations. No stage, no studio audience, no introductions. Just one continuous musical film. This was before MTV, mind you, and even before music videos. The special, *Movin' with Nancy,* was broadcast in prime time on two different networks. Jack won the Emmy for it. He'd asked me to write it for him. The guest stars would be Nancy's musical collaborator, the songwriter Lee Hazelwood, and, oh—Frank Sinatra, Dean Martin, and Sammy Davis Jr. (More about the making of the special in the next section.)

Jack had a brief encounter with almost every young actress in Hollywood, or at least tried to. I was hoping to run him a close second at the time. He was seriously involved with women only twice: with Nancy first, and later with Liza Minnelli, whom he married.

Nancy Sinatra was and is a sweet, loving person. I've known her off and on for more than forty years. She and Jack fell in love on the show and soon afterward were engaged. Jack asked me to be his best man. There was a prewedding dinner at Chasen's, attended by both families and friends. This had to be the most Catholic dinner ever held outside the Vatican. Jack Haley Sr. was a Knight of Malta. He and his wife, Flo, had donated a small fortune to the church. The Sinatras were Italian, enough said. Even I was Roman Catholic. At the dinner, George Schlatter (the producer of the wildly popular *Laugh-In* and a close friend of the Sinatras) rose and observed: "Thank goodness these two young people both worship the same God—Frank."

The wedding date was rapidly approaching. I was asleep in my beach house one night when the phone rang. It was Jack. He was audibly upset and told me I had to come over right away.

"Jesus, Jack, that's a forty-five minute drive. What the hell is it?"

"I can't go through with the wedding."

Total silence on both ends. "Are you sure?"

"Yeah. We could be in a lot of trouble."

"What's this *we* shit? I'm only the best man."

"Just get in here, will you?"

I did exactly that. Jack had tracked Nancy down at a movie with friends. No time like the present to let her know. Somehow, she eventually understood. She remained loving and loyal to him. I really think she was his most indispensable friend.

Movin' with Nancy

Shot on film—on 16 mm film (the first network show ever to be so)—with a French Éclair camera. There was very little dialogue. For my part, the writing was concentrated on setting the songs to their proper backgrounds and locations, telling the story. Jack and I would stay up nights plotting out the sequences. He had a deep love for and encyclopedic knowledge of movie musicals, plus a genuine knack for shooting inventive visuals to tell the story. He richly deserved his Emmy. "Sugartown" was shot at the base of a waterfall near Santa Barbara; "Who Will Buy This Wonderful Morning," at a crumbling, abandoned amusement park ride. For "Up, Up and Away" we used a real racing balloon owned by Jay Fiondella, the owner of Chez Jay's, a popular restaurant in Santa Monica. We hung Nancy in a balloon basket off a crane on Mulholland Drive for most of the number, then put Jay in a blond wig to actually fly the balloon. He crash-landed somewhere in Thousand Oaks, to the north, but we got the footage we needed.

Dean Martin

Dean Martin worked only one night, at the L.A. County Museum of Art. He played Nancy's "fairy godfather" and brought mannequins to life with a tap of his magic wand as he sang "Just Bummin' Around," written by Bobby Darin. I found Dean strangely unlike his public image. He was more complicated than I anticipated, full of questions and suggestions. His onscreen nonchalance, which seemed effortless ("I was so drunk last night I had to buy a movie star map to find out where I lived"), was in fact a carefully crafted persona. We worked for six or eight hours that night. He never had a drink.

Sammy Davis Jr.

Some great entertainers have a primal need to perform. With Sammy it was nothing less than an utter compulsion. Frank Sinatra once told me: "Sam would have had the greatest act ever seen in a club if he only knew when to get off. Audiences are like women. You want to leave them begging for one more. Sam gives them *two* more, then more after that till they're exhausted." Frank also famously said of Sammy: "He gets up in the middle of the night for a glass of water and goes down to the refrigerator. He opens the door— the light goes on—he does twenty minutes."

Sidney Korshak (more about him later) was a hugely powerful lawyer with definite ties to organized crime. His impressive client list included the Dodgers, the Hilton Hotels, and Gulf & Western, but it was his position as head legal honcho for the Teamsters union and their pension fund that gave him real clout. Nobody fucked with Sidney, not even Frank. The story everyone supposedly "knew" about him was this: When Sammy was having a major affair with Kim Novak, she was Columbia Pictures' biggest star. Studio head Harry Cohn was beside himself with worry. If word got out, Novak's career would be over and he'd lose his most important leading lady. Sidney was sent to Vegas to visit Sammy, who was performing there at the time. Reportedly, he told Sammy that if he ever saw Novak again, his other eye would be put out. This account was universally accepted by Hollywood "insiders." Some years later I was writing the James Bond film *Diamonds Are Forever* in Las Vegas. Sidney was close to the producer, "Cubby" Broccoli, and costar Jill St. John, and therefore close to the movie. Late one night, while I was drinking in a group that included Sidney, someone brought up Sammy's name and I stupidly observed: "If it's about Sammy, maybe you'd better check with Sidney." What an unnecessary smartass remark. I immediately blushed, realizing I'd made a colossal blunder. Sidney smiled. "You're referring to we'll put your other eye out? Actually, I threatened him with something far worse. I told him if he ever saw her again he'd never play another major nightclub in this country for the rest of his life." In those days the mob could deliver on that threat. Moreover, Sidney was right. Sammy *would* rather have gone blind than stopped performing.

Sammy was whiplash smart. He could sing. He could act. Boy, could he dance (he was Michael Jackson's first hero). He played several musical instruments. Pound for pound, there was no entertainer to match him, but he was still desperate for acceptance. From everyone. Other entertainers, civil rights leaders, politicians, high society, and "the Hood." He screwed around with and married white women and black women. I'm convinced the principal reason he converted to Judaism was to gain more acceptance in establishment Hollywood. He was one of the most avid and knowledgeable movie fans I ever knew and was always screening films at his home.

He loved the James Bond movies. While I was writing them, he would pepper me with questions about everyone involved and ask how every stunt scene and chase was shot. No detail was too small. When I went to see him in a club, he would introduce me from the stage as "the James Bond screenwriter" and then say: "You'd let me live next door to you, wouldn't you, Mank?" I'd always answer back, "I can't afford your neighborhood, Sam," and he'd roar with laughter as if hearing it for the first time.

One night in New York, Sean Connery came to see him at the Copa and went backstage afterward to pay his respects. Sammy reacted like a kid with his hero. Sean, for whom golf was a religion, was playing the next morning at Forest Hills Country Club, the home of the U.S. Tennis Open. He asked Sammy to join him. Sammy used to joke that his golfing handicap was being "an extremely short, one-eyed black Jew." Little did he know how prophetic that description would turn out to be. The following morning they went to Forest Hills and were sitting in the bar, waiting for their time to tee off, when a flustered and visibly embarrassed club manager approached. He explained apologetically to Sean that a terrible mistake had been made, that they'd had no idea Mr. Connery would be bringing Mr. Davis with him. Quite simply, Mr. Davis wasn't allowed to play at Forest Hills. Those were the club rules. Sean exploded angrily: "Do you mean to tell me that in this day and age at supposedly one of the finest clubs in the country a black man can't . . ."

"No, no, Mr. Connery, that's not it. We have several black members. Mr. Davis is Jewish."

Everyone forgets how shabbily the Rap Browns, Eldridge Cleavers, and Stokely Carmichaels who took over the civil rights movement during the sixties treated the African Americans who paved the way for equality. Even Martin Luther King Jr. wasn't exempt from their disapproval. Hell, he wanted laws passed by white people that gave civil rights to blacks. Those rights weren't theirs to give, they had to be *taken*. I saw their point, but the dismissal of the contributions of a Sammy Davis Jr. and yes, even a Sidney Poitier, was totally inexcusable. Sammy sold out nightclubs where black people weren't even allowed to sit down. Why didn't Sammy refuse to play them? Why didn't Willie Mays quit baseball when he couldn't stay in the same hotel as his white teammates? Why wasn't Willie Mays *angry*? Why wasn't Joe Louis *angry*? During their lives they underwent discrimination the younger generation could barely conceive of, and they prevailed. Unfortunately, when Sammy hugged Richard Nixon after receiving a national honor from him, his reputation among the militants was sealed.

It's all come full circle by now. When Sidney received his Lifetime Achievement Award from the Academy not that long ago, the standing ovation was endless and deafening. Every black actor was visibly tearing up while applauding, and rightly so. Sammy's reputation was almost fully restored by Michael Jackson and others shortly before Sammy's death from cancer. He was finally being recognized and honored as he always should have been. Hell, Sammy just wanted everyone to love him. He just wanted everyone to love everyone. He meant it when he sang "I Wanna Be Me." He just didn't know who that person was.

Frank Sinatra

Gee, no one's ever written about Frank before. I'd met him as a kid, but I first got to know him during *Movin' with Nancy*. He'd never quite forgiven Dad for not casting him as Sky Masterson in *Guys and Dolls*, but thank goodness they struck up a genuine friendship after that. Frank wanted to sing a song directly to Nancy on the show. We'd film it in a recording studio with a full orchestra. Frank, who'd started in the big band era, only sang with all the musicians right there. He had an incredible ear. He could hear the second trombone hit a tiny "clam" while thirty instruments were playing and he was singing. Sometimes even the audio engineer thought he was wrong, but when they played back the tape—there it was.

Frank wanted to sing "Younger Than Springtime" to Nancy: "It's such a pretty song and no one really sings it anymore." Guess what? We decided on "Younger Than Springtime." On the day of shooting I was absent-mindedly leafing through the song sheets while we waited for Frank to arrive. Something odd about some of the lyrics caught my eye: "Warmer than winds of June are the gentle lips you gave me." And later: "Angel and lover, heaven and earth . . ." This was clearly a man/woman song, not a father/daughter one. I pointed it out to Jack. It sounded a bit like incest to him too. "You're right," said Jack. "Tell Frank . . ."

"Hey, you're the director. *You* tell him."

"*You're* the one who found it. *You* tell him."

Frank arrived. I showed him the problem. He agreed, then said: "You're a writer. Change the lyrics."

"But Frank, this is Oscar Hammerstein!"

"Oscar's dead. And Dick Rodgers'll kiss my ass for singing it. Let's go."

I made the two changes. They were serviceable, if hardly inspired. The gentle "lips" became the gentle "love," and "Angel and lover" (forgive me) became "Sunlight and moonbeams." He sang it beautifully, needless to say. I sat off to one side, still having misgivings about altering the words of the great Oscar Hammerstein. Frank noticed. As he was leaving, he came over to me. "Forget about it. You're Adolf Eichmann. You just followed orders."

"Frank? Eichmann's dead." He grinned and left.

The lyric of the song was everything to Frank. Someone (Tony Bennett, I think) once said: "Before Bing Crosby, singers sang *at* people. Bing was the first who sang *to* them. Frank was the first to actually *share* the song with them. When he sang a sad song, *you* were sad with him. When he was happy, *you* were happy too." His phrasing was unique. Unless you know his version of a particular song by heart, it's impossible to sing along with him. He holds on to certain words longer than you would, clips off others, extends vowels until he seems to be swallowing them. He's more than a singer, he's a wonderful storyteller.

Frank was thrilled with Nancy's show and invited me and Jack down to his desert compound in Rancho Mirage numerous times. It was brilliantly planned out. Frank's actual house was too small to entertain in, ensuring his privacy. The guest houses were circular turrets, most surrounding the pool and stocked with every kind of toiletry, robe, and different size of comfortable footwear to pad around in. Across the tennis court sat the Christmas Tree House, which had earlier been built specifically for President John Kennedy. There was a helicopter pad next to it and downstairs quarters for the Secret Service. Kennedy never stayed in it. When his brother Bobby was attorney general, he warned Jack that he might be indicting some Mafia types with at least social ties to Frank. It wouldn't look good for the president to be spending the holidays there. Frank never forgave Bobby for that. But no matter. When Kennedy came out to Palm Springs for Christmas, he stayed at Bing Crosby's during the day but spent every night partying at Frank's compound. Needless to say, any social secrets he had would be safe there. The building that saw all the action was a huge, separate structure, large enough inside to screen 35 mm films. It had several different spacious seating areas, AP and UPI news tickers, and a lengthy bar with a sign over it proclaiming: "Living Well Is the Best Revenge."

I remember one particular party. Jack and I had been drinking steadily as we scanned the assembled guests. They included Sam Giancana from Chicago, then the Mafia "boss of bosses." Giancana was talking to "Three-Fingered" Tommy Lucchese. We later looked him up in *The Green Felt Jungle:* multiple indictments for just about everything—no convictions. Frank came by and noticed us staring at them. He leaned down, smiled, and said: "Listen, if Vic Damone could handle a lyric, they'd be at *his* house."

He was serious about Damone and lyrics, once telling me: "Vic's got the greatest set of pipes in the world and I'm crazy about him. But he's been singing for more than twenty years and doesn't have one great song he really owns, one that's identified right away with him. He sings the song great, but he doesn't tell the story." Another time, I was walking out of a Vegas casino bar with Frank. Barbra Streisand's hit "People" was playing over a speaker. I asked him if he'd ever sung the song. He shook his head. "Three reasons: First, it's the girl's song. She sang the hell out of it. Second, it's got a great start and a great finish but it kind of falls apart in the middle. Most important, the lyric's a fucking lie. People who need people are *not* the luckiest people in the world. People who love people are. People who are loved. But people who need people are unhappy people, trust me."

It's difficult to describe the aura that surrounded Frank in those days. He was genuine royalty and treated as such. I remember sitting in a large booth with him and several others at Sorrentino's in Palm Springs one night. When you were with Frank, if you ordered a drink, a whole bottle was brought to the table with your own bucket of ice. An inconspicuous bodyguard made sure you weren't disturbed. That night the place was packed. The manager came over: "Frank, excuse me, but the new sheriff of Palm Springs is at the bar. He wanted to know if you'd buy him a drink."

"Tell him to go fuck himself. Tell him I never did a favor for a cop in my life. Tell him exactly that."

We watched as the manager went back to the bar, swallowed, then gave the plain-clothed sheriff the message. The Sheriff laughed loudly, turned, and raised his glass to Frank, who returned the gesture, then said: "I knew it. That asshole thought I was making a joke."

Nancy called me one day and asked if I'd like to come down to hear Frank record a terrific new song. I was having lunch with my friend David Hemmings, and she said it was fine if I brought him along too. The song was "My Way," forever after identified as Frank's anthem. Don Costa was the arranger-conductor leading a full orchestra. I can't remember whether it was the second or third take, but when it was over, Frank turned to the booth, grinned at Costa, and said: "If you don't like *that,* babe, you don't like black-eyed peas." He left without hearing it back. He knew he'd nailed it. David and I were astounded.

Frank really loved what he did best, singing, and worked hard at it. Music *was* his life, and he was the master. The same couldn't always be said for other creative pursuits. He had the talent to be an exceptional actor. When he worked for Fred Zinnemann, Otto Preminger, John Frankenheimer, or my father, he showed it. On many other films, like *Tony Rome* or the Rat Pack movies, he was a one-take wonder. He'd say the lines, tell the director to print it, and move on, often to the frustration of other actors, who had to do their close-ups without Frank reading his lines off camera. One day Jack Haley and I got the brainstorm idea of doing a Broadway musical of *The Great Gatsby.* We wanted Burt Bacharach to write the score. There was only one perfect musical Gatsby in the world—Frank. We mentioned the possibility to him. He agreed he'd be perfect casting but said: "You know what? I'd have to show up nine times a week, week after week, month after month, and say the same fucking lines and sing the same fucking songs every night. I love you guys, but I couldn't do that. I'd break your heart."

I saw only the good Frank, the one full of humor, hospitality, and unbelievable charity toward others. A friend of Jack's and mine, a young actor named James Stacy, was costarring in a popular TV series called *Lancer*. Jim had his leg severed in a motorcycle accident. His career was effectively over and he was facing huge medical bills, some of which would continue for decades. Jack and I decided to throw a benefit for him. The Beverly Hilton Hotel donated their ballroom and agreed to eat the charges for waiters and food. Liza Minnelli and others, including Frank, agreed to get up and sing. But Frank insisted on at least fifteen musicians. He wanted Nelson Riddle to conduct. Only the Musicians' Union refused to perform for nothing, "lowering" their fees to between $15,000 and $20,000. Frank barely knew Jim, but when he heard about it he wrote out the check.

I once asked him what other singers he listened to, if any. He mentioned several females, starting with Billie Holiday. I asked about the men. Any male singers? "Sure. A little Tony Bennett, a little Mel Tormé, and a whole lot of Nat King Cole." The line of his that still sticks in my mind? After Judith Exner published the exposé of her affair with John Kennedy, Frank said: "Hell hath no fury like an ex-hooker with a press agent."

The Beat of the Brass

The second musical special Jack Haley and I did together, this one for A&M Records and Herb Alpert and the Tijuana Brass. A&M stood for Alpert and Jerry Moss. The two of them met when Jerry was an independent music promotion man and Herb was playing the trumpet at weddings and bar mitzvahs, trying to pick up "extra" work in movies. They decided to join forces in a fledgling company. Each of them put a hundred dollars into a joint bank account. They wound up owning the largest, most successful independent record company in the history of music. It couldn't have happened to two nicer guys. When they finally sold the company to Polygram decades later for an absolute fortune, they still had never signed a formal contract with each other.

Indeed, "trust" was the magic quotient, the real currency at A&M. I remember my first meeting with Jerry and Herb. I was getting $15,000 to write the special, which was top dollar in those days. In fact, a fee that size for an hour-long show was customarily split between multiple writers. At that time, I was in a small personal financial hole, having run through what money I had. At the end of the meeting I somewhat embarrassedly asked them if it would be possible for me to get half my fee up front—right then, that day. Herb smiled that mischievous little grin he has: "You're not going anywhere, are you?"

I said, "No."

He turned to Jerry: "Hell, let's give him the whole fifteen thousand." Jerry nodded. It was the only time in my life I would ever be paid 100 percent of my salary before I'd even put a ribbon in my typewriter. That's how they did business.

At the time I worked with them, Herb and the Brass were selling more records worldwide than anyone except the Beatles. It had all started with the smash single record of "The Lonely Bull." The combination of mariachi music filtered through jazz proved irresistible to the public. This "mariachi" music was conceived, written, and marketed by American Jews. "The Lonely Bull" was written by Sol Lake. Herb was a graduate of predominately Jewish Fairfax High School in Hollywood, and Jerry was a smart young ex-promotion man from the Bronx. Don Rickles used to joke: "Have you seen this new Mexican group, the Tijuana Brass? I met them last night: Herbie Alpert, Julius Wechter, Sol Lake, Ken Kaplan . . . they oughta be called the Tijuana Briss."

The *Beat of the Brass* album went gold, as did every album the Tijuana Brass ever recorded. The show got great ratings, and once again we shot nonstop musical numbers on location: on deserted, crumbling Ellis Island, where Herb's parents came through at the turn of the century; at a rodeo; at the annual Mardi Gras parade in New Orleans, in which Herb was the grand marshal; and all over the country.

Herb was an extremely handsome guy. He was also naturally shy. He performed wonderfully, but at the end of almost every show, his shirt was wringing wet from the tension he felt. I remember one night, after we'd shot part of a musical number in downtown Las Vegas. Herb, Jack, and I returned to the Sands Hotel where we were staying. We walked through the casino and decided to unwind by playing a little baccarat. The table was roped off, which made it easier on Herb in terms of privacy. We started playing. Jack had the "shoe" and couldn't win a hand to save his life. I, thank God, bet against him on every hand. Herb was backing him. He was betting modestly, but soon ran out of what cash he had. He asked the guy in the high chair how he could get some more money. The man "clicked" his clicker loudly. Jack Entratter, who ran the Sands, arrived instantly. "Yes, Mr. A, what do you need?"

"Could I get some more money?"

"How much?"

Herb got that little smile again. "How much *could* I get?"

Entratter paused. "Well, it's Saturday night, the banks are closed tomorrow so we can't check on anything . . . I'll give you a million dollars for now, okay?"

Herb blinked. "How about . . . a thousand?" Entratter smiled, pulled the money out of his pants pocket, and handed it to him.

A&M had bought the former Charlie Chaplin Studios on La Brea and Sunset. There was a huge gold trumpet over the studio gates. The former sound stages had been redesigned to become the finest recording studios in town. Herb and Jerry were on a roll. They'd already signed Burt Bacharach, Quincy Jones, and Sergio Mendes and Brasil '66, and the hits and new acts just kept on coming. Two young kids who won the All-American Talent Show became the Carpenters. Herb wanted to sing a song in the special. He had a musical voice, but with limited range. We decided on a song by Burt Bacharach called "Close to You." At the last minute Burt came up with another idea. He'd written a ballad for the musical *Promises, Promises,* which he loved, but there wasn't room for it in the show. The song was "This Guy's in Love with You." It was gorgeous, and Herb sang it wonderfully, playing on the record as well. "Close to You" was given to the Carpenters. Both were smash hits. Herb and Jerry couldn't lose.

Jerry had a house at the beach near mine. We'd play gin rummy at night, and he'd put on the new records they'd just cut at A&M. "Stuck in the Middle with You," by Stealers Wheel, was later a particular favorite of mine. We were playing one night shortly after Jerry had just returned from London. He'd just signed two relatively unknown acts. Their names were Cat Stevens and Joe Cocker. The *Mad Dogs and Englishmen* tour added Leon Russell and Rita Coolidge to the list. It would continue that way for decades, right through Styx, Peter Frampton, Janet Jackson, and the Police and Sting, among many others. Jerry commonly signed the acts with a handshake, an absolutely impossible way to do business today. But his word was as good as his bond, and A&M was the place to be. They even dabbled in movies, and guess what? They were successful, backing such hits as *The Breakfast Club* and *Birdy.*

I've had a continuing relationship with Herb. Most important for me, Jerry Moss became as close a friend as I've ever had in my life. From 1968 to this day I don't suppose a week's gone by when we haven't talked or seen each other at least once.

Liza Minnelli

When I first met Liza, she was a frenetic cocktail of talent about to explode, Krakatoa before a major eruption. She'd been a minor sensation on

Broadway in *Flora the Red Menace* and was about to perform in Las Vegas for the first time at the Riviera Hotel. She asked Jack Haley and me to help her out with any ideas we could come up with. We all went up to Vegas together. The entertainment world was waiting to see just how much of an entertainer Judy Garland's daughter really was. There must have been enormous pressure on her. The brass at the Riviera didn't consider her a "headliner" as yet—she'd have to share the marquee with someone, preferably a comedian. An old Vegas warhorse, Jack Carter, was selected. His name was just big enough to advertise without distracting the audience from Liza's debut. Carter proved to be a problem. He'd been a Vegas fixture. He wanted top billing on alternate days. They had to flip a coin to see who would close the show on opening night. Liza won, thank God. The entire audience had come to see her anyway. Carter performed interminably. I thought he'd never get off. There were even audible calls of "Liza! Let's see Liza!" She finally came onto the stage and knocked 'em dead. When one fan yelled out, "Sing 'Over the Rainbow'!" Liza yelled back, "It's been sung, pal!" Clearly, this was a young lady to be reckoned with.

We got to know each other well in those days. After she'd won the Oscar for *Cabaret*, Bob Fosse put together a show called *Liza with a Z*, which may have been the best nightclub act ever. It was beautifully paced and brilliantly choreographed, an hour and a half of singing and dancing with one show-stopping number after another. She toured Europe with it. When I was writing the screenplay for *The Eagle Has Landed* in London in 1975, I flew to Hamburg, Germany, and hooked up with Liza and her troupe for the final few European concerts. Hamburg was famous for its Reeperbahn district—reportedly the most sexually free-fire zone on the continent. After her concert we were taken on a private tour. I remember the two of us being taken to a club where a naked woman did strange and wonderful things onstage with a python. It was followed by live intercourse between two attractive people which never seemed to end. At one point, the man (extremely well hung) lifted his partner in the air with his penis still inside her and carried her down into the audience. They must have been tipped off about Liza, because they headed straight for our booth. They sat down next to us, naked, with the coitus still uninterrupted. Liza remarked, "Oh, dear, this is more than I expected."

I said to her, "We don't see enough of the Schmidts, darling. We should do this more often."

The last stop on the European tour was Barcelona, a toddling town, complete with all-night flamenco dancing, great fun. Then a flight out of Lisbon to New York. The pilot invited Liza and me into the cockpit and let her fly the plane for a while before kicking us out as we reached the eastern tip of Long Island. God, flying was fun back then. Believe it or not, people actually dressed up to get on a plane, and you could walk right on without taking off your shoes or handing over your eyedrops.

Liza had a steel backbone and a dedication to performing that was unshakable. I remember staying with her in Vegas for a few days while she was playing the Riviera. We'd eat at McDonald's around five o'clock in the afternoon. She'd devour orders of french fries and milkshakes, anything loaded with carbs. She had two shows to do, and *Liza with a Z* was so exhausting to perform that she sweated away several pounds a night. After the late show, her dressing room was packed with well-wishers and celebrities. Liza would shut herself inside her private makeup area to wind down. I joined her in there. She'd whap back a triple brandy, check herself in the mirror, then go out and join her guests.

Liza married Jack Haley Jr. at the same tiny church in Santa Barbara where her mother had married Vincente Minnelli. The wedding party consisted of five people: Jack, Liza, me, the great lyricist Fred Ebb (*Cabaret, Chicago,* and many more), and Sammy Davis Jr. Fred was Liza's semiguru and her "best man" for the day. Sammy and I shared the same duty for Jack. We drove up together in a limousine. When we got to Oxnard (about halfway), Sammy had to take a piss. We stopped at a gas station. He got out dressed in a psychedelic Indian blouse with multiple strands of love beads, something of a culture shock to that community. As he exited the men's room he caught the attention of a young couple in a convertible, getting gas. "Hey! Are you Sammy Davis?"

"Yes, I am."

"Really?"

Sammy immediately started to sing and dance for them. He might as well have been at the Copa. When he finished, everyone in the service station gave him an ovation. As he returned to the limo I lowered the window and threw a handful of loose change out into the street. "Congratulations, Sam. You just made the Arco Hall of Fame." Everyone in the car laughed loudly. Sammy, bless him, didn't think it was quite that funny.

I always thought the main reason Jack didn't marry Nancy Sinatra was that his career had barely started. His house was action central for young Hollywood, and he was eager and ambitious. Clearly, Nancy would want children and a relatively normal, if privileged family life. Jack didn't want kids. He adored Nancy, but he had places to go where he hadn't been yet. Liza was another matter entirely. Their marriage always seemed to me to have been a happy, convenient partnership of sorts. They were both constantly on the go. Her career had exploded. He was starting to direct features. They caromed from coast to coast like out-of-control pool balls: New York, L.A., Studio 54, Halston, Europe, premieres, Vegas, the whole spectrum of "being there." They were sometimes together, but progressively more often by themselves or with an escort. Their careers were taking on different arcs. Jack's movies were indifferently received, and for good reason. Let's face it, neither *Norwood* nor *The Love Machine* is taught in film schools these days. For a creative guy with his talent and acumen, I couldn't believe the kind of material he picked out for himself. Liza seemed unstoppable, the toast of (fill in the blank). When she filmed *New York, New York* with Robert De Niro for Martin Scorsese, things started to take an ominous turn.

In the seventies, between the Bond films, *The Eagle Has Landed*, *Superman,* and *Superman II,* I was practically commuting from London to L.A. Most of "happening" Hollywood was into cocaine by then. Marijuana was almost passé. I didn't do coke much. It made me incredibly hostile for some reason. Someone would say, "Hey, Mank, how are you?" I'd say, "What the fuck do you mean by that?" My friends begged me to stick with my Jack Daniel's, and I took their advice. During the filming of *New York, New York,* I remember one large party in particular where there were lines of blow on almost every table. Famous noses were scarfing them up. As I looked around the room I spotted someone I knew—Sergeant Rudy Diaz of the LAPD. Rudy'd been attached to many cop films as a technical advisor. I'd worked with him twice. Somehow his name had wound up on the guest list. He looked at me, smiled, then took a seat at the coke table. As the famous noses introduced themselves, Rudy took out his badge and identified himself. The instant look of sheer terror around the table was palpable. Rudy: "Lucky for you guys I'm Homicide, not Vice. How all you people can have so much talent and be so fucking stupid at the same time is just incredible."

Shortly afterward I was in Calgary, Canada, where we were shooting the Smallville sequences from *Superman*. Liza was doing a new Kander and Ebb musical called *The Act.* Surprise, surprise, it was being directed by Marty Scorsese. I had heard and read rumors that he and Liza were having an affair. I checked in regularly with Jack by phone, but he never brought it up. I never asked, feeling that if he wanted to talk about it, he would. The phone rang in my Calgary hotel room very late one night. It was Liza. She was in San Francisco where the show had opened to less-than-sparkling reviews. She wanted to know if I'd stop by San Francisco on my way back to L.A. and give whatever thoughts I had on how to help it. They were next headed for the L.A. Music Center and then on to Broadway. I told her I would. "Does Marty know I'm doing this?"

"Yes."

"Do Kander and Ebb?"

"Yes."

"How about Jack?"

"No, he's seen it, he's busy at home. We'll get a car to pick you up at the airport and a suite in our hotel."

I had to let Jack know I was coming. He was my friend. I told him over the phone. He seemed fine with it. He said he couldn't make it himself but whatever ideas I had would be more than welcome.

I arrived in San Francisco and saw the show. Boy, were there problems. Not the least of them was that Marty, one of the master film directors of our age, didn't seem to be ideally cut out for staging a Broadway musical. While he was giving notes to the rest of the cast and crew, Liza and I returned to her dressing room. She sat at her mirror and matter-of-factly told me that Jack had decided to come up after all. He was taking a late flight and would be there any minute. Then we got to the show: "What do you think it needs most?"

"I think you should close it."

"Don't say that."

"Liza, that's my honest opinion. There's so much work to be done and you're opening in L.A. in less than two weeks. Shut it down, rework it till everyone's happy, and put it on when it's ready."

She stared up at me, grabbed my forearm, and squeezed hard. "Don't tell Marty that. Whatever you say, don't tell him that. Promise?"

"I promise."

Jack arrived. We all went to dinner at Ernie's. There were so many levels of tension around that table I could barely count them. The show was in real trouble. Jack must have made suggestions previously that were rejected. The opening conversation was painful: "Gee, it's cold up here for this time of year, isn't it." "How's *Superman* coming, how's that kid, Chris Reeve?" "Have the steak, it's the best in town." Everything but "How about those Dodgers?"

Then a silence. Marty looked over at me. "You think I should close it, don't you." Liza had obviously told him my opinion after making me promise not to.

"Yes, but on the other hand, I haven't directed *Mean Streets* and *Taxi Driver*." It was the most uncomfortable dinner I'd ever been at. I could have kicked myself for having seen the show in the first place. I returned to

Canada and then to New York for more shooting on *Superman*. Sometime before the L.A. opening, Marty left the show. Gower Champion took over directing in L.A. and then on to Broadway, where it received very mixed reviews. Everyone loved Liza (what else was new?), but it closed after a short run.

Jack and Liza's marriage deteriorated quickly. He began drinking heavily, finally destroying his liver. The grin was still there, the snappy remark, but there was a deep sadness too. His career had a brief resurgence when he put together the brilliant history/compilation of the movie musical *That's Entertainment,* still the bible for any enthusiast of the genre. It was released as a feature and was deservedly a big hit. He finally needed a liver transplant if he was going to stay alive, but couldn't get a new one because of his advancing age. He became somewhat of a hermit, not even seeing close friends that often. A few times when I called him in the morning he was already obviously drunk. I felt so sorry for him. Shortly before he died, Dick Donner and I went over to the house to see him. Jack was in bed, barely "there," but God, did we laugh a lot. We reminisced about the good old days, the women, the projects that flew and those that didn't. It was the Three Musketeers having a final reunion. As Dick and I were leaving, Nancy Sinatra arrived. She had been so loyal and loving to him during those days. It would be Oscar time soon. Nancy told me she asked Jack what screener he wanted to see. She suggested a film starring Michael Douglas called *The Wonder Boys.* "They just left," he replied. He died several days later.

The Sweet Ride

My first feature as a screenwriter. I was barely twenty-five years old. Fox had picked up the option on my original screenplay, loved the dialogue, and had a fairly low-budget picture they wanted to make about young people living at the beach. I was a young person living at the beach. Sure sounded like perfect casting. It was based on a pretty good novel by William Murray (who later wrote several wonderful books about horse racing and the track). The problem was (with the picture too) it tried to touch all the bases at once: drama, comedy, porn, dropouts, surfing, true love, a touch of perversion, and the general malaise of 1960s young people. Frankie Avalon and Annette it definitely wasn't. My director was a Canadian, Harvey Hart, who was filming Fox's hit TV series *Peyton Place* at the time. Harvey was delightful to work with, patient and contributive to me.

The producer was Joe Pasternak, a legend for his longevity as much as the quality of his films, many of them musicals: from Deanna Durbin in the thirties to Mario Lanza, Kathryn Grayson, Fernando Lamas, and even Elvis, they seemed to be his specialty. He'd recently made a hit, *Where the Boys Are*, about young love on spring break, and seemed well suited for our film. Unfortunately, Joe had recently suffered a massive stroke and had progressive Parkinson's disease to boot. His face and hands trembled, his voice was halting and gravelly, and he shuffled rather than walked. By all rights he should have been home under a nurse's care. We shot the film on a practical location, a house on a cliff past Malibu, and I think he was physically able to visit the set only a couple of times. *The Sweet Ride* was, I believe, Joe's 105th film. It was also his last. At a later Masquers Dinner honoring him and his career I was a speaker and pointed out that producing just one screenplay of mine had put this legend out of business.

The male star was Tony Franciosa, an extremely intense and talented actor with a hair-trigger temper that always bubbled underneath an apparently cheerful surface. He'd been nominated for an Oscar for his supporting performance in *A Hatful of Rain*. Tony became a good friend and stayed down at my beach house with me from time to time. He'd been involved with several strong women in his life, among them Anna Magnani and Shelley Winters, whom he married. His temper was his worst enemy. Near the start of Don Rickles's career, everyone was flocking to see this outrageous new insult-comic who didn't mind taking on members of his audience, no matter who they were. Don was playing a club called the Slate Brothers on La Cienega Boulevard at the time, and one night Tony and Shelley Winters were in the audience. When the time came for celebrity introductions, Don pointed out Shelley Winters, the multiple Oscar-winning actress, and asked her to rise, which she did to loud applause. He then introduced the up-and-coming young star Anthony Franciosa and asked Tony to rise. As the applause died down, Don said: "Tony, could you remain standing for just a minute more? I want everyone in the room to get a look at the only guy who'd marry a broad who looked like that." Tony's eyes flashed instantly. He vaulted two tables filled with seated customers, trying to get to Don before being tackled by a gaggle of waiters and bouncers while Rickles beat a hasty retreat. Several years later, on a TV series called *Fame Is the Name of the Game*, Tony (a true professional) was late one morning. The production manager ragged him about it. Tony asked him to stop. He didn't. Tony decked him, knocked him flat with one punch. The secret was watching the eyes. If you watched Tony's eyes, you could always tell when you were about to cross into potentially dangerous territory.

The Sweet Ride "introduced" Jacqueline Bisset through a lucky accident (as happens so often in the movie business), and by the time the film was through shooting, before it was ever released, through a series of unforeseen circumstances, she was almost guaranteed to become a movie star. I've never seen anything happen quite like it in more than forty years since.

We couldn't get the kind of female lead we wanted for our film because the budget was so low that we simply didn't have the money for the Yvette Mimieuxs of the world. We read several "unknowns" without success. One night, Harvey Hart and I went to a screening of Stanley Donen's *Two for the Road* at Fox. At the beginning of the film, while hitchhiking his way across France, Albert Finney runs into a bus filled with British schoolgirls and is immediately smitten by a brunette with an absolutely magical look to her. She instantly contracts chicken pox and is left behind to recover while Finney "settles" for Audrey Hepburn and the story actually begins. Both Harvey Hart and I found her look as magical as Finney did in the film. We checked up on her. It turned out she was already under contract to Fox. I called Stanley Donen (whom I knew through Gene Kelly) in England and asked if she could act. His reply: "I have no idea. But she's a knockout, isn't she?"

We flew Jackie over, tested her, and found her to be more than acceptable for the part. Outside of being wildly attractive, she was also fun and hard working. I've known her on and off ever since and worked with her again some ten years later while doing a rewrite on *The Deep* in the Caribbean. At first Fox was worried that because of her given name and especially the spelling of her last name, the American audience would think she was French. This resulted in a classy move on the part of the Fox publicity department. In promotional materials to the press (but not on the poster, thank God) it said: "Introducing Jacqueline Bisset—rhymes with Kiss It."

While we were shooting, Frank Sinatra was at Fox and had a problem: Mia Farrow was meant to play his wife in a film called *The Detective*. But she was shooting *Rosemary's Baby,* which was going wildly over schedule and seemed like it would never end. Someone told Frank about this gorgeous English girl who was shooting a surfing movie at the studio. He looked at some rushes and hired her. Some weeks later (we were still shooting), Peter Yates was looking for a young woman to play Steve McQueen's girlfriend in his new film, *Bullitt*. He was told about Jackie, saw the rushes, and hired her as well. So before *The Sweet Ride* had ever been released, Jackie was already cast opposite Frank Sinatra and Steve McQueen in her next two films. Not a bad way to break into Hollywood. As I said, I've never heard of anything quite like it before or since.

One interesting postscript to Jackie. These days, I teach a course in filmmaking to graduate students and use *Two for the Road* to illustrate inventive ways of flashing forward and backward, the film taking place simultaneously in five different time periods of a marriage. Every time I see Jackie and hear her voice at the start I realize she's been "looped" by another actress. That's not her real voice. I guess Stanley didn't even trust her with five or six lines.

The film opened to decidedly mixed reviews. As I mentioned earlier, it tried to touch all the bases at once and wound up confusing the audience no matter what kind of film they expected to see. A good lesson for the future. At any rate, I had my first feature under my belt and guess what? Now I was headed for Broadway.

Georgy!

In 1947, when asked whether he believed the rumor that Hitler was still alive and living in South America, George S. Kaufman replied: "I have no idea. But if Hitler is still alive, I hope he's out of town with a musical."

Looking back, I'm still somewhat hazy about the details of how *Georgy!* came together. Columbia Studios wanted to do a Broadway musical of their surprise hit movie *Georgy Girl*. Not a bad idea. I'd written Emmy-winning musical specials, had a feature under my belt, and was as young as the untried composer, George Fischoff, and the lyricist, Carole Bayer, later Carole Bayer Sager, a major talent who collaborated with so many different and wonderful composers from Peter Allen to Burt Bacharach (also one of her husbands). There were two "pros" involved as well. Fred Coe, the producer, had a string of stage hits from *Two for the Seesaw, The Miracle Worker,* and *Wait Until Dark* to *A Thousand Clowns.* And the director would be my friend Peter Hunt, with whom I'd worked at the Williamstown Summer Theater. Peter had just won the Tony for directing *1776,* his first Broadway show. The cast was talented, if unknown. Georgy was played by a wonderful, tiny, and charming girl, Dilys Watling, who wound up being nominated for the Best Musical Actress Tony along with Katharine Hepburn (good luck with that, Dilys). John Castle, an excellent and versatile British stage and film actor, took the male lead, Joss. The secondary female lead was played by Melissa Hart, who'd done mainly television but was also Tony nominated for Best Supporting Musical Actress.

We opened in Boston to encouraging audience reaction and somewhat less encouraging reviews. All of the out-of-town clichés in the Busby Berkeley musical films turned out to be true: songs were replaced, scenes were rewritten, new choreography inserted, and everyone who was invited up to see the show knew exactly how to "fix" it. The first act is great—the second needs a lot of work. Or: all your problems are in the first act—the second just flies by, leave it alone. Or: her wardrobe. They just don't relate to her in those mousy colors. She practically disappears. And so on, and so on. Then we went down to our last stop before New York, the Schubert Theater in New Haven, the city where I'd been to Yale and where at the time I'd watched so many shows pass through on their way to New York and Broadway.

I was happy as a clam. I liked the show a lot. Sure, it needed some nips and tucks, but those would come. I was having an affair with one of the dancers. She was delightful and supportive, and her legs went on forever. I ran into André Previn (whom I knew from L.A.) one day. He'd written the music for *Coco,* a musical starring Katharine Hepburn that was following us into the Schubert. He'd seen our show the night before and was jealous of the wonderful shape we were in.

Unfortunately, Fred Coe's outlook wasn't quite as rosy. Fred drank heavily and had a curious warning sign when he did: for some reason he never wore stays in his shirt collars and the more he drank, the more the lapels seemed to rise, almost involuntarily. If Fred approached you with a vertical "Captain Hornblower" collar, you knew you were in for a broadside. Either the new song stunk or the set (by the multiple Tony-winning design legend Jo Mielziner) was "a goddamn erector set," or—worst of all—why didn't my Tony-winning writer friend Peter Stone come aboard to "punch up" the book? Before I could object, Peter had already been invited up (without anyone consulting me). I was in no position to argue. He and I were friends. We had a great relationship. There was never even a suggestion he would seek any form of credit—this was between us—and some of the gags he added did get laughs. But this one-time experience was so professionally deflating for me. Indeed, I have never been rewritten by anyone before or since for the rest of my entire career.

Our tiny musical with no stars opened in the cavernous Winter Garden Theater, at least twice the size of the house we should have played. But *Mame* was closing there after a run of six or seven years, and it was the only theater available. Opening night I followed the tradition of the time and reserved a table at Sardi's to wait for the reviews. My date was my friend and sometimes girlfriend Carol Lynley. At first, only one or two acquaintances joined us, and somewhat reluctantly. Then—the *Daily News* hit the stands. The review was a rave! Suddenly, my table started filling up. Extra chairs were added. Everyone ordered drinks, especially champagne. I remember David Frost (very popular at the time) suddenly appearing magically in the seat next to me, effusive and congratulatory. The *Mirror* and the *Herald Tribune* were next—both were positive. My table was now "action central." Then—dum de dum-dum—came the *New York Times,* the one review that could make or break a show like ours with no stars and a tiny advance sale. Clive Barnes killed us. He wasn't too tough on the actors or the book, but the last line of his review said: "I left the theater humming the title song from the movie." That was more than enough to kill us, just that one last line.

Suddenly, Carol and I were once again alone at the table. Gee. Where the hell had David Frost gone? The check arrived. I looked down at it and gulped. It was more than $1,000 (this was in 1969). God, they'd all ordered expensive champagne. You know, you don't get a fee up front to write a Broadway show—just a piece of what it grosses. I'd been living off what little capital I had for months. Reluctantly, I pulled out my American Express card. And then came divine intervention in the form of a human hand—the hand of Vincent Sardi, who had clearly seen everything that had been going on at my table. He plucked the check out of my hand and smiled: "Thank you for your contribution to the theater, Mr. Mankiewicz. Please come back to us again soon." It was as classy a gesture as I've ever received in my life.

I returned to my beach house in a deep depression. I didn't call people or answer the phone. I was almost broke. My last two projects had been a perverted surfing movie and a flop Broadway show. After a couple of days there was a knock on my door. It was dear Natalie Wood. "You're going to have to come out sometime, Mank. Did you ever see *The Burning Hills* with me and Tab Hunter? I had to go out to lunch the day after it opened."

I started to feel better. My phone rang. It was my agent, Malcolm Stuart. "How'd you like to write the next James Bond film, Mank?"

"Please don't fuck with me, Malcolm, I'm not in the mood."

"I'm serious. It's far from a sure thing, but Cubby Broccoli (the producer) wants to see you at his house tomorrow afternoon. I swear."

Unbeknownst to me, a series of circumstances had been set in motion by people I didn't even know that was about to radically change my life and career. Somewhere in the Great Beyond, "Pop" must have been smiling to himself. I was about to become (in show business terms, anyway) "somebody."

5

The 1960s Gallery

Milton and Ruth Berle

Milton was smart, competitive, always "on," an inveterate cigar smoker and great friend of the Sinatras, Frank in particular. His wife, Ruth, was strong willed, fearlessly funny, and very well may have extended Milton's life span by a decade. I remember a birthday party for Nancy Sinatra at her sister Tina's house. Milton and Ruth were there, as were Frank, Jack Haley Jr., I, and several others. I was sitting next to Nancy on a couch when Frank gave her his present. It was a box that contained a smaller box, which contained an even smaller box, which contained a check. Nancy's eyes widened: "Oh, Daddy . . ."

She passed the check to me. I looked at it. Wow! Ten thousand dollars. I looked again: no, I'd missed an extra zero, no, two extra zeroes. Stunned, I passed the check to Ruth Berle, who looked at it: "How about that," she said. "It was my birthday last week and Milton gave me a sweater."

Milton Berle and Steve Lawrence

Milton was widely reputed to have had one of the largest penises in show business. Steve Lawrence (a delightful human being, an underrated actor, and a great friend of Milton's) told me this story: Steve and Eydie Gormé were going on a sold-out concert tour and asked Milton to join them. Milton would open the show, then Steve and Eydie would perform, and then the three of them would finish up together. Milton agreed on a price. Steve asked for the name of his agent or lawyer. Milton told him to forget the middleman—just send the papers directly to him and he'd sign them. After the opening concert they congregated back in Steve and Eydie's dressing room.

Steve: "All right, Milton, let's see it."

"See what?"

"Your penis."

"Are you crazy? I'm not going to show you my penis."

Steve pulled out their agreement. "It's right here in your contract, Milton, on page 3." He read: "Upon completion of the first engagement, Mr. Berle shall show Mr. Lawrence his penis." Milton's eyes bulged. Steve persisted: "This is a legal document, Milton, signed by you and notarized— I expect you to live up to your contract." Milton absolutely refused.

Steve repeated his request after every concert with no luck. Months later, he and Eydie were at a party at Milton's house. After dinner, with much booze freely flowing, Milton suddenly caught Steve's eye. He gave him the high sign and gestured with his finger to follow him into the next room. Once they were alone, Milton silently dropped his pants. Steve stared: the penis was enormous. Milton smiled, then said: "And it's—at rest."

Bobby Darin

I've been fortunate enough to have seen many great entertainers in my life. Right up there with Sammy Davis Jr., Judy Garland, Marcel Marceau, and Frank Sinatra I would rank Bobby Darin. If you're surprised, you probably never had the good fortune to see him onstage.

I met Bobby through Peter Stone, who'd suggested to both of us that we'd like each other. Peter was right. Bobby and I became fast friends immediately. When Bobby wanted something, he got it. Sometimes through bullying, but mostly through seduction. If Bobby wanted you to like him, well goddamnit, you loved him. He was sharp as a tack, infectious, and funny, and pursued friendships with the same energy he spent performing. He'd just divorced Sandra Dee. I had a house at the beach. He loved the beach. I was trapped in town late many nights. He'd just bought a place on Rodeo Drive in Beverly Hills. We exchanged spare house keys and used each other's homes when we felt like it. Bobby had a serious heart condition. He knew he wasn't going to live long. That's why everything had to be at warp speed for him, including friendships. At that time Bobby wanted to learn how to play tennis so he could become part of the group who played around town. I got him a lesson with Alex Olmedo, the pro at the Beverly Hills Hotel. Two days later Bobby proudly showed me three different kinds of rackets, wrist bands, books on the history of tennis, and several different kinds of tennis shoes. He always jumped into the deep end of the pool. He needed to know everything right away. He went back to Alex for more lessons, then asked how long it would take to become a good social tennis player. Alex told him if he kept at it, maybe within a year. Bobby quit. He decided it would take too long. Also, he felt if he wasn't going to be really good—really, really good—it wasn't worth doing at all.

Bobby wrote terrific songs, both music and lyrics, some of them big hits. He played the gut guitar especially well. When he was about to go on the road at one point, he wanted to play a steel guitar in his act. I remember him practicing so furiously that his fingers bled. He told me they had to bleed so that they could heal and calluses would form. If you didn't have thick calluses, you couldn't play a steel guitar worth shit.

Bobby played in a western called *Gunfight in Abilene*. He took lessons from a quick-draw professional so he could become the fastest gun in southern California. Never mind that he didn't really have to be able to draw a gun that quickly. He needed to know that he was the best and practiced until he felt that no one was faster.

I think Bobby always felt like an outsider in life. Someone looking through the window, wanting desperately to get inside where the others seemed so safe and warm and happy. This feeling was reflected in his best performances as an actor: *Too Late Blues, Pressure Point* (playing a racist opposite Sidney Poitier), and *Captain Newman, M.D.*, where he played an emotionally troubled soldier opposite Gregory Peck and was Oscar nominated for Best Supporting Actor.

Knowledge and "class" were important to Bobby. He grew up as Walden Robert Cassotto in New York and Philadelphia, never knowing his father and with no formal education to speak of. His mother raised him on welfare. He marveled at the fact I'd gone to Exeter and Yale, and wanted to know all about the experience. At the time I got to know him he was having an affair with Diane Hartford, the tall, beautiful, if somewhat vapid wife of Huntington Hartford, heir to the A&P fortune and owner of Paradise Island in the Bahamas. Diane was crazy about Bobby and not shy about carrying on the affair in public, something he reveled in. This was Bobby as "the Great Gatsby," the kid from the wrong side of the tracks who didn't really "belong" sticking it to the upper class. I never thought Bobby cared for Diane as much as he did for the fact that she was Mrs. Huntington Hartford. If Bobby couldn't be in that "class," at least he could irritate the hell out of it.

Bobby liked to organize other people he considered to be at loose ends in life. He would host Christmas Eve dinners at which he'd collect five or six guys: some old friends, some that had worked with him, and on two occasions—me. At those dinners Bobby was host, Santa, and Papa, all rolled into one.

In 1968 Bobby fell passionately in love with the persona of Bobby

Kennedy. The senator was running for president, and without having met him, the other Bobby felt he was his soul mate. I could see the parallels: As a politician, Bobby Kennedy was like the champion of the little guy. Both of them were quick to have sudden flashes of anger, which died just as quickly. Both were headstrong and compassionate at the same time. My cousin Frank was Bobby Kennedy's press secretary. Through Frank and Paul Ziffren, a powerful attorney and member of the Democratic National Committee who was a neighbor of mine at the beach, I got Bobby introduced to the Kennedy campaign. Bobby appeared with Senator Kennedy several times. He performed to raise money for him and occasionally flew with him on the campaign plane. He was totally devastated when the senator was assassinated that fateful night at the Ambassador Hotel. Bobby never truly got over it. Disillusioned and desperately wanting to fulfill what he thought to be his new persona, he made a lot of changes.

Bobby began calling himself "Bob" Darin. Gone was the big band/rock 'n' roll swinging performer. He performed solo with a guitar, singing contemporary folk songs, some of which he'd written. Needless to say, his traditional audience was unappreciative of this change in style. He composed and distributed an album titled *Walden Robert Cassotto*. Just Bobby and the guitar. It contained ten or so songs he'd written. Some of them, like "Long Line Rider," were absolutely first-rate.

He later moved to northern California. I didn't see him with the same frequency. I remember visiting him in New York when he was performing at the Copa. He knew I was coming and told me I'd be in for a big surprise. The surprise to me was not that he was singing folk songs—I knew he would be—but that the audience was impossibly rude, yelling "Sing 'Mac the Knife'!" and "Where's the band?" Through it all, Bobby kept right on singing, just him and the guitar, being the man he was determined to be. We had dinner after, then went back to his suite at the Pierre Hotel. Bobby's folky stance onstage did not extend to his living arrangements. I remember walking into his bedroom and seeing half a dozen pairs of ripped blue jeans on the bed ready to be packed, all of them ripped in precisely the same way.

Time was soon running out for Bobby. His heart problem had increased dramatically. He went to the world-famous Dr. Debakey at Baylor University in Waco, Texas, for open-heart surgery. I hadn't seen or talked to him for maybe a month or two after that. I assumed he was back in northern California. Then one night I went to a party given by one of the Everly Brothers. It was outside in a garden, at night. Suddenly, there was Bobby. He motioned me over. We hugged. He told me he was going to need a second operation. I asked him, was Debakey sure? Bobby nodded. At that time no one had ever survived two open-heart surgeries. Debakey told him if he didn't have the operation, he'd be dead within the year. If he did have the operation, the odds were three to one he'd die on the table. I was stunned. My eyes started to glass over. Bobby suddenly grinned, reached out, and squeezed my cheek between his fingers. Then he winked and gave me a kiss. It was the last time I ever saw him. He was thirty-seven years old.

Henry Fonda

The quintessential American actor and star of the first film I worked on after college, *The Best Man*. In the more than twenty features and twice as many television shows I've participated in since, I never worked with anyone as considerate, hard working, and professional. He was a hero of sorts to me, perhaps because of the films I saw him in while growing up, or perhaps merely because of that warm, exploding grin he had that emotionally undressed you. Hank called me "Tommy." He seemed so wonderfully uncomplicated. It never occurred to me that someone who'd been divorced five times must have had more than a few ups and downs in his personal life and issues with his children as well. But, quite simply, he was Young Mr. Lincoln or Wyatt Earp to me.

I was everyone's assistant on *The Best Man* (primarily to Larry Turman and Stuart Millar, the producers), and my $125-a-week salary rated me a small office without a secretary. Part of my duties was to screen actors for smaller parts and send my candidates upstairs. One day there was a knock on the door. Hank opened it and entered, clutching a copy of the *New York Times* Sunday magazine. It was open to a picture of a beautiful blond woman in an ad. "Tommy," he said, "you know how we don't see the character of my wife anywhere during the film until the very end when she walks into the convention with me? She doesn't even have any lines." I nodded. "I want this woman to play her. Can you find out who she is and get her out here?"

I stared. "Sure, I guess . . . Let me make some calls."

"Thanks. Let me know, okay?" He was gone. I sat there, infinitely shocked that Henry Fonda might want to put someone in his movie just because he wanted to screw her. She got the part, of course. And the rest, I suppose, was up to him.

Months later I was at a small gathering at John and Linda Foreman's house. John, who later became a prolific producer, was Hank's agent at the time. Hank had had a bit to drink that night and suddenly started railing about his daughter, Jane, who had famously lived in New York with a homosexual actor followed by a homosexual acting coach. Hank was convinced she was on some weird campaign to convert gay America and that all she really needed was to be fucked by "a real guy." He turned to a twenty-one-year-old Tom Mankiewicz. "Tommy, would you like to fuck my daughter?"

"Hank, I would love to fuck your daughter. But I'm not sure Jane would let me."

Famous actors are always asked if there's any part they wish they'd played but didn't. Hank told me about what must have been a horrifying experience: He and John Foreman attended an early performance of *Who's Afraid of Virginia Woolf?*, then the most celebrated play to have hit Broadway in years. Hank was devastated by it, and in particular the performances of Arthur Hill and Uta Hagen as George and Martha. At intermission Hank said to John: "I've got to play this part. It's as if George was written for me. And Arthur Hill is so fucking good."

John was unimpressed. "Jesus, Hank, it's just a bunch of nasty characters hurling insults at each other, what's the big deal?"

After the performance, Hank said to John: "I'm going backstage to congratulate Arthur Hill."

"But Hank, you don't even know Arthur Hill."

"Oh, somehow I think he'll see me . . ."

Hank started down the alley to the stage door. John stopped him. "I might as well tell you now since I know Arthur Hill knows—you were offered this part." Hank stared, frozen. "I read it and thought it was a showy piece of crap and I turned it down."

Hank told me: "I loved John, he'd been a wonderful agent and friend to me for years, but if I'd ever been capable of strangling another human being, that would have been the moment to do it."

Judy Garland

I've already mentioned Dad's lengthy affair with Judy Garland at MGM. It continued one way or another for a long time, even after both were married. Around 1962, I was sleeping in my room at Yale one night. The phone rang around 3:00 A.M. I picked it up, groggy. A voice at the other end said faintly, "Tom . . . is this Tom?"

"Yes."

"Tom, this is Judy Garland."

At first I thought someone was putting me on, but as she kept speaking I recognized the voice, slurred as it was. She sounded in trouble and asked for Dad's number. I gave it to her. Half an hour later my phone rang again.

It was Dad, pissed because I'd given Judy his number. "She gets hopped up on pills and starts calling people. She won't get off the phone, she won't seek proper help, and those two bastards who pretend to be taking care of her, Freddie Fields and David Begelman, are robbing her blind." Dad changed his home number the following day.

I finally met Judy about three years later. I was beginning life in Hollywood as a production assistant on *The Best Man*. One of the first people I met in L.A. was Guy McElwaine, at the time a press agent working for Jim Mahoney, among whose clients were Frank Sinatra and Judy Garland. Guy later went on to become a major agent and top executive at several studios. Judy was doing a television variety show at the time, directed by a young Canadian named Norman Jewison. (Years later, Norman became my neighbor in Malibu. He's a terrifically talented nice man who just won the Directors Guild Lifetime Achievement Award for films such as *In the Heat of the Night* and *Moonstruck*. Just recently, we had lunch at his beach house.) The musical supervisor on Judy's show was Mel Tormé, who had known her since their days at MGM and whom she loved and respected musically. Guy had mentioned to Judy that I was living in L.A. and that he knew me. "Oh," she said, "bring him down, bring Tom Mankiewicz down, I want to meet him."

I went to CBS for the taping one night. When we arrived, I could see her motor home in a cavernous hallway. It had fake grass, a picket fence, and a little yellow brick road up to the door. Guy and I walked onto the set, where a packed audience had been waiting for Judy over an hour. The crowd was getting restless. Judy had apparently refused to leave her motor home, upset about something she wouldn't divulge. Even Norman and Mel couldn't get her out. Guy had an idea. He took me out into the hallway. We walked up the yellow brick road to her door and knocked. "Whoever it is, get the hell out of here, leave me alone!"

Guy spoke softly: "Judy, I brought Tom Mankiewicz down here. Remember you said you wanted to meet him? Well he's right outside. He wants to say hello."

There was a silence. The door suddenly opened and Judy Garland stared at me. "Hi," I said. "I'm Tom Mankiewicz."

She grabbed me in a bear hug and started sobbing on my shoulder. I was terrifically embarrassed, but it's a moment I'll never forget. She took me by the hand and led me onto the stage. The audience roared for her. She flashed a huge smile, got on her mark, and performed lights out as if there'd never been anything wrong. *Showtime!*

It seemed Judy was always broke later on in her tragically short life.

Even though she was highly paid, somehow she never had any money. Liza told me that when she traveled with her mom, they had a foolproof scheme, especially in the larger cities where Judy was so adored and respected. They would first check in to a suite at, say, the Pierre Hotel. Judy would be playing Carnegie Hall or somewhere equally prestigious. From the moment they arrived, every time they went downstairs to the car that took Judy to rehearsals or to dinner, they would bring some of their belongings with them in an overnight bag. By the time they checked out, none of their things were left in the suite at all. They'd go down in the elevator, get in the car, and drive to the airport, skipping out on the bill. Most hotels simply ate the charges since she was so loved and respected and they were proud to have had her as a guest.

When Judy made her famous "comeback" concert at Carnegie Hall, Frank Sinatra said to me: "She's the only singer in the business with the balls to finish with 'Chicago' while playing New York. Here's a broad who 'owns' a dozen classic songs, and none of them is 'Chicago.' If you're going to sing it, you do it in the first twenty minutes, the first set, unless you're actually playing in Chicago." What a monumental talent she was. Once-in-a-lifetime stuff. And at the time I met her, what a terribly sad human being.

Cary Grant

I was introduced to Cary Grant by my friend Peter Stone, who wrote the screenplays for *Charade* and *Father Goose* (which won the screenwriting Oscar) starring the great actor. Cary was shooting *Father Goose* at the time. Peter brought me onto the set. The cast and crew were working up high on a parallel. You had to walk up a ladder to reach them. Peter went first. I could see him taking Cary aside as I'd almost reached the top rung. Cary walked over, looked down at me, and said: "Are you Joe Mankiewicz's son?"

"Yes, I am."

He extended his hand: "Here, let me help you up. That must be an enormous burden."

Cary Grant had a reputation for being cheap, and while he was a charming man and a living legend, I saw nothing to disprove it. Peter and I had lunch with him at least three times, and I remember us picking up the check all three times. The Italian actress Claudia Cardinale was an international star then. Universal (where Cary had an exclusive deal) asked him if he would consider doing a romantic comedy with her. He was thinking about it. One day at lunch he said to me: "You're a bright lad. Peter (Stone) says you can write. See if you can come up with a premise for me."

God, I worked hard. My story began with a "cute meet" for them in an elevator that suddenly loses power and stops, trapping the two leads inside. I won't bore you with the details, but Cary finally calms down a frightened Claudia by kissing her. When I told Cary this, he smiled at me: "No, no, Tom, I'm sure you meant she kisses *me*."

"Excuse me?" I said.

"The woman always kisses me first. Even when it seems like a mutual idea, she actually kisses me." In other words, Cary was the love object. He was so smart about himself. In the eighties (as you'll see) I had roughly the same experience with Robert Redford while rewriting *Legal Eagles*. He'd taken a page from Cary Grant's book. Cary never did do a picture with Claudia Cardinale. In fact, after *Father Goose* he did only one more film.

Cary was also the ultimate clothes horse. His suits were handmade by an anonymous tailor whose identity was a state secret. Martin Landau played James Mason's chief henchman in Hitchcock's classic *North by Northwest*, starring Cary. Hitchcock had a wonderfully warped sense of humor. He told Marty he'd found out who Cary's tailor was and would be sending Marty to him to have his suits in the film cut in exactly the same way as Cary's. *Exactly*. It would be their little secret. Marty's first scene was in the Chicago train station. There was a full crew and lots of extras. He'd never met Cary Grant. Marty was sitting in his chair waiting to work when he was approached by one of Cary's elegant posse: "Excuse me, Mr. Landau, but Mr. Grant wants to know where you got that suit."

Marty looked across the station. He spotted Cary through crisscrossing people some fifty yards away. "I got it in Wardrobe, at Universal, a month or so ago."

The man nodded, walked over to Cary, then crossed back to Marty again. "I'm sorry, Mr. Landau, but Mr. Grant says that's not possible." Incredibly, Cary had been able to recognize the distinctive cut of his own tailor, even from that distance.

I once ran into him at Carroll & Co., a high-end clothing store in Beverly Hills, at their annual sale. There he was in the crowded shop, picking up some socks and underwear. Everyone pretended to shop, but they all watched Cary out of the corner of their eye. I asked him: "Doesn't this bother you a little, all of these people staring?"

"A little," he said, "but if they ever stopped, I'd be absolutely panic stricken."

But that never happened to him. He *was* Cary Grant. And keenly aware of it. Every time he entered the Universal commissary to take his table next to the back wall, the room stopped dead. Cary would walk briskly down the aisle of front tables, muttering under his breath as he went by: "Yes, it's me, it's me, it's me, it's me, it's me, it's me . . ."

The Tin Man

Jack Haley Sr. played that iconic role in *The Wizard of Oz*. Buddy Ebsen was cast at first, but his skin couldn't tolerate the silver makeup, so the part fell into Jack's lap. He and his wife, Flo, had come out to Hollywood after a long career in vaudeville. They were on "the road" for what seemed like forever, he told me. They never had a real home until they settled into the San Fernando Valley in the thirties. MGM put him under contract, usually for musicals and comedies, typically as the hero's best friend. He was getting a healthy weekly paycheck and decided to invest it in land. One acre in the Valley cost about a hundred dollars then. In the Antelope Valley (virtually uninhabited at that time) an acre went for twenty-five dollars. Jack bought several acres a week, every week, every month, every year. He told me: "I never really realized how much I was worth until my yearly land tax bill exceeded a million bucks by the late forties." He became an independently wealthy land baron for the rest of his life.

Jack and Flo were devout Catholics. Jack became a Knight of Malta and donated millions to the church. When I met them through Jack Jr., they had a home in Beverly Hills and two cars: a Rolls-Royce and a station wagon, each with a plastic baby Jesus dangling from the rearview mirror. Flo, an absolutely dear woman, was trying to raise money for her local church (where I'd been christened in 1942) by driving nuns door-to-door in the neighborhood. She told me she was appalled at how cheap everyone was. Most of them wouldn't give her a nickel. Something suddenly occurred to me. I asked: "Flo, you aren't by any chance taking the nuns door-to-door in the Rolls-Royce, are you?"

"Yes. Why?"

"Well, if a group of Sisters piled out of a car like that in front of my house, asking for money . . . Why don't you try the station wagon?"

She did. Things instantly started to look up.

Jack told me wonderful stories about the making of *The Wizard of Oz*: "We were shooting 'Follow the Yellow Brick Road.' Ray (Bolger), Bert (Lahr), and I were such hams. We started dancing down the road with Judy and Toto. Soon, the three of us were gesturing wildly, fighting for position, elbowing each other, and gently kicking the little mutt in the ass if he got in the way. Victor Fleming (the director) yelled, 'CUT!' We stopped. He looked down at us from a crane. 'You know what, guys? I can't see the little girl.'"

The 1960s Gallery

Every year Jack would give a Sunday open house for all the vaudevillians still alive and working. I never missed it. I could sit on the living room couch all day, for once with my mouth shut, and listen to Ray Bolger, Jackie Gleason, Milton Berle, George Burns, and many others, swapping hysterically funny stories about an era gone forever, but certainly not forgotten in that room.

David Hemmings

Perhaps the most voracious, omnivorous consumer of life I've ever known. Wildly talented in uncountable areas, David only knew how to pursue life in excess. I saw him first (along with most of the moviegoing public) in Michelangelo Antonioni's *Blow-Up*. He looked like a Botticelli painting, a beautiful young man who was also clearly a wonderful actor. I first met him at a party at Peter Lawford's beach house when David was playing the evil Mordred in the movie version of *Camelot*. We bonded instantly. He was impossibly inquisitive, sopping up knowledge like a human sponge. He was a gifted artist, especially at caricatures, had a great sense of humor, and furiously consumed everything put in front of him. One didn't have "a" brandy with David, one had an entire bottle. He chain-smoked, screwed everything that moved and some things that didn't. He was an excellent guitarist, cofounded an important independent production company, Hemdale, owned and managed prize fighters, and directed Marlene Dietrich. His early career as a child operatic star ended abruptly when his voice cracked for all time onstage in Paris while he was singing the title role of Billy Budd in Benjamin Britten's opera.

David fell in love with Gayle Hunnicutt, an actress then under contract to Universal. They decided to get married. He asked me to be his best man. The wedding took place at the Beverly Hills home of Jack Hanson, the ex–minor league shortstop who, with his wife, Sally, became owner of the then ultra-chic haberdashery Jax, the equally trendy Daisy Discotheque (the first ever in Beverly Hills), and *Cinema* magazine. David stopped by my beach house in the morning to drive into town for the ceremony. He had so much brandy in my car on the way he could barely stand when he got out at Jack's house. My major function as best man was to keep him on his feet during the wedding.

We became even closer in London in the seventies, during which I was working on six films. David asked to meet me one night at an after-hours club on the King's Road, where he made me a unique proposition. He was part of a small group that was about to stage a political coup in the Seychelles, a popular resort destination in the Indian Ocean. I believe it was being done with the secret cooperation of a hotel chain. David's group needed money to bribe the country's tiny army and were a bit short on funds. Here was the proposition: if I came up with £5,000 (about $12,500 then) and they succeeded, I would become minister of culture. I swear. I wouldn't have to live there or become a citizen, but I would be the minister of culture. The irony of my being the screenwriter of the James Bond films at the time wasn't entirely lost on me, but I begged off. Too many bad things could happen to me as a result, and David wasn't exactly known for dotting all his i's and crossing all his t's in situations like this. As it turned out, the tiny army did take over the islands' only radio station, declared a new government, then were promptly arrested by the islands' equally tiny police force. Sic transit my potential ministry.

Years later I was directing the season opener of HBO's hit cable series *Tales from the Crypt*. It was a five-day shoot, popular to do at the time among fairly celebrated actors and directors, even though everyone got "scale" (union minimum pay). I had a part for a crazed, evil apartment building "super" who lived in the basement and gave Andrew McCarthy a love potion to make Mariel Hemingway go nuts for him. It was only a day's work. David was living in Idaho at the time, married to a woman named Pru, and I thought of him instantly. He immediately got on a plane, flew down, and gave an exquisite performance filled with wonderfully inventive bits of "business." God, it was fun seeing him again. Even more fun to work with him. It would be the last time I ever did either one.

David remained an outrageous high-liver, brimming with new projects and propositions. His body simply gave out on him while he was shooting a film on location, I assume from sheer exhaustion. He was only sixty-two. He was an original, bless him, and could have existed only during the time in which he lived.

Dennis Hopper

Brooke Hayward and Dennis Hopper were married in the chapel of a Park Avenue cathedral in New York City. It was the early sixties. Being aware of how adamantly Leland Hayward opposed the relationship, I didn't expect him to come. Then—surprise, surprise—he suddenly appeared at the rear of the chapel just as Brooke was going to start down the aisle. He put his arm around her and whispered in her ear. Better late than never, I thought; what a good guy. I found out later he was telling her there was still time to back out.

Dennis and Brooke left for California and settled down (in a manner of speaking) in a house on Crescent Heights, above the Sunset Strip. When I arrived in L.A., they were welcoming and kind. It was great fun hanging out at their place. I was honored when they asked me to be a godfather to their daughter, Marin. Dennis was extremely thoughtful, talented, and certifiably nuts. For a while he had a Formula One racing car with no headlights or tail lights that he roared up and down the hill with impunity. He also had perhaps the keenest eye for modern art in the entire country. The house was filled with paintings and sculptures from as-yet barely discovered artists: Ed Ruscha, Robert Rauschenberg, Roy Lichtenstein, Edward Kienholz, and Billy Al Bengston, to name just a few. He took Warhol seriously, unlike most people in those days. At the time I wouldn't have given him a hundred bucks for everything. Boy, was I wrong.

Dennis was the ultimate consumer of any substance that distorted reality. He really did live in a private world. I always considered *Easy Rider* to be a wonderful cinematic accident committed by extremely talented potheads. I remember running into Dennis and Peter Fonda in New Orleans at Mardi Gras. Jack Haley Jr. and I were shooting a musical TV special with the Tijuana Brass. Herb Alpert was the grand marshal of the parade. Dennis and Peter were shooting taster footage to raise money for a low-budget project called *Easy Rider*. They asked if they could borrow our cameraman—they were shooting with ten cameras—which was impossible because we were shooting all day every day on a tight schedule. They were permanently stoned, totally disorganized, and changing the script every day. No matter how haphazardly the sausage was made, *Easy Rider* became a landmark film, symbolic of a new generation.

Sometime in the mid-sixties Dennis and I took off for Mexico, for the bullfights or jai alai or both. Neither one of us had ever been to Disneyland, so we decided to check it out. We were both in altered states when we got inside our cup on the Mad Hatter's Teacup Ride. There was a metal ring in the center. By pulling on it you could make the cup spin faster. What a golden opportunity. We pulled so hard, got the cup spinning so fast, that our heads were hanging out backward as we whirled around. An announcement came over the PA system: "Would the two men in cup number eight please slow down!" We didn't. The ride was over. We were ejected from the park. As we left, Dennis mused sadly, "Thrown out of Fantasyland . . . what a complete bummer . . ."

As I write this, Dennis has just died of cancer. Through a life filled with high highs, low lows, a sea of drugs, and multiple marriages, from Crescent Heights in Hollywood to Mabel Dodge's legendary home in New Mexico, then back down to the beach in L.A., he's been a total original. An outsider who had his modern art collection exhibited at the Hermitage in Saint Petersburg. An insider who began as a contract player in the fifties, knew his craft well, and finally left his own special mark on the motion picture. Godspeed, Dennis.

John Huston

A great friend of Dad's. Married five or six times, he alternated between being broke and a millionaire. What a talent. It seems to me now that directors such as Huston, Welles, and Lean would be impossibly politically incorrect these days. Their lives weren't spent on red carpets and inside agency offices putting "packages" together—they put their excesses on the screen through the stories they told and the characters who inhabited them. Their films have real juice in them because their lives did. I first met John at a poker game in New York. He was everything I expected him to be: womanizer, gambler, hard drinker, storyteller, and charmer. I was young, and the stakes we were playing for actually made a difference to me. Halfway through the game I found myself alone in a pot, betting against him. I had a pretty good hand. I raised. He raised me back. I smiled nervously: "You know, playing against you, I really should be betting two hookers and a copra plantation."

He smiled back: "That's very nice of you, Tom, very charming. Just put the money in, we'll chat later." Needless to say, he won the hand.

After the game, I said: "If you're ever playing in another game while you're here, let me know . . ."

He grinned at me: "Oh, I'll send a car for *you* . . ."

John told me two things that are so important for directors to know. One: "If you get what you want on the first take, print it and move on. So many directors seem to do several more takes just for the hell of it. They don't even know what they want, but they do it anyway, as if something magical may happen. What a total waste of time." Two: "If an actor (or actress) is giving a wonderful performance, don't interfere by directing them. Let them have their head. If they're talented and doing well, halfway through shooting they'll know more about the character than you do." This lesson was brought home to me by Robert Mitchum one night. Bob's first film with Huston was *Heaven Knows, Mr. Allison*. He played a marine accidentally trapped with a nun on a tiny Pacific island during World War II. The nun was played by Deborah Kerr. Bob: "It was my first time working with John and I guess I was a tiny bit nervous. I wanted to please him. After the first week of shooting he hadn't said a word to me about my performance. I asked him if I was doing okay. He said: 'You're fine, Bob, just fine.' I kept checking in with him and he kept saying that. Toward the end there was a particularly important scene. The Japanese were invading the little island and bombing it first. I was supposed to push Deborah into an empty shell hole and jump in on top to protect her. Our characters had developed a deep relationship with sexual undertones, and here I was, lying on top of a nun. It was a delicate moment, and my expression reflected it. After the first take John leaned down into the hole and said, 'More, Bob.' I said, 'More?' He said, 'Even more.' That was the only piece of direction I got from him through the entire film."

Danny Kaye

One of the most wildly talented performers ever. *The Secret Life of Walter Mitty* and *The Court Jester* (among others) are still comedic classics. Everyone knows of his prodigious talents for singing, acting, and dancing, but Danny's other accomplishments cast a wide net as well. He was a pilot—not just a putt-putt pilot: by the sixties he'd been checked out on jet airliners.

He loved sports and bought a minor league baseball team in Seattle that eventually became the Mariners. Whenever I went to Dodger Stadium I'd always see him engaged in deep conversation on the field before the game with Walter Alston, the Dodger manager at that time. Players were showing him their batting grips or sliding techniques. From time to time he actually sat in the dugout. Danny had to know everything, had to speak from real knowledge. He was also as close to being a physician as you could get without having gone to medical school. He studied all diseases, trivial or exotic, and how to cure them. He even had the American Medical Association's huge physician's dictionary, which pictured every conceivable pill in the world and explained its proper use. Dad knew Danny well and was something of an amateur doctor himself. He was jealous of Danny's AMA volume. When a doctor on Aunt Sara's side of the family passed away, Dad asked her to pretend to the AMA that he was still alive and had merely changed his address, so he could get his hands on that book. For years it was sent to a "Dr. Emanuel Aaronson" at Dad's house.

Danny's real passion was cooking. He was a world-class chef and had the diplomas and culinary awards to prove it. My good friends Leslie and Evie Bricusse lived just across the street from him. Danny was an admirer of Leslie's music and lyrics. He and Evie became regular dinner guests, and they brought me along with them on occasion. The dining table was in the kitchen. Danny would cook over the huge wrought-iron stove in his chef's outfit, aided by uniformed sous-chefs. He would keep a nonstop monologue going, filled with funny reminiscences, as one piping hot dish after another was transferred to the table and was instantly devoured. His favorite cuisine was Oriental. I've never had better Chinese food in my life.

Danny had a variety show on television at the time. I knew a couple of his writers, who told me that he was a demanding prick. But he paid top dollar and knew good work when he saw it. He was also reputed to have had a roving sexual appetite. His wife, the wonderful lyricist Sylvia Fine, had apparently learned how to live with it. I never met anyone so intent on learning everything about everything and so proficient at it. Had Danny lived more than a thousand years earlier, he truly would have been a Renaissance Man.

Gene Kelly

Along with Fred Astaire, *the* singular talent of the American musical film. One sat back and marveled at Astaire, at his dazzling style and grace, but there was something almost patrician about him. Gene was everyman, a brilliant dancer and choreographer, but someone the average guy could identify with. His contributions to the musical were singular and inventive. Gene was the first to dance with himself onscreen (*Cover Girl*), the first to do a major number with an animated character (Jerry the mouse, in *Anchors Aweigh*), and the first to seriously inject ballet into the genre (*An American in Paris*). He codirected and starred in *Singin' in the Rain*—by near unanimous consensus, simply the best musical ever made.

He was also the most competitive man I've ever met. Whether it was at charades, Scrabble, tennis, or dancing—he had to win. He was so kind and generous to me, an irascible Irishman with a quick grin forever giving me paternal advice. I met him through Jack Haley Jr., the godfather of his daughter, Bridget. Gene was also a great friend of Robert Wagner's, whom I'd worked with. The three of us played tennis several times a week with Pierre Groleau, the assistant manager of the celebrated Hollywood eating mecca Ma Maison. Many of our games were held on the court of Joe Pasternak, who would later produce my first screenplay, *The Sweet Ride*. Gene was obviously athletic and covered the court with grim determination. If you aced him with a serve just inside the line, he'd say: "I'm not sure. It might have been just out. Take two." This usually worked with me, but not R.J., who'd say, "I don't want to take two, Gene, I just aced you." I'd grin. Gene would drop his racket in frustration: "Well, if we're not even going to play fairly . . ." Sometimes rackets were thrown, insults were hurled across the net, but we always had a great time.

We played for bottles of Lafite Rothschild wine. R.J. and I were always going for the big play and too often missing. We'd insist on going double or nothing, then blow it again. After a couple of years we owed Gene and Pierre thousands of bottles of the world's most expensive wine. They insisted we pay up, so we decided to take them to the Bistro in Beverly Hills for dinner. We ordered one bottle. The sommelier brought it and poured. Gene tasted it, wrinkled his nose, shook his head, and sent it back. The next bottle was deemed acceptable. When we left the restaurant, the maître d' handed Gene the first bottle we'd ordered. Gene turned to us: "I knew you cheap bastards would try to get away with one bottle. Well I'm giving a small dinner tomorrow night, and this one will go down exquisitely." Gene had won again. He had to.

He was equally competitive at Scrabble. Gene had memorized dozens of bizarre words from the dictionary and would use them, hoping you would challenge him and lose your turn. We were in a tight game one night. He put down the word *xyst*. I frowned: "I challenge." Son of a bitch, it was in the dictionary, part of an ancient Greek portico or something. I lost my turn. We were virtually tied. Gene put down another totally unrecognizable word. I didn't challenge, not wanting to lose another turn. He won the game, then said: "You should have challenged. That word doesn't exist, I made it up."

"Gene, that's cheating."

"No, it isn't. The rules say you can challenge. If you're right, I lose my turn and have to take back the letters. I'm just playing by the rules." Technically, he was right. But as to being fair . . .

Gene was rapidly losing his hair at that time. He was almost bald. He had three different toupees made for him. One was quite modest, his "I'm just sitting around with friends" toupee. The next was slightly fuller, his "I'm going into Beverly Hills or having lunch in a public place" toupee. Finally, there was what I called the "Looms of Mohawk" rug. That fuller-than-full toupee was reserved for awards ceremonies or television appearances and made him look twenty years old. After playing tennis one day we returned to Gene's house on Rodeo Drive. Gene was in shorts, sans any toupee at all. As we were talking on the sidewalk a car suddenly stopped. Two women inside were staring out at him. "Excuse me, are you Gene Kelly?"

"Yes, I am."

They weren't entirely convinced. Gene smiled, then suddenly hopped up onto the top of a four-foot wall that ran along the side of the house. He started singing "It's Almost Like Being in Love" from *Brigadoon* as he incredibly tap-danced away down the wall in sneakers: "What a day this has been, what a rare mood I'm in . . ." The women swooned.

But dancing had always been a deadly serious business to Gene. One night at Jack Haley Jr.'s house, Debbie Reynolds told me that when she met with Gene about *Singin' in the Rain,* he told her: "You can dance, but not as well as Donald (O'Connor) and I. You're going to have to keep up. I'm not dumbing down any numbers to accommodate you." Debbie rehearsed and worked until her feet bled. She kept up. What a talented, wonderful performance she gave in that film. At another time later, he performed with Julie Andrews on television. She'd already starred and danced in musicals on Broadway and in film, but her dancing was apparently not quite up to his standards. Julie told me: "We rehearsed and rehearsed until I actually began to resent him. Then I saw the number on television and called to thank him. I'd never danced that well in my life."

Gene told me that when he was in London casting *An American in Paris,* he interviewed an enchanting young British/Dutch actress who hadn't played a major film role yet. Her name was Audrey Hepburn. "I knew she was magic. And she could dance a little. But she was a hoofer. I needed someone who could also dance ballet. The next thing I know, Willy Wyler casts her in *Roman Holiday* and the rest is history. Damn."

His favorite partners? For all-around dancing, Cyd Charisse. The most fun to dance with? Rita Cansino (Rita Hayworth to you), Judy Garland, and Shirley MacLaine. Best hoofer? Donald O'Connor, hands down.

Arthur Loew Jr.

Legendary playboy, sometime producer, friend, and one of the funniest men ever. He was the son of Marcus Loew, film pioneer and founder of the huge theater chain. Arthur was well known for his affairs with Elizabeth Taylor, Janet Leigh, Natalie Wood, and Joan Collins—among many others. After a divorce from Tyrone Power's widow, Debbie, Arthur finally married a delightful young actress named Regina Groves and stayed this way for the rest of his life. The story (perhaps apocryphal) was that she had refused to sleep with him until they got married. The wedding party was held at the Daisy. Arthur acted as his own emcee. After having introduced several others who spoke, he finally zeroed in on the man who was definitely the guest of honor, the legendary Adolph Zukor, founder of Paramount Pictures and former partner of Marcus Loew. Zukor had been very close to Arthur, who referred to him as "my grandfather." Zukor, who was then in his late nineties, rose to tumultuous applause and started for the microphone. There was one small problem: while his legs were pumping up and down, whatever muscles he needed to make him go forward weren't functioning. He was walking and walking, but only painfully inching his way to the mike. The applause continued interminably. Zukor finally arrived. As he was about to speak, Arthur leaned in front of him and said: "Thank you. My grandfather gave up a lot to be here. Tonight's his bowling night."

While Arthur was engaged to Natalie Wood, the three of us were sitting around her living room one day. There was a lull in the conversation. Suddenly, a repetitive loud noise. We looked: one of her dogs was vigorously licking its private parts. The dog kept at it and at it. We stared. Arthur turned to Natalie and said, "You know, if I could physically do that, I'd have never asked you out in the first place."

Sophia Loren

In the mid-sixties David Wolper sent me and Jack Haley Jr. to Rome to do a documentary on Sophia Loren for prime-time television. Sophia was everything one expected and more: earthy, funny, smart, self-taught, and fluent in several languages. She was so stunning to look at your hair hurt. She and her husband, Carlo Ponti, had seen the Nancy Sinatra special that Jack and I did and for which Jack had won the Emmy for Best Director. I was sent on ahead with a cameraman to gather material. Jack was to join us later.

I covered Sophia as she was shooting a film on nearby locations in Rome. She was practically worshipped by the public, who routinely called her "La Madonna." Several brought their babies and small children to be blessed by her. My cameraman was a very young John Alonzo, whose talent with our 16 mm Éclair camera was so evident I was hardly surprised when he later became a major cinematographer and shot *Chinatown*. Sophia watched him work from the corner of her eye and asked to see our rushes, which she was thrilled with. Nothing got by her.

Ironically, "La Madonna" and Carlo were having major problems with the Catholic Church. The Vatican did not recognize Carlo's Mexican divorce from his first wife, so his marriage to Sophia was not legal in their eyes. Carlo was lobbying the College of Cardinals in the way special interest groups lobby our Congress—different red hats were constantly being invited to their beautiful palazzo in Marino, a small town outside of Rome, for a little "friendly persuasion." As fate would have it, one of the most powerful and conservative princes of the church was Cardinal Frings of Cologne, a relative of Kurt Frings, a major Hollywood talent agent whose clients included Elizabeth Taylor.

The situation came to a curious head one day at the inauguration of a small soccer stadium in Marino for which the Pontis had provided most of the funds. Sophia was to preside at the opening game when the local Marino team was to play Naples, one of the major soccer powers in Europe. This matchup would be the equivalent of the Harvard baseball team playing the New York Yankees, but since Sophia came from Pozzuoli, a suburb of Naples, it was arranged. The inaugural ceremony was in the middle of the playing field. A small but capacity crowd was held back from the field by fences. The mayor of Marino gave a rousing speech lavishing praise on Sophia, who looked staggeringly beautiful in a deep-red turtleneck sweater underneath a black fur coat. The local monsignore was asked to bless the field with holy water. He hesitated. The crowd began to mumble. Sophia walked up to him. He turned away. Clearly, he didn't want to bless a location in the name and company of someone whom his church regarded as living in sin. The crowd started to boo him, yelling angrily. Sophia smiled broadly, walked straight up to him, and extended her hand in friendship. He stared. If it hadn't been for the fences, I think the locals would have torn him to pieces. Alonzo and I were thrilled—we grinned as he kept shooting. What an incredible piece of film we were getting. The game finally started and Naples politely kept it close. Late that afternoon when we returned to the villa, Sophia had already told Carlo what happened. He asked for the film, confiscated it, and had it destroyed. It was his right by contract (they had final approval of everything), and he was already in enough trouble with the church. But I'll always remember Sophia's gesture with the offered handshake. She was a natural-born star.

A short while later came one of the most unforgettable lunches I ever attended. Louis Nizer had just been appointed the new head of the MPAA (the Motion Picture Association of America). He was on an international tour to introduce himself, and the Pontis were asked to give the welcoming lunch for Italy. Sophia asked if I would like to come, and whom I wanted to be seated next to. The guest list was staggering: Vittorio De Sica, Federico Fellini, Marcello Mastroianni, Luchino Visconti, Alberto Moravia, and so on. I told her I thought Fellini was the greatest director in the world. It was settled. I would sit next to "Federico."

Before the lunch started, Sophia introduced me to him. "This is the young man who thinks you're the greatest director in the world," she told him in English.

"Aahh!" he replied, and promptly kissed me on the cheek.

During the meal I was absolutely stunned at the dazzling array of talent spread around that table. Could life get any better than this? Sophia was no fool, as usual. She was the only woman at the table. I soon discovered Fellini spoke better English than he let on in public. I began to ask him questions. Why, I wanted to know, since he and the Pontis were such good friends (Carlo had produced *La Strada*), had he never made a film with Sophia? Everyone coincidentally stopped talking when I asked him. The question almost boomed across the table. Sophia gave a wicked, tiny smile and said in English, "Yes, Federico, why haven't you ever made a film with me?"

"Because, Tom," Fellini replied, "I am northern Italian; I make my films from here—" He tapped his forehead. "Sophia is southern Italian, Neapolitana; she makes her films from here—" He tapped his heart. "If you want this shit," tapping his heart again, "talk to Vittorio." He pointed across the table at De Sica, who laughed louder than anyone.

Unfortunately, this wonderful experience came to an abrupt end. Sophia had a miscarriage. We weren't even aware she was pregnant. Her picture shut down and she took to bed. I later found out it wasn't her first miscarriage. It seemed so sadly ironic—this woman who looked for all the world as if she could drop a baby in a field and keep on working suffering through such difficulties in having a child. She asked to see me to say good-bye. I went up to her bedroom. She was lying under the covers, for the first time looking truly vulnerable and sad. We talked briefly. She smiled and gave me her hand. "Ciao, Tesoro," she said.

Years later Sophia and Carlo asked me to do a major rewrite on a film they were making, *The Cassandra Crossing*, costarring Richard Harris, Burt Lancaster, and Ava Gardner. It was at the height of the "disaster movie" craze. In this case, hundreds of European passengers were trapped and sealed inside a train filled with a deadly virus intended for biological warfare. Privately, I called it "the Towering Germ." While it was certainly no one's best film, it was a certified financial hit for its two young producers, Andy Vajna and Mario Kassar, who went on to form the hugely successful Carolco production company. Most important for me, it was a genuine thrill to hear an actress of Sophia's talent, one I remembered so warmly, delivering my dialogue on the screen.

E. G. Marshall

When Dad came up to Williamstown in the early sixties, I had a small part in a play called *The Visit*. The stars were E. G. Marshall and Nan Martin. That summer, E.G. had earlier starred in *The Skin of Our Teeth*. Almost twenty years later he played the president of the United States in *Superman II*. I was down on the set discussing some dialogue I'd written for him when his eyes suddenly narrowed: "We know each other from before somewhere, don't we?"

I smiled. "In a way, yes."

"From where? No, wait—don't tell me. I want to figure it out for myself."

For the rest of the day's shooting he constantly looked at me out of the corner of his eye. Just before we wrapped, his face suddenly lit up as if he'd just discovered radium. He came over. "We've actually been onstage together, haven't we." I was astonished that he'd remembered such an insignificant performance in such a small role so long ago. "Were you any good?" he asked me. "You couldn't have been terrible or I'd have remembered you right away."

Yvette Mimieux

A wonderful free spirit whom I've sadly lost contact with over the years. She's survived treks into every nook and cranny of the earth and multiple relationships with all sorts of people from show business to big business. We went out from time to time in the sixties. I distinctly remember her jaguar—not the car, the animal. A fully grown adult named Zareen who lived with her off Benedict Canyon. Zareen was a dividend from a relationship she'd had with an animal trainer at Jungleland. The big cat was missing his front fangs (thank God), but when he latched onto your calf or ankle, he could gum you to death. He loved to play, which usually meant you falling backward along with your chair when he jumped into your lap.

Leslie and Evie Bricusse gave a large party one night in Beverly Hills. Yvette and I went. So did Zareen, on a leash. When we entered the living room, everyone took a cautious step back. Yvette reassured them: "Don't worry, he's friendly and housebroken, he loves everybody." She unhooked the leash. Zareen immediately went under Leslie's piano and took a dump—the kind steam rises from. He glared defiantly at the guests, then hissed at them, exposing the impressive teeth he still had. Everyone gasped. The room was silent. Then Peter Stone said, "All right, who's going to rub his nose in it?"

Anthony Newley

Tony Newley was an explosive bundle of talent, energy, and humor. He was a magnetic performer and first-rate composer and lyricist, mainly in collaboration with his longtime partner, Leslie Bricusse. By the 1960s they'd already assembled an impressive catalogue, from the lyrics to "Goldfinger" to the words and music for "What Kind of Fool Am I?" and "Who Can I Turn To?" Tony had a unique voice, unmistakable in its affectation and idiosyncrasy, but warm and friendly, with great range.

He'd been in show business his entire life. As a child actor in the forties he played the Artful Dodger in David Lean's *Oliver Twist*. His little girlfriend in the film was Petula Clark, later famous for singing "Downtown" and many other hits. Tony made a huge impression on Broadway playing Littlechap in *Stop the World*, followed by *The Roar of the Greasepaint—the Smell of the Crowd*. Both musicals were written with Leslie Bricusse and directed by Tony. He had married the gorgeous Joan Collins. She was about to deliver a child. So when Tony arrived in L.A. to begin work on Leslie's film *Doctor Dolittle*, all systems were definitely go.

I met Tony and Joan through the Bricusses. We became friends. They bought a large house on Summit Drive, and Joan loved to entertain. She'd been on the verge of becoming an important actress without ever having really made it. It wasn't until she played Alexis in the TV series *Dynasty* more than a decade later that she truly became a recognizable star. For now, Joan was gregarious and popular, had a wicked tongue, and could entertain lavishly and often. Tony, on the other hand, had no stamina for parties. Most nights he would disappear upstairs around ten o'clock, never to be seen again. He was an introspective sort and I think personally tortured by many insecurities, which actually played to his advantage in his warm and touching performances. He always seemed to be reaching out to the audience for reassurance and love, and they always responded enthusiastically.

Among Tony's personal demons was his predilection for teenage girls. It had to have been a factor in his soon-deteriorating marriage to Joan. I remember a knock on the door of my Malibu beach house one day, early in the morning. It was Tony and a young girl who looked no more than fifteen. They'd spent the night at the Madonna Inn in San Luis Obispo and were on their way back into town. Tony asked to use the powder room. The young girl and I sat facing each other in my small living room. She was chewing gum and staring at me. After an uncomfortable moment or two she said, "Can I ask you a question?"

I said, "Sure."

She gestured off at the powder room. "Did he write 'What Kind of Fool Am I?'"

Later on, when Tony was making his outrageous, semiautobiographical musical film *Can Heironymus Merkin Ever Forget Mercy Humppe and Find True Happiness?* (a truly bizarre film), he asked me to collaborate with him on the screenplay and lyrics. Leslie Bricusse was up to his ass in his own projects. My screenwriting career was just starting to take off, and I felt the material was so autobiographical that it was too difficult to relate to. In retrospect, it would have been great fun to work on. Tony didn't lack for confidence. There's a scene in the film where he stands on the edge of a high cliff in a flowing robe and sings to God: "It's me, I'm all I need."

Tony semiretired after an acrimonious divorce from Joan. He'd starred on Broadway and in films, cowritten songs that were genuine standards, and played to sold-out rooms in Vegas, but seemed oddly disillusioned by the whole thing. I remember running into him before he died at much too early an age. He was remarried to a warm, pretty woman named Dareth. She was a flight attendant he'd met on an airplane. They had me over to dinner one night. They seemed so happy. I hope that toward the end Tony found some of the peace he seemed so desperately to be seeking. He was such a major talent, and so kind to me.

Merle Oberon

One summer during the sixties, Merle Oberon rented a house in the Malibu Colony. I used to see her walking on the beach, clearly past her prime, but still stunning. She always wore huge picture hats, scarves, and dark glasses and was accompanied by a very large dog and/or her much younger boyfriend, a man named Rob Wolders. One day while I was writing on the patio, Rob walked up my steps. He explained that someone had told him I'd gone to the Yale drama school and that I had hundreds of plays in my bookcase. Merle wanted to tour in summer stock. She needed an ideal part for herself. Could I think of one and if I could, would I please call? That night I took a look and decided on Shaw's *Candida*. The title role is a sensational one for a mature woman. Rob seemed to be an actor, and if he was, there was a great part for him as well. I called him. He dropped by to pick up the play. Merle had never read it. The very next day, Merle Oberon walked up my patio steps. She had the copy of *Candida* in her hand. She sat down and said: "I read the play. It's a great play and a great part, but frankly I don't have the talent. I couldn't begin to play a character this complex, but thank you anyway for suggesting it." I remember thinking I'd never heard an actor or an actress say they weren't talented enough to play a certain role. Indeed, I've never heard it since. It's simply not in their nature.

J. D. Salinger

Earlier I said the only celebrity I ever accosted, spoke to without an invitation, was Willie Mays. There was one other. I was in New York, drinking with friends at P. J. Clarke's. It was packed every night then, and usually sprinkled with famous people. Our waiter came up and said: "You'll never guess who's sitting at the little table in the corner. J. D. Salinger."

My head whipped around. Son of a bitch, it was him. That was the face on the back of my literary bible, *The Catcher in the Rye*. Fortified by several shots of Jack Daniel's, I got up and walked over to him. I cleared my throat. He looked up: "Mr. Salinger, I'm sorry to bother you, but I just wanted you to know I think you're the greatest living American writer."

He nodded. "That's very nice of you, kid. Now why don't you get the fuck out of here."

I smiled and left. On the way back to my table I started to grin. What a perfect reaction. I'd have expected nothing less from my hero.

Edie Sedgwick

Andy Warhol's "It" girl of the sixties, the star of many of his films. Edie was exquisite-looking with fine, elegant features. She was also deeply troubled and came from a largely dysfunctional family. When I first saw her at a party, my radar for distressed actresses started beeping in overdrive. There was a fear factor involved with her. I could tell it would only take a little something to light the fuse. One night we went to a large gathering at Gil and Susan Shiva's in the Dakota. Halfway through the evening I glanced over at Edie. I could see a major storm on the horizon. I asked her if she wanted to leave. She nodded. She took me to the Factory, Andy Warhol's famous headquarters. I thought of myself as a reasonably hip guy at the time, but I was unprepared for the absolute zoo I saw in there. Weird, really weird music, all kinds of drugs in the air, and open sexual activity between consenting adults and some semi-adults. I survived. Unfortunately, Edie did not. She eventually committed drug- and alcohol-induced suicide even though she'd tried to clean up many times with the help of friends and family.

One night during the time I knew her, she accidentally and mysteriously set fire to her apartment. Paramedics wheeled her out the front door of her building on a gurney. There was a picture of it on the front page of the *New York Daily News*. I was back in California. Peter Stone tore off the front page and sent it to me with the handwritten inscription: "There, but for the grace of God . . ."

David O. Selznick and Jennifer Jones

Question: Who produced (to name just a few) *King Kong, Dinner at Eight, A Star Is Born, The Prisoner of Zenda, Anna Karenina, Intermezzo, Rebecca, Spellbound,* oh, and *Gone with the Wind*? Answer: David Ogden Selznick.

Shortly after arriving back in L.A. in 1963 I was fortunate enough to become a frequent guest at the beautiful Tower Road home of David Selznick and Jennifer Jones. It was its own world, in which David was the ringmaster and impresario. Everything that went on there was conducted under his personal direction. If you engaged in sport, swimming in the pool, or playing croquet on the huge back lawn, David was there to officiate, sometimes with a whistle around his neck, calling a "foul" as Louis Jourdan or Jean Negulesco hit a ball out of bounds. One day there was an improvised water polo game going on in the pool. Hope Lange, who was merely swimming at the opposite end, was actually whistled out of the water by David when he mistakenly thought she'd committed an infraction of the rules.

David's primary passion was the game of charades. He would often organize charade evenings in advance, handpicking the teams. Or if he was at home, bored, and suddenly got the urge, he would call restaurants like La Scala and Chasen's, find out who was eating there, and get them to come up to the house for an impromptu game. No one else that I ever knew in Hollywood had that kind of residual power. Since I had some talent at the game and lots of free time, David asked me over frequently. The games were spirited. Many famous people played, sometimes for stakes up to a dollar a second. David never played. As usual, he was the "official" in charge. He made up all the topics to be acted out for both sides. He kept the time.

One night, the writer-director Richard Brooks was among those playing. Richard could be extremely crusty, and this particular evening he stopped the room cold by suddenly asking David: "David, why is it that you never play? I think you ought to play tonight."

Everyone in the room started to applaud enthusiastically. David was reluctantly convinced to play. Richard took over the topics and the timekeeping. The one that David had to act out was "Checkpoint Charlie." The Berlin crisis was in full swing at the time. Checkpoint Charlie was the gate into the American sector. He got up and signaled: "Two words." Then he gave a silent Nazi salute. His team responded: "It's German . . ." David started turning an imaginary steering wheel. "You're driving in Germany . . ." He gestured at supposed buildings around him. "A German city . . . Berlin? You're driving in Berlin . . ." David gestured up at an imaginary curved structure and ducked. "You're driving under an arch in Berlin . . . It's a gate in Berlin!" David nodded. All of this was done in thirty seconds or so. David was really quite good. Someone yelled out, "The Brandenburg Gate!" David shook his head angrily. "The gate . . . the gate . . ."

David suddenly blurted out: "It's Checkpoint Charlie, for Christ's sake!"

He sat down. The room was totally silent. Richard Brooks looked at his watch: "That's very good, David. Forty-three seconds." No one said a word.

I remember a party at David's when I told him Natalie Wood was going to be directed by Serge Bourguignon in an upcoming film called *Cassandra at the Wedding*. Serge had directed the Oscar-winning (Best Foreign Film) *Sundays and Cybele*. The script for *Cassandra* had been written by Natalie's former secretary and close friend Mart Crowley, later to write the barrier-breaking play *The Boys in the Band*. Natalie, her then fiancé Arthur Loew Jr., and I watched *Sundays and Cybele* at a screening set up for her. When Bourguignon's name came up on the screen, Arthur remarked, "How about that. This picture's been directed by an entrée." It was wonderful.

I told David I thought Serge was a "brilliant" director.

"Why do you say that?" David asked.

"Have you seen it?"

"Yes," he said.

"Didn't you think it was brilliantly directed?"

"I did," he replied. "But you called him a brilliant director. I only call a director that after seeing four or five of his films. Tom, if the only movie you'd ever seen in your life was *I Am a Fugitive from a Chain Gang*, you'd think Mervyn LeRoy was a brilliant director."

David's parties were legendary. I felt lucky to have been invited to so many. It was a chance to meet celebrated people, not merely in show business but in politics, the other arts, medicine, almost any field. I met and talked to Aldous Huxley and Igor Stravinsky at David's. He seemed to know everyone, and no one seemed to turn down his invitation. He doted on Jennifer like an old bull mastiff with a beautiful puppy. Jennifer had a few quirks of her own. She would sometimes disappear in the middle of the party and then reappear twenty minutes later dressed in an entirely different outfit. Some nights she'd change clothes two or three times. Jennifer was one of the first people in Hollywood to get into yoga in a serious way. When engaged in conversation with you, she had a habit of suddenly dropping into a yoga position on a chair or a couch with her legs screwed up at all angles. It was disconcerting but also quite endearing. One day I came over and was ushered out onto the patio, where David joined me. He said, "We have to stay out here till Jennifer's finished with yoga. She's inside with the 'Pure Souls.'"

"The 'Pure Souls'?" I asked.

"Those are the people who teach her. That's what they call themselves, the 'Pure Souls.'"

We went on talking. Finally, Jennifer came out. "Oh, David, we had such a beautiful time again." She turned to me: "You know, these people are genuine altruists. They want nothing from anyone. They have no ambition, no sins, no greed."

"How did you find them?" I asked.

"Well, they sent me this brochure," she replied.

David told me one night that at one of his parties in the forties, Samuel Goldwyn arrived late, having just previewed one of his films. David asked him how it went. Goldwyn said: "Fantastic. David, I've never gotten such a wonderful reception to any film I've ever made. They were cheering, they were laughing, they were clapping."

David looked at him and said: "Sam, I was there. I sneaked into the back. I just got home myself."

Goldwyn quickly replied: "Don't worry, we can fix it."

David was extremely protective of Jennifer. He and Dad had never worked together. They had a healthy mutual respect but no real affection. In the early sixties David wanted to make F. Scott Fitzgerald's *Tender Is the Night*. He thought Dad would be the ideal writer-director for it and was probably right. They discussed the project. Dad was very interested. He wanted William Holden to play Dick Diver. Dad thought Bill was the ideal casting for any Fitzgerald hero, including Gatsby. The main stumbling block was that David insisted on Jennifer playing the colead, the emotionally troubled Nicole Diver. Dad frankly didn't think she was a good enough actress to handle the part. He strongly urged David to let him hire a young actress named Joanne Woodward. David made it plain that using Jennifer was a condition of making the film. Dad backed out.

David then offered it to a talented young director named John Frankenheimer, who agreed to Jennifer but wanted to offer the supporting part of Rosemary to Natalie Wood. David was close to Natalie personally, but he and Jennifer balked at making the offer. Natalie was an up-and-coming star, and they were afraid she might overshadow Jennifer. Bill Holden was eventually eliminated too. Then Frankenheimer backed out of the project. David settled on Henry King, a good, competent director who'd directed Jennifer in *Love Is a Many-Splendored Thing* (oddly enough, costarring Holden), which had been a hit. Jason Robards Jr., a superb actor, was dreadfully miscast as the handsome, dashing, and charismatic Dick Diver. Jennifer's last film had been five years earlier, *A Farewell to Arms.* She played opposite Rock Hudson, who was much too young for her. John Huston started the film as director but quit early on because of what he thought was excessive interference from David. A press release was issued. In it, David modestly declared: "On my films I think of myself as the conductor of the orchestra. The director is my first violinist."

Huston replied, "What Selznick really wants is a piccolo player."

David could be gruff, but he also had an insecure streak when he didn't feel in control. I was keeping company with Tuesday Weld at the time. She had a house near mine up the Old Malibu Road. David was coming down to the beach one day, and I asked him if he wanted to meet her. Tuesday had a reputation of being somewhat of an enfant terrible, and David was interested. I'll always remember this giant of a man sitting on a little couch in a small beach house, looking extremely uncomfortable. Tuesday was charming with him. David spotted a framed drawing of a tree on the wall. Very intricate, with dozens of branches and many more leaves. "Who did that drawing?"

"I did," replied Tuesday.

"I'll give you a thousand dollars for it."

"It's not for sale," said Tuesday. "But I'll give it to you."

She took it off the wall, handed it to him, and kissed him on the forehead. David blushed. He left without taking the drawing with him. If David couldn't pay for it, it wasn't really his.

David's eye for young talent was remarkable. He remained enthusiastically involved in discovering people until he died. One day he told me: "I just read a wonderfully smart and funny story about a girl going undercover as a Playboy Bunny. The young woman who wrote it is a first-class writer. Her name is Gloria Steinem. I'm optioning it for a film." David died before he could move the project forward.

David was not above trying to control the lives of young people as well. He was utterly convinced that the only girl in the world for me was Candy Bergen. Beautiful, smart, another child of show business, what a *perfect* fit! Candy and I actually went out a few times and got to know each other fairly well. David may even have introduced us. She was and is an absolutely delightful human being. For years, whenever we ran into each other, we asked how the "kids" were, depending on whatever "divorce" settlement we were inventing at the time.

David Selznick was wonderful to me. He encouraged me and believed that I would make it as a successful writer and director. He was a giant Energizer Bunny, never stopping to catch his breath, filling his days furiously with phone calls, memos, stories, and pieces of advice. I was honored when Jennifer asked me to be an usher at his funeral.

Inger Stevens

One of my first real crushes after arriving in L.A. My radar for troubled actresses must have been working overtime in Inger's case. She was a beautiful, total joy to me, and underneath, one of the most desperately unhappy human beings I've ever met. We were both shooting at Columbia, she on her hit TV series *The Farmer's Daughter* and I on *The Best Man*. We were introduced by a young actor, George Furth, whom I'd cast in a part in the film. (George, who was wildly gay, became a very observant, funny writer and famously wrote the book for Stephen Sondheim's production of *Company* on Broadway.)

Inger and I spent parts of virtually every day together. Her dressing room on the lot was my second home. We constantly made each other laugh, even as the sadder details of her life became apparent: a broken, meaningless marriage to an agent, aborted major romances with Bing Crosby and especially Harry Belafonte while they were shooting *The World, The Flesh and the Devil* in Hawaii. In those days, if it ever came out that a blond, blue-eyed, wholesome TV sweetheart had had a passionate affair with a black man, even Belafonte, her career would have instantly been over. I soon found out that she was also secretly married to a black musician named Ike Jones. He wasn't treating her well, and she didn't know what to do about it. She was spiraling downhill mentally, but so good at putting on a cheerful persona that few people noticed. We slept together one night, or tried to. It was a total disaster. She was high on booze and antidepressants that no longer had any real effect on her. I was drunk. Tears rolled down her cheeks. Then the actual sobbing began. I didn't know what to do. I hadn't been that terrified since I was twelve years old, facing my mother in the middle of the night. Poor, dear, sweet Inger committed suicide at thirty-five.

Harry Truman

Although I never personally met the former president, he came to Yale while I was there to address a combined group of political science classes and remembered a moment that I found singular and touching. After he observed that a president's typical day is so busy he "didn't have time to take a piss in the White House," someone asked him about his final day in office. How did it feel, after winning World War II, dropping the atomic bomb, carrying out the Marshall Plan, founding the CIA, integrating the armed forces—how did it feel to stand there watching Dwight Eisenhower take the oath of office, and in an instant, cease to be the president? Truman paused briefly. "You know what moment I remember best? I got in a car with a couple of Secret Service guys to drive to the airport for my flight back to Missouri. On the way, the car suddenly came to a stop. I asked what the hell was wrong. They explained it was a red light. We had to stop for a red light, just like everyone else. I hadn't stopped for a red light in seven years."

Jack Warden

In the mid-sixties Malibu was still a small town. The people who lived there year-round were fairly well known to the Malibu sheriffs, who had a small station opposite the pharmacy, just outside the Colony gates. If you were pulled over for drunk driving within the city limits in those days and hadn't hurt anyone or done any physical damage, especially if you lived in the Colony or on the Old Malibu Road, they'd let you sleep it off in their little two-cell station without putting it on your driving record. In the morning they'd go across the street and get you breakfast at the pharmacy café and, after a stern admonition, let you go home. The talented actor Jack Warden (*Twelve Angry Men, Heaven Can Wait*) was a frequent guest at the sheriff's station in those days. He woke up one morning extremely hung over and found himself staring at a cellmate who had been arrested during the night. The guy squinted at him and said "*N.Y.P.D.*, right?"

Jack nodded. "Yes, I was in *N.Y.P.D.*"

"Lemme ask you something. You ever work with Peggy Ann Garner?"

Jack thought, then said, "Yeah, as a matter of fact I *have* worked with Peggy Ann Garner."

His cellmate grinned: "I fucked her maid."

6

The 1970s

Arrival

Every screenwriter worthy of the name has already directed his film when he has written his script.

—*Joseph L. Mankiewicz*

Diamonds Are Forever: Reinventing Bond

In 1970, I was a Bond fan like everybody else. There was a screenplay called *Diamonds Are Forever,* and Sean Connery had turned it down. Albert "Cubby" Broccoli, producer of the James Bond movies, said: "We need a big rewrite and I want to have an American writer because it takes place in Vegas and the Brits write really lousy American gangsters. And I want the writer to be young. We gotta get young. But he or she has got to be able to write in the British idiom because we've got Bond and Moneypenny." And David Picker, head of production at United Artists, said: "I saw a play the other night. A musical of *Georgy Girl.* I loved the book. It was written by Mankiewicz and I don't know him so he must be young. He's American and all the characters were British. And I thought it was written really well. So, why don't you add his name to your list?"

So I went up to Cubby's house. Met the director, Guy Hamilton, who took a shine to me. They gave me the script. I had a good meeting. I was signed on a two-week guarantee for $1,500 a week. Even in those days, for a Bond movie that was nothing. They were willing to invest $3,000 in me. Cubby said, "I want you to rewrite the first thirty pages and hand them in, and let's see what we do." I went down to the beach and worked my ass off. I thought, okay, this is your test. You ought to be able to write James Bond. You think you're this wonderful kind of cocksman. You love the movies. You think you write good dialogue. I turned it in, and waited. The phone rang one day and a female voice said, "One moment for Mr. Broccoli." He got on the phone and said two words: "Keep going." And hung up.

I said, "All right, goddamnit, this is what you do for a living now. You are a writer. You are going to keep going and write a good screenplay. Here we go. Nobody's going to relieve you of your command, and you're going to see this thing through." And son of a bitch, they sent Sean Connery my first sixty pages and he agreed to do the movie. They kept all of that from me because Cubby didn't want me to have a big head. As far as I was concerned, Sean was always going to do this, but John Gavin was signed as the backup Bond in case Sean didn't do it.

I'm writing, and the pages are flying, and they're prepping the movie. I'm sitting in the bar of the Riviera Hotel with Cubby. I'm twenty-seven years old. The production manager, Milton Feldman, stops by. Cubby said, "Milton how is Sean's suite?" He was arriving the next day.

Milton said, "It's great, Cubby. I got the golf clubs in there. I got the Glenlivet scotch." Sean had the presidential suite.

Cubby turned to me and asked, "How's your suite?"

I said, "Cubby, I don't have a suite. I have a double room, but it's wonderful. I'm happy as a clam. It overlooks the Strip. Everything is great."

He said, "Milton, get Mankiewicz a suite."

Milton said, "But Cubby—," and then looked at me and said, "No offense, Tom. But, Cubby, if we get him a suite, that's more money than we're paying him a week."

Cubby said, "I didn't ask you what it costs, Milton. He's writing the fuckin' movie. Get him a suite." I thought, goddamnit, that was another nail that was pounded into the board. That's right, I am writing the fucking movie. This isn't something you're dabbling in. There is a big engine going down the track here, and you're part of it. This is what I want to do.

It's a strange thing when you are the son of somebody famous, especially somebody who was a writer and a director. You have tremendous advantages in that you can get people on the phone that you couldn't if your name was Tom Schwartz and you came from Kansas. But at the same time, there's a whole constituency that's really rooting for you to fail. Well, he's not his father, is he? Or, the only reason he got that was because he's Joe Mankiewicz's son. Or whatever. Writing was the perfect vehicle to refute all of that, because nobody buys a script because you're Joe Mankiewicz's son. Frankly, I wouldn't have gotten on *The Best Man* with those two young producers if I wasn't Joe Mankiewicz's son. They met me and liked me and said, "Fine." But writing is the final proof, getting asked back because of the quality of your work.

Genetically, the Mankiewiczes have something about writing. Uncle Herman wrote *Citizen Kane,* Dad wrote *All About Eve.* My cousin Don wrote the pilots for *Marcus Welby, M.D.* and *Ironside* and a Harper Prize novel. My cousin John, who is younger than I am, was one of the original writer-producers of *House* and is now doing *The Mentalist.* He goes all the way back to *Miami Vice.* So the Mankiewiczes have had a proclivity for writing. It's something in our DNA. Every Mankiewicz has good dialogue. Mankiewiczes are not as good at structure. But you can learn structure. You can't learn to write good dialogue. It's like you can go to acting school, but you can't learn how to be a wonderful actor. You either have something in you or you don't have something in you. You can shape it. You can use your craft. I always marvel when I look at Marlon Brando—and when I finally wound up working with him on *Superman*—and see the greatest actor of my lifetime on the screen. He has unbelievable talent, but he has unbelievable craft as well. I watched him take scenes back from people through his craft. He's also got terrific talent. Jack Nicholson also has terrific, terrific talent. He's not Jack Nicholson for nothing. Writing is a tremendous craft. But if you don't have the talent, all the craft in the world won't save a series or movie.

Writing James Bond films was a total accident, and so many things in show business are. It was a product of a meeting between David Picker and Cubby Broccoli. I had nothing to do with it. If David Picker hadn't been in one of the four audiences to see *Georgy!,* I'd never have gotten that phone call. That's so true of so much in show business, where people are accidentally picked. The wonderful part of that accident was these were films that were nothing like the films that my father had made, which were very intellectual, almost plays. Magnificent work. But I had my own little corner of the sky. I could probably write James Bond better than Dad could no matter how good he was. It was more my generation, my time, and my kind of thing. That phone call was the most pivotal phone call because I had this grasshopper quality about me which was, all right, I'll do a little of this, I'll do a little of that. A couple of musical specials and a little surfing movie and then I'll try Broadway, but whoops, that didn't work. Then, all of a sudden, comes that time when you gather yourself together. I don't know what would have happened to me if Cubby had called and said, "I read the pages; thanks, but no thanks. We're going to go with someone else." I don't know what I would have done. Done a Norman Maine from *A Star Is Born* and walked into the ocean. Or said, "Fuck it, let me try and be somebody's assistant."

The Bond movies started with *Dr. No* and *From Russia with Love,* which were fairly small in story and budget. The big fight between Sean and Robert Shaw was in a train compartment. Lotte Lenya had a little knife in her shoe. In *Goldfinger,* when that Aston Martin started firing machine guns and squirting oil and had an ejector seat, it gave the audience an appetite. You couldn't go back after that. The cars and gadgets were not in Ian Fleming's books. They were inventions of the screenwriters because Bond became almost a PG-13 family film, meaning that the audience wanted to be entertained; they wanted to roar at some outrageous device. Q became a hugely important character. *Goldfinger* was responsible for the whole thing when that Aston Martin appeared. Now, all bets were off with Bond.

Harry Saltzman and Cubby Broccoli were the producers. They traded first billing. Traditionally, one of them would take the next film and produce it principally. So, *Diamonds Are Forever* was Cubby's film. More important, Sean Connery loathed Harry. There was actually a clause in Sean's contract, which was hidden from Harry, that said, "Mr. Connery is never to see Mr. Saltzman while he's working." Sean thought a lot of money had been stolen from him. As we got ready to shoot in Las Vegas, Harry showed up. He was a very volatile, pudgy, short guy. Tremendously smart. Like a shotgun, Harry could give you five rat-tat-tat ideas. Three of them would be no good, and two of them great, but he couldn't differentiate between them. He thought they were all great. He was Canadian, and he had produced new-wave British films—*Saturday Night and Sunday Morning,* *The Entertainer* and *Look Back in Anger.* Harry looked at the Bonds and the enormous success and all the money he was making as a bankroll to become Howard Hughes. When he showed up the day before shooting, everybody's going, "Oh, Christ." He said, "No actor is gonna tell me whether I can be on the set of my movie or not."

The first night of shooting was in downtown Vegas. A car chase and a red Mustang. In Sean Connery's huge motor home were Guy Hamilton, Jill St. John, Cubby, and me. Just as we were about to do the first shot, there was a knock on the door and Harry walked in, defiantly. Sean stood up and grinned and said, "Harry," and went over and kissed him on the cheek. Harry just stood there immobile, and left the next day. We never saw him again. Cubby and Harry had two different lifestyles and different sets of friends. Michael Caine was very loyal to Harry, for example. Harry had done *The Ipcress File* and helped Michael out a lot. Cubby and Harry had a company together called Danjaq, which still exists, named for their wives, Dana Broccoli and Jackie Saltzman. As they kept making pictures, Harry decided to become Hughes-like. He bought the Éclair camera company, which quickly went belly up. Then he decided to buy Technicolor. He went to board members privately and offered them all kinds of things, and suddenly they threw out the chairman of the board and Harry was now chairman of the board of Technicolor. Technicolor's stock was selling at thirty. When Harry was ousted two years later, it was selling at eight. Harry said to me, "Those bastards, I just walked in there one day and I'm out the fuckin' door. How can people do something like that?" I thought, Harry, that's just what you did. You fucked the last guy, they're not going to fuck you?

Diamonds Are Forever was shot principally in Las Vegas under the watchful eye of Sidney Korshak, who was Cubby's great friend. Mr. Korshak at the time was, shall we say, "keeping" Jill St. John. God, Jill was beautiful. She's been a great friend over the years. At the time, there was going to be a national Teamsters strike, and Cubby said, "Jesus Christ, Sidney. We're shooting. This is gonna kill us."

Sidney said, "Don't worry, Cubby, there won't be one here." He was the head legal advisor for the Teamsters union and ran the pension fund, which was hundreds of millions of dollars way back then. It was the biggest money pot in the world. Sidney was such a quiet power. He never threw his weight around that way that you could see. A few years after the Bonds, I was taking a girl to Vegas. We had a nice suite at the Riviera, because the Riviera was an old home to me. Eddie Torres ran the Riviera on a daily basis. (The father of Dana Torres, the Olympic swimmer—the older woman with a body you could strike a match on.) I walked into the Riviera with my girl, and Sidney was just checking out. He said, "Tom, how are you?"

I said, "Fine, Sidney."

He looked over at the desk and said, "Are the guys taking care of you?"

They said, "Yes, we are, Mr. Korshak."

He said, "Great. Well it was great to see you. I've gotta go to the airport." All of a sudden, I was upgraded to the presidential suite. There was no charge. Just because I was lucky enough Sidney was standing by the desk. Those days are long gone. I don't think that happens anymore.

Cubby was a huge gambler. He would sit down and play baccarat every night. Cubby would never win or lose less than $10,000 or $15,000 a night. I would sit with him. The limit was $2,000. Minimum bet was $20. Cubby would put his $2,000 down, and I'd put my twenty bucks down. I noticed that when he lost, and he got up, he always tipped more heavily. One night I asked him, "Cubby, why do you tip more heavily when you lose?"

He said, "Listen to me. In your life you're going to have a lot of successes and you're going to have some failures. You're going to have wonderful things happen to you and a couple of disasters. It's gonna go up and down. But you know what? First, you've got to be a gent."

Behavior was really important to Cubby, that you're a gentleman. You treated people well in that old-world, maybe Italian way. He couldn't stand it if somebody wasn't a gent. What Cubby didn't like about George Lazenby (who played Bond in *On Her Majesty's Secret Service*), outside of the fact that he wasn't that great as Bond, was an incident in Switzerland, where they were shooting. Lazenby walked into a store and wanted to buy a Walther PPK firearm. The saleswoman said, "You can't buy it, unfortunately, because we can't sell to foreigners." He started to charm her and said he was James Bond and blah, blah, blah. She sold it to him. He got in trouble because he showed it to somebody and the police came and they went to her. And Lazenby's thing was, "She didn't have to sell it to me." Cubby couldn't forgive that. He said, "I can't imagine that guy would try and let that girl suffer. He's the one that tried to buy the fucking gun. He's not a gent."

It's wonderful when you have a book nobody's heard of that has a wonderful plotline but isn't really working as a movie and you can make it work. In many ways, the James Bond movies were like that, because those books were really three-reelers. You used them as a springing-off point. *Diamonds Are Forever* the book probably coincides with the movie for forty-five minutes out of the two hours ten minutes of running time. Cubby had once worked for Howard Hughes. (Cubby had been an agent. He had lots of odd jobs.) The plot in *Diamonds Are Forever* is that Blofeld has taken over billionaire recluse Willard Whyte's hotel, the Whyte House, and it's the perfect cover because no one's seen the man in twenty years. How do they know that he isn't the billionaire? He has a voice box that makes him sound like Whyte. But that's not in the book at all, and that's the whole plot, really. Whyte lives on the hotel's secure top floor, and Bond must get to him. So Bond stands on top of an outside elevator and fires pitons into the exterior wall to reach the penthouse.

I Gambled My Way

Howard Hughes owned five Las Vegas hotels at one point. He had just taken over the Sands, and Frank Sinatra was playing there. He and Hughes did not get along. Frank went up to the casino window and said, "Give me $50,000," and they said, "We're sorry, Mr. Sinatra. According to Mr. Hughes, we don't do that anymore."

He said, "I don't think you understand me."

They were scared of him, but they said, "I'm sorry, Mr. Sinatra, but we don't."

Then the pit boss came over and said, "Frank, you can't do that." And Frank hit him. He got in a little golf cart that was in the lobby and went right through a plate-glass window, went across the street to Caesar's Palace and signed a deal.

Eddie Fisher was a compulsive gambler. He owed a lot of money at various hotels. Eddie Torres called him one day and said, "Eddie, you owe us $250,000."

Eddie said, "That can't be. I don't owe you $250,000."

What the hotel bosses had done is buy up all his markers. No hotel thought they'd be paid. So they bought up all of his markers for fifty cents on the dollar and said, "You're going to be playing in the big room." Fisher asked for how long, and Torres said, "We'll tell you when you're through."

Cubby Broccoli took me downtown one night. Binion's Horseshoe was one of the big places downtown. Famous because it had $1 million cash in the quadruple-ply window, and it was all insured. Benny Binion, who ran it, was elderly then. He's no longer with us. They still have the world championship of poker there. Cubby, Guy Hamilton, and I had drinks with Benny. He was talking about the old days, and about the million dollars in the window. He said, "You know, I came here in the forties. I'm a fairly cheap hood. The mobsters were all killing each other over the Strip, so I came downtown to open up a place to get out of their way. I got the idea of putting the million bucks in the window. The truth was that it wasn't really a million bucks. There was a lot of paper in there. So I rented ten grand and called it a million and painted the rest of it green, and it looked great in the window. Today it's really a million dollars.

"We have a slogan that we will accept any bet up to a million dollars. Now, there's nobody in the world in 1947 who's going to bet a million dollars or anything close to it, especially downtown. We got penny ante gamblers. All the big guys are up on the Strip. So one night, this guy's shooting craps. And he's doing pretty well. He says to the pit boss, 'I'd like to bet one million dollars.' He's coming out on the next roll of the dice that he either rolls a seven or makes his point. He put a million dollars on the pass by. The blood drained from our faces. We didn't have a million dollars. We didn't have anything like a million dollars. But it says in the fuckin' window that we accept any bet up to a million dollars. And I thought, all right, fifty-fifty, maybe the guy will crap out. And what am I going to do? I can't say I'm a liar. So I said okay.

"The guy rolls a seven, and he wins a million dollars. And I'm thinking, Okay, let me see, after I get beat up . . . All of a sudden, the guy says, 'Let it ride. I'd like to go again. Another million.' I said, 'What the hell, I didn't have the first million. Yeah, go ahead.' And that guy stayed for another hour and he lost $200,000. But for that one brief moment, my life was over. Like every gambler, he just couldn't take his million and go home."

During *Diamonds Are Forever*, Barbara Broccoli, Cubby's daughter, was thirteen years old. Cubby was a big backgammon player because he was a big gambler. Milton Feldman fancied himself a really good backgammon player. He kept saying to Cubby, "I'll play you, Cubby, any stakes you want." Cubby would say, "Milton, we're making a picture here. I'm the producer. And you're just the fuckin' production manager. How's it gonna look that I'm taking money from my own production manager?" But Milton would say, "You won't take money from me."

One day Cubby said, "I'll tell you what I'll do; I'll back my thirteen-year-old daughter, Barbara, against you, and you name the stakes." Milton wouldn't do it. And Barbara could play. Everybody in the Broccoli family knew how to play backgammon. Barbara's now producing the movies.

Sean Connery: Actor, Unselfish Actor

Sean Connery was just absolutely delighted with and complimentary of the script I'd rewritten. I met with Sean the first night that he was back in Las Vegas. Sean is a very complicated man; he doesn't suffer fools gladly. Sean's passions in life are first golf, there's no question, then a split between women and drinking, and then acting. But he is a single-minded kind of fellow. He made an extraordinary deal—nobody's really had a deal like this. He got $1.2 million to come back. That was huge. Elizabeth Taylor had gotten a million bucks for *Cleopatra*, but nobody had gotten a million dollars outside of that. Also, he wanted to make films. So United Artists gave him $1.2 million, plus he could make any two films he wanted up to a budget of $2 million. He made a film called *The Offence* in which he played a detective. It was a great film with Ian Bannen, directed by Sidney Lumet, who made another memorable film with Sean called *The Hill*. He did four or five films with Sidney. He just loved Sidney—he worked fast, and Sean liked to work fast too. Sidney was all about a lot of rehearsal, and then, when the gun sounds, off you go.

Sean gave away more than half the $1.2 million to a Scottish educational trust that he founded for Scottish painters, poets, writers, and actors. It was $800,000 he put in. This is in 1970. Twenty-five thousand dollars tax free, which was very good in those days if you were a poet. Twenty-five thousand dollars tax free in Scotland—my God, it's like getting $100,000. Sean said, "But, they have to stay in Scotland. I'm not paying for some young Scottish poet to live in fuckin' Paris." He was such a passionate nationalist. It stopped him from being knighted for a long time, because there was a Scottish separatist party. He was knighted after Roger Moore and Michael Caine because of the Scottish problem. The proudest moment in his life was when the queen opened Scottish Parliament, and walking down High Street in Edinburgh was the queen, and walking next to her was Sean Connery in his kilt.

During *Diamonds Are Forever,* the consummate Vegas entertainer at the time—I know there were Elvis and Frank—was Tom Jones. He was playing at Caesar's Palace in the big room. Tom Jones did a wonderful thing. It was Oscar time, and we were shooting up there. He flew up every British nominee for a special show. Of course, everybody from the Bond movie was invited because it was a Bond movie and we were in Vegas. Jill St. John and Sean Connery were keeping company at the time, and Sean didn't want to walk in with all the lights on. Sean was probably the biggest movie star in the world at the time, being James Bond. So he said to me, "Boyo, why don't you go with Jill, and I'll join you before the show starts." (He always called me "boyo" because I was so much younger, and I guess that's a Scottish expression.)

I said, "Great." I went to the gift shop at the Riviera and bought Jill what looked like a twenty-karat diamond ring. It was fake. It cost $4.25, but when she put it on her finger, people would say, "Wow, look at that ring" because it's Jill St. John.

Tom Jones was great. That was the era when women would run down and throw their room keys and underwear on the stage. That was not staged, it was real. It was this mania. Now, Sean slipped in after the second number. I couldn't believe it: he was wearing Farmer John overalls with a shirt, and not wearing his toupee. Sean lost most of his hair very early. He wasn't bald, but it was a pronounced receding hairline. In Bond, he always wore a toupee, but he didn't in other parts. He never walked around with a toupee on. Tom Jones was introducing people. "And now, ladies and gentlemen, I'm about to lose all of my fans, because sitting in the audience tonight, I don't know exactly where but I'm told he's here, is Double-O Seven himself, James Bond, Mr. Sean Connery." And then the place went nuts. A light came on in the booth, and Sean stood up, and we heard all these people say, "Look, Ethel, he doesn't have any hair." I just loved him for it. He could have whapped it on, but that's the way Sean was. I had a great respect for him because of that. Sean would say, "We're going to make a movie like *The Hill*? Fuck it, I'm not wearing a toupee. This is what I look like." I don't know many actors who would have done that. Another actor would have said, "Look, I don't mind walking around without my hair during the day, but if I'm appearing in front of all these people, I should put the toupee on." But not Sean; fuck 'em.

Everybody talks about the good old days. Las Vegas was a different town. When you look at *Diamonds Are Forever* now, when Sean swings his red Mustang out onto the Strip, you can see desert in the distance, which is now all condos and skyscrapers. Then, there were eight, nine hotels there. There was a downtown. But if you wanted to bet on the dogs, you'd go downtown. People on the Strip were larger than life. Women wore mink coats. Men wore suits.

In the downtown Vegas car chase, Bond's in the red Mustang, and he's being followed by a sheriff in a police car. Ford gave us all the cars for the car chase. In return, Bond had to drive the red Mustang convertible. Mustang sales went crazy after that car chase. Bond goes down a narrow alleyway in his car, and there is a tiny, tiny opening. He says to Jill St. John, "Quick, lean this way," and the car goes up on two wheels and goes through sideways, and the police car crashes. We shot the car coming out of the alley in Vegas. When it came time to shoot it going in the alley, that was on the back lot. Everett Creech, who did most of the car stunts, could get the car up on two wheels, but he couldn't aim it. So he cracked up a couple of cars just trying to get through that space. He said, "There's a guy I know down south who can do this. His name is Joie Chitwood."

We called him. "Everett Creech says you can get a car up on two wheels and aim it."

He said, "I sure can. How much are you going to pay me?"

"Five thousand dollars."

"I'm on my way to the airport."

He finally got there, but it was three days later. We were shooting other stuff and people forgot how the car came out of the alley. This was the script supervisor's fault. The car came out in Vegas with Sean down and Jill up. When we did the entrance, Sean was up and Jill was down. Now, it's impossible to go in one way and come out another way in this tiny space. It's physically impossible. Joie Chitwood was already on the plane back to

Louisiana, and we said, "Oh, fuck, he came in the wrong way." The script supervisor got chewed out, because that's their job, to say, "He's going in the wrong way. He should be going in that way." It's about as lame as you could get. Part of it is also Bond in a suspension of disbelief in the first place because you're having fun and the car chase is fun. But if you did that in *Serpico*, everybody would notice and say, "You can't do that."

The picture was a delight. Suddenly, I was in the big time. The score was going to be by John Barry, who became a friend. The picture was designed by Ken Adam, one of the legendary production designers. Everything was first cabin. It wasn't like you were doing your little surfing movie. Suddenly, you're working with world-class people, not the least of which was Sean Connery. This has only happened to me a few more times in my life. Sean asked for a meeting with me right away, and went through the script. Most of his suggestions or questions were about other people's parts. I've never met such an unselfish actor. Most of the time, when you go through a script with an actor, 100 percent of it is about him or her. "Do I have to do this? Do I have to do that?" Then, there's the next scene in which twenty-seven people die, but if they're not in it, they don't care. Sean would say, "Now, here when he turns around, why does he do that? How can we make that a little clearer?" That really surprised me a lot.

Regarding his Scots accent, there's a scene in the beginning when he first meets Jill St. John and she keeps changing her hair color as she's going in and out of her room. She came in with red hair, which Jill had, and Sean said, "I don't care too much for redheads. Terrible tempers."

Guy Hamilton, who was very much a to-the-manor-born guy, said, "Sean, could we try to cut down on the rolling *r*?"

In the next take, Sean said, "Don't care too much for redheads. Terrible tempers. Oh, I can't do it!" And that was an interesting thing, because Ian Fleming wrote James Bond as being very English. It was the gunmetal cigarette case and the blend of Virginia tobaccos. Almost a snob thing. The ideal casting for Bond would have been a young, more muscular David Niven. Bond was terribly English. When they cast Sean, Fleming, in the beginning, called him "that Scots lorry driver." And then, of course, Sean completely won him over and was James Bond. The last book Fleming wrote was *The Man with the Golden Gun*. In that book, Bond retires. Fleming gave him Scottish ancestry, and he goes back to Scotland to retire. That's how much Fleming loved Connery.

Roger Moore was the original choice for Bond, but he was unavailable because he was doing a series called *The Saint*, which was a huge hit in

England and the United States. Roger got three cracks at the apple, because when Sean decided to quit after his fifth one, *You Only Live Twice,* the producers went back to Roger again, but he was doing a television series that nobody remembers with Tony Curtis called *The Persuaders.* He was unavailable. After *Diamonds Are Forever,* third time's a charm. Harry Saltzman wanted Burt Reynolds, who was a star at the time. Cubby had a big thing about Bond being tall. He said, "I've stood next to Burt Reynolds, Harry, and he's a shrimp."

Harry said, "He's not a shrimp!"

Cubby said, "And the other thing, over my dead body is Bond going to be anything but British. He's not going to be American."

Mel Gibson wanted to play Bond. He could have a good British accent. He was a big star. As a matter of fact, the head of United Artists called me and said, "Would you talk to Cubby? Mel Gibson wants to play Bond, and boy, this is going to be wonderful."

Cubby said, "Let me tell you something. I don't want Mel Gibson."

Paul Newman even inquired; his agents said he would like to do it once. A lot of actors thought they'd like to do it once. In this case, Mel Gibson had said that if the picture grossed over $100 million—and this was back in the early eighties—he would do another one. Cubby said, "It'll stop being a Bond movie. It'll be a Mel Gibson movie, and I don't want a Mel Gibson movie, I want a James Bond movie." And that's the difference. And he was absolutely right about that. But Roger finally got his crack on *Live and Let Die.*

London Town

The production moved to London. I was the luckiest twenty-seven-year-old. I could fuck my brains out. I was writing James Bond, I was reasonably attractive, I was young and could crack a line or two, and I made many friends. It was during that time when you slept with somebody as a thank-you for a wonderful evening, and in no place more than London. This little country, England, was the cultural leader of the world in everything that mattered. Their actors were Richard Burton and Peter O'Toole and Tom Courtenay and Albert Finney. Models, Jean Shrimpton and Twiggy. The great fashion photographer, David Bailey. The fashion, the miniskirt. Music, the Beatles and the Stones. Theater, John Osborne. That little country suddenly exploded on the cultural scene. In those days, when you had Oscar nominees for the five best actors, three of them were British. It was the center of the world then, the way Rome was when Fellini made *La Dolce Vita.*

Everybody who was anybody was there. I could get a table at the White Elephant for lunch because I was the fuckin' James Bond writer. I was so happy. When you're that age, things like that mean a lot to you.

I stayed on *Diamonds* for forty weeks. I was dating up a storm and going out. One day, Cubby said to me, "I'm going to have to let you go. We'll talk about writing the next one."

I said, "Let me go?"

He said, "United Artists has called me a few times saying, 'Hasn't that guy finished writing the script yet? Because we're paying his living allowances.'" I had a nice allowance I was living on.

David Picker, who was a very nice guy, said, "Cubby, between you and me, didn't Mankiewicz stop writing like twenty weeks ago?"

Jill St. John, God bless her. She and I were quite friendly. I told her I was going to have to go home. She said, "Oh, don't be silly. Move in with me. I've got a wonderful flat. Don't go. Guy Hamilton wants you here, everybody wants you here. Just move in. I've got a spare bedroom." Jill and I never had a thing. So now I'm Jill's roommate.

Jill was going out with Michael Caine, and then Frank Sinatra came to London to do concerts and she was going out with Frank. My bedroom was very near the front door. Jill and I only had one key, and we'd leave it under the mat. One night, I'm still up in the bedroom, and she and Frank are coming back to Jill's place. She obviously kneeled down to get the key under the mat, and I heard Frank say, "You leave your key under the mat?"

She said, "Well, that's for my roommate and me."

"Your roommate?"

"Tom Mankiewicz."

There was a pause, then Frank said, "I'll break his fuckin' pencil."

I happen to be going out with—not a huge, passionate affair, but going out with—Diane Cilento, an actress. She played Dirty Molly in *Tom Jones* with Albert Finney. Very attractive. And she's the ex–Mrs. Sean Connery. His first wife. Sean has already married Micheline (Roquebrune) during *Diamonds Are Forever,* and he's still married to her, although he has had every leading lady and some supporting ladies, too. I'm with Miss Cilento over a one-month period, but it's very memorable, because a couple of people heard about it. Ken Adam said to me, "Oh, I wouldn't go out with Sean's ex-wife. One day you're gonna get killed." Diane and Sean didn't get along at all. I never knew if he knew about it. I ran into Sean in a restaurant in L.A. ten years later, with Micheline and his son by Diane Cilento. I kissed Micheline. Sean said, "And this is my son." The son said to me, "Oh, I remember you." I'd spent the night at the house a few times when he was a kid. He must have been five or six. I went, oops!

The Audience Speaks

Cubby was always the voice of the audience. In *Diamonds Are Forever*, I wrote a line in a scene toward the end. Bond is held prisoner by Blofeld on an oil rig. He says, "Well, Blofeld, it looks like you've won." And Blofeld, played by a very sophisticated actor named Charles Gray, says, "As La Rochefoucauld once observed, Mr. Bond, humility is the worst form of conceit. I do hold the winning hand." Cubby read this and said, "La what?"

I said, "It's La Rochefoucauld. He's a French writer, sixteenth, seventeenth century. Wrote maxims like Humility is the worst form of conceit."

He said, "Get it out."

Guy Hamilton, the director, said, "Oh, no, Cubby, it's wonderful."

He said, "No, no, get it out." And every draft would come back and there was still La Rochefoucauld. Eventually, Guy shot the scene in such a way that it could not be cut. The only coverage is Blofeld saying the line. It was shot and there was nobody to cut to. Cubby was just furious. As we started *Live and Let Die*, Guy Hamilton said to him, "Cubby, I want you to know I saw *Diamonds Are Forever* in Paris, and the La Rochefoucauld got a big laugh."

Cubby said, "France is the only place we didn't make any fuckin' money."

He was like a foster father in films to me. The other thing in *Diamonds Are Forever* was there's a coffin that arrives via airplane. Sean is pretending to be a guy named Franks, and he's looking at the coffin with the CIA agent, Felix Leiter. The diamonds are being smuggled in in the coffin. Felix Leiter says, "I give up. The diamonds are in there somewhere, but where?" Sean says, "Alimentary, my dear Leiter," meaning the alimentary canal. The diamonds are stuffed up his ass. Cubby said, "No one is going to know this 'alimentary.'"

I said, "You know 'It's elementary, my dear Watson'?"

He said, "Yeah, I get it, but nobody's gonna fuckin' know this."

So Guy again, who loved all these things, said, "Oh goodness, Cubby, let us have it. Sean likes it."

He said, "All right, Jesus Christ, alimentary, my dear Leiter."

Diamonds Are Forever is playing at Grauman's Chinese, and Cubby and I go, and we're standing in the back. It's a full house. Sean says, "Alimentary, my dear Leiter." And two people just laugh like hell out of the hundreds. Cubby turns to me and says, "Big deal, two doctors."

Richard Maibaum wrote a lot of Bonds. He was a great friend of Cubby's. A sweet man to me. Just wonderful. Always very complimentary about me. We shared credit on *Diamonds Are Forever* and *Man with the Golden Gun*. Dick was a good deal older than I was. He has more Bond credits as a writer than anybody. Somebody said, "Well, maybe Dick's written himself out. This is his tenth." We shared credit, and he gets first credit because it's alphabetical. M-A-I, and M-A-N. We shared credit without ever having met, but later on I met him at Cubby's, and he was a wonderful guy. And a good writer. I felt so lucky to have my name on a James Bond picture at that point in my life.

Live and Let Die: Presenting the Next James Bond

Thank God, the picture was a hit, and Cubby and Harry were going to ask me back for *Live and Let Die*. They thought, we'll take one last shot at Sean. During 1971, I'd already doped out a lot of the script. Harry produced most of *Live and Let Die*. He called me one day and said, "Here's the scene. Sean's asleep. He thinks he's in bed with Solitaire. He feels something, wakes up, and there's a crocodile in bed with him. Isn't that great?"

I said, "Harry, let me ask you a couple questions. First of all, if the crocodile's in bed with him, why didn't the crocodile eat him? He's asleep, I mean, the crocodile would munch on him."

He said, "I don't know. You're the writer."

"And the other thing, they have these tiny little legs. How did he get on the bed? Is there a ramp or something that he walked up?"

"I don't know. You're the writer." This was Harry.

So I went to lunch with Sean. I told him about ideas for the new script, including the crocodiles and whatnot. Sean leaned toward me. "You know what I hear, boyo, all the time? It's my obligation to play Bond." He was the only Bond as far as everyone was concerned. Except for George Lazenby, he had been Bond in every movie and the audience loved him. Sean said, "When is my obligation over? After eight Bonds? Ten Bonds? Twelve Bonds? When do I stop having an obligation to play Bond? There's only two things in my life I've ever wanted to own: a golf course and a bank, and I have both." He had a little Scottish bank, and he owned a golf course in Marbella, Spain. You could understand completely. There were so many different parts that he wanted to play, and he wanted to work with people like Sidney Lumet. But the audience says, "No, you owe it to us." Like Bobby

Darin singing "Simple Song of Freedom" and people are yelling, "Sing 'Mack the Knife'!" like it's your obligation.

So here comes Roger Moore. *Live and Let Die*. Harry said, "Let me negotiate with Mankiewicz's agent." Cubby said, "Be my guest, Harry. We want him, Guy Hamilton wants him."

I had kept company, as they say, with Harry's assistant, Sue Parker, who's just a beautiful girl and a wonderful person. Sue said, "Your agent, Robin French, is calling tomorrow at ten. Why don't you come to the office, and you can listen in to the phone call from outside?"

I said, "I'd like to."

On the phone, Robin said, "All right, here's the deal, Harry. Tom wants $100,000." Now, that was a lot of money in 1971 for a screenplay. One hundred thousand dollars for a kid who's twenty-nine years old. All right, I've written *Diamonds Are Forever*, but $100,000 put you in a certain league.

Harry said, "What did we give him on this picture, $1,500 a week or $1,250 a week? Tell you what. We're willing to step forward. We'll guarantee him $50,000."

Robin said, "No, he's gonna need a hundred, Harry."

"I'll have to check with Cubby," Harry said. "We might go as high as sixty, I don't know."

Robin said, "Here's another way we could do it, Harry. He'll do it for fifty."

"Oh, good."

"And he wants 2 percent of the net profits."

There was a silence. Then Harry said, "Well, let's not talk science fiction. Okay, he'll get one hundred."

I lived at the beach in Malibu until 1971. When I got *Live and Let Die*, I said, "I'm going to buy a house." I'd been renting this kind of shack in the Malibu Colony. The heat didn't work, it was tiny, and it made the least use of the little lot. It was forty feet wide. On the beach. To show you I've never been a great businessman, I asked the owner, "If I were to buy this house, what would you charge me?" I'd lived there for seven years.

She said, "I'd make you a good deal, but I'd have to charge you what I think it's worth, $85,000."

I said, "You must be out of your mind. I'm not paying $85,000 for this house." I was renting it for $500 a month. I'm pissing away $6,000 a year on this house.

When she said $85,000, I came into the city and looked. I was getting good money for *Live and Let Die,* and I found the house that I'm in now. It was on a dead end with a great view. I could see all the way to the ocean. There was no dining room. It had a tiny little kitchen. I put the office in. Over the years, I've just added and pushed out. When I started to make really big money, a couple of times I said to myself, "I'm going to look for another house." I'd look around and say, "You know what? I come home and I'm happy here." I just am. Two minutes away from Sunset. Five minutes away from Beverly Hills. It was not that chic. Now it's very chic. Lots of actors live up here. Forty years ago, we had foxes and snakes, and a couple of mountain lions would come down. It wasn't as built up. Lots of wildlife, which has gradually been pushed out as it has around the world. So I've always been very happy here.

I made a little compound for the cats. I love cats because they're highly affectionate and full of mischief, but they're also independent. They sack out a lot of the day, and they want their own time. They gradually take over the house, and it becomes their place. They can go in and out of their compound all day, and no predator can ever get to them. I have this strange communication with cats. Lenny Bruce, whom I met a few times, just before he died, used to say, "The difference between a dog and a cat is you work all day, your boss is yelling at you. You get home, your wife starts yelling at you. It's just a terrible day. You get in a chair, try to read the paper, and here comes a dog with a rubber ball in his mouth, and you hit him on the head with the newspaper. Five minutes later the dog's back again with the rubber ball in his mouth." He said, "You hit a cat in the head with a newspaper and you don't see him for six months. Never put up with that shit."

At this time, Dad was living in Pound Ridge in Westchester County. He had a beautiful thirty-acre estate with a pond. He always wanted to live up there, and he was an easterner. Every time I went to Europe on the Bonds, which was a lot, I would stop by. I would fly to New York and spend the night up in Pound Ridge. Then I'd take the Concorde the next morning, which was just three hours and twenty minutes across the Atlantic to London. It was the most wonderful plane ever. It was *Live and Let Die* time, and by then, instead of renting a car or taking a cab, I had a limo with a driver. United Artists was paying for it. I arrived at the house in a limo to spend the night, and Dad was out in front of the house in this little circular driveway of the estate. I got out of the limo and said to the driver, "Ralph, tomorrow at seven o'clock."

He said, "Absolutely, Mr. Mankiewicz," and took off.

Dad looked at me and said, "Wow, a limo."

I said to him, "Yeah, everybody who makes a couple hundred thousand a year takes a limo now and then." Which was really stupid and crass. He grinned. What I was trying to say was, "I'm independent." It's the stupidest thing I ever said to him.

Boyo

Ian Fleming was still alive for the first two Bond films. He had a house in Jamaica called Golden Eye. Cubby would tell you the reason the Bond movies got started in the first place was Harry and Cubby had optioned all of the books except *Casino Royale* and *Thunderball*. They couldn't get those two because they were already optioned by two separate parties. But all the other books they got. They had a deal with United Artists, and *Dr. No,* the first one, was made for $1.2 million. Sean got $25,000. Nobody had ever heard of him. And United Artists was almost unwilling to put up the $1.2 million, saying, "God, we don't know, there's never been a picture like this." John F. Kennedy was elected president of the United States. It was 1960. He was charming the world, and he had written *Profiles in Courage*, which won a Pulitzer Prize. Somebody asked him in a press conference, "What do you read for relaxation?" And Kennedy said, "Well, when I really want to relax and have some fun, I read the exploits of a British secret agent named James Bond." No one had ever heard of the books. All of a sudden, everybody was buying James Bond books, and United Artists said, "Let's go."

Cubby always said they might have gotten it off the ground anyway, but still, "I've got to thank President Kennedy for getting the financing for the first one." Charlie Feldman made a picture of *Casino Royale* with five James Bonds and Woody Allen, but it was not a hit. The Broccolis finally bought it back and made it with Daniel Craig. *Thunderball* was owned by a man named Kevin McClory. He knew to play ball with Cubby and Harry because, by that time, *From Russia with Love* had been made, *Goldfinger* had been made. It was clear you weren't going off with your own James Bond. The world was in love with Sean Connery. *Thunderball* says, "Produced by Kevin McClory, Executive Producers are Broccoli and Saltzman."

Later on, McClory and Sean decided to make a picture called *Never Say Never Again* that was based on *Thunderball*. Broccoli and Saltzman sued and went to court, and the court ruled that McClory and Connery could make *Never Say Never Again,* but it had to be a remake of *Thunderball*. Other Bond characters that were in the other books and had been in movies were not allowed to be in it, like Q, the guy who made all the gadgets, who was not in *Thunderball*. Sean asked me to write it. I said, "I can't." He was fighting with Cubby. "The Broccolis have been so wonderful to me, and for me to go off and write the picture now . . ." I told Sean I thought he was fabulous and I wished him luck. Sean understood.

When they finished the picture, Sean called me and asked, "Would you take a look at the rough cut? We're going wrong in some places." It was for Warners, and I was at Warners.

I called Cubby and asked, "Do you mind if I take a look at the picture?"

He said, "Please do, and give him every suggestion."

I saw the movie and it wasn't bad at all. I had a couple of ideas. We all went back to Bob Daly's office. Bob Daly and Terry Semel were running the studio. Terry started off. "It seems to me the problem is—" and Sean said, "Now, quiet. Let's hear from boyo there." I'm a little older, but still I'm boyo to him. "Boyo wrote *Diamonds Are Forever*, which makes no fucking sense at all, and it was wonderful."

Sean returned to James Bond, and Kevin McClory was the producer, a snake in the grass to do that. That's the kind of behavior Cubby wouldn't tolerate. That was not gentlemanly, not ethical behavior. Sean had sued Cubby and Harry and United Artists for money he thought was owed to him. Sean's way of getting back at them. I had always talked to Sean about if you ever really want to hang it up as Bond, you should do a farewell to Bond film where he is just a step slower and he realizes the villain that he's up against is a little faster, and he has to use his wits. The leading lady should be somebody your age, like Sophia Loren, who was still so beautiful. At the end of the picture, you do what Fleming wrote. You go back to Scotland and retire with Sophia. He didn't do it.

At Different Stages

The only time my father and I ever worked together on the same lot, on different movies—it was toward the end of his career—was when he was doing a picture called *Sleuth* with Laurence Olivier and Michael Caine at Pinewood, and I was writing *Live and Let Die*. We would drive in together, and we had a totally different relationship then because I was free and clear. I didn't need anything from him, and we really got along wonderfully. He had one soundstage for *Sleuth*. It was that one magnificent set by Ken Adam, the house. Two actors. That's the whole movie. The Bond film had seven soundstages.

Dad walked onto our stage, which contained a big underground cave, a lagoon, a mechanical shark swimming around, guys with machine guns, and a rubber inflated version of Yaphet Kotto. Dad looked at it and he said, "My God, what do you people do in here all day?"

Roger Moore, God bless him, said, "Oh, please don't tell him, Tom. He'll just go out and make a film exactly like it." It's now called the James Bond stage. You can flood it, and we later used it on *Superman* for the Fortress of Solitude. Revolutionary at the time.

Back in London, a car would always drop Dad off five blocks from the hotel so he could walk. He liked to walk. One night we were walking, and he said, "Tom, I think if this one works out, I just may hang it up."

I said, "Oh, Dad, you're just tired."

He said, "No." And son of a bitch, *Sleuth* was a big hit. Olivier was nominated. Michael Caine was nominated. Dad used to joke, "The only film I've ever done where the entire cast was nominated." He was nominated for Best Director. I think he thought, okay, this is a way to go out after forty years of doing this.

After that he pretended to be interested in making films. Redford came to him with *All the President's Men*. Paul Newman, who lived nearby in Westport, Connecticut, brought lots of projects. Dad would always find an artificial reason not to do them. I knew now he was never going to do another picture. So Sleuth was the last one. *Cleopatra* pretty much did that to him: it was such a physical ordeal. He took so many drugs on the film to get through it. For a year and a half, he was a half-assed junkie taking pills. He was always a master of self-control. I don't think he ever drank too much. His one vice was his pipe. He used to talk about when he was a compulsive gambler, but I don't think he ever was a compulsive gambler. He was always very measured. So for him to be a half-assed junkie before he got off it, I think was humiliating for him. It was a terrible ordeal.

While I was writing the script in London, I got into tarot cards. A lot of scenes are with the lovers and the hanged-man death cards. I started to do people's tarot. I was pretty accurate. Things happened. (Obviously, it's pure luck.) Michael Caine and I were friends. He had a house just outside of London, on the Thames. He was having a big Sunday brunch all day, and he asked, "Bring your tarot cards, will you? Everybody's asking, they want to get their tarot done."

It was no fun in the beginning, because everybody was drinking and having a great time, and I was in the corner at a table doing people's tarots. I got through with all of it except for this little girl that Michael was banging. She was very shy. I knew he was going out with her. She was Miss Guyana. I said, "Well, I guess I'm finished."

She said, "You haven't done mine yet."

She sat down, and I started doing the cards, and I said, "You're presently in love."

Michael was listening, behind her. She said, "Yes, I am."

Michael was giving me the high sign, like "Look out." I said what the cards said: "You're going to marry this man."

He was shaking his head, like "No, no, no!" She said, "I am?"

I said, "You're going to have a child." And he was going crazy. That girl is Mrs. Michael Caine, Shakira Caine. They got married, and they had a child, and they're still married. Shakira is one of the most beautiful women in the world. She played a small part in *The Man Who Would Be King* with Michael and Sean. She is still convinced I have some higher power. I run into them every couple of years, and she'll say to other people, "He knows things."

Location, Location

We started the picture with Cubby, but Harry took over the actual producing. Cubby and Guy and I went to New Orleans and Jamaica to find locations. A lot of the Bonds were written on the fly on those trips. You'd see something, and all of a sudden it would become a sequence. We were driving around Jamaica on the back end of the island, and we saw a wall and fence and a sign—"Warning, trespassers will be eaten." We screeched to a stop. It was a big crocodile farm. The now-famous sequence where Bond hops over the tops of the crocodiles was born. The guy who owned the farm was named Ross Kananga, a white guy. The villain played by Yaphet Kotto was Dr. Kananga. I named it after him.

When you were in New Orleans, everything was fine. The minute you went out into another parish, it was like going back a century. The local sheriff ran everything. (You saw what happened after Hurricane Katrina, how miserably black people were treated in the parishes outside of New Orleans.) There was a big boat chase in the picture going through the bayous, and we were going to shoot in one particular parish and drop a million dollars, which would have been huge. We met with the sheriff, and he was thrilled to have us: "James Bond, goddamn." He said, "I understand there's a lot of nigras in the cast."

We said, "Well, yes."

He said, "Now are there any nigras on the crew?"

We said, "Yes, we will have some on the crew."

He said, "We're happy to have you shoot here, but I don't want nigras behind the wheels of your trucks driving. It could upset some folks to see a lot of black people driving."

Cubby said, "Well, sheriff, I guess we'll just have to spend our million dollars in another parish." God bless him for saying that.

The sheriff said, "No, hold on, hold on. Okay, but keep it down to a dull roar, will you?"

And Cubby said, "We'll keep it down to a dull roar." As we were leaving, he said to the transportation captain, "I want a black guy behind the wheel of every vehicle. Fuckin' cracker."

That's 1972. You're in the back country. You're not in New Orleans with the big city folks anymore. The rules were different out there. When Dick Donner shot *The Toy* with Richard Pryor, there were many death threats on Pryor. They were shooting outside of Baton Rouge in that parish. They had police and state troopers living in the motel where Richard was. They were scared.

Cubby and Harry staged a huge press conference in Jamaica, where we were shooting. Press from all over the world came because Roger Moore, who was quite well known, was starting his career as James Bond. There must have been four or five hundred press. The first question was inevitable. "What does it feel like to take over from Sean Connery?" Nobody mentioned George Lazenby. Next up—"Why are you doing this?"

Roger answered, "When I was a young acting student at RADA, the Royal Academy of Dramatic Arts, I was in a play and we were lucky enough to have Noel Coward in the audience. After the play was over, Noel came backstage and said to me, 'Young man, with your devastating good looks and your disastrous lack of talent, you should take any job ever offered you. And, in the unlikely occurrence you're offered two jobs simultaneously, take the one that pays the most money.' And, here I am." He disarmed everybody. Noel Coward had just died. He said, "And pity Noel couldn't be here to watch me as Bond, because when he saw me in the play, I only had four expressions. Now I have six." Well, you just had to love him.

One of the first days shooting, Roger was supposed to run for a double-decker bus. There was a bus chase, and the top half of it was sheared off by a low bridge or something. Guy Hamilton said, "All right, Roger, just run across the square and hop onto the bus and that's a cut."

Roger said, "I think I ought to tell you something, Guy. I can't run."

Guy said, "You can't run?"

Roger said, "Well, of course I can run. But when I run, I look like a giant twit."

Guy said, "All right then, run for us." And he ran. Roger has such long legs that he bounded when he ran, sort of like Bambi. He was perfectly in shape, but it did look kind of odd. Guy said, "All right, then, Roger, on action, walk briskly toward the bus." Oh boy, look at James Bond, he can't run. But Roger was absolutely a delight.

Now, the big thing about *Live and Let Die* was in the beginning, I wrote Solitaire black. In the book she was white. I made some changes. Fleming believed in the British Raj. He was, in essence, a racist. In the kindest way. It wasn't vituperative racism. In the book *Goldfinger,* it says, "The swarthy Yid lifted his eyebrow," referring to Goldfinger, who was clearly Jewish. In *Live and Let Die,* a lot of it took place in Harlem, and it was African Americans. But the last movie Fleming must have seen with African Americans in it was *Gone with the Wind.* This was 1972, and they were making *Superfly* and *Across 110th Street.* In the book, the black people were saying stuff like, "Sho'nuff." Waiting on the levy. Waiting for the *Robert E. Lee.* Cubby and Harry asked me, "Which one do you want to do next?" I thought *Live and Let Die* was great because it was black, and it was of the times.

So I wrote Solitaire black. She was the leading lady. And Bond would have to sleep with her. As a matter of fact, she's a virgin in the book, and he deflowers her. Diana Ross was interested in being in a Bond movie. She had been in one movie already, and she could act. As all of this is going on and we're working on the screenplay, David Picker reads the screenplay. He goes, "Whoa, whoa, whoa. Everybody, we're going to have a meeting here. I can't have this. Solitaire can't be black." I asked why, and he said to me, "Don't be such a Jane Fonda about this, will you? Listen." He gave his reasons, which, if I were David Picker, I would have made. He said, "This is Roger's first movie, and I think he's going to be wonderful. But Diana Ross is one of a kind. What if she blows him off the screen? She's hot, and you bet she's going to be singing the title song, and she's in the movie, and we got a new Bond. But secondly, and most importantly, there are about eight countries in the world where I cannot release this film if they sleep together. And the biggest one is our second-biggest-grossing country in the world, Japan. They don't allow race mixing in Japanese movies. They don't like Koreans, they don't like Chinese. Now they don't care if white superheroes are with Japanese girls, but black and white, Chinese/Japanese, it's just anathema. They're not going to do it. Now, South Africa is also a big-grossing place for us. There are Middle Eastern countries. And also, when you have James Bond deflowering a black virgin played by Diana Ross, I'm not so sure you guys want to go to the Detroit opening of this movie either."

So we said, "Okay, okay." In the script, Rosie Carver was white and Solitaire was black. Now, Solitaire was white and Rosie Carver was black. Jane Seymour had been in a British miniseries. I still think Jane looked too young in the movie, but it made her. Jane was cast as Solitaire.

We were shooting in Jamaica, and Harry said, "You've got to get guards in Jamaica, it's dangerous. So I've taken the liberty of getting us all guards for our houses." The first night we were there, we went out to dinner and all our guards robbed our houses. So things didn't work out for Harry a lot.

We got to the crocodile farm, and there came the time when we had to do the stunt with Bond hopping over the tops of the crocodiles. Their little legs were tied down underwater, but their mouths and tails were free. The stuntman, Bob Simmons, dressed as Roger, hopped off the island onto the first crocodile and slipped. The crocodile turned its head and went *whap*, and just missed him. The stuntman said, "My fault, my fault." He got back on the island. New set of clothes. He did it again, and he slipped on the second one, and the second one got his shoe. Just ripped it off. He said, "That's it, sorry. Not doing it."

Harry went berserk. "We've got Bond on the island surrounded by crocodiles, how do we get him off?" He turned to me and said, "You're the writer. How do we get him off?"

I said, "Harry, I don't know. A helicopter comes by?"

All of a sudden, a grip spoke up. "I have an idea. Why don't you go into Kingston into a sporting goods store? What if you got track shoes with cleats?"

So we got a pair of track shoes. Painted them to look like Roger's beautiful shoes. And the stunt that's in the movie is the very first take. He hopped over all four and got to land. I learned, keep your ears open. People on the crew have suggestions. Here's big Harry Saltzman, the big producer; me, the hot young writer; and the great stuntman, and a grip said, "How about if you had cleats on your shoes?"

In those days, there was no CGI. All the stunts were real. I would have to okay every stunt that I was writing with Bob Simmons. I'd say to Bob, "And it goes into a second-story window." He'd say, "No, we can't, no ramp, we can't get up into a second-story window. We can go into the golf course." For the boat chase, Jerry Comeaux set the record for the world's longest boat leap on film. It was ninety-eight feet. It went up and over

Sheriff Pepper and everybody. Then, Bond is chasing the villain. Jerry played the villain, then Bond chasing him. There were no black stuntmen at the time who drove boats. So unfortunately, all of the black boatmen who are chasing Bond are white guys in blackface. We had black stuntmen who started to object, and then Guy Hamilton asked, "Well, would you like to take the jump?"

They said, "No fucking way we're gonna take that jump. We don't know how to do that."

Guy said, "Well, we've got to have the jump in the movie."

Now, of course, there are black stuntmen that can do everything. That stunt was a big specialty. The unfortunate thing was, Jerry Comeaux did it twice, and then said he could do it better. And Guy let him. The boat flipped in midair, and Jerry broke his back. I found out later, when I was directing, if you've got a stunt to do and it's done well and the guy says, "I can do it better," say, "No, thank you. I've got what I want." Just take it.

In the script that United Artists had, it said, "There follows the most terrific boat chase you ever saw." Then it says, "Exterior. Hotel. Morning. Bond wakes up." So finally we were already starting to shoot, and David Picker called and asked, "Could I actually read the most terrific boat chase I ever saw, because I think you guys are shooting and we just wanted to read it." The boat chase itself written out was fifteen pages. I was doing it shot for shot. Almost storyboarding on paper.

Walking the Tightrope

In *Live and Let Die*, we had a wonderful character called Sheriff J.W. Pepper who's after Bond the whole time. I made him a racist southern sheriff. A wonderful actor from New York, Clifton James, played him with an accurate southern accent and a pot belly. We were shooting out in the boondocks in the bayou, and all the local sheriffs would come by and watch us shoot. They'd laugh like hell at him, and they all looked and talked exactly like him. When he stops one of the black hoods, he says, "Whirl around, boy. Ten fingers on the fender." Then he spits between the guy's legs and says, "I don't imagine this is exactly your debut at this sort of thing." The black audiences I saw it with were like, "Whoa." Then he becomes a comical character, because everything happens to him and he never can catch anybody. But that, in many ways, was my proudest moment writing Bond. Vincent Canby in the *New York Times* gave me a wonderful review: "How did Mankiewicz write this screenplay with things the way they are racially in this country? All the villains are black and all the heroes are white, and he makes it work." It worked great with black audiences. They loved that movie. It was walking that tightrope.

Yaphet Kotto, who was a real up-and-coming black actor, was very worried at the start of the film about the dignity of the black man. At the end of the picture, his character gets inflated like a rubber ball and bursts. I had a long talk with him. He had just been in *Across 110th Street,* which was very much a blaxploitation movie in the best sense of the word. I said, "Everybody knew Goldfinger was Jewish, but nobody thought he represented an anti-Semitic character. This is not anti-black, it's a Bond movie." And he was wonderful in it. He and Guy Hamilton didn't get along very well. Guy was very reserved, and Yaphet was like an open cut in terms of talking about people. Guy didn't like to say very much. Very British Raj. So in that sense, a very good director for Roger. Guy and Sean almost said nothing. By the time Sean did *Diamonds,* he'd played the part so often, there's no great mystery in those scenes as a way to play it. And Sean knew the way to play it.

Moore McCartney

John Barry had been such a great composer. Cubby was good friends with John, but it was a new Bond, and John Barry had a particular sound that reminded you of Sean. So Cubby had the idea of going for Paul McCartney. They made a deal with McCartney whereby McCartney owned 100 percent of the song, but United Artists could put it on the album. In those days, a movie soundtrack album sold a lot. So UA owned the album, owned the song 100 percent for the album. McCartney owned the rest to it; the single, the publishing. He was so huge at the time.

Cubby loved Jerry Moss, my friend at A&M. He'd met Jerry a couple of times with me in L.A. and then in London, when Jerry was signing artists. There was a scoring session, and Cubby said to me the next day, "Well, we got taken. This is crap."

I said, "Play it."

Cubby put on a cassette. It was "Live and Let Die." I said, "Cubby, I think it's pretty good. I'm not just saying that."

He said, "Oh, I think it's a pile of crap."

I said, "Jerry Moss is in London."

"Yeah, let's play it for Jerry Moss."

So we played it for Jerry, and Jerry said, "You don't like the song, Cubby?" He said no. Jerry said, "Well, I'll tell you what. For whatever rights you have to this song, I'll pay you a million dollars, because this song is going to go platinum. This song is gonna win the fuckin' Oscar."

Cubby asked, "You really think so?"

Jerry said, "I really think so. I'm quite serious: if you want to negotiate with me, I'd love to take this song off your hands."

Starting the next day, Cubby said, "And we have the greatest fuckin' song you ever heard! This is unbelievable!" It wasn't his kind of music. Cubby liked Sinatra.

Live and Let Die, to my knowledge, is the only James Bond film that was ever written end to end by one writer. I have sole credit. Nobody else touched it. Today they hire Paul Haggis to do the final rewrite, and they get different teams to write different scripts, and they pick the best one. Sometimes there are great sequences from scripts that they own, and they stick them in the one that they're shooting. It's a different way of doing it now.

Writing for Roger Moore is different from writing for Sean. Roger is really an actor in a theatrical way. Where Sean would throw away the throw-away lines, Roger would play with them. The difference between them is that Sean could sit at a table in a nightclub with a beautiful girl and either lean across the table and kiss her or stick a knife in her gut under that table and then say, "Excuse me, waiter, I have nothing to cut my meat with now." Roger could kiss her, but he looked nasty if he was going to stick a knife in her, because Roger looks like a nice man. Sean looks, in the best sense of the word, the best movie-star sense of the word, like a bastard. There's a twinkle in his eye and there's violence in his eye. When he comes into a room, you think, okay, look out. With Roger, you have to write the entrance more. He is much more Fleming's Bond. That's exactly who Fleming thought of as Bond. He's very English. Big and tall. Sophisticated. Roger looked like a nice guy. So the kinds of sadistic things that Sean could do that the audience roared at, Roger couldn't do.

But Roger was a very sophisticated actor with a presence. For instance, in *Live and Let Die,* he's being chased in an airport by thugs, and he hops into a place where a little old lady is waiting to take a flying lesson. He says, "I'll be your instructor today, Mrs. Bell," and they go. They never leave the ground, but they smash through hangars, destroy things. And at the end of it, she's passed out and the wings have been sheared off the little plane. Roger looks at her and says, "Same time tomorrow, Mrs. Bell?" Well, he could do that and be charming. That's not a good line for Sean. Roger could play those lines. When the bad guys are going to feed Bond to the crocodiles—Roger is their prisoner, he's touring around the crocodile farm—the bad guy says, "Now, this is the time I like best. Feedin' time."

Roger says, "I suspect the highlight of the tour." He could do it in a wonderful, English, sophisticated way. But that would not be a line for Sean. So you wrote for them differently. You just got into their rhythm.

The Lizard

After *Diamonds Are Forever* and *Live and Let Die,* back in L.A. I had a relationship with Elizabeth Ashley. In 1973 I was feeling pretty hot because *Diamonds Are Forever* had been a hit and *Live and Let Die* was completed, and I was going to do another one. Elizabeth had received a Golden Globe nomination for *The Carpetbaggers* and had appeared in *Ship of Fools* and on Broadway in *Barefoot in the Park.* She was nuts, high strung; just perfect for me. She had gotten divorced from George Peppard. And George was a real piece of work. He was a heavy drinker. He would come over, and sometimes he'd be drunk. He came over once when I wasn't there and fired his gun into the ceiling. He had terrible drinking problems. He was a really good actor, he did *Breakfast at Tiffany's* with Audrey Hepburn; he should have been a big movie star. But booze really, really hurt him.

I was living at Elizabeth's off and on. George said to me, "You know, my agents tell me this movie I'm doing needs a rewrite, and they said, 'Tom Mankiewicz would be good.' And I'm not even aware of the fact that he's a good writer; all I know is he's fucking my wife."

I'm not a brave man. Maybe I'm not cowardly, but I'm certainly not brave. I said, "Well, George, what can I tell you? Your agent's right and you're right." It came out before I'd even had a chance to think about it, and I thought, he's going to kill me. He just smiled and sat there. It's one of the few times in my life where my mouth was so far ahead of my brain.

George and Elizabeth had a son named Christian who looked exactly like George. Elizabeth used to joke, it's the only child in the world where they wonder who the mother was. One day, Christian had a young friend over. They were maybe five years old. The two boys were swimming in the pool and they had life vests on. Inside the house, Elizabeth and I were arguing about something. All of a sudden, Christian came in and said, "Mommy, Johnny's at the bottom of the pool." We ran out, and there was Johnny. He had taken his life vest off. We were so selfish arguing we never noticed. Elizabeth was already in the water. She dove down, pulled him out, and did CPR. He threw up, and he was fine. It was the closest in my life I'd ever been to death right in front of me. Elizabeth saved his life. His parents came over to pick him up later, and we thought the only fair thing to do was to tell them what happened. It was our fault. We didn't notice because we were so full of ourselves at the time. Whatever the nattering was about, it wasn't anything that important.

The Man with the Golden Gun and The Spy Who Loved Me: Run, Run, Mank

So *Live and Let Die* opens. Now here comes *Man with the Golden Gun.* We all knew that was going to be the next one. I'd already written a lot of the script. In 1973 I got the call to come over to Hong Kong, where Cubby and Guy were. Then Bangkok. There was a famous man named Run Run Shaw who ran the Shaw Studios, where the chop-socky movies were made. He started Bruce Lee. He was the first Asian ever to be knighted. Run Run could get you heroin, bazookas, tanks, or the best suit in Hong Kong. He had three Rolls-Royces, all with the same license plate, Run Run. Nobody knew which one he was in because he never wanted people to know where he was. A member of his family had been kidnapped before we arrived. The police couldn't find him, but they found the kidnappers' bodies hacked to death in the back of Run Run's car. It was fine. He had a brother in Singapore named Runme, and Runme could also help you in Southeast Asia in the same way. I turned them into characters called Hai Fat and Lo Fat.

We stayed at the beautiful Peninsula in Hong Kong. Cubby had a suite that had four separate bedrooms, a communal dining room, and its own staff of three people that were there twenty-four hours a day. If you got up at three in the morning and you wanted a Jack Daniel's, the guy would get up and make it for you. We also went to the Bottoms Up Club, where you could get a blow job while you were sitting there. Hong Kong was the big R & R place for the American fleet. We went from there to Bangkok.

Here's an example of Harry starting the movie and Cubby taking over. At one point, I was going to write a series of articles for *Playboy*, "Being on the Road with Bond." The title of my first one was going to be "Your Elephant Shoes Are Ready." We went up to northern Thailand, where the elephants in those days worked the teak forests pulling logs. Harry, with that mind of his, was looking at thirty elephants when he said, "An elephant stampede. We're going to have an elephant stampede in the movie. And Bond will be on the lead elephant."

The guy who ran the teak forest said, "Mr. Saltzman, these elephants don't stampede, and if they do, you can't stop them. They'll just destroy everything in their path. They're not trained elephants that way."

Harry asked, "What's that on their feet?" They wore leather shoes because there were so many sharp things in the forest and they were working all day. Harry said, "We're going to have elephants, goddamnit. Fifty of them." He turned to Claude Hudson, who was the production manager, and he said, "Claude, get me fifty sets of elephant shoes." That's two hundred shoes!

So Claude said, "Yes sir, Mr. Saltzman." He ordered two hundred elephant shoes.

Well, Harry went back to London. Cubby and I found this wonderful place called Phuket down south, and there was nothing there. It's like Miami Beach now, but then, we couldn't find anyplace for anybody to stay, not even the crew. We flew down in helicopters from Bangkok every day that we shot down there. James Bond Island is still there, where Bond and Christopher Lee had their face-off. After the movie came out, because the locale was so staggering in the film and it was a Bond film, somebody thought about building a hotel there. And then, hotels just started sprouting up.

So we were staying at the Oriental Hotel in Bangkok. One of the most elegant hotels in the world, on the river near the floating market. Cubby and I were having a drink in the outdoor bar, and somebody came up and said, "Excuse me, Mr. Broccoli, your elephant shoes are here."

He asked, "What elephant shoes? There's not an elephant in the movie."

I said, "Oh, shit, Harry ordered two hundred elephant shoes."

One of the great things about Bond was, as a young guy who was barely in his thirties by now, I was going to Hong Kong, Thailand, Egypt. We stopped in Calcutta, and the poverty was so overwhelming that we decided that was not a Bond kind of city to shoot in. I was seeing the world. Then we got back to London. Guy and I had a couple of disagreements. I was also feeling really tapped out on Bond. This was my third in a row. I wanted to make other pictures.

I went over to see Cubby. I said, "I think I should get off this. It would be best for the picture. I've done nothing for three and a half years but James Bond."

Cubby was just terrific and he understood. He said, "Okay, does this have to do with Guy?"

I said, "Well, a little bit. We're just not getting on in the same way we were, but we're not disliking each other. I could stay on."

So I went home, and Dick Maibaum, whom I had taken over for on *Diamonds Are Forever,* finished up. We always got along great. When they finished shooting, the first thing Cubby and Guy did was invite me over to dinner at Cubby's house. The Bonds were a club. Cubby made it that way.

The same soundmen by and large, a lot of the same cameramen. The same people on the crews. Cubby knew everybody's name, the names of their kids. So you belonged to a big club. Terence Young directed the first two. Then Guy Hamilton. Then Terence. Then Lewis Gilbert, then Guy, Guy, Guy, then Lewis Gilbert. There were a few directors. Ken Adam designed just about all of them. You were part of a fraternity. It was amazing. You would hear stories about the other Bond pictures from the people who were on them.

A few years later, after I'd done the first three pictures, Cubby asked me to rewrite *The Spy Who Loved Me*. He said, "Now, here's the deal. This has got to be done away from the Writers Guild because I need a big rewrite. Under the Eady Plan, we already have our three non-British subjects on this picture"—the Eady Plan stipulated that to receive governmental tax credits and financial help on a film produced in the United Kingdom, only three non-Brits could be involved in any capacity—"there's me, somebody else, and Barbara Bach. So you can't get credit because we'll lose our Eady Plan eligibility. And if it goes through the Writers Guild, you're probably going to get a credit because I'm asking for a big rewrite, but you can't have a credit, so I'm going to get into trouble with the Writers Guild. So nobody can know that you're on this picture. I'm going to pay you cash."

We made the deal. Nobody knew that I was rewriting that picture. The first thirty pages went off to England, and Roger Moore called Cubby and asked, "When did Mankiewicz get on this picture?"

Cubby said, "He's not on the picture, Roger."

He said, "Of course he is. He's on every fucking page. Tell him he's doing a good job."

Catherine Deneuve wanted to be in a James Bond movie. She had won every award in the world, but she was getting older, and she wanted to be in a worldwide hit. Her price was $400,000 then. I was at Cubby's house every day rewriting *The Spy Who Loved Me*. The pages were flying. He got a call from her agent saying she wanted to do it and her price was $400,000 but she'd do it for $250,000. She'd love to have a lark and do it. Cubby said to the agent, "First of all, please tell her I am so flattered that she wants to do it, but I've never paid more than eighty thousand dollars for a James Bond girl in my life. None of the girls, with the possible exception of Ursula Andress, ever went on to be a star or have a career. I'd rather take the extra hundred seventy thousand and put it up on the screen somewhere. I'm very flattered that she wants to do it, but I can't pay a Bond girl two hundred fifty."

Of Human Bondage

Obviously, the best actress in a Bond film was Diana Rigg. She was in the Lazenby one. Peter Hunt directed it, and he had been the editor of the Bond movies. Cubby always regretted letting him direct *On Her Majesty's Secret Service*. He said, "It was very well directed, but by giving him that job, I lost the best editor I ever had, because once you make them a director, you can't ask them to edit anymore." Diana Rigg hated Lazenby. The last shot of the picture, Rigg's last shot, she said, "This is my last take?"

They said, "Yes, it's the last take on the picture."

She did it, turned around and spit at George Lazenby, and walked off the set. That was the good-bye.

Fleming did write wonderful character names like Pussy Galore and Goldfinger and Plenty O'Toole, who was in *Diamonds Are Forever*. So there were an awful lot of funny names that we, the writers, just picked up on. Sex and violence in the Bond films was very interesting, especially in the seventies. In *Diamonds Are Forever*, the very first scene, Mr. Wint and Mr. Kidd get a package of diamonds in the middle of the desert from a dentist. In my script, Mr. Wint said, "Oh, doctor, could you take a look? I have something wrong with my tooth." The dentist said, "Say ahh," and he said, "Ahh," and they popped a scorpion down his throat. Now, the British said that cannot be in a PG. They were very strong on violence. We couldn't put it in. In the movie, they drop it down the back of his neck. But with Americans, any violence was just fine for a PG. They had no problem. But if you had a sexually suggestive sentence, they'd cut it out. With England, it was just fine. Anything sexual. Lana Wood plays Plenty O'Toole in *Diamonds Are Forever*. For one and a half seconds, you can actually see her breast as she's being thrown out a window. Censors went crazy in the United States about that, but it was the only coverage we had, and they let us keep it.

My favorite lines in Bond that I ever wrote were cut out of *The Spy Who Loved Me*, and they were Roger Moore's favorite lines as well. At a bar, he runs into Barbara Bach, who plays a Russian colonel. The two of them know who the other one is, but they've never officially met. Bond says, "For the lady, a Stolichnaya." She says, "And for the gentleman, a vodka martini, shaken not stirred." He turns to her and says, "I must say, you're much more beautiful than the pictures we have of you, Colonel," and she says, "I'm afraid the only picture we have of you, Mr. Bond, was taken in bed with one of our agents, a Miss Tatiana Romanova," who was the girl in *From Russia with Love*. Bond says, "And was she smiling?" And the colonel says, "As I recall, her mouth was not immediately visible in the photograph." Bond says, "Ah, then I was smiling." They wouldn't let us do it. They said, "You've got to cut that out." Censorship was so silly. I would say, "God, if anybody understands that, we're not protecting them from anything. A twelve-year-old won't know what the hell we're talking about." Sometimes what you did, and everybody did it on purpose, you would write twenty things you knew would never pass to try to negotiate and get the four you really wanted in. It was like that then. So they would say, "The following twelve lines are completely unacceptable." And after Cubby would yell and scream, they would say, "Okay, these four but not the other eight." If you were lucky, they were the eight that you never wanted anyway.

Cubby and Harry could do outside films. Cubby did films like *Chitty Chitty Bang Bang*. More family entertainment. Harry was a Canadian, and he wanted to be knighted. So he made *The Battle of Britain* with every known actor in the English language. Each actor had about two lines. This was Harry's bid at knighthood. Some critic said, "Never have so many done so little." Harry got into more and more business troubles, and he started getting loans from people and putting up his stock in Danjaq as collateral. That was illegal according to the bylaws of Danjaq. Cubby knew about it and just let Harry keep digging his hole. At one time, Harry was a man with at least tens of millions of dollars. But he had cross-collateralized himself into a real hole. The reason the Broccoli family controls the Bonds today—starting with Pierce Brosnan—is Harry had to sell out. Cubby had him by the short and curlies, and would always say, "Harry keeps forgetting I'm from Sicily."

Cubby got United Artists to buy Harry's half. Cubby said, "In the old days, I could vote yes. Harry voted no. And United Artists had the deciding vote. Now, under this deal, I vote yes, United Artists votes no, and then I vote yes again." Now, you can't make a Bond film unless you go through the Broccolis. Michael Wilson, who is Dana Broccoli's son by a former marriage, and Barbara Broccoli, the youngest daughter, produce the films. They call all the shots. It was very sad for Harry. Jackie Saltzman got cancer. They went all over the world trying to find cures. Harry finally wound up living in Florida. But as partners, they were amazing. In the days when I went to work for them on *Diamonds Are Forever,* they had the world by the tail. Bond was the only real movie event. There was no *Raiders* yet, no *Superman,* no *Lethal Weapon*s, no *Star Wars,* no anything. The world waited for the Bond movie to come out every eighteen months or so. This is how important they were: Cubby had a Rolls-Royce and his license plate was CUB1. Suddenly, during *Diamonds Are Forever* or *Live and Let Die,* the British government now recognized Cuba. The Cuban ambassador was entitled to the license plate CUB1. The British government told Cubby that he couldn't have that license plate anymore. He got crazy. He said, "We'll find out who's more fucking important in England, me or the Cuban ambassador." And son of a bitch, I don't know how he did it, but CUB1 stayed on Cubby's Rolls-Royce. Maybe the Cuban ambassador had CUB2. It was a big deal. On the other hand, the Bond pictures were made in England. Hundreds of people were employed. Millions were spent. It was great for the economy.

When *Casino Royale* came out with Daniel Craig, his first Bond, I was driving down Sunset Boulevard and a car was right on my ass. A big black SUV. I pulled over to let it go by, but it stayed right behind me. I took a right, it took a right. I took a left, it took a left. I pulled over. And the car pulled over behind me. It was Barbara Broccoli. She had seen MANK2 on the license plate. She jumped out and we hugged. She said, "So, what do you think of the movie?"

I said, "The title song sucks. You've got to do better."

She said, "I agree."

"And the movie's twenty minutes too long, but every movie's twenty minutes too long today as far as I'm concerned. Daniel Craig, you should keep him and lock him in a cellar and don't let anybody else have him. He should do fifty of these."

It was a wonderful movie. I didn't like *Quantum of Solace* because I couldn't follow it. I didn't know who was fighting who and what was going on. One critic said it correctly: Bond should introduce himself with "My name is Bourne, Jason Bourne." This is *The Bourne Identity*, and that's not Bond. The idiosyncratic wit that's in Bond. The car that swims underwater. Those things are missing. And the audience misses them. You miss Q and the preposterous, the bizarre that's in Bond. The thing that differentiated Bond from *Lethal Weapon*, from *Bourne,* was its sense of humor. It's bizarreness. You could just stop the movie dead with a huge belly laugh at a remark of Bond's. I thought the writers were so smart in *Casino Royale* to make it all about Bond, because this guy's in here for the long haul. He's a wonderful actor. Daniel Craig can play anything. Now if they can just get some of that fun back. Guy Hamilton was a great instructor for me in terms of getting the bizarreness. He said, "Never forget, Tom, in a Bond movie, if you want to start a fire, first you call the fire department. Everything works backward."

Sean remains, to me, the best Bond because he was Bond when the audience broke in with him. But also, he had that glimmer of violence in his eyes. When Sean is in physical fights onscreen, you'll notice he's smiling a lot. It's not a big smile, but it's like he's enjoying it. He looks like a bastard. If you were a woman, you would never want to marry Sean Connery, but boy, would you like to spend a weekend with him in Brazil. Sean had that violence and excitement in him. Roger was Fleming's Bond, and did a great job. Pierce Brosnan was neither great nor terrible. He was just Bond. He was fine.

The best actor they ever had playing Bond was Timothy Dalton. Cubby asked me at the time, "What do you think of Tim Dalton for James Bond?"

I said, "How about Tim Dalton for a James Bond villain?" There was something slightly androgynous about him, and evil. A wonderful actor. He only did two. A very good friend of Cubby's. An interesting guy who would go to the Arctic Circle and help wildlife, and he had a long affair with Vanessa Redgrave.

Daniel Craig is just terrific. He was a shot in the arm when Bond really needed it, because it's an amazing series. It's been going fifty years. *Dr. No* was 1962. I saw it when I was in college. I saw *From Russia with Love* when I was in college, and *Goldfinger* the year after I got out of college. There have been twenty-two of these. Nothing like that's ever happened in the history of film. Bond went great with the times. Sean was the guy for the sixties. The seventies got Love, Love, Love and marijuana. It was a bit more freewheeling, and what I brought to the Bonds was a lot of humor. I think I was right for the seventies. Then all of a sudden, it got too much. By the time *Moonraker* was made, they became silly pictures.

And Away I Go

I was now a hot writer. But I was really tapped out on Bond. You can only write so much of the same thing for so many years. Jackie Gleason, who had been in vaudeville, was a giant when I was growing up. *The Jackie Gleason Show* from Miami Beach—"A little traveling music, Ray"—and Reggie Van Gleason. He was fabulous. The hottest producers on television were Bud Yorkin and Norman Lear, who had *All in the Family, Maude,* and *Sanford and Son.* I got a phone call from Norman Lear one day in 1974. He said, "Listen, you'd be the ideal guy for this. I'm going to do a series with Jackie Gleason; he's coming back. And he's going to play a conman. I mentioned you to Jackie, and he loves the idea."

I flew to Miami and a car and driver picked me up, and I went to Jackie's house. He had a big sunken bar, and he started to make a drink. I was looking at Jackie Gleason, and there was something very aggressive about him. He was, after all, "the Great One." He was the guy at Toots Shor, he had done *The Hustler,* Minnesota Fats. Now he was doing *Smokey and the Bandit* playing the sheriff. We were talking about the show. It was going to be called *Panama Fargo.* I said to him, "Jackie, I've got some ideas for some supporting characters that—"

He said, "Oh, fuck those supporting characters, pal." He called you "pal" all the time. "They get too famous and they have too much to do."

"Really? Because they were terrific in *The Honeymooners.*"

"That's what I'm talking about. This will just be me."

I said, "I have one specific idea. When the main title comes on and it says 'Panama Fargo'—"

He said, "Let me interrupt you, pal. That's not the title of the show."

"That's not the title? Because Norman told me—"

"No. The title of the show is 'The Great One Is Panama Fargo.'"

I said, "Okay. All right."

So we talked for a couple of hours. He said, "I look forward to seeing the page."

I got back to the Jockey Club and called Norman. I got his assistant because Norman was on the set. I said, "Tell him I'm coming back. I thank him very much. I don't want to do this. And I think if he really talks to Mr. Gleason, he's not going to want to do it either."

I got back to L.A. about ten hours later and I had a message from Norman Lear saying, "You're right. I just talked to him. I don't want to do it either." And that was the end of it. Still, you gotta love Jackie Gleason.

Columbo

I got a reputation as a fixer. I'd done the Bonds. That's where Peter Falk got my name. I had met Peter a couple of times, but I really didn't know him. It was the strangest job I ever had. Peter Falk was doing Columbo. It was a big hit internationally. He threw a snit at the studio. He said to Universal, "I want somebody on this show to look at the scripts and to make sure that everything is right. That the clues are at the right time. Independent; not our staff." He had great writers; William Link and Richard Levinson and others. He said, "Here's who I want: either Len Deighton"— a novelist who had written *The Ipcress File*—"or Tom Mankiewicz." Where he got Len Deighton from, I don't know. He'd seen my name on three straight Bonds. It was a demand for renegotiating.

My then agent, Ron Mardigian at William Morris, called. "I got the strangest call from Universal. It's an offer but a nonoffer. Peter Falk apparently wants you to read *Columbo* scripts. But Universal is saying, 'Forget it, we don't pay writers to read; we pay them to write.' I said, 'Look, he's doing features. He's obviously not going to go on *Columbo*.'"

Apparently, Peter Falk made a big stink, and Universal called Ron back and asked, "Well, what would he want to read a script?"

Ron had checked, and the writers got $15,000 for *Columbo*. He said, "Mankiewicz would want five thousand to read it. A third. He'd read it and supervise it."

They said, "You're out of your mind," and hung up on him. Then Universal called back and said, "All right, seventy-five hundred a script. Take it or leave it."

Ron joked, "If we'd turned them down again, we might have gotten ten."

So, for one year of *Columbo*, I read scripts. I apologized to Link and Levinson. I said, "You guys are doing a great job. I watch Columbo all the time."

They said, "No, no, we understand."

I got along fine with Peter. We were having lunch one day. It was the day of the Emmys. He was nominated for Best Actor in a Long Form. I asked, "So, you going down to the Emmys tonight? You're knocking off early?"

He said, "I don't think I'm gonna go."

"Why, Peter, for Christ sakes? You're going to win."

"Yeah, but I'm only up against Dennis Weaver for *McCloud*. It's just the two of us, so if I win, I just beat Dennis Weaver."

I said, "Look, you want to be loved by the audience?"

He said, "Yeah."

"If you win, come up and say, 'Sorry, Dennis, it came up tails,' and they'll love you."

He said, "That's not a bad idea. I'm going."

I'm getting ready to go out to dinner—I'm putting on my tie and my jacket or my Nehru jacket—and I'm watching the Emmys. The presenter says, "And the winner is, Peter Falk." Peter gets up and says, "Sorry, Dennis, it came up tails." The audience gives him a round ovation, and he says, "Thank you, Tom Mankiewicz."

I get to my dinner, and everybody says, "Boy, we had no idea you were so intimately involved with *Columbo*. Peter Falk won, and he thanked you first."

I said, "No, no, that's not for Columbo, that's for the line!"

I've never been actually paid not to write or direct or produce but just to read. I would go into the office with Peter and say, "I think you could hold back discovering the bloody handkerchief and it would be more effective at the end of act three." I would feel I wasn't earning my $7,500 unless I had some ideas. They were wonderful scripts because he had a great writing staff. He was just exercising some muscle. Television, unlike features, is the medium in which supporting actors can become big stars. Telly Savalas, always a supporting actor. *Kojak,* huge star. Peter, *Columbo,* huge star. Dennis Weaver was doing *McCloud.* He would never have been a leading man, but he was a huge star in television. One of the great character actors who was in *The Sopranos,* Joe Pantoliano—Joey Pants, as he was called—said, "You know why we have a good show? Everybody in it's a supporting actor. It's just good fucking actors." In film, the director is everything. In series television, it's the writing and the stars. Let's say you go out and direct *Columbo;* if Peter doesn't like you, you don't do another *Columbo.* I counted on *NCIS* thirteen different producing credits. It says co-producer, co–executive producer, supervising producer, co–supervising producer. Most of those are writers. They get that credit because you can't list the writing staff. My cousin John fixed *In Plain Sight,* a series for USA. It says: "Co-producer, John Mankiewicz." He didn't do any producing, he just fixed the scripts. So in television, it's writing and the stars.

No Thanks, CIA; Hello, Mother

I made one stupid decision: I said, "No, I don't want to write *Three Days of the Condor.*" That was a wonderful movie. I wish I had done it, but it was CIA and I thought, oh, God, here we go again. John Huston said, "All your films are your children and you love them all equally." I don't think that's true. There are films you love more.

Joe Barbera of Hanna Barbera, the huge cartoon place (Yogi Bear, all of that), wanted to do a film about ambulance driving. He got some young guy to write a script at Fox. They were very happy to give Joe development money because he had a lot of money himself. This kid did not deliver. I said, "Boy, that's really interesting, ambulance driving, because there's so much you could say about society." Joe Barbera heard that I was interested, and he was very interested in me because I was a James Bond writer. I said, "Can I ride in an ambulance for a couple of weeks and just see?"

He said, "Sure." He got me to the Schaefer Ambulance Company. I rode in an ambulance with a driver named Tom "Hap" Hazard and his partner. It was just amazing.

On the Sunset Strip, we pulled up and a guy with a stab wound was bleeding to death, but he wouldn't go with us. Hap said, "We can't take him against his will. Under the law, that's kidnapping."

The sheriff's deputy said, "He's a material witness to a stabbing. Take him."

We took him to UCLA, and he tried to attack the attendant on the way down. We found out it was going to be his third strike. There was a warrant out for his arrest, and he didn't want to go to the hospital because he knew they'd find out who he was.

We went to an old people's home where there was a guy dressed as a four-star general who was losing it, and his wife was calling because she was afraid he was going to kill himself. We went to heart-attack victims. I said, "Boy, there's a terrific movie in there." So I wrote an original called *Mother, Jugs & Speed* about this little ambulance company run by a crook in an unincorporated area. It was a wild group of people. I was at a party at Natalie Wood's—she was a great friend of mine at the time—and I met a British director named Peter Yates, who had directed *Bullitt* with Steve McQueen. He was hopping a red-eye that night, leaving at ten thirty for New York. We were talking, and I asked, "What are you going to do next?"

He said, "I'd love to do a comedy, but I'd love to do one with a little bite to it."

I said, "Well, I happen to have one in the back of my car."

He said, "Really? Can I read it?"

So I gave it to him. He got on the plane and called me the next morning from New York and said, "Let's do it." Things like that happen. I could have easily not had it in the trunk of my car, or he could have read it and not liked it.

So we now gave it to Alan Ladd Jr., who had just taken over as head of Fox. I knew Laddie. Laddie read it and said, "This is about the most offensive script I've ever read in my life. There is no group you don't insult in this movie. Can you guys make this for three million bucks?"

"Yes," we lied.

We thought Gene Hackman was the perfect guy to play Mother because he was a mother hen. I knew Gene a little bit, and I flew down to Baja California, where he was shooting a movie called *Lucky Lady* with Liza Minnelli and Burt Reynolds. Stanley Donen was directing it, and when I got down there, it was clear everybody was hating the experience. Stanley said, "Did you come down here to fire me? Is that why Fox sent you down?"

I said, "No, no, Stanley, it's all right."

I met with Gene Hackman, who'd read the script. Gene said, "Listen, I'd love to do this, but I can't do it until September or October, and let me tell you why. I have worked nonstop since *The Poseidon Adventure*. I've done six or seven movies in two years, and if this stinker doesn't put me out of business . . . My wife wants to divorce me. My son is on drugs. I've got to spend a couple of months with my family."

I said, "You're our first choice, but Peter said we can't wait till September."

Hackman said, "I saw a man on television last night who would be wonderful. He was a black comic named Bill Crosby."

"You mean Bill Cosby?" I said. "He did a series once called *I Spy* with Robert Culp, and he's pretty good. Nightclub star, comedy star, and a wonderful actor."

We called Laddie, and he said, "That's really interesting." We flew up to see Bill performing in Lake Tahoe. He'd read the script.

He said, "I'd love to do this. I have one question. I understand this was offered to Gene Hackman. Gene and I are not usually cast in the same part. So how would you change this for me?"

I said, "I'm not intending to change one line."

He said, "Then I definitely want to do it." It was a part written entirely for a white person.

Cosby took deferred money. Harvey Keitel, who played Speed, took deferred money. We wanted Valerie Perrine to play Jugs, but she wouldn't defer any money. We thought, it's unfair for other people to defer money and not her. Raquel Welch, her tongue hanging out to play Jugs, would defer money. So we had this crazy group of people: Bill, Raquel, Harvey, Larry Hagman, Chicago Bear Dick Butkus in his first part, Allen Garfield (whom Vincent Canby called "the Laurence Olivier of American sleaze"), Bruce Davison, performance artists like Toni Basil, and the weirdest cast in the world. We shot the whole picture on location out of something called a Cinemobile. We found a pool hall that was being condemned and turned it into the ambulance company in Venice. We shot the whole movie really fast and came in at 2.99999 because we had to juggle the books. We got Charlie Maguire, who was Elia Kazan's first assistant and one of the great production managers of all time, to be the associate producer to make sure we were on track.

Raquel was very insecure in the beginning, and she had five women who worked for her. Makeup, hair, public relations, wardrobe. I called them the Raquettes. They would always say, "Raquel wants to see you." In the beginning, I was going out once a day, "Yes, Raquel?"

She said, "My motor home is supposed to be the same size as Bill Cosby's."

"It is, Raquel." We're sitting in it.

"His looks much bigger. I was in there."

I said, "Raquel, that's because you wanted a ceiling-to-floor mirror, and the only place to put it is right in the center, so it tends to cut your motor home in half, but it's exactly the same."

She said, "There must be a larger motor home available."

Charlie Maguire told me what to say. He was giving me producing rules. I said, "I'm sure there is, Raquel, and if your staff finds one, have them bring me the info and we'll take a look."

She said, "Okay."

Charlie said, "Her staff's never going to find one. She was waiting for you to say, 'Okay, we're going to bring three here tomorrow and you pick one.'"

Larry Hagman, who was totally nuts, would arrive on the set one day dressed as an astronaut and the next day as a World War I French general. This was Dick Butkus's introduction to filmmaking. Allen Garfield was a compulsive gambler, and when we hired him, we didn't know he was. One day, he called me and asked, "Can I have all of my money?" He was signed for ten weeks at $5,000 a week.

I said, "Allen, I don't know if I can do that. Let me see if I can help you out."

I called Laddie, who said, "Hell, no, he can't have all his money. He's getting five thousand a week for ten weeks."

Garfield's wife's lawyer called saying, "Don't give him the money, because he'll just gamble it away."

We were looping the picture at the end of shooting. Peter and I were waiting for Allen in the looping theater, and he was very late. All of a sudden, two guys who look like they're from the national company of *Guys and Dolls* came in and said, "Mr. Garfield here?"

We said, "No, he's not. Are you looking for him?"

They said, "Yeah, we're looking for him."

"We're looking for him, too." Poor Allen, shit.

It was such a liberating experience being out on the streets, working with such diverse talent as Cosby, Keitel, Hagman, and L.Q. Jones. During the shooting of that film, Peter Yates and I were walking to lunch one day and passed a guy leaning up against the wall with a big beard. He looked like a bum. He said, "Peter?"

Peter turned around and said, "Oh, my God, Patrick?"

He said, "Yes."

Peter said, "What's happened?"

He said, "No, no, I'll be all right. Just nice to see you."

It was Patrick McGoohan, the *Prisoner, Secret Agent* man. It was booze. I didn't recognize him at all, but the minute Peter said, "Patrick?" I said, "Oh, my God, it's Patrick McGoohan." Obviously, he recovered from that, because he went on to do many things.

Peter was a delight to work with. He had in his contract that it was a "Peter Yates production." But he said, "Since you're writing it and we're both producing it, why don't we call it a Yates/Mankiewicz production?" Nobody's ever offered me a credit like that. When the main title came out and read "a Yates/Mankiewicz production," Peter said, "Oh, I wish I hadn't done that, because Mankiewicz is such a long name. I look like a fucking strawberry."

I made a deal with Jerry Moss and A&M. We had Peter Frampton, Brothers Johnson, Quincy Jones, Herb Alpert. They gave us all the music and the rights to use it and score it with A&M music. The picture opened huge. We made that film for $3 million, and it grossed about $17 million. In those days, ticket prices were about two bucks. Everybody got their deferred money. It won two festivals in Europe because they thought it was anti-American, and anything that was anti-American was automatically nominated. To open a picture in those days cost you $2 million. Today it costs $15 to $20 million to open a movie properly. Laddie says, "Now, today, if I'm running a studio, I'm not going to have seventy million dollars in a little ambulance picture. But then, my reasoning was, I've got Tom Mankiewicz, who writes great, and I'm laughing in spite of the offensive nature of his picture. I've got Peter Yates, who directed *Bullitt*, and Bill Cosby, Raquel Welch, and Harvey Keitel. I'm making this for three million bucks. What's the worst that can happen to me? The picture only grosses a million, five, I've lost a million, five. If it does what it did, if it grosses seventeen, and then I sell it for another three, this is hugely profitable to me. Then it has a life forever on tapes and DVDs."

I get a profit check every year for *Mother, Jugs & Speed*. I went to a screening of some film a few years ago, and Elvis Mitchell, who is African American and was a film critic for the *New York Times,* said to me in the lobby before, as we're all having a glass of wine, "You know a picture of yours that is so terrific and really wasn't treated with the respect it should have had when it came out?"

I said, "It's *Mother, Jugs & Speed*."

He said, "You're right. And it's also Bill Cosby's best performance ever."

I said, "I love that picture."

Two weeks later, I'm down at the Music Center. I was talking with Leonard Maltin, who writes film reviews, and he says, "You wrote a movie that I gave a bad review to, but I saw it again the other night on cable and I'm changing my review."

I said, "*Mother, Jugs & Speed.*"

He said, "That's right." It now says, "Hilarious black comedy."

The first half hour of that film is very funny. Then, Bill Cosby and his partner, Bruce Davison, get a call down to a junkie's house. There's little Toni Basil with a shotgun, and she says, "I want drugs." Bruce Davison says, "I'm hip, but lady, listen, we don't carry the kind of drugs in our rig that you want, but we'll get you some." She says, "Liar," and blows his head off. Cosby's got a gun stashed in his rig, and he says, "Hold it there, lady," and she puts the shotgun in her mouth and pulls the trigger and kills herself. Our first preview was in Saint Louis. Twenty people got up and walked out. They thought this was going to be a rollicking ambulance comedy with Bill Cosby. Afterward, Peter, Laddie, and I went for a drink, and Laddie asked, "Do you really need the scene with the shotgun? You saw what happened. This is Middle America. Do you really need that?"

And Peter and I said, "We really, really do. That's really what the picture's about."

Laddie said, "Okay, let's keep it in." Laddie knew that it was important to the movie and important to us, and that was his movie. A stupider studio head would say, "Guys, I'm afraid I really have to insist. It's our three million dollars, and let's just say that Bruce Davison disappears and we throw in a line that he's on vacation and we just go on." But Laddie was a wonderful studio head. The first two pictures he green-lit were *The Omen,* directed by Dick Donner, and *Mother, Jugs & Speed.* We were a little hit, and *The Omen* was huge. But if you made it for $3 million and you grossed $17 million and you sold it to ABC for $3 million more—if they could invest $3 million and get $20 million back—it was almost seven times your money. Later, Scorsese did *Bringing Out the Dead,* but it didn't work. Marty is no good at comedy, and I'm saying that about a guy who's one of the best directors. Every time he tries to do an elegant film or a funny film, God bless him. But *Raging Bull* is one of the best films ever made. He finally won an Oscar for *The Departed.* This guy didn't win for *Mean Streets,* for *Raging Bull,* for *Goodfellas.* Just one after the other. I would say *The Departed,* which is a perfectly good film, is probably his fifth or sixth best.

Jerry Oppenheimer, who is Jule Styne's adopted son, is married to an old friend of mine named Gail Oppenheimer. They were having a small dinner party and Tony Martin was there. He got up during dinner to relieve himself, and as he came out of the bathroom, he suddenly slumped and hit his head, and was down. It was scary. Gail said, "We have to call 9-1-1."

Blake Edwards was there with Julie Andrews, and Blake was in a crotchety mood that night, which he can be at times. He's wheelchair-bound now. He said, "Don't call 9-1-1. They don't know what they're doing." Someone called 9-1-1. Those guys were there in ninety seconds. It was unbelievable. Beverly Hills. They were hooking Tony up, and Blake was saying, "They don't know what the fuck they're doing."

I said, "Blake, they know what they're doing. These people are lifesavers. I did a whole movie about this once."

The guy who was hooking Tony up asked, "What was the movie?"

I said, "*Mother, Jugs & Speed*."

He said, "Are you kidding?" He turned around and said, "Hey, this guy did *Mother, Jugs & Speed*! What'd you do?"

I said, "Well, I wrote it and produced it."

He said, "Jeez, every EMT in the city knows that movie. Every ambulance driver knows that movie." As he looked past me, he said, "I'm sorry, are you Julie Andrews?"

She said, "Yes, I am."

He said, "And it's Julie Andrews and the guy who wrote *Mother, Jugs & Speed*!"

Tony's vital signs were good, and to show that he was fine, he started singing! So Tony Martin's on the floor singing, *Mother, Jugs & Speed* is a hit with the EMTs, guy wants Julie Andrews's autograph. I said, "This is a medical emergency in Beverly Hills. This could never happen in Omaha."

The EMT, as he was leaving, said, "I'm serious. Every EMT in the city knows *Mother, Jugs & Speed*. Every ambulance driver knows *Mother, Jugs & Speed*. That's our movie."

These kinds of films were my corner of the sky. Dad couldn't give me advice on *Mother, Jugs & Speed*. He loved the movie, but the streets of L.A. with ambulances at night, it was nothing he knew. The kinds of movies I was doing weren't up his alley. The only movie I ever did that he said, "Now, there's a movie I might have made" was *Ladyhawke*. He thought it was so sophisticated, and he loved it. There was no, "I'm so proud of you." But to other people my dad would say, "Well, I can't even keep up with Tom anymore; I don't know what movie he's on, and they all seem to be doing very well." Peter Yates and I gave a screening of *Mother, Jugs & Speed* for the cast and crew of *Saturday Night Live*. They all wanted to see it. Later on I did *Dragnet* with Danny Aykroyd, and he remembered that screening. My dad didn't say so, but he was so impressed that these hip people on television loved this movie and his son wrote it. But we were not a family like that.

American Germs

This was the age of the disaster movie: *Earthquake, The Towering Inferno.* Two producers who became very famous, Andy Vajna and Mario Kassar, later Carolco, put together a package and a script called *The Cassandra Crossing.* American germs—germ warfare—were on a train and suddenly got loose, and the whole train was quarantined but it kept moving. It was kind of anti-American: the implication at the end was that the Americans sent it over a faulty bridge for everybody to die. So it was a fight against time with everybody trying to save themselves. And they couldn't get off the train. The script needed a rewrite, and Peter Guber (the wunderkind head of Columbia) said, "There's only a couple of people who could do this, but you've got to do this quick."

The director was George Cosmatos, who would later direct *Rambo.* George smoked four packs a day. This picture was his whole life. They had signed Sophia Loren, Richard Harris, Ava Gardner, and Burt Lancaster. Sophia said, "We want top writers here. This script isn't right." So they gave her a list, and she said, "Tom Mankiewicz. He was here ten years ago. Get him, I love him."

I received a cable I still have from Carlo Ponti saying, "Sophia and I are wondering, could you come over for a few weeks and do some work?"

I said, "Absolutely. Why don't I send you pages right now, because I'm producing a picture"—*Mother, Jugs & Speed.* "I will also call Burt Lancaster, who's in L.A."

Although he's only in the first twenty minutes of the movie, Burt hated his part. I'd written some pages and sent them to his agent. My assistant very breathlessly came into my office and said, "Burt Lancaster's on the phone!"

I was almost as impressed as she was. I'd grown up with *Trapeze, Brute Force, Elmer Gantry,* and *From Here to Eternity.* I mean, he's Burt Lancaster. I got on the phone. He talked just like Burt Lancaster. "These pages are good, kid. They're very good. Much better. I have a few suggestions."

I said, "Please, anything."

"Could I stop by your office at Fox?"

"Absolutely, any time."

"Say about ten in the morning."

"I could come down to you."

He said, "No, no, I'll be in town. I'll come to you. Ten o'clock. Oh, and Tom, don't forget to leave a pass at the gate." I thought, God, Burt Lancaster driving up to any studio, you don't need a pass; you're fucking Burt Lancaster!

So he arrived the next morning for our meeting. And he was wonderful. He said, "I'm going off to Europe now, but you'll send the pages to me."

I said, "Absolutely."

He said, "It's very nice to meet you."

I said, "Could you do me a favor before you leave?"

"What is that?"

"Some people today are being brought up on Dustin Hoffman and Robert Redford, but I was brought up on Burt Lancaster and Kirk Douglas. Before you leave, could you just laugh for me?"

He said, "You mean like ha, ha, ha?" And he went, "Ha, ha, ha, ha, ha," like in his movies, and I started laughing. He went louder, "Ha, ha, ha, ha, ha, ha!" And he backed out of my office going, "Ha, ha, ha, ha!" It was just wonderful. I was in hysterics. The only time I ever met him. I don't care whether my father was in the movies or not, when you run into one of your heroes, it elicits the same reaction every time like when I was seventeen and turned around and there was John Wayne. You're a movie fan. I was so thrilled to be in the same room with Burt Lancaster. If he had said about the script, "No, here I think I should rape five people," I would have said, "Yeah, good idea, good idea!" because I'm with Burt Lancaster.

So during *Mother, Jugs & Speed,* over six or seven weeks, I did some work on the *Cassandra* script. It had an all-star cast: Ingrid Thulin, who was one of Ingmar Bergman's leading ladies; Ava Gardner, who'd done *The Barefoot Contessa* for my father; Lionel Stander, who was a blacklisted actor at the time and later wound up playing Max for me in *Hart to Hart;* and the first part for O.J. Simpson. This is how silly the movie was, O.J. Simpson played a priest. George Cosmatos was so thrilled. He said, "I got O.J. Simpson." Richard Harris was the male lead (they wanted Peter O'Toole, who sensibly turned it down), and Sophia. I never visited the set. I was never in Europe. I just kept sending pages, and then I would get notes and I'd get on the phone with Sophia. I was getting a nice piece of change for this. Carlo Ponti called me and said, "Listen, tell your agent to make the deal for half the amount of money. And I'll put the other half in a Swiss bank for you, and no one will know about it. Tax free. Be drawing interest for the rest of your life."

I said, "Jesus, Carlo, that's illegal, isn't it?"

I've often thought that if I'd put that money in a Swiss bank, which would now be over thirty-five years ago—and it was a nice chunk of money—what it might be worth today. But then, you have to go get it. That's how a lot of business was done on European films. It was a huge hit in Europe. Mario Kassar and Andy Vajna made a pile off it. It was toward the end of the disaster cycle. Everybody had destroyed everything.

The Eagle Has Landed

The Eagle Has Landed was a big bestseller by Jack Higgins. It was going to be a Paramount movie. Lew Grade was the executive producer. It was produced by a guy named Jack Wiener, very bright, smart, and British. His partner was David Niven Jr., who's the most charming guy in the world but knows absolutely nothing about producing movies. He was just hanging on. And I did the screenplay. I was so excited because they got John Sturges to direct it. *Bad Day at Black Rock. The Magnificent Seven. The Great Escape.* I met with him. He had a patch over one eye. A tough old guy. He liked the script a lot. It was about a plot to kidnap Churchill in World War II. The best part was the undercover IRA agent, which Donald Sutherland played. We offered that part to Michael Caine. Michael called me and said, "Listen, I love the script. I'd like to be in this movie." He said, "I'm forty-two years old. I had my first child only four years ago. I'm happily married. I don't want to play an IRA agent. There are so many crazy people, and if they think I'm playing it wrong or somebody takes offence . . ."

I said, "It was in the Second World War."

He said, "But still, it's the IRA. On the other hand, I'd love to play the German colonel."

I said, "I'm sure we'd love for you to do it. Let me talk to John Sturges."

Michael said, "Isn't it amazing? Here we are only thirty years after the Second World War, and a British actor would rather play a Nazi colonel than an Irishman."

So he played the colonel. Donald Sutherland said, "What are they going to do to me? I'm fuckin' Canadian!" So Donald played the IRA agent.

There were some wonderful actors: Robert Duvall; Judy Geeson; that terrific woman from *Upstairs, Downstairs,* Jean Marsh; Larry Hagman. It was, in many ways, easily the best script I'd ever written. But John Sturges, for some reason, had given up. Michael said on the set, sometimes, if he was behind, he would say, "We don't have to shoot that scene." This was a heartbreak for me. It's my cousin Ben Mankiewicz's favorite movie, and it gets a great review in Leonard Maltin's book, another *Mother, Jugs & Speed.* My new favorite critic. But there were scenes missing. I wasn't there for most of the shooting. I was just there for the beginning, and everything was fine and everybody was happy. Donald and Michael were wonderful. But when it was over, John Sturges didn't even edit it. He got on a boat and went to the Mediterranean.

The picture is as good as it is because Anne V. Coates was our editor. She edited *Lawrence of Arabia*. She was David Lean's editor. I didn't know her. She was screening a rough cut for some executives in a big theater. I was invited. Rough cuts are always difficult. Francis Coppola said, "No movie is ever as good as the rushes or as bad as the rough cut." You watch the rushes every day and say, "Boy, we nailed that. They're gonna love that." Then, you put the whole film together and you say, "Oh, boy, are we in trouble." Every time. I sat there, and I was frankly a little disappointed. Some of my favorite scenes or little moments weren't even there. The executives liked it a lot.

Anne Coates came over to me and introduced herself. "You're Tom Mankiewicz, right?"

I said, "Yes."

She said, "Are you terribly disappointed?"

"Just a little."

"I thought you would be. I read your script."

She said some of it was unexplainable. In the picture, Michael goes around recruiting with a letter from Hitler authorizing him to do whatever he wants in terms of getting into England. There's a scene with Donald Pleasence, who plays Himmler, where Michael finds out that the letter he's been carrying is a fake. Hitler knows nothing about it. You've got to cut to Michael's face when he finds out. There was no close-up of him. I said to Anne, "You've got to cut to his close-up."

She said, "There isn't one."

I said, "That's impossible."

She said, "There isn't one."

Sturges never directed again. Some of the actors told me he was drinking very heavily on the movie and would sometimes come in in the morning hung over, and then he would start to drink in the afternoon. I don't mean to vilify him in any way, because he's one of my heroes as a director. I was so thrilled he was going to be on it. But he never directed again. That was his last movie. He took off on a boat, and Anne Coates said that's the last she saw of him. He just gave up.

But the actors were so good. John Standing, who played a priest in the film, said, "You know the thing about Michael Caine? We were all in that church in the movie, and there's all of these wonderful actors, and we're all

Rosa Stradner (mother) and Tom Mankiewicz (age one year), Los Angeles, 1943

Chris Mankiewicz (brother), Joe Mankiewicz (father), and Tom Mankiewicz (age two years) at home in Los Angeles, 1944

Unless otherwise noted, photos are from the collection of Tom Mankiewicz.

Tom, Timber, and Chris at home in Los Angeles, 1940s

Rosa, Tom, Chris, and Joe, movie premiere, New York City, 1953

Tom, Rosa, Joe, and Chris at home in New York City, 1950s

Tom and Joe, Yale graduation, 1963

Tom and Mia Farrow, 1960s (courtesy Dominick Dunne)

Tom in his twenties

Joe, Chris, and Tom, 1970

Harry Saltzman and Tom on location in Jamaica for *Live and Let Die*, 1972 (courtesy United Artists)

Tom and Roger Moore on location in Jamaica for *Live and Let Die*, 1972 (courtesy United Artists)

Tom, Peter Yates, and Bill Cosby on the set of *Mother, Jugs & Speed*, 1975 (courtesy 20th Century Fox)

Tom and
Liza Minnelli,
1975

Marlon Brando, Richard Donner, and Tom watching video playback on the set of *Superman*, 1977 (courtesy Warner Brothers)

Jackie Cooper, Margot Kidder, Richard Donner, Tom, and Sarah Douglas in the makeup room of *Superman*, 1977 (courtesy Warner Brothers)

Margot Kidder and Tom at *Superman* premiere, 1978

Tom, 1979 (courtesy *Broadcast Week*)

Natalie Wood and Tom at Wood's home, 1979

Jack Haley Jr. and Tom, 1980s (courtesy Nate Cutler)

Don Hunt and Tom, Kenya Game Ranch Club, Kenya, 1985

Christopher Plummer, Tom, and Dabney Coleman on the set of *Dragnet*, 1986 (courtesy Universal City Studios, Inc.)

Tom and friend, Kenya Game Ranch, Kenya, 1985

John Candy and Tom on the set of *Delirious,* New York City, 1990 (courtesy MGM/UA)

Tom, John Candy, and Joe L. Mankiewicz on the set of *Delirious,* West Fifty-Seventh Street, New York City, 1990 (courtesy MGM/UA)

Tom and Jerry Moss, 1990s

Ben Mankiewicz, Sidney Poitier, Martin Landau, Sid Ganis, Tom, John
Mankiewicz, and (bottom left) Rosemary Mankiewicz, C. O. "Doc"
Erickson, Academy of Motion Picture Arts and Sciences tribute to Joe
Mankiewicz, Beverly Hills, California, 2009 (courtesy AMPAS)

Tom at sixty-eight, 2010

Tom's ashes, over Kenya Game Ranch, Kenya, 2010 (courtesy Ron Mardigian)

acting up a storm. And Michael Caine is doing nothing. I'm thinking, poor sod. I watched the rushes the next day, and he's doing everything. He knows how to act on film. He doesn't overact, he just listens."

My cousin Ben, who is the weekend host on Turner Classic Movies, ran *The Eagle Has Landed* once. He asked, "Did you write that line for Duvall about the girl at the party?"

I said, "Yes, I did."

He said, "That's the greatest, most complicated line."

All of a sudden, they find out that Churchill's going to be spending the night in the country at this little house in two weeks. Duvall starts thinking. His lieutenant says to him, "Surely, Oberst, you don't think this can be carried out." And Duvall says, "A wink from a pretty girl at a party rarely results in climax, Carl. But a man is a fool not to push the suggestion as far as it can go." Duvall said, "I love this line." *Newsweek,* which didn't like the movie, picked it out as stilted dialogue. Richard Schickel in *Time,* who really liked the movie, picked that line out as the level of sophistication that was so wonderful.

Actually, the best line in that piece I waited a long time to write. The IRA agent played by Donald Sutherland pretends to be a game warden. Jenny Agutter, a very good British actress, is much younger than him and has a huge crush on him. She doesn't know he's IRA. They're about to sleep together for the first time, and he's on top of her. She looks up at him. He looks down and says, "I'm no good for you, dear girl. That's not to make you want me more; that's the truth." And he fucks her. Women always swoon when the man says, "I'm no good for you." But it was the truth. He was an IRA agent who was going to fuck her and leave town. As I wrote the screenplay, I would have said both those lines out loud, especially the Duvall one, because it's almost a tongue twister. You say to yourself, "Is this too complicated now?" A lot of times you write a line that's too complicated, and you really have to simplify it. Larry Hagman always played assholes better than anybody. He's an asshole colonel. Treat Williams plays a captain who is supposed to intercept Churchill on the Walsingham Road. He says, "But, sir, I don't think he's on the Walsingham Road. I think we're being sent on a wild goose chase." And Hagman says, "Captain, if you're not out there on Walsingham Road to meet Churchill in exactly one hour, this country is going to hang you from Big Ben by your balls." It went over great opening night in London.

The problem with adapting a famous novel, a bestseller, is the book is, let's say, 400 pages long. If you write that as a screenplay, you've got a six-hour movie. There is a real science to trying to glean out six scenes that are pivotal. Then you have to figure out how you're going to do this in 125 or 130 pages. It really is a complicated process. The question is not whether you're going to lose something from the novel, but how much. The novel works at 400 pages. You've got to make your movie work in two hours. I'm really adapting 140 pages of that book. Oddly enough, for me, it's easier to write an original, because at least you can go where you want to go. It should be easier to adapt, because there's the story. But you feel very guilty when it's a book like *The Eagle Has Landed,* which was a bestseller. You say, "Boy, I hope I do this justice, because lots of people really like it." It would be like *The Da Vinci Code.* People are going to say, "I thought the movie was fine, but I really loved the book." When a book becomes a big best-seller, it's very difficult to make a successful movie. The picture was a huge hit in Europe. Perfect European subject matter with that cast and a plot to kidnap Churchill by the Nazis in World War II. Juliet Mills, a great friend of mine, who did *Nanny and the Professor,* called me and said, "That's my favorite movie of all time."

For the London opening, I stayed at the snootiest hotel in the world, the Connaught. The opening night for *The Eagle Has Landed* was going to be a command performance for Prince Charles and Princess Anne. I walked into the hotel lobby and said to the concierge, "John, I'll need a car tomorrow night."

He said, "Yes, Mr. Mankiewicz. Will a Daimler suffice?"

I said, "I'm sure a Daimler will be just fine."

Behind me, I heard a tut-tut noise. It was the hotel manager, Bill Gustav. He said, "Mr. Mankiewicz, please. When one goes to one's own royal performance, one always arrives in a Rolls." And he leaned past me and said, "Get Mr. Mankiewicz a Rolls."

I said, "Thank you, Bill."

He said, "Not at all, sir. Reflects on the hotel, you know."

He was the quintessential hotel manager. He let me walk through the lobby in blue jeans during filming because I was leaving at six in the morning, but he asked me, very nicely, if I could use the rear entrance to the hotel when I came back at six o'clock in the evening, because he didn't want people with blue jeans going through his lobby. And you respected him. He asked Paul Newman to leave because there were fans out in front of the hotel and he didn't feel it was fair to the other guests to have to walk through those fans in and out. Dad stayed there. Henry Fonda and David Niven were the two actors that he allowed. There were never any fans out in front.

I was going at the time with a British actress named Suzy Kendall who was just beautiful. She was in *To Sir, with Love.* I had just arrived in London, and she was going to spend the night in the hotel. I was checking in, and she was standing next to me. Bill looked at her and said, "Welcome back, Mr. Mankiewicz. And how long will Mrs. Mankiewicz be staying with us?"

Suzy said, "Just visiting, thanks."

He said, "Very good, madam."

He knew damned well who she was because she was quite popular at the time and she was Dudley Moore's ex-wife. But *News of the World* would be by, and that would be a no-no for his hotel. Not fair to the other guests. Dick Donner would say, "You have to hold a mirror under people's noses to see if they're alive here." I was going to have a drink at the Connaught bar with Christopher Plummer, a friend of mine (later, I directed him in *Dragnet*), who was at the National Theatre. You were not allowed in the bar without a tie on. They had three Mankiewicz ties ready to wear depending on the color of my shirt. It was a wonderful hotel, and that was London in the seventies. It was snootier than Claridge's and very small.

Suzy Kendall was just a dream. One of the things I really missed in life was not having any kids and never having a bad marriage. Suzy, for some reason, couldn't have children. She and Dudley tried. I tried so hard to give her a kid. When Dudley married Tuesday Weld, Dudley, Tuesday, Suzy, and I would have dinner. There's something rather sick about that. Suzy lived in Hampstead. Beautiful little house. I don't know what happened to her. I haven't seen her in a long time. She was just adorable.

Going Deep

In 1976, right after *Mother, Jugs & Speed*, Peter Yates committed to direct *The Deep*, which was Peter Benchley's next book (after *Jaws*). Peter Benchley was a friend of mine, since we went to school at Exeter. He was one of those guys, like Elmore Leonard, oddly enough, who insisted on writing the first draft. He's not a very good screenwriter. It's a different kind of writing. Mario Puzo never finished a screenplay: he was a wonderful novelist, but he wasn't a good screenwriter. One is written through the ear with the dialogue, and one is written through the head. Peter Benchley had written the first draft, then they got somebody else on it.

It was Peter Guber's first picture as a producer. He did something that I've never heard of before or since in movies. He got Robert Shaw, Jackie Bisset, and Nick Nolte to sign off the book. They never read a script. Guber said, "We're going to lock you in. Peter Yates is available, the script's being written now, and here's Benchley's book." Peter Yates was unhappy with the script, but not like Robert Shaw was unhappy. When Shaw got to the

Caribbean, he said, "We're not going to shoot this." So Peter Yates and Peter Guber called me. "You've got to come down here. You're the doctor."

They sent me the script. I said to Peter Yates, "It's really not very good."

Peter said, "I know. That's why we want you down here. If it was very good, we wouldn't have sent it to you!"

So I said, "Okay."

The production was in Tortola, British Virgin Islands. I left L.A. in such a hurry I forgot my passport. The flight went from L.A. to Miami to San Juan, and then San Juan to British Virgin Islands. I got through Miami to San Juan because Puerto Rico's an American protectorate and you didn't need a passport. Peter Guber had somebody go to my house to get my passport. It was handed to a Pan Am pilot and flown down to San Juan, where I stayed at the San Juan Hilton for two delightful days waiting for it.

Peter Island is a small island, and most of it was the Yacht Club. At the top there were four interconnecting bungalows with a courtyard. The four bungalows were Peter Yates, Jackie, Derek Cracknell (the assistant director), and me. The pages started flying. Peter Guber wrote a book about the making of *The Deep*. He wrote, "Thank God, Mankiewicz is here and he and Shaw just love each other."

Shaw was so smart. He was a huge drinker. In his contract with Columbia, it said that he couldn't drink. Terrible alcohol problems. He had ten kids. He had been married to a beautiful actress, Mary Ure, who died the opening night of a play. She was in *Look Back in Anger* with Richard Burton. He finally married the nanny, which was great because she took care of all the kids. He died at fifty-two years old. Heart attack. Sean Connery told me about when they were doing *Robin and Marian* and Shaw played the sheriff of Nottingham. He'd be drunk in the fights. But he was so smart and had a great sense of humor. He could be very cutting. He said, "Now, this line, it's a little complicated for Jackie."

I said, "A little complicated?"

He said, "Well, words aren't exactly the only thing that belong in her mouth."

Nick Nolte worshipped him. One day, Nick came on the dive boat and he had a copy of the BBC *Radio Times. Rich Man, Poor Man* was being run in England, and there was his picture on the cover. Nick asked, "You're from England. Is this good?"

Robert said, "Why yes, I would say more people per capita get the BBC *Radio Times* than get *TV Guide* in America. You can safely be assured your picture will be on everyone's coffee table in the United Kingdom this week."

Nick grinned. Shaw said, "I'm so happy for you, dear boy. Now, perhaps, finally, I can stop explaining to people who you are," and walked away.

Nick said, "Isn't he great?"

I finished half the script and we were all reading it. I was never a big Nick Nolte fan. Not a bad actor, but Jesus, a human being out of control. Robert was making good notes. Nolte said, "Now, this line; I would never say this line."

Before I could say anything, Robert said, "Nick, are you saying you wouldn't say it or the character wouldn't say it?"

And Nick said, "Well, I guess I'm saying I wouldn't say it."

Then Robert turned to me and said, "You know, that's the trouble with young actors these days. They don't want to play anything. They just want to be themselves."

I asked him about Steven Spielberg. "Is Spielberg really as good as I think he is?" They had, of course, done *Jaws* together. Shaw said the most prophetic thing. "Young Steven has exquisite taste. He is a wonderful director. But he has one problem: a rather plain-looking fellow, and they're already sending private jets for him and he's going out with actresses. Steven will never be able to make a film about a man and a woman. Ever. He'll never know what it's like to sing under a lady's balcony and have a hot tub of shit poured on your head. Never going to happen to him." Shaw was absolutely right. Spielberg is a master filmmaker: *E.T., Saving Private Ryan, Schindler's List, Close Encounters, Jaws.* He tried one relationship film called *Always.* Didn't work. He's never had a love story between a man and a woman. Robert saw it right away. By the way, Shaw's in my favorite James Bond film, which contains one of the best fights ever, the vicious fight in the train compartment between Shaw and Sean. *From Russia with Love.* That's my favorite Bond. I love that picture.

I would spend days with Robert. He never wrote a line, but he wanted to talk to me about all the scenes. He had written a great play called *The Man in the Glass Booth* about Adolf Eichmann. He said, "I'm not going to write this fucking script."

I said, "No, I know that."

He said, "Nor do you want me to, but we'll talk."

Peter Yates would come back from scouting locations at three in the afternoon and Robert and I would still be there, Robert drunk. Visibly. Peter asked, "How can you let him do that?"

I said, "Peter, I don't know where he gets it. There's no booze here. He either hides it in his pants or it's prehidden inside the bathroom."

Howard Curtis, whom I was later going to work with—he was R.J.'s stunt double on *Hart to Hart*—was Robert's stunt double for diving. Robert had to dive every now and then so they could get pictures of him through his face mask underwater. I tried to go under, but I would use up my forty minutes of air in eleven minutes. I was just panic stricken down there. By the way, Jackie Bisset learned how to scuba dive in the swimming pool of the Peter Island Yacht Club. She was just so wedded to Al Giddings, the underwater photographer. He would say, "Don't worry about the one barracuda. But if you see a school of barracuda, get out of the water as soon as possible. If you see a shark, just get behind me." I was down there one day, and a shark came swimming by. Suddenly, there were eighteen, twenty people behind this one guy. He just swam right up to the shark and bopped him right in the nose, and the shark went away.

There was one day on the dive boat at ten o'clock in the morning when Robert Shaw was drunk. He was going to go under, and Howard Curtis said, "Robert, you're not going down. You're pissed."

Robert said, "I am not. I haven't had a drink. I'm going down."

Howard said, "No, you're not."

Robert said, "Get out of my way, Howard," and Howard coldcocked him. He really protected him because you could die if you go down when you're drunk. And Robert just adored him, loved Howard for that, that he would do that. A lot of stuntmen would say, "Oh, fuck him. He's a big star, let him go down. If he gets the bends or has a heart attack, I tried to stop him." Howard was terrific.

The writing credits for the film read Benchley and a very good writer who didn't do a particularly good job on this, Tracy Keenan Wynn (Ed Wynn's grandson). Peter Guber and Peter Yates were so surprised because they thought Tracy Keenan Wynn was going to turn in a corker. But they were not satisfied. I don't want to run anybody else's work down, but Robert was absolutely adamant about it. He said, "We can do better than this." So my reputation as a script doctor kept growing. Today, there are famous script doctors—for instance, *Crash, Million Dollar Baby,* Paul Haggis. He rewrites the Bond movies for a million bucks. They bring him in to do what I did on *The Spy Who Loved Me.* I started *Moonraker.* Cubby asked, "Can you help me and Lewis Gilbert out? We have a premise about a space shuttle being eaten at the beginning of the picture. Can you come up to NASA with us in San Jose for a few days and write some stuff down on a couple of pages?" Which I did because I was so loyal to Cubby. And, Lewis Gilbert, who directed *Alfie,* was a good director.

The Deep grossed more than $100 million in 1977, which would be like grossing $350 million today. Whether you get credit or not, everybody knows you were down there doing it: Peter Yates knows, Peter Guber knows, Robert Shaw knows, Jackie Bisset knows, and the studio knows. Peter Yates had a big piece of *The Deep:* 10 or 15 percent of the profits. David Begelman, not the most honorable fellow, but a good executive who was running Columbia at the time, was a good friend of Peter Yates's. They were offering Peter another picture. Peter went to see David one day. He said, "First, David, let me just say, my business manager and my agent say that you guys owe me six million bucks from *The Deep.*" There was a silence. He said, "Six million. They've looked at the grosses."

David said to him, in essence, "You're probably right. We probably do owe you six million dollars. We're going to offer you two; take it or leave it." And Peter took it because he knew the alternative was to be in court with the studio for years. He said, "If I go on *The Tonight Show* and say two million wasn't enough, people will throw food at me. On the other hand, Begelman just cheated me out of four million dollars." So you always have to make that decision when you have monkey points.

Clint Eastwood was a cash cow at Warner Brothers. They treated the people that they had deals with so wonderfully. But Clint finally went to them one day and said, "Here's the deal. I'm going to take Screen Actors Guild minimum. Take Screen Directors Guild minimum. When the picture opens and the theaters keep their 30 percent, it's 'hello partner.' No deductions of any kind; not publicity, not cost for opening it, not interests, not loans, just 'hello partner.'" A "hello partner" deal is when a studio partners with an actor to share box office gross on a film from dollar one. And they made a "hello partner" deal with him. He was the only guy who could do it then.

The best deal ever made was by two people who changed television and movies. Desi Arnaz and Lucille Ball wanted to shoot *I Love Lucy* in L.A. because they lived there. It was going to be more expensive by—and we're talking the early 1950s—$5,000 an episode, and a whole episode only cost $40,000. And, Desi wanted to do it on film. He was a very smart guy, not the second banana to her, a really good business man. He said to the network, "I'm going to film it."

They said, "No, you can't film it, for God's sake. Everything's on tape, on kinescope."

Desi said, "I want to film it. We'll put up the five thousand extra every week, Lucy and I, and we want to own the negatives."

The network said, "Absolutely." They laughed at him because there were no reruns in those days. There were no videotapes, there were no

DVDs, there was no ancillary market at all. Nobody could ever imagine rerunning them. All of a sudden, Lucy and Desi owned the shows. That was a big event.

I was watching *NCIS* and now it says, "Producer: Mark Harmon" in the eighth year. *Gunsmoke* is one of the longest-running series in the history of television. At a certain point, Jim Arness, playing Marshal Dillon, had to sign up again for three years. He said, "I want a piece of the show and I want to be executive producer." Bill Paley was running CBS at the time. Another CBS executive said, "If we do this, we're opening a door that can never be closed." The executive didn't talk with Paley, and John Meston, a producer-writer on the show, was hired in secret to write the show where Marshal Dillon is killed. Burt Reynolds, who was in the series at the time, becomes the marshal, and they'll just go on and call it *Gunsmoke*. The executive went to Bill Paley and said, "Here's the situation, Mr. Paley. This is what Mr. Arness wants, and his contract's up in three months. We had an episode written and we can kill him."

Paley said, "You mean *Gunsmoke*, that's been on already for twelve years, and my kids' favorite show? Let me ask you a question: If we give Arness a piece of the show, his production company, are we still going to make money?"

The executive said, "Oh, yeah, we'll make money."

Paley said, "Then do it." And that started the trend where you see an actor's production company having a piece of the show.

Rewriting *Superman*

At this point, in 1977, I had rewritten *The Deep* and *The Spy Who Loved Me*, among others. I was the fixer, and I didn't really want to be the fixer. I wanted to do screenplays like *The Eagle Has Landed* or *Live and Let Die*, where I was on from start to finish. Dick Donner had been a really close friend for so long. I was lying in bed, it was five o'clock in the morning, the phone rang, and it was Donner with the most unmistakable voice in the world. He never has to introduce himself. He said, "Get up, get up. I'm in Paris."

I said, "Jesus Christ, Donner, it's five in the morning."

"I know. I'm doing *Superman*, and so are you."

"No, no, no. I'm not doing *Superman*. What is it, the Superman comics?"

"Absolutely, and you're going to do it, and there's a lady on her way to your house right now with the scripts. *Superman* and *Superman II*. It's two scripts. Two movies. And you're too nice a guy. I told her you'll come down and open the door."

I said, "Oh, shit."

The doorbell rang. I hung up on Dick and went downstairs. Here was this nice lady. The two scripts, which anyone can see in the "Making of *Superman*" featurette on the DVD, were between five hundred and six hundred pages long. I just looked at them and put them down on the hall table. I went upstairs and the phone rang again. It was Dick. "Are you reading?"

I said, "No, they're too heavy to get upstairs, Dick."

He said, "I'll be back home tomorrow. Read them."

I read them and they were very campy, although there was some wonderful stuff too. Mario Puzo had written a first draft. He was not a good screenwriter. But then the producers got Robert Benton and David Newman with Mrs. Leslie Newman. They're very smart writers. Benton is a wonderful writer. But the script went on forever. No comic-book character had ever been out on the screen successfully in the history of movies. And here I was rewriting again. I was taking somebody else's script.

When Dick got back, I called him and I said, "Look, I'd love to work with you, we're friends, but this is not the—"

He said, "Come over to my house," which was very close. "Come over."

I went over, rang the doorbell, and there was no answer. I went around the side of the house. I knew his house very well. There was Dick, standing in his garden, looking out at a view of Los Angeles, dressed in a Superman suit that they'd given him. He turned around and looked at me. I couldn't believe it. He said, "Just try the suit on and you'll do it." He started running at me, the cape was billowing out, and I was laughing. Dick has got that infectious enthusiasm. He said, "If we can get the love story right, it'll work." It was not stunts or flying, it was if we can get Lois and Clark and Superman right, and make them real, we'll really have a picture.

We had to work for the Salkinds. Alexander Salkind was the old man, and his son, Ilya, was the nominal producer, along with a kind of a hit man they had, named Pierre Spengler. The Salkinds weren't really producers; they were promoters. They had the idea to do *Superman*. Warners thought it was a lousy idea and let them have it for a negative pickup, which means, you go make the movie and we'll distribute it. As promoters, the Salkinds asked, "Who is the most famous writer in the world?" It was Mario Puzo at the time, because of *The Godfather*. They got him, and they went out and got Marlon Brando and Gene Hackman to commit by paying them a lot of money: Brando was guaranteed $3 million, Hackman was guaranteed $2 million. This was 1977. At the Cannes Film Festival, they had helicopters with banners saying, "Superman, Puzo, Brando, Hackman." I got to know Hackman fairly well during *Superman*. We talked about it one night. He said, "You know, I came from New York from the stage. I don't know how I ever became a leading man. I was just going to be a supporting actor for my whole life, and I was happy as a clam." But then, two films were released: *The French Connection,* where he isn't playing a romantic lead, but he was the lead and he was fuckin' great; and *The Poseidon Adventure,* where again, he was the lead but he wasn't a romantic lead. All of a sudden, he was a movie star.

Gene was delighted with the pages I was writing. Benton and Newman wrote some good stuff for him, but some of it was silly—not that Lex Luthor's part isn't silly. Gene had a mustache when Dick met him in L.A. Dick said, "You've got to lose the mustache, Gene."

Gene said, "I don't want to lose the mustache. I love the mustache."

Dick said, "Yeah, but here's the whole thing about Lex Luthor: he doesn't have any hair."

Gene said, "You're just going to have to live with that," and Dick said okay.

So the first day of makeup tests, Dick walked in wearing a mustache. It was the first time Gene had seen him in London. Dick said, "If you can't lick 'em, join 'em."

Gene said, "You look great with that mustache."

Dick said, "I'll tell you what, Gene; I'll shave mine if you shave yours." Gene said okay. They put some lather on it and they shaved Gene's mustache, and Dick pulled his off. It was a fake mustache. Gene was fucking furious. Furious! And then he laughed because Dick really got him. He knew it was best for the part.

The picture started with Guy Hamilton as the director. They figured they'd get a Bond director. Guy would have been disastrous casting for *Superman* because he was a cynic. That's what made him so wonderful for Bond. He was also rather snobby; exactly wrong for *Superman*. But this is what I mean about the Salkinds being promoters as opposed to producers. They had no idea how to cast a director for it. They were going to shoot the picture in Italy, but all of a sudden the lira got more expensive and the pound was collapsing, so they decided to move to England. They figured they were going to save millions. They said to Guy Hamilton, "You'll be very happy, Guy; we're shooting this movie in England now, so you can be home."

Guy said, "I'm sorry, but I'm a tax exile from England. I'm only allowed ninety days a year in the United Kingdom." He was officially a citizen of Malta.

They said, "Okay, good-bye." So Guy was paid off.

The reason they went to Donner was that *The Omen* was a smash, and it was opening in Europe and he was right there. When Dick came on, they'd already spent $5 or $6 million. I don't think the Salkinds ever raised more than $16 million, and they were going to do two movies, plus pay Dick and me a lot of money. It is the only film I've ever worked on or ever heard of where the director was never shown a budget or a schedule. They couldn't show him a budget because they couldn't tell him how much money they actually didn't have. There was a sequence from *Superman II* where the three super villains come through the ceiling of the White House to take over and there's a gun battle with marines. That was scheduled for a day and a half. Dick said, "Are you crazy? If they come through the ceiling of the White House wrong, that's going to be a whole day to put that back. You can't shoot this in a day and a half. I'll tell you what: Why don't you schedule the rest of the film for four days, and I'll be nine months over? It doesn't really matter. This is all fucking fiction." The Salkinds had no idea how to make a movie. They'd been very lucky with *Three* and *Four Musketeers* because Dick Lester, the director, did know how to make a movie.

Donner liked to smoke marijuana. It was all very careful. The house he had on Floor Street—and I eventually moved into that house—was next door to Margaret Thatcher. She was the head of Her Majesty's Loyal Opposition at the time, as the Labor Party was in power. She had cops in front of her house. We were asked over to a big Tory party at Mrs. Thatcher's. We went and met her.

It was the seventies, and people weren't drinking, they were smoking grass. One night we were out with John Standing, an actor friend of mine who was in *The Eagle Has Landed*. Dick rented the house that we were in from John's ex-wife. At the end of the evening, John gave us each a Thai stick as a gift. I was never a big drug taker, I was a big drinker. The next morning, Dick and I are up at six thirty. We're taking a flight to Zurich so we can have breakfast with Salkind, who didn't fly. We're at Heathrow, Dick's going through the metal detectors, and I'm waiting to put my brief-case on the conveyor belt. I open it up, and there's the Thai stick, right on top. And I know Stacy Keach is doing two years in prison. I snap the brief-case down and start coughing. I'm playing like I'm not feeling well. I open the briefcase, snatch the Thai stick, and stuff it in my sock; I don't know what to do. Dick is saying, "What's going on? Will you come on, we're going to miss the plane."

I go through security and say to Dick, "There's a Thai stick in my sock," as we're getting on the plane.

Dick says, "Oh, Jesus. Switzerland is worse than England. It's in your sock?"

I said, "Yeah." And I did one of the shittiest things I've ever done in my life. We were in first class. It was a small first class, eight seats. Across the aisle from me was a little old guy in his seventies. At one point during the flight, he got up to take a leak and I took the Thai stick and jammed it in the back of his seat. He looked like such an honorable man. I thought, when they're cleaning the plane, if they do find it, they'll blame it on this guy. So maybe he gets arrested, but he looks like an honorable guy, so I'm sure he can get out of it, whereas I look like an absolute asshole in my thirties.

I told Dick, "I jammed it in his seat." I hated that.

He said, "Oh, you prick."

I said, "What am I supposed to do, try and get through Swiss customs?"

Alexander Salkind lived in the Grand Dolder Hotel in Zurich. He looked like a little gnome. He was about four foot eleven with flowing white hair. I used to call him Margaret Rutherford. He was married to this Mexican woman named Bertha. Bertha was nuts. She told Dick and me at the beginning, "You know, my son, Ilya, is a god."

We didn't like Ilya too much. I said, "A god, Mrs. Salkind, really?"

She said, "Yes, he was the product of my first lovemaking. And in Mexico, we believe that the product of your first lovemaking is a god."

Dick said, "Well, tell God to watch out or he's going to get kicked in the nuts on this picture."

We started from scratch. Dick threw out everything that Guy had. He signed a new production designer, a genius named John Barry. Not the composer. He designed *Star Wars*. Obviously, Brando and Hackman were going to stay. And we set about trying to start this movie. We wanted Miss Teschmacher, Lex Luthor's girlfriend, to be Goldie Hawn. But Goldie was a big star, and she said, "I want two million dollars just like Gene. I'm as big a star as Gene Hackman."

The Salkinds didn't have the $2 million. Goldie Hawn would have been so wonderful as the loopy Miss Teschmacher. The Salkinds said, "She's too expensive." So Dick and I went to see Ann-Margret, who was our second choice. She was delightful and terrific, and we thought, okay, she's going to be great. And Ann-Margret only wanted $1 million for the two movies. So that's half the price. We were having preproduction meetings at the Grand

Dolder Hotel. Pierre Spengler came into the bar where we're sitting and said, "I just got off the phone. Congratulations, we just signed Ann-Margret for Miss Teschmacher."

Dick and I said, "Thank you, Alex," to the old man.

He said, "You see, Mr. Donner, what you make me do? The things you make me pay for?"

So we were having a drink and talking about other elements of the movie. Suddenly, Pierre came back in and said, "We've just signed Valerie Perrine for Miss Teschmacher."

I said, "Excuse me? We just signed Ann-Margret."

He said, "Yes, but Valerie Perrine is brilliant." And she was. Wonderful actress. Spengler said, "And, she's willing to do it for five hundred thousand for the two pictures."

I said, "But I thought you just closed with Ann-Margret."

And the old man said, "She can sue." I thought, boy, these are the people we're doing business with.

Then we had to go up and see Brando. This was one of the most memorable meetings we'd ever had. It was in Los Angeles in the late summer, but it was one of those weeks where it was a hundred degrees. Dick had a little Porsche with no air conditioning. The top was down. We got up to Mulholland Drive to Brando's house. He shared a driveway with Jack Nicholson. There was a gate, and we got onto the motor court. The front door opened, and all of a sudden, four Dobermans and Rottweilers ran out. We were pulling up the top on the car, and they're "Arr, arr." In the doorway appeared Marlon Brando in a caftan. He clapped his hands and the dogs came running to him. I said, "Dick, I think there's a power imbalance going on here."

I hadn't seen Marlon since I was a little kid and he'd done two films for my father: Shakespeare's *Julius Caesar* and *Guys and Dolls*. We had called Marlon's best friend, Jay Cantor, who had been an executive with Universal, MCA. He'd been Marlon's agent, and was really close to Dick. I knew him well too. We had said, "Tell us about Marlon." Cantor said, "On every picture, Marlon's either at your feet or at your balls. So just be yourself, because if he senses fear . . ."

So Marlon was sitting there. We all had coffee or a drink. He said, "You know, I've been thinking. We're up there on Krypton. Maybe we don't look like people." Dick and I sneaked a glance at each other. He said, "Maybe we look like bagels or green suitcases." Oh, God. We just signed Marlon Brando for $3 million and he's a green suitcase. He said, "And maybe we don't speak." To say this to a writer. He said, "Maybe we just make electronic sounds, and there are subtitles on the bottom of the screen." We were sitting there dying. He said, "They're paying me a lot of money, and my kids really want me to do this. They want me to be Jor-El. It's funny, because when you tell a kid a story—they all know the story of Superman. You tell a kid a story, and you say the fox was behind the wall, and then he went and hid behind the tree. The next night, the kid says, 'Tell me the story about the fox, Daddy.' Well, the fox is behind the tree. The kid says, 'No, no, Daddy, the fox is behind the wall. Then he went behind the tree.' Kids remember everything."

Dick suddenly burst in and said, "That's why you can't look like a green suitcase and you can't make electronic sounds, because everybody knows Jor-El was on Krypton."

Marlon started to roar with laughter. He had been testing us. He just wanted to see who he was working with. He wanted to see if we were two assholes saying, "Yes, that's very interesting. Electronic sounds, hmm, and what would they sound like, Marlon?" He wanted to see if we were that kind of guy or the other kind of guy. He laughed so hard when Dick yelled at him because it had all been a huge put-on.

Dick and I were coming back from the studio one night—this was still in prep. We knew we were dealing with the Salkinds. We didn't know how much money they had or didn't have. We didn't have a Superman at that time. We didn't have Lois Lane. We had a start date with Brando and Hackman. We thought both films would cost $30 million, and this is back in the seventies. Dick had a driver named Brian. I'd had a few Jack Daniel's. Dick had had a couple of joints. We were driving in silence in the car. Dick said to me, "Penny for your thoughts."

I said, "I'm thinking we could be presiding over the greatest financial disaster in the history of film. That's what I'm thinking." And we just went on in silence.

The car dropped Dick off at his place, which I later moved into. Brian dropped me off at the Connaught Hotel, and as I got out of the car, I asked him, "Brian, would you give the two guys who were just in the back of your car thirty-five million dollars to do two movies?"

He said, "No, sir, I wouldn't."

I said, "Thank you, Brian." I went upstairs, called Dick, and said, "Even Brian wouldn't give us the money. We're in a lot of trouble."

So now we're casting in New York. Dick had seen Chris Reeve. He had a small part in a play with Katharine Hepburn called *A Matter of Gravity*. We couldn't find anybody to play Superman. We found either wonderful actors who didn't look remotely like Superman, or really great-looking guys who just couldn't act. We got so desperate at one point that Skye Aubrey, who was married to Ilya Salkind at the time, said, "You know who could do this and who is so handsome and great? My dentist in Beverly Hills." To make a long story short, we flew the dentist over to London. We had him work with Jeff Corey, a well-known acting coach, for a week, and we tested him. And you know what? He wasn't bad. He wasn't very good, but he wasn't bad. Dick and I were watching the screen test the next morning in the screening room at Pinewood, and I said, "You know, the guy's not all that bad."

Dick said, "You want to put thirty-five million bucks behind this dentist?"

I said, "No."

And he said, "Okay."

We tested some of the most beautiful women for Lois Lane: Anne Archer, Deborah Raffin. We approached Jessica Lange, but she didn't test. Candy Bergen came to London to meet with us. She wasn't going to test either. Susie Blakely, who was a big TV star, tested. Lesley Ann Warren tested. Anne Archer and Deborah Raffin were so beautiful. Of those two tests, Dick said, "As the mother of my children, yes. As Lois Lane, no."

It got down to a tie between Margot Kidder and Stockard Channing. They had a sense of comedy about them. I had written the scene where Superman lands on Lois's balcony. They sit down and she interviews him. That was one of the test scenes. In the Benton and Newman version, it was about two pages long, and I turned it into eight pages. It really became a scene of courtship. It was a wonderful test scene to have, and it was in the picture. Both Margot and Stockard just nailed that part so well. The reason we hired Margot was that she paired better with Chris Reeve when we found him. He was so young looking, and there was a kind of goofy quality to Margot, whereas Stockard looked like she could have had Chris for lunch. The ideal Lois Lane would have been a young Natalie Wood. She would have been great, but she was too old at the time for Chris.

We had now tested the dentist, and Jon Voight was in the wings if we couldn't find anybody. He was willing to play Superman for another $2 million. But Dick and I were determined, very much like Cubby with Bond saying, "I don't want to have a Mel Gibson movie, I want to have a James Bond movie." Dick and I agreed with him 100 percent. Superman was going to be Superman. It wasn't going to be Burt Reynolds in the Superman suit. He was going to come on the screen as Superman. We had Brando, we had Hackman. So there would be enough for a big marquis. Chris Reeve was, I don't know, seventeenth on the list. It had been a while since Dick had seen him. He said, "Today's your lucky day. You're coming over to test for Superman."

Chris said, "Oh, jeez guys, I'd love to, but I'm in an off-Broadway play."

Dick said, "Get your understudy to go on."

And Chris said, "I don't have an understudy." It was a ninety-nine-seat house. In the late seventies, it was three dollars a ticket. So we bought the house for two nights to fly him to London.

There was just something wonderful about Chris. He put on the Superman suit, and he was so nervous. He was sweating, and the sweat came through his Superman suit, his armpits, and Dick said to Yvonne Blake, the costume designer, "We'll have to take care of that. If he shoots on a hot day . . ."

Chris hopped off onto the balcony and said, "Good evening, Miss Lane." The minute he said, "Good evening, Miss Lane," Geoffrey Unsworth, the cinematographer, turned and looked at me like, is this the man? Then Chris sat down and said, "I suppose you'd like to know a lot about me." There was this wonderfully shy quality about him. He was testing with Holly Palance, Jack Palance's daughter. She lived in London and was a good actress. She helped us out by doing Lois Lane.

At the end of the test, Dick and I looked at each other like, this is the guy. Dick said, "Okay, Chris, just hang in there for a second. Boy, this is really good. Chris, you're staying here for a while."

He said, "I can't do that because I've got an apartment in New York."

Dick said, "We'll bring your apartment here. We'll bring your girlfriend here, we'll buy out the rest of the run of the show. Where's your plane ticket?" He said it was in his jacket, and Dick ripped it up and said, "You're not going anywhere."

We sent the test back to Terry Semel at Warner Brothers and said, "This is the guy we want," and they looked at it and said, "Great, go with him."

For General Zod, the villain, our first choice was Albert Finney. Finney was a star. We could work it out so that he could work for fifty days and not eight months. We met with Finney at Tramps, the big discotheque in London. They had a private room where you could hear the music but you could talk. Finney said he'd love to do it, and we said great. He said, "But here's the thing: I have to be off by five o'clock." He was doing the British equivalent of summer stock in a town like Birmingham. He said, "I told them I would do it. They're doing eight plays, so the curtain goes up at eight o'clock, but to get there, I should leave by five or five thirty."

And Dick said, "I can't do that. I can't guarantee you. If we're going late one night, I can't let you go." So he couldn't do it.

Second choice was Christopher Plummer, who was the leading man at the National Theatre that year. I knew Chris. I got him over to the Connaught to meet with Dick. Chris had the same problem. He would do it but he was in the National Theatre. Dick and I didn't realize that that meant he was in almost every play that year. He was the leading man. Terence Stamp was our third choice. He had played Billy Budd onscreen, then he had gone a little cuckoo and gone to India to seek inner peace, but he'd come back. He was a terrific guy. Anybody's first choice. Valerie Perrine was signed and Ned Beatty, one of the most versatile actors in the world. In *Network*, he plays the head of the corporation. "You are fooling with the forces of nature!" And he could play the little guy who got buggered in *Deliverance*, and he could play a dummy like Otis. He could play anything.

And then, there was the editor of the *Daily Planet*, Perry White.

I knew Jason Robards had just won the Oscar for playing Ben Bradlee, editor of the *Washington Post*, in *All the President's Men*. I said to Dick, "You know who'd be a great idea for Perry White: Jason Robards. He's gruff like Perry White, and it would be a wonderful thing to go from Ben Bradlee to Perry White."

He said, "Great idea."

I called Jason up. I said, "I'm doing *Superman*, and I don't know if you're familiar with the comic strip, but there's a newspaper, the *Daily Planet*, and there's an editor."

Jason said, "You're doing *Superman*, the guy with the cape from the comic book?"

"Yeah."

"Why are you doing that?"

"Well, Jason, it's going to be a terrific picture."

"You're doing the guy with the big *S* on his chest."

"That's right."

"And you're actually doing a film. This is a feature film."

"That's right, Jason. Marlon Brando and Gene Hackman are doing it."

He said, "Well, that's their problem."

I said to Dick, "I don't think Jason is going to do it." There was that attitude, that this could only be a turkey.

After Krypton, the only set that was ready was the Daily Planet. That was a big set. I was in a particularly difficult position because I was trying to write every scene that took place in the Daily Planet in *Superman* and

Superman II even though I wasn't sure about a lot of things in *Superman II.* I had to get those scenes written because once you're in the Daily Planet, you've got to shoot the Daily Planet. Then you strike the set and that's it. You don't rebuild it. We were going to start on Monday in the Daily Planet. And on Wednesday, our Perry White arrived—it was Keenan Wynn, who was a wonderful actor, gruff. Famous as Colonel "Bat" Guano in *Dr. Strangelove* for saying, "You're going to answer to the Coca-Cola company," when Peter Sellers asks him to shoot the Coca-Cola machine. Keenan Wynn arrived in London on Wednesday at Heathrow and promptly had a heart attack at the airport and was taken to the hospital. Thank goodness, he lived. But we were without a Perry White.

Dick was calling people. Jesus, it's going to be Thursday tomorrow. We start shooting Monday. Jackie Cooper was on the list. Dick called him at home. "Hello?"

"It's Dick Donner."

"How are you, Dick?"

"I'm here with Tom Mankiewicz."

"Say hi to him."

Dick said, "How'd you like to play Perry White in *Superman?*"

He asked, "When does that start?"

"Uh, Monday."

"How long am I going to be there?"

"I don't know, four months, six months, eight months. A while. But you're not in everything. You're at the Daily Planet. Probably take a vacation then."

Cooper said, "But Monday. What am I offered?"

Dick said, "Don't worry, we'll work it out. It'll be fair. Oh, very important, Jackie. Do you have a passport? If you don't have a passport, we don't have time, you can't play Perry White."

Jackie said, "Hold on." He went running upstairs and came back and said, "Yeah, I got a passport."

Dick said, "Great, you're Perry White. Get your ass on a plane tonight." That's how Jackie Cooper got it, and he played Perry White in all four Superman movies.

The United States has cameramen, but the Brits have what's called lighting cameramen. So Geoffrey Unsworth, who did *Superman* and *2001,* and won Oscars for *Cabaret* and *Tess,* was a lighting cameraman. Peter MacDonald, his operator, was really the guy that Dick Donner would talk to on the set of *Superman.* He was the guy you would line up the shots with. It was

Geoffrey's responsibility to light the scene. Days would go by where Geoffrey never even looked through the barrel of the camera. Later, Peter MacDonald became the lighting cameraman, then he became a director. So there is that progression in British cinema that does not exist in American film. Geoffrey and Dick were absolutely in love with each other. The picture is dedicated to Geoffrey because he died before it came out. He was a genius. And so was John Barry, who designed it.

Barry came up with this wonderful idea one day. He said, "You know what Krypton is? The whole planet is one giant crystal. So when it's destroyed, it shatters like crystal, and all you see is great chunks of crystal flying all over the place." Of course, this is before CGI.

Yvonne Blake said, "I have these costumes that, when you hit them with light, they glow."

Then, Geoffrey came up with this idea that *Superman* is three movies. It's shot in three styles. It's written in three styles. On Krypton, everything is shot through a fog filter. It's white. It's cold. And they speak in almost mock Shakespearean English. Then, when they get to Smallville, where he's growing up, everything is shot in pastels like Norman Rockwell. The dialogue is, "Hey, ma and pa," and "gosh." Then, when you get to Metropolis, bang, there are the red reds and the green greens, and it's Lex Luthor, and the lines are flying. It was always designed that way. Jack Kroll picked it up very easily when he put us on the cover of *Newsweek*.

There was such a collegial spirit. Dick and I got along with everybody, and Dick was the leader. This picture is a tribute to him. It was a high-class version of the old Mickey Rooney–Judy Garland films—"I've got costumes, my folks have the props, we'll put it on in the barn!" We were doing stuff for the first time, and everybody knew we were under the gun because nobody knew how much money the Salkinds had. Wally Veevers was head of special effects, and Derek Meddings did all the miniatures. You look at that film today, and what they did without CGI was so incredible for 1977.

Dick said to me, "You've got to write like it's real, like it's really happening. I don't want the audience to be once-removed from watching it. I want them to be in it." That notion comprised a lot of what I did. The basic plot, which was a wonderful idea, of Luthor stealing missiles to break off California because he liked the coastline property, stayed. There were a lot of things that I kept. Benton and Newman are wonderful writers. (I never saw a Puzo script.) And, by the way, because Benton was a good friend of mine, I didn't go on the picture without calling him. I asked, "Bob, do you mind if I go on *Superman*?" And, he said, "Not at all. I have no emotional attachment to it." That was clear from the script, which was very outwardly funny and smart, but you were never inside it. I'm not talking about the big bones of the story, like Krypton, but I probably wrote 65 percent of what you see on the screen. The basic story was theirs. But we had ideas like getting Noel Neill, who played Lois Lane in the television series, for an appearance, and, as a kid growing up, Clark jumping over a train. Inside the train is Noel Neill, and her little daughter says, "Mommy, I just saw a boy jump the train." And she says, "Oh, Lois Lane, you and your . . ." So we got this idea that Lois had seen him by accident when she was very young. Rex Reed, who was a very famous critic at the time for the *New York Daily News,* runs into Clark going into the *Daily Planet.* "Hello, Clark." "Hi, Rex."

We got such a wonderful reception in New York. When we were doing the location scouting, the Daily News building was just perfect for us because they had a huge globe in their lobby like the Daily Planet. So we asked if we could make it the Daily Planet. The Daily News was just thrilled that we were there. They had a lively group of writers like Jimmy Breslin. We were shooting in front of the Daily News at night. It was the scene where Superman rescues Lois hanging from a helicopter. When Dick and I were at the Daily News the first time, we saw a phone booth, but it was the half phone booth that you have in New York, with a little cradle. I said, "Donner, take a look." We both started laughing. Superman and the phone booth was a big thing. Of course, the first thing that happens when Clark sees Lois hanging from the helicopter is he starts to unbutton his shirt as he runs to a phone booth, which is a half phone booth so he has to go change somewhere else. So it was adding that kind of stuff.

Anyway, we were shooting in front of the Daily News. We had our generators and all the lights on the building. Quite a crowd and a lot of cops. Geoffrey Unsworth needed more light, more power than the generator could produce. One of the cops heard it and said, "Tell you what, Mr. Unsworth. You unscrew the plate on the street light, and you can plug right in there. Nobody knows, but you can do that." As he plugged in the plug, the lights went out in New York. It was the blackout. We had nothing to do with it, but Geoffrey was convinced for months that he had caused the New York blackout. The cops commandeered our generators because they could provide light. All the police radios were going. One of the detectives who was with us and some uniformed cops went up to Harlem because there were stores being bashed in.

Margot Kidder and I were going together at the time. Keeping company. A minibus took us back to Fifty-Ninth and Fifth because a lot of people were at the Plaza. Margot and I were living in Lorne Michaels's apartment at the Mayflower on Central Park West. We were standing in front of the Plaza surrounded by hansom cabs, the horse-drawn carriages. I asked, "Could you take us to the Mayflower?"

The guy said, "Tonight, we can go anywhere."

There were no lights. We picked up people who asked, "Could you take us down two blocks?" We took people to their apartments. It was a magical night in New York. Obviously, it was a dreadful night for some people. The guy took us the long way around. We went up Broadway over to Central Park West. He was thrilled because he could never do that.

Margot had a little girl, Maggie, who was two at the time. We were sort of a traveling act, Margot, Maggie, and me. Once, we were shooting in Canada, and somebody from the press said, "I want to interview Mankiewicz. Where is he?"

Dick famously said, "Find the motor home with the baby food on the bumper."

Maggie was going to spend a week with her father, writer Tom McGuane, as part of the divorce visitation agreement. The night before she left, Maggie was upset and crying, and Margot went into the next room where her crib was. I heard her talking to Maggie, and she said, "You are a very lucky little girl because you have so many people who love you. Mommy loves you, Daddy loves you, Tom Mank loves you." Maggie was calming down, and Margot said, "All right. Who does Daddy love?"

Maggie said, "Maggie."

"And who does Mommy love?"

Maggie said, "Tom Mank."

One of the most important elements in the picture was obviously trying to make Superman fly. Nobody had ever flown onscreen well. In the old *Superman* television show, they just hung him and let the scenery go by. So it was a real challenge to all of the technical crew. We tried everything in the beginning: a little animation, tilting the sets, a catapult to throw him up in the air. Early on, we were shooting in New York, and we had Chris hung from a crane. There was a sequence about Superman's first night in Metropolis, where he arrests crooks. One of the things he does is to take a cat out of a tree. We were swinging Chris into the tree, and he was getting scratched, and the fake cat kept falling off the branch. New Yorkers are just so great. They were leaning out of windows yelling, "You can get that cat, Superman!" We finally gave up and shot him taking the cat out of the tree on the back lot of Pinewood in England. By then, we knew how to make him zoop up. In New York, when he was hanging from the crane, there was a helicopter traffic guy who said on the air, "Ladies and gentlemen, I'm not drunk, but there's a guy with a big red cape flying up in the air down below us, and he's got a big *S* on his chest." It was still new that we were doing *Superman*.

Dick loved to play practical jokes. Months earlier, when we were location scouting for *Superman* in New York in Times Square, I was wearing those boots you wore in the seventies, those little short boots that were part of that bullshit fashion. My feet were killing me. We took a break, and we were going to have lunch somewhere with Geoffrey Unsworth. There was a Florsheim shoe store nearby. I said to Dick, "You guys go on. I'll join you in a minute. I've got to get out of these shoes."

Dick said, "You can't get shoes at Florsheim's."

I said, "Yes, of course I can, Dick."

Dick, being a New Yorker, said, "That's really low class, Florsheim."

So I got my Florsheim loafers and I was very comfortable. I walked into the restaurant and sat down. The waiter came over and asked, "Would you like a drink, sir?"

I said, "Yes, I'll have a Bloody Mary."

The waiter looked down and said, "Excuse me, but are those Florsheim shoes?" Dick had put him up to it.

Everywhere we went in New York, Dick called ahead. At the Empire State Building, the elevator operator said, "All the way to the top for you guys, right, Superman?" We said yes. He said, "Hey, those are Florsheims aren't they?" Couldn't believe it. Everywhere we went. Dick would break up because he loves that kind of stuff.

So when Marlon was shooting the long speech where he and Susannah York put the baby in the capsule, halfway through the first take, Marlon said, "I'm sorry. I can't say this crap."

All the blood drained out of my face because we had talked about it and rehearsed it. I walked out to him and asked, "Marlon, is there some adjustment I can make?"

He said, "Yeah, you could adjust just about every—" and he looked down and asked, "Are those Florsheims?" Dick collapsed, and Marlon collapsed, and they had done it all for the gag. They were two incredible practical jokers.

Brando's Valentine

The capsule speech was very long, and Brando wanted everything on cue cards, because at that stage in his career, he was reading most of the time. I said to him, "How about that speech in *Last Tango in Paris* where you're standing over your dead wife's coffin; that long speech?" He said it was all written on the bottom of the coffin. I said, "How about in *Apocalypse Now?*"

He said, "The ear you can't see has got a little speaker in it, and I pre-recorded it."

I'm getting really disillusioned. So we played a joke on him and mixed up the cue cards. And he gave the speech beautifully. I said, "You fraud. You son of a bitch, you have memorized it."

He said, "What?" He looked around and he started to laugh.

Before Brando started to shoot, I asked a very simple question of Dick: "Why is there an *S* on Superman's chest?"

Dick said, "Well, he's Superman."

I said, "Yeah, I know he's Superman, but he came from Krypton with that *S*. So he's not Superman on Krypton, because everybody's got the same powers on Krypton."

Dick said, "Holy shit. You're right."

I said, "Look, maybe we don't even have to deal with it."

He said, "No, you brought it up, we should deal with it."

So on Krypton, everybody in the Council of Elders has a badge on his or her chest, an inverted triangle, with a different letter. Jor-El's is an *S*. Maria Schell has a *D*. That's a family crest. Everybody has a crest with a different letter, and *S* happens to be their crest. We explained it to Marlon. Dick said, "Also, Marlon, Superman has a spit curl. So, you're going to have a spit curl too. That's another family thing."

Marlon said, "No, I'm not. I draw the line there. No spit curl."

The very first day of shooting, Dick walked into makeup and he said to the hairdresser, "Do the spit curl. If he objects to it, we'll live with that and we don't use it. But I'll betcha it'll be okay."

She just went ahead, and she was doing his hair. She shaped the spit curl. He looked at it and said, "Oh, what the fuck."

Marlon was such a fascinating man, and probably the best actor. He and I were reading the capsule speech together. This is a couple of days before he shot it. There are lines in there that say, "They're a good people, Kal-El. They wish to be. They only lack the light to show the way." This is what he's saying to the baby before putting him in the capsule. Marlon said, "They only lack the light to show the way. Hey, that's iambic pentameter. It's the structure that Shakespeare wrote in. If music be the food of love, play on. Now is the winter of our discontent. Friends, Romans, countrymen, lend me your ears. They only lack the light to show the way." I had written it, and

I didn't realize it was iambic pentameter. I thought, what kind of a mind must he have that, twenty-five years after *Julius Caesar*—he'd never done Shakespeare again and he'd never done it before—he could pick out iambic pentameter. So something was going on in there that was extra special. With Brando aboard, we took Krypton much more seriously. In the original script, Jor El did not have a speech to his son. He just put the kid in the capsule. We wanted to make this a mission.

One day, Brando comes on the set and says to Dick, "I heard *The Omen* is really good. I never saw it."

Dick says, "You never saw it? You should see it. I'm sure there's a print in London; I'll get you a print." So Dick calls Fox in London. They don't have a print in London, but there's one in Paris. Dick arranges to have it put on a plane that day, because Marlon's got to see it. Then, they've got to find a place to show it. They get the Odeon Leicester Square, the biggest movie theater in London. Marlon is a night owl. The last show is over at midnight, and they're going to run *The Omen* at midnight for Marlon Brando.

The next morning, in comes Marlon. "Morning Dick, morning Tom." Doesn't say a word about the movie.

Dick is saying to me privately, "He hated it."

I say, "Dick, he couldn't have hated it. It's a wonderful movie."

Marlon is just not saying anything. Dick goes running into his office at the first break. He gets the home phone number of the manager of Odeon Leicester Square. He says, "Did Mr. Brando see that movie?"

The manager says, "Yes, sir."

He says, "You're sure it was Marlon Brando?"

He says, "Mr. Donner, I know what Marlon Brando looks like. He was there. He was with a Chinese girl" (who he was living with at the time).

And Dick says, "Oh, fuck, he really did see it, and he hated it."

All day long this goes on. The last shot of the day, Dick's on a crane and the Council of Elders is below. Trevor Howard, Maria Schell, Harry Andrews, wonderful group. And Dick says, "Action."

Marlon looks up and says, "How'd you get all those baboons to attack that car?" and just starts to laugh.

And Dick, I'll give him credit, says, "I yelled, 'Action!'"

Marlon said, "It's a great fucking movie." But he held him all day. He just loved it. Give some back to Dick. He was a wonderful guy that way.

On the Council of Elders, originally Paul Newman was going to be chairman, and Joanne Woodward was going to play Mrs. Jor-El. Then Orson

Welles. But the British Actors' Equity got crazed about hiring British actors. They said they've got to be British. I was in a meeting with Dick, and I said, "This is all so fake, because you know we're going to hire Susannah York and Trevor Howard. They're only going to be working a week anyway, and they do five movies a year."

Susannah York was fine. Trevor Howard was so funny. He had played Captain Bligh to Brando's Mr. Christian in *Mutiny on the Bounty*. Trevor really had a drinking problem. He would be in his cups by about nine in the morning. At the opening of *Mutiny on the Bounty*—it was a royal command performance—the limos were pulling up, and here's Trevor Howard, Captain Bligh. They opened the door, and he just fell out onto the street, he was so fucked up. A brilliant actor and a nice man, though.

So one morning, Trevor is drinking pretty good in makeup. We're shooting the Council of Elders line as the chairman says, "Enough. This discussion is terminated." We're rolling, and he says, "Enough. This discussion is determined." Then he says, "That can't be right."

We say, "No, it isn't, Trevor; this discussion is terminated."

"All right, keep rolling, I've got it. Enough! This determination is discussed. No, that's not right."

All of a sudden, Marlon looks at him and says, "The whistle of the whip." And Trevor and Marlon burst into laughter, and they're both on their knees pounding the floor. We don't know what's going on. Apparently, this happened to Trevor a few times on *Mutiny on the Bounty*. He had a line where he said, "Mr. Christian, if the men persist in this rebellion, they shall feel the whistle of the whip." But he couldn't say it.

Marlon had a wonderful sense of humor. We got along with him very well. Marlon was at our feet in that way. In his contract, it said that no press could be on the set when he was working. One day, Jack Kroll of *Newsweek* was in London, and he wanted to come on the set. We asked Marlon if that was okay. He said, "Absolutely."

Jack Kroll walked on and asked, "So, what do you think of the picture, Marlon?"

We just held our breath. Marlon said, "This picture is a fucking valentine, is what this picture is." He was wonderful to us.

When I was a little kid, I may have shaken hands with Marlon when he worked with my dad, but I had no relationship with him before *Superman*. He was wonderful about Dad. He loved him. The only movie that Marlon directed, *One-Eyed Jacks,* was hugely long when he finished it, three hours and twenty minutes. He called Dad. "Will you take a look at it? This is so long, and I need some suggestions." If you remember the film at all, he's a villain and he gets his hand smashed by Karl Malden, and he can't pull a gun. He goes to this Chinese fishing village. There was an hour of him falling in love with a Chinese girl, then she dies and he goes back.

Dad said to him, "Marlon, the Chinese girl, the whole story, you don't need it. Just lift it and you'll have a wonderful picture."

He said, "I can't do that. His whole redemption is with the Chinese girl."

Dad said, "I'm telling you, Marlon. Just lift it."

Marlon said, "I'll think about it."

Then Marlon called Stanley Kubrick and ran the picture with him. Marlon said, "Joe Mankiewicz thinks I should lift the entire Chinese girl, which of course is ridiculous."

And Kubrick said, "Not so ridiculous. I happen to think Joe Mankiewicz is right."

So he lifted it. He never wanted to direct again.

You get a chance, I don't care how fleeting it is, to work with Marlon Brando, and he's playing your dialogue—I don't care whether it's terrible or brilliant—he's saying your words. If you love movies, and you love being in movies, and you love writing, and you love directing, then that's just a big privilege. And the fact that he treats you like a colleague, the way we all got on in that picture.

When Marlon completed shooting, he was the only actor I ever asked for an autograph. I asked him to sign the title page for *Superman II*. It was the only thing I happened to have at the time. It said, "Tom Mankiewicz Draft" on it. He crossed through it and wrote, "Should be Tom Megawatts." Then, something in Spanish, Marlon.

Marlon may have saved my life. The last day that he worked, he wanted to go out to dinner with me and Dick, the three of us. We said great, and off we went. The Salkinds had invited him to dinner, but he hadn't responded or something. They were trying to find out where we were eating. We went to a place on Kings Road. All of a sudden, the Salkinds—Bertha, the old man, and Ilya—and Pierre Spengler walked in. They really were forcing themselves on us. Bertha was drunk, visibly under the influence of something. She got into the booth between me and Marlon. Bertha had been sending me rewrites. I kept saying to Dick, "What do I do with these?" He said, "Just put them in a drawer and keep going." They were not very good, to say the least.

So we were sitting there at the table, and she suddenly said, "Mr. Mankiewicz. I kept sending you rewrites, and I never hear from you. Why is that?"

I said, "Mrs. Salkind, I'm so terribly sorry. I've been so busy."

She said to everyone, "You know how much my husband is paying this man to write?" And she announced my salary to the table. I couldn't believe it. She said, "You ought to get on your hands and knees and thank my husband for hiring you in the first place."

You have to remember, Alexander Salkind is about four foot eleven. I said, "Mrs. Salkind, I'm always on my hands and knees when I'm talking to your husband."

She picked up a steak knife and went right for my heart. I was shocked. One split second. Marlon, quick as a cat, grabbed her and pushed her down in the booth. He said, "Will you behave?" And this little tuft of hair could be seen going up and down, like yes. Marlon let her up, and she went right after me again with the knife. Marlon grabbed her again.

The next morning, I was on the set and Alexander came in and apologized to me. He said, "Mexicans shouldn't drink."

I said, "Look, Alex, I thought about just heading for the airport. Nobody's ever done this. But, can I make you a deal that, while I'm on the picture, I don't see your wife. She can't be on the set when I'm on the set. She tried to fucking kill me twice."

He said, "Absolutely. Absolutely."

Two weeks later, Dick and I are called over to the Salkinds' home for a meeting. We go over, and I think Bertha's going to be there. What the fuck, it's two weeks later. So we go in, and she's not there. The old man and I are talking, and Dick has to take a pee. So he leaves. He's about to go in the bathroom when he hears, "Psst. Psst!" He looks down the hall, and it's Bertha. She's in her bedroom, and she says, "Mr. Donner, come here. Mr. Mankiewicz is a wonderful writer, and I should not have insulted him, and I should not have attacked him."

Dick says, "He knows that. I think it'll be fine."

She says, "You know I'm just trying to help with the rewrites."

And he says, "We know that, Bertha."

She says, "Some people call me the Shakespeare of Mexico," and she closes the door.

Dick came back to the meeting, and I said, "Where have you been?"

He said, "I've been talking to the Shakespeare of Mexico."

I said, "Oh God, Donner, what did we let ourselves in for here?"

We called the picture "Close Encounters of the Salkind." What I went through was nothing compared to what Dick went through, because he was on that picture shooting every day forever.

Marlon was signed for ten days and wound up working for thirty days. He gave us free days because he really liked the picture and he was enjoying himself. At that time, if he wasn't enjoying himself, he would absolutely phone it in and just take the money. He could never be bad. He threw himself into scenes and he was so collegial with the other actors, which was amazing to me. Chris Reeve had only one line with Marlon onscreen. It was when he tells him about the rules: "You're forbidden to interfere with the laws of nature. Your name is Kal-El, and you grew up on the planet Krypton." But at the beginning, he says, "Speak, my son," and Chris says, "Who am I?"

Dick said, "That's really going to be your only line with Marlon, or I could do it as part of Marlon's bit."

Chris said, "No, no, please, I've got to have a line with Marlon Brando." For two days before we shot the scene, you could hear Chris going, "Who am I? Who am I? Who am I?"

So the day came, and Marlon said, "Speak, my son."

Chris said, "Who am I?"

And Marlon said, "Are you going to say it like that?"

We put him up to it. Chris turned the color of a Coke machine, bright red. Marlon was having fun. We got a genuine buzz and genuine enthusiasm off him.

People are absolutely right when they say he phoned a lot of it in. He got to a point in his life where he wanted to live in the South Pacific. He wanted to help the Indians. There's another actor completely unlike Marlon who had the same philosophy, Bill Holden. He did a couple of really good parts like *Network* when he was older, but he said, "There comes a time in your life after you've done it a lot, no matter how much you love it, when it seems to be a pretty silly way to make a living. Pretending to be somebody else." But Bill, for instance, owed the government back taxes. He did a lot of pictures like the one with Paul Newman and Jackie Bisset for Irwin Allen in Hawaii, *When Time Runs Out*. It was about an exploding volcano. Bill was drinking a lot. When he came back, I said, "So, how was that?"

He said, "I have no memory of having made the film."

Marlon always needed money in the sense that he lived expensively and had foundations. If Marlon didn't need the money, on the whole, he'd just as soon live in Tahiti. He had a family there. He loved Dick, though. He could do the *Omen* gag with Dick, pretending not to have seen it, because he liked him, not because he didn't like him. He was waiting to burst with laughter.

When Marlon came in to loop, I asked, "Marlon, you're good at this, right?" Donner was in England. Brando was finished shooting. Dick would say, "Just loop it. You be there. You direct it." I wasn't a director yet, but he would trust me to do that.

Marlon said, "When you loop, it's not whether or not you lose in performance, it's just how much." That was for him because he liked looking at the other actor, and he always locked eyes with you like a German shepherd, even when he was just telling you a story. I would agree with him. I don't think any good actor is ever as good on a looping stage as he is in a scene.

Close Encounters of the Salkind

Dick and I were told, if you're going to work for the Salkinds, get your money in escrow in a Swiss bank before you begin to work, and a certain amount is released to you every week. When we were shooting in Canada—Clark Kent growing up was shot in Canada because we had a British crew and it was easier to work in Canada—the Salkinds announced to the crew they were only going to get half their salary for the time they were there, which was going to be six weeks, judging correctly that they'd rather have half the salary and get the other half when they got back than try to go back to London and be unemployed. They would pay people a check on a Swiss bank. You deposited it in your bank in England, but it had to go back to Switzerland to be cleared before it came back to your bank, so it was always three weeks late. Jack O'Halloran, one of the villains, two weeks into shooting said to Pierre Spengler, "I want my money. I need money to live on. I've got to go paycheck to paycheck. I can't wait a month for the first check to clear."

Pierre said, "Well, that's the way it is."

This was on the stage. Jack put Pierre Spengler up against the wall and said, "I want my money by five o'clock tonight. I want the money for the two weeks' work I've done. And if I don't get it, I know where you live." And that night, he got paid.

Dick and Ilya Salkind were the ones who completely didn't get along. The old man steered clear of Dick. He knew Dick was doing a good job and that Ilya hated him and Dick was a pain in the ass with him. The quality of what Dick was shooting helped them raise more money.

At one point, I was asked to go to Zurich to see the old man. Dick and I were told the Salkinds have to abide by everything in your contract. If you give them an inch, they'll take a mile. We had money released to us from the Swiss bank every week, and in my contract, it said that wherever I went on the picture, I had to have a suite in a hotel. That was not out of grandiosity, but I always wound up writing in the hotel. The maid comes in to clean, I'm trying to write, I could always go to another room, and that was very important to me. So, I go to the Grand Dolder Hotel in Zurich. There's a message for me to meet Alexander Salkind in the bar at five. I get into my room, and it's a single room. It doesn't matter. I'm just there for the night. I'm not writing. The phone rings, and it's Salkind. He says, "Mr. Mankiewicz, you see what your friend, Mr. Donner, has done to us. Here I am calling you in your single room from my single room. See you at five o'clock."

So I take a walk along the lake, and later, as I'm walking up the main staircase of the hotel, I hear Alex's voice yelling. I go down the hall, and there he is in this beautiful suite, talking to investors in French or German or something. I peek in and keep walking.

We met at five o'clock. We sat down for a drink, and I said to him, "Before we even start talking, why did you say, 'Here I am calling you in your single room from my single room'? I've seen your suite. Why did you do that? It's such a tiny little lie; why would I care whether you were in a big suite or a single room? You just lied."

He said, "I can't help it." And that was so honest. That was his hallmark. He was a hondler through and through. A promoter who made a lot of money. At that meeting, he asked, "What if I put you on as a producer? Would this make the production go faster? Would we have more cooperation from Mr. Donner?"

And I said, "Alex, that would sentence me to be on this picture for another year or more than the year I've been on it."

He quickly said, "Besides, every time there was a disagreement with me and Mr. Donner, you would side with Mr. Donner, wouldn't you?"

I said, "Probably, Alex, because let me be very honest with you. He knows how to make a picture, and I'm not sure if you or Ilya know how to."

He said, "All right, let's not talk about it anymore." That was that.

I told Dick later, "If I was the producer, this thing would cost eighty million dollars and I'd let you get away with everything." The final budget for the two pictures—and this is really expensive in the late seventies—was between $30 million and $40 million. But the costs are so different now. For instance, to open with a big picture costs $40 million or $50 million. You keep seeing the trailers on television and the ads in the newspapers, not only in the *New York Times* and the *L.A. Times,* but in the *Cedar Rapids*

Gazette as well, and the one-sheets in every theater. The costs have just spiraled like crazy.

Superman and *Superman II* were shot at the same time. So if we were shooting in Lois's apartment, scenes from both pictures would be shot. Warners was very explicit: make sure the actors know it's two pictures. This wasn't going to be one extremely long *Superman* where the Salkinds were going to pay everybody once like they tried to pull off on *Three Musketeers* and *Four Musketeers*. Warners was looking at the rushes and got increasingly interested. They said, "Wait a minute, instead of a negative pickup, we'd like to have a piece of this." So they kept putting in more and more money. It was becoming a Warner Brothers picture, even though the Salkinds had control like Cubby with the Bonds. But the Salkinds needed their money. Before the first picture came out, they held Warners for some ransom. We were going to open at Christmastime. In November, they refused to release the negative for prints unless Warners bought four territories, including South Africa and Germany, from them. It was clear the Salkinds owed a lot of people a lot of money.

It came time for the score, and John Williams. One of the nicest men in the world, a friend of my close friend Leslie Bricusse's. He came over to London and saw the rough cut of *Superman*, which was almost three hours. We were sitting in the screening room afterward and John asked, "Okay, so, what do you hear when you hear the theme from *Superman*?"

Dick said, "I don't know, that's why you're here."

I said, "I'll tell you what I hear. We're opening around Christmas, and about a month later is the Super Bowl. It's halftime at the Super Bowl, the band comes out of the tunnel, they're playing the theme from *Superman*."

Then John said, "I got you." He wrote such a beautiful score; a beautiful love theme. When we first heard the score, it just sent us through the roof. He helped that movie a great deal. Such a joy to be able to work with talents like that.

We opened in Washington, D.C., for the Congress when Jimmy Carter was president. Lois says to Superman in the scene where he visits her on her terrace, "Why are you here?" And—I had to put it in—he says, "For truth, justice, and the American way." It went down big with Congress. They loved it. Then we had New York and California openings. It went very well. Old man Salkind was not allowed in the country for those openings because there was a warrant out for his arrest for fraud.

The Salkinds fired Dick as soon as the picture opened. There was about 30 percent left to shoot for *Superman II*. I've always said if *Superman* had been a flop, the Salkinds would have made Donner finish *Superman II* as a punishment. But the picture was a big hit, and the Salkinds figured anybody can finish *Superman II* now. They had 70 percent of the movie already in the can. Hackman was wrapped. Ned Beatty was wrapped. Valerie Perrine was wrapped. They'd all done their work. Dick Lester, who'd done the *Three* and *Four Musketeers* for the Salkinds, had a big piece of the profit of those films and never got any money from the Salkinds, so he sued them. He won in court, but he won against a Lichtenstein company that was part of a holding corporation that was broke, and he couldn't get any money. He was pursuing it, and the Salkinds said to him, "If you'll finish *Superman II,* we'll give you the money we owe you." So Lester finished it. Again, terrible casting for it because Lester's a cynic. He was not like Dick Donner.

Lester called Dick and said, "We should split credit on the second movie."

Dick said, "I don't split credit, so you take the credit."

The cast was devastated. Terry Semel, who ran Warners distribution then, met with me and said, "Dick Lester would like you to go on and finish *Superman II* with him."

And I said, "Terry, I can't do that. Dick is my friend and he brought me on, and I'm completely loyal to him."

Terry said, "I understand. Could you go to London and accidentally run into Lester and talk to him about it?"

I said, "No, I couldn't do that either." So they got David and Leslie Newman to come back. Benton was not interested.

I got a phone call from David Newman saying, "My God, we saw the picture yesterday. You made a silk purse out of a sow's ear. My God, you did a great job. Thank you so much. I'm so proud to have my name on it."

I said, "Thank you, David. Really appreciate the phone call, because you guys are terrific." Benton was my friend, actually.

Then that Sunday in the *New York Times* there were interviews with lots of people, including David Newman, who said, "Well, basically it's just our script. They just cut it." And they went on and wrote the screenplay for a little classic called *Sheena, Queen of the Jungle* with Tanya Roberts, and I thought, okay, serves you right!

The Directors Guild said that Lester couldn't get sole credit on the picture unless he shot 40 percent. So they started writing scenes that were not necessary and arbitrarily changing scenes that had been shot. *Superman II* came out and it was fine. There were some phony reviews because Dick

Lester was very much the critics' darling. David Denby, who was a critic for *New York* magazine at the time, wrote, "You can tell the difference between Richard Lester and Richard Donner because in *Superman II,* Gene Hackman has a fine edge, and he's funny." I wrote a letter to *New York* magazine saying, "Just for the record, Gene Hackman did 100 percent of his work with Dick Donner, and it was all written by me." Never printed the letter.

Superman III, which had Richard Pryor in it, was made. Terry Semel came down to my studio bungalow one day. I always knew when they wanted a big favor. If the mountain was coming to Mohammed . . . He asked, "What's wrong with *Superman III*?"

I said, "Terry, there's nothing really wrong with it, but it's a Richard Pryor movie. It's not a Superman movie, and that's not Richard Pryor's fault."

Semel said, "What would it take to get you and Donner back to do the next one? Price is no object." By this time, Warners had invested in *Superman* heavily and could call the shots. Ilya was still listed as producer, though.

I said, "Let me talk to Dick."

We went out and had dinner, and we decided we didn't want to do it anymore. We did the first two. We'd gone to Krypton, Smallville. Kryptonite had destroyed his power. He'd become a human being in *Superman II* and gotten beaten up, then regained it. We thought, there's nothing else to do. At the time, Chris Reeve was dead set on *Superman IV: The Quest for Peace.* He gave the script to me and said, "I need your help." In this one, Superman goes to the United Nations.

I said, "Chris, here are the rules. You can't deal with anything that Superman could take care of. Superman could disarm this whole planet in half an hour. You can't have a tsunami in *Superman,* because with his super breath, he'd blow back the waves. You can't allow tens of thousands of people to be killed. You can't show anybody starving to death in a Superman movie because he could grow crops that would feed the entire planet. You don't get into that because somebody's going to say, 'Well, why doesn't he just fuckin' do it?'" Whereas with *Batman,* which I wrote the first draft of, I said, "Batman, completely different, because he's a human being and he dresses up at night. Batman can do all kinds of things. But Bruce Wayne as Batman is powerless to do anything about nuclear weapons or hunger or the tsunami. But Superman has got super powers, so stay out of that. You can't come to the UN. If I were an ambassador to the UN, I would say, 'Well, why don't you do it, flyboy?'"

The Donner Cut

The reason for *Superman II: The Donner Cut,* which was released on DVD, was there was an arc—I hate to use a pretentious word like that—that ran through the two pictures, which was in the relationship with his father. In the beginning, the father sends him to Earth; it's God sending Christ, Allah sending Mohammed. When Lois is trapped in the earthquake in the first one, she's being crushed to death, and Superman's got to do something about it. Brando appears in the sky and says, "It is forbidden for you to interfere with human history." Superman screams, flies up in the air, and turns the world backward to before there was an earthquake, and Lois is alive. He's disobeying his father. Jor-El would always visit his son in the Fortress of Solitude, the vision of Brando. When Superman decides to become a human being for the love of Lois in the second film and he gets beat up for the first time and realizes what a mistake he's made, that he's betrayed his father, he comes back to the fortress and says, "Father, forgive me." This is not in the *Superman II* that was released. This is a scene that's only in the Donner Cut. When Superman sleeps with Lois in the Fortress of Solitude, Brando appears. Chris says, "Father, I have sinned. I have disobeyed you." Margot is watching, they've slept together, and she's wearing the Superman tunic like a little nightgown. She's scared, peeking around the corner, and Brando's eyes flash at her like, you bitch. It's really dramatic. As Jor-El commits suicide to give his son new life as Superman, he says, "You'll never see me again." He reaches out and touches his son like God touching the hand of Adam in the Sistine Chapel. And Superman becomes Superman again.

The Salkinds knew they had a big hit with *Superman II* coming up, and that Brando got a piece of the gross; a fairly small piece of the gross, but it was going to add up to a lot of money—but not if he didn't appear in *Superman II*. So what did the Salkinds do? They sideswiped it using Susannah York, a perfectly good actress, to do all the scenes, and Brando was completely cut out of the second movie. We just couldn't believe it. The Salkinds started this fiction, which was, "It was too expensive to get him back," which they kept up until the release of *Superman II*. There was no question of getting him back: he'd shot all the scenes; they were already in the can. He'd looped, he'd done everything when he was first there. So you give Marlon 5 percent of the gross. It was Marlon Brando. The Salkinds really fucked with what the pictures were about. I don't want to say this is some great, classic novel that can't be fooled with, but that was the intent of the films. We were really angry at them for cutting him out arbitrarily even though they were going to make a lot of money. They were in the chips. The reason for the Donner Cut was to put Brando back into the movie. That was the way it was intended to be. Those scenes were so effective.

In fact, we put all of Dick's footage back in. Some sequences had been cut to give Lester more footage so he could be eligible to be called "director." There's a sequence at the beginning of *Superman II* that was never in the movie release, but it's in the Donner Cut. Lois is alone with Clark in Perry White's office. Superman's photograph is on the front of the *Daily Planet*. She's looking at Clark and she starts to put glasses and a hat on Superman. It's Clark. They're supposed to go to Niagara Falls for a story on honeymooners. Lois says, "Well, it wouldn't be a problem, would it, Clark? We could just zoom right up and just fly right back." And Clark says, "Oh, Lois, are you getting on to that stupid thing about me being Superman again?" She goes to the window and she opens it. He says, "Lois, we're thirty-five floors up." She says, "Don't worry, Superman, you won't let me die," and she jumps out the window. She flies through the air, and Clark, with his x-ray vision, pops open an awning. Lois hits the awning, bounces up, and lands in the garbage truck. She looks up at Clark Kent leaning out the window saying, "Lois, are you crazy?" And she faints. It was a great way to open *Superman II*.

The actual test scene for Chris and Margot is in the Donner Cut. They're getting ready to go to dinner. Clark's standing behind Lois, and she says, "You are Superman, aren't you?" He says, "Oh, Lois." She turns around and she's got a gun. He says, "Lois?" She goes, *bam;* she fires it at him and nothing happens. Clark sets his jaw and says, "If you'd been wrong, Clark Kent would have been killed." And she says, "How? With a blank?" It was not live ammunition. He looks at her and she says, "Gotcha!" It was a cute scene, and they were so great together.

When *Superman II: The Richard Donner Cut* premiered at the Directors Guild, Brandon Routh, the new Superman, was there with *Superman Returns* director Bryan Singer. Margot came down from Montana, and we went together to the screening with Dick and Lauren Shuler Donner. Onstage, we had a symposium with Jack O'Halloran, Sarah Douglas, Margot and Dick, the remaining people. Ilya Salkind was there. I couldn't believe it. He said to me afterward, "Yeah, it works. It works that way, too."

Everybody worked so hard on those movies, and it really was the arc with Brando all the way through that made the father/son thing, Jor-El and Kal-El. When Brando was putting the baby in the capsule, and he kept saying, "I send this with you and I send this," Susannah York, a perfectly nice person, said, "What does the mother send? The mother sends dick. I'm just standing there."

I said to her, "When you get three million dollars for fifteen days' work, you can send everything." And there was the Salkinds' *Superman II* without fucking Jor-El in it. They just didn't want to pay the money. There would never have been a Donner Cut if Brando had been in *II*. It was Warners' mistake in the first place to go with the Salkinds. The Salkinds wanted to do it, and they were right about that, but Warners should have said, "Look, we own it"—because they owned DC Comics. "It'll be a Warners picture instead of a negative pickup." As Warners became more invested, it gave them an excuse to reissue all four Superman films plus the Donner Cut on DVD.

The *L.A. Times* loved the Donner Cut, but they said the gem is the commentary by Donner and Mankiewicz to *Superman*. They had us do the commentary at Dick's house as they ran the movie on his TV. It was very irreverent. "That's the *Daily Planet* newsroom. See the girl in the second desk? God, she balled everybody, didn't she? Even Hackman, I think, got her." We cut a lot of that out. "Valerie was so drunk in Calgary. She memorably said once, 'I'm going to go out and get me a cowboy,' because it was during the Calgary Stampede."

Superman Forever

In the early nineties, Dick was honored by the Directors' View Film Festival, which had the Joseph L. Mankiewicz Award for Excellence. Robert Benton had won it, Merchant and Ivory had won it, and it was a very eastern award, but they decided to give it to Dick for his lifetime achievement. I did a ten-minute film of Donner, clips from his movies, that is just a corker; it's the best reel you've ever seen, with music scores from his films. We flew with Jerry Moss on his Gulfstream, landing in White Plains, and went to Stamford, Connecticut, where the big celebration was. Chris attended with his wife, Dana. He was in his wheelchair, which really wasn't a wheelchair. Margot flew in. I hadn't seen Chris in years. Even Danny Glover flew in. Mel Gibson sent something from Australia. Lots of people were coming up; Lauren Bacall and people from New York.

Chris and Margot started nattering at each other just like it was back on the set. He was funnier and smarter than when they worked together. It is just a terrible thing to say, but I think that his accident made him so introspective. It sharpened everything in him. He was a better person because, instead of just being that good-looking guy who was going from picture to picture, he had really faced something incredibly dramatic in life. I was sitting across from Chris—the air was being pumped into his lungs all the time—and he said, "Hey, Mank. Look at this." On the table, he moved his finger; one finger. It was like a miracle, and he'd been working hard so he could move a finger. He had an incredible attitude. What happened to him was a freak accident. How many people fall off horses every day and that never happens to them?

I was so moved by all of us getting back together again with everything that had happened to all of us. Margot had had some terrible episodes because she was bipolar and nobody knew it. Chris had had, obviously, a terrible thing happen to him. Dick had been through six more hit movies, but this still was the thing that kept a place in his heart. It was like a class reunion. Chris died the next year, and then, inexplicably, his wife, Dana, died a few years after at forty, lung cancer and had never smoked. I don't know where that came from. She was just wonderful. But he was a terrific guy. I'd never seen that in my life, but I thought he was so much a better person. That night, Chris's eyes danced in a different way, like he had been through hell, but he was dealing with it and was convinced he was going to get out of it.

We were just starting to shoot *Superman,* and Chris was so worried that he was going to be typecast the rest of his life. He kept saying to me, "I've got to talk to Sean Connery. You know Sean Connery, and he's not typecast as Bond." But he was typecast as Bond. I ran into Sean somewhere. "By the way, the kid playing Superman, he wants to talk to you about being type—"

Sean said, "Oh, fuck, I don't want to talk to him about that."

About three weeks later, we were at this big party and Sean was there. So I went over to him. "Listen, the guy's over there. You've got to talk to him."

He said, "Oh! Okay." So he went over and said to Chris, "Well, first of all, if boyo is right in that you're probably in trouble and it's not going to be a hit, don't worry about it. You're going to be able to start fresh. If it is a hit and you are Superman, the next two things you do: number one, find a movie that is completely opposite and do it right away"—which Chris did, a picture called *Somewhere in Time,* which was a love story—"and the second thing, because we're talking about if it's a hit, get yourself the best lawyer in the world and stick it to 'em." That was his advice.

The thing that made Chris work so wonderfully as Superman was his natural shyness, which meant that he could play Clark Kent almost better than Superman. I said to him, "It's really simple when you think about it.

Just make it a mantra. You are Superman. You are playing Clark Kent, but you are Superman. I'm writing it that way, that everything Clark does is Superman playing that." I said to Dick once, and I don't mean this derogatorily to Chris, "You know, you take the *S* off his chest, his balls fall off." Meaning he's a supporting actor. He's not a leading man cut of the jib of real leading men. That's what made him so great as Superman. Here was this shy, disarming guy who was good looking, but he was a supporting actor playing a leading man. I'm sure people think of Chris as a leading man. I don't in that way.

A few years later, he was in a movie called *Monsignor* with Geneviève Bujold. I just wanted to check up on Chris. I went to the noon show in Westwood, and there were maybe twenty people in the whole audience. Geneviève Bujold's in love with him, but she thinks he's a priest so she can't sleep with him. But he's not really a priest. He turns to her and says, "I've been keeping a terrible secret." Some guy three rows down yells, "I can fly." All twenty of us just burst out laughing. The funniest thing I ever heard in a movie theater. It shows you what Chris was worried about. Sean knows that even if Sean is elected prime minister of Scotland and wins five Lifetime Achievement Awards, his obituary will begin with "Best known for James Bond." It just will. And Chris was Superman.

Mank Rules

The Tom Mankiewicz rule in the Writers Guild was created because of *Superman*. I got a separate credit, creative consultant, in the main title, and Dick Donner put it *after* the writers. The Writers Guild went berserk over the placement. Everybody knew I'd rewritten both pictures, *Superman* and *Superman II*. I'd stayed on them for over a year and a half through the casting, the editing, the scoring, the location scouting, and holding Dick's hand and head sometimes, working with the Salkinds. Dick said, "You deserve a separate credit on the picture." He invented the credit "creative consultant," which is now very common. We went to a hearing with lawyers and a judge, and I showed them fourteen roundtrips to London after I'd finished writing, meaning working on the picture. They ruled in my favor because the movie was about to come out. But I had to agree that on *Superman II,* my name would come just before the writers in the main title. It goes today: writer, producer, director. The Writers Guild claims to own the rights to the word "creative" on the screen. I've always said, "Jesus, a lot of great cinematographers and designers and so on might disagree with you that 'creative' only applies to writing." When *Superman II: The Richard Donner Cut* was premiered at the Directors Guild, I was sitting with Margot right behind Dick in the audience, and here it comes, "Written by Bob Benton and Newman and Mrs. Newman," and son of a bitch, I'm after the writers again. Dick stuck me after the writers. I said, "Oh, my God." And I heard from in front of me, "Just shut the fuck up."

It won the Saturn Award for the best DVD of the year from the science fiction, horror, and fantasy people. Bryan Singer was very helpful with the DVD. He was doing *Superman Returns*. He said, "I want to get this picture back to the sensibility of the first Superman film." He would come down and visit us in the editing room. He hadn't started shooting his yet. He said he was doing *X-Men* up in Canada: "In my motor home, I had one picture, *Superman*, and I would watch it every day all day."

Back from Krypton

In my personal life, as I've mentioned, I was always attracted to women who had tremendous psychological problems. As Natalie Wood (one of the greatest friends I ever had in the world, man or woman) said, like a pig with truffles, I just knew how to find them. They were almost always actresses. Not only did I know how to find them, but they find you, too. They know that you're receptive. I would go to a party and see somebody, and I knew right away, and they knew I knew. That would haunt me my whole life. With the exception of a couple of them, we're still friends. The one thing I miss in my life is not having children. I wish I'd had an unhappy marriage and two kids, because I think I would have been a really good father. I wish I had just absorbed the pain. At a certain point, I just gave up. I thought, if the right thing comes along, I'm still prepared to get married at seventy. But I got so exhausted in my life.

I went to Natalie Wood's analyst, who was a very good guy. I was just starting with Kate Jackson, and we were going to go to Mexico together, and then she couldn't and I was really pissed. In the analyst session, I said, "I'm really mad at her."

The analyst said, "Let me get this straight. Three days ago, you didn't know this person. And the first night you're together, you decide to go to Mexico. And now, you're really angry, and this is based on what, the twenty-four hours' knowledge?" It sounded so silly I couldn't believe it. But it could drive me crazy because I had found a different version of Mother again. I knew there was something wrong with Katie. I don't mean wrong like she was going to kill somebody, but there was a lack of balance there, and it was wildly attractive to me.

I'll tell you how loyal Natalie Wood was as a friend. This was the late seventies. There was a New Year's party. Natalie was back with R.J. I told her, "I'm feeling a little philosophical, and I think I'm going to stay in on this New Year's."

She said, "Fine, okay."

About an hour later, Margot Kidder was in town, and I had been with Margot during *Superman*. She said, "Mank, come on down to the beach. We'll have a New Year's thing."

And I said, "Sure, okay." I don't know why, and I went down.

The next morning, New Year's Day, I was still down at the beach with Margot, and Natalie called my house and there was no answer. She called again, and she said to R.J., "I don't like it. Something's wrong. He was depressed."

R.J. said, "Oh, I'm sure he's fine. He's probably out."

She said, "He wouldn't be out. It's New Year's Day." She called again. Then she called my business manager. She said, "I'm worried about him. Can you get into his house?" Then she called the alarm company. I came home about eleven o'clock in the morning and there were police cars in front of my house, and my business manager was in there, and the alarm company had opened the front door. That's how fiercely loyal she was to her friends. I adored her.

Years later, after William Holden died, I was going out with Stefanie Powers, who was in *Hart to Hart*. Robert Benton came down to visit me on the set, and he talked to Stefanie, and I said, "See, I'm cured. There she is."

He said, "No, you're not. But you're getting better."

Hart to Hart: TV Repair

Television has the most repeated concepts in the world. When I was a kid, there was Dr. Ben Casey and Dr. Kildare. The lawyers were *The Defenders.* And it was *Medic,* with Richard Boone. Now it's *Grey's Anatomy, ER, Law and Order.* Law, medicine, and cops are the story lines that keep going. I was at Warners fixing everything. The studio asked, "Could you do a new series with James Garner?" He was thinking about it and hadn't done one since *The Rockford Files.* He was huge. It was going to be called *MVP,* an ex–most valuable player who is now a detective. We had a meeting. Garner said, "You know, I'm in such bad shape, I wear a girdle. You know that scene in every show where somebody slides a note under the door? If I lean down to pick it up, we shut down for six months. We've got to be very careful with me." I liked him a lot. He said, "Is there any way I could just be in ten minutes of every episode?"

I said, "I don't think so; it's the Jim Garner show."

He said, "You know, these wusses today, they shoot twenty-two episodes, twenty-two hours. By the seventeenth hour, their asses are dragging. When I did *Maverick,* we shot thirty-nine. I was in fights in saloons, I was hopping on horses. That's where my back problems started, all those years as Maverick."

MVP never happened.

I'm blessed and cursed by being the fixer, by being Dr. Mankiewicz. Leonard Goldberg and Aaron Spelling were huge, successful television producers. I knew Leonard socially, and we got along well. He called me one day and said, "Listen, I know you want to direct."

I said, "Yes, I do." My favorite cartoon in the world is Bimbo the Talking Dog, sitting on a stool talking to his agent. On the walls, it says, "Bimbo, Box Office Smash in Chicago," "Bimbo Sells Out in New York," "Bimbo Talks!" And he's saying to his agent, "Of course, what I really want to do is direct."

Leonard said, "We've got this old script of Sidney Sheldon's called *Double Twist.* Basically, it's *The Thin Man,* but we haven't been able to sell it. If you can rewrite it so we can sell it, we'll let you direct the two-hour movie."

I said, "Great." So I started rewriting like crazy. Sidney Sheldon's "script" had the couple as car burglars living in a Century City condo with a John Gielgud butler. It was for a small slice of the audience. So I made it *Hart to Hart;* the couple lived in a sprawling ranch house, she was a professional writer, he owned something called Hart Industries, which was anything we said it was. They had a butler/housecleaner, Max, an ex–prize fighter. We made it that you wanted to have dinner with the Harts. I did a wholesale rewrite.

Fred Pierce was the president of ABC; a big, tough guy. I went to see him with Leonard Goldberg after I had rewritten the piece. What bothered Pierce was franchise; you are a detective, you are a doctor, you are a cop, a lawyer. Everybody's got a franchise. We didn't want to make them detectives. My mind was racing like crazy in Pierce's office. I said, "Fred, you know the little dog, Freeway?"

He said, "I love that little dog. That's a wonderful touch, that dog."

I said, "In the morning, here's what happens. Freeway goes out to get the morning paper."

Pierce said, "I'm way ahead of you. They get their cases out of the paper that Freeway brings. There's the case. Now, you're talking."

Everyone said, "Terrific."

Freeway never got the paper; not in the pilot or any other time. Leonard said, "That makes Fred happy. He'll forget. As long as we do a good show, don't worry about it."

Robert Wagner was the biggest male television star; he'd done *It Takes a Thief* and a series with Eddie Albert called *Switch*. He was the small-screen Cary Grant. I knew him quite well. He was in the *Bob Hope Presents the Chrysler Theatre* rewrite I had done in the mid-sixties. I knew him and Natalie separately, and they were back together again. ABC sent him the script, and he said, "This is terrific. Get Mank out here; we're going to talk about it."

I was dispatched to Hawaii, where he was doing a miniseries called *Pearl* with Angie Dickinson. R.J. and Natalie and I went to dinner at a very fancy place, the Outrigger Canoe Club, on Oahu. I said, "ABC would like to make this a long form, about ninety minutes, like *Columbo* or *McCloud*, with the Harts, and they'd love to have you and Natalie do it."

R.J. said, "Let me tell you something. I sell soap. My wife sells tickets. But if you put me on one network and you put her up against me, I'll kill her in the ratings. On the other hand, nobody will walk around the corner and pay ten dollars for a movie anymore that I'm in, and they'll pay for her. Why don't we just do a regular series? Let's get a costar and let Natalie sell tickets. Let her do what she wants."

I think he really wanted to wear the pants in the family. He was going to make a lot of money from this series, and she could work if she wanted to. George Hamilton was hot, and Aaron Spelling said, "You know what? The audience will resent him as Hart for being that rich. But nobody will begrudge R.J. a nickel."

Now we're talking about who should play Mrs. Hart. Suzanne Pleshette was a big contender. Aaron and Leonard wanted Kate Jackson because Katie was a lot of trouble on *Charlie's Angels* and they thought they would move her to another series. R.J. didn't want that. He said, "There is somebody I worked with in two *It Takes a Thief*s. Stefanie Powers. We got along great as actors."

They said, "Absolutely not. She has no TV-Q. *The Girl from U.N.C.L.E.*, a series she was in, faded in one year. She was in a series called *Feather and Father* that flopped after six episodes."

And R.J. said, "I think she'd be great."

Everybody knew she was really good looking and she played comedy well. Spelling and Goldberg forgot—they didn't really forget, they just didn't acknowledge—that R.J. had costar approval in his contract. One night, we were drinking at R.J.'s house, and he called up Tony Thomopoulos, who was overseeing ABC's primetime programming at the time. He asked, "By the way, Tony, how's the thing going with Stefanie?"

Tony said, "What thing with Stefanie?"

R.J. said, "You know, the only actress I approve. We don't have to do the series, Tony."

Stefanie read the script: it's Spelling-Goldberg, who had five series on the air, and Robert Wagner. Stefanie's agent asked for $20,000 a week. Spelling-Goldberg said, "It's impossible because the girls, *Charlie's Angels*, are getting $20,000, and they've been on the cover of *Time* magazine. This girl has no TV-Q. We're going to have to bump the Angels up."

Aaron said to me, "Tommy, go see Stefanie." I knew Stefanie from the sixties, we would go out. I hadn't seen her in seven or eight years. He said, "Go see her and get her all excited and then we'll come back and offer her twelve-five."

I said, "Aaron, I can't do that. You can't ask me to get her excited to get her price down."

So he called her up and said, "I guess you must be a little nervous about Mankiewicz, first-time directing?"

She said, "No, I think it's high time. I think he should have directed a long time ago."

He said, "Well, you've got questions about the script. You and Tommy will have to sit down, probably."

She said, "No, I don't have any questions. I think it's a great script. Really happy that he's directing. Couldn't be happier that it's R.J. I guess it's just about the money, isn't it, Aaron?" They finally made a deal where she got $15,000, but she got a pay-or-play *Movie of the Week* for $250,000 that would make up the difference. They knew she wasn't going to do the movie because she was going to be unavailable. It was supposed to start in February, but we would still be shooting in February.

When I was casting the *Hart to Hart* pilot, Marcy Carsey, who later joined Tom Werner to produce *The Cosby Show*, was a fairly high-level executive at ABC, and she was very, very concerned. She said to Leonard, "Mankiewicz is casting women who are too old." This was the time of *Charlie's Angels*. As Mrs. Hart, Stefanie was thirty-four, thirty-five, and in the pilot were Jill St. John, in her late thirties, Stella Stevens, in her late thirties, Natalie Wood, in a cameo, in her late thirties.

Aaron said, "Don't worry about this. I'll take care of it."

We were shooting in Palm Springs. I told the women, "Marcy Carsey doesn't think you're young enough." They said, "Ah, fuck." I was walking by the pool at La Quinta, and there, sunning themselves, were Jill St. John and Stella Stevens and Stefanie Powers, looking like a fucking million dollars. Jill yelled, "Hey, Mank! Don't us old chicks look great?!"

R.J. wanted Sugar Ray Robinson to play Max. He knew Sugar Ray, who was so loved in this country and, pound for pound, the greatest fighter. ABC said, "No. We're worried about this. Even though he's their friend, he's also the driver, he also cleans up, and it's Sugar Ray, who's also black." I had written the pilot, and the tag was them on safari in Africa. It was at night, there were lions roaring in the distance, and suddenly, jungle drums were heard. They're around the campfire, and the last line of the original pilot script was R.J. saying, "What do the drums say, Max?" And Sugar Ray says, "I can't tell until I hear the piano." That wasn't going to work. ABC decided they were taking too big a risk because the Harts are very rich, and what does that look like? R.J. was going to lose that one.

We didn't know who was going to play Max. One day I was having lunch in the commissary about three weeks away from shooting. You could smoke in commissaries in those days. Standing in line for a table was Lionel Stander with a silly hat on and a big cigar sticking out of his mouth. I said to whoever I was with, "That's Lionel Stander. He was in *The Cassandra Crossing*. He looks like Max."

The person I was with said, "That might not be a bad idea."

I walked up to him in line and said, "Mr. Stander, my name is Tom Mankiewicz."

He said, "Oh, I've heard of you."

I said, "I'm doing a series, kind of like *The Thin Man,* with Robert Wagner and Stefanie Powers. There's the part of Max, the butler, who's also their friend and driver."

He said, "Here's the thing. I'd like to do the least amount of work for the most amount of money."

I said, "I think this part is right up your alley, Lionel." So I called Leonard and said, "I'm sending Max over."

Lionel went over to the Spelling-Goldberg bungalow, opened the door, looked at Leonard, and said, "Hi." Leonard called me back and said, "That's it."

Lionel had been blacklisted in the fifties. The part was really a godsend to him because he made a lot of money and he had a stable family and a home for the first time. He would always say to me, "You know, I was a pretty distinguished actor in the thirties. I was in the Group Theater. I did Shakespeare and Chekhov. And now people say, 'There's Robert Wagner, there's Stefanie Powers, and there's Max.' It'll be on my fucking tombstone: 'Here lies Max.'" But he loved it. He had most of his scenes with Freeway.

Casting the dog was interesting. I wanted a mixed breed, and I worked with a great animal trainer, Bob Blair. I saw a lot of dogs, and most of them looked too purebred. One day, in walked Charlie, a mixture of five or six breeds; adorable. Bob said, "We just got him from the pound. He's smart as hell but, so far, all he can do is sneeze on cue. He's a little green."

I said, "No, no. That's the dog." The very first thing in the pilot, he had to be on the couch next to R.J. Charlie kept hopping off the couch before the scene was over. After a couple of takes, I said, "Jesus, what are we going to do?" We taped him on the couch with double-faced tape! If you've ever seen the pilot, the last thirty seconds, he's just straining to get off the couch.

Lionel and Charlie didn't get along. Charlie liked R.J. and Stefanie most. Stefanie was magical with animals. At home she had a German shepherd, a really tough male cat, a bush baby, which is a little monkey, and a parrot. And they lived in a beautiful ecological balance. There was a scene in the Harts' Gulfstream where Charlie was supposed to stay seated but kept hopping off. Stefanie finally picked him up by the scruff of his neck, put him in the seat, and said, "You stay there now. Stay." And his eyes went wide. In the scene, he was right there. It was perfect. I would say, "God, I wish the actors were like Charlie." When Lionel and Charlie did something right together, Charlie would get a treat and Lionel would get a Camel cigarette. That was his treat.

What I Really Want to Do . . .

I told Dick Donner, "I'm going to direct," and Donner said, "Why? If you're good at it, I'm going to lose my best writer."

I said, "Give me some tips. What am I looking at here?" I had worked on crews, I'd produced movies.

He said, "Don't overprepare, you'll lose your spontaneity. Know the direction you're shooting in. Rehearse the scene, but leave yourself open for all kinds of things that are going to occur, because you're also going to be rewriting while the scene's going on because you're a writer. Don't have a shot list. You know enough about movies, for God's sake. You've worked on them in every area. That's number one. Number two, don't worry about going over a little. Don't worry about making a schedule. If you're on time and on budget and the show's no good, all they'll remember is the show wasn't any good. If you're a little over budget and a little over time and the show's wonderful, all they'll remember is the show was wonderful. And remember, it's very difficult to fire a director once you start shooting; very difficult. It happens very seldom." And the last thing Donner said, "Don't admit you're wrong to the crew. They'll turn on you like a bunch of Dobermans. Just say, 'No, I was right, but we can do it another way.'"

When you're on a feature and shooting two and a half pages, you don't need as much spontaneity as you do when you're flying by the seat of your pants on a television episode shooting eight pages a day. I know orderly writers, good writers, who literally do their screenplays in advance, scene by scene on three-by-five cards, and they move them around. I'm much more spontaneous. I know two or three key points in the screenplay that I'm going to do: she finds out that that's not her mother, and later on, she almost drowns. I've never written a treatment in my life. I tend to start writing. Dick knew that because I've never written a treatment for him. He said, "You're spontaneous and that's your strength, so do that. The best directors are spontaneous directors. Suddenly, an actor has an idea and it's a good idea. If you're all locked up and you've got your shot list, you don't know what to do with that good idea."

I couldn't have had a more welcoming and easier time of starting to direct with people who were total pros. We started shooting, and the very first day, I was so psyched up, so overprepared, I thought, boy, this is going to be a tough day. But I was through with R.J. at three o'clock in the afternoon, and there was another little scene I could shoot. I turned to him and said, "That's all, R.J., you're through. I'm going to go around the corner and shoot this other scene."

He said, "Old fellow"—we always called each other "old fellow"; I don't know where it started—"can I give you some directorial advice?"

I said, "Sure, please."

He said, "Never look an actor in the eye and say, 'You're through.' Say, 'That's all for today, R.J. See you back in the morning, R.J.' But never say, 'You're through.' It sends a chill right through you."

I'm a big fan of five- and six-page scenes between people, like Superman landing on Lois's balcony. There's a long scene in bed with R.J. and Stefanie early on in the piece. She sneaks in his window with a gun; you think she's going to kill him. She gets into bed and they have this long scene. Now, because of the way the sets had to be built and how we had to schedule the shoot, this was the third day, and Stefanie got into bed with R.J. Normally, you wouldn't want to shoot a scene like that until they'd been working together for a couple of weeks. Bob Collins was the cameraman. He finished *Superman* and *Superman II* after Geoffrey Unsworth died. Collins was in his twenties; very, very good. I asked him, "Can't you shoot two overs at the same time?"

He said, "No, you can't do it, because if you light her, you can't light him."

I said to Bob, "There's got to be a way to light both of them."

He said, "No, there isn't. Not inside. Outside we could try for it. But if you're going to light her, and she's beautiful, and you're going to be shooting over him, if you want me to light him over her, it's going to look like hell. I know what you want, but you can't do it. If they're lying on the grass in the sunlight, we'd put silks on both sides and we could try that. But not in here."

I said, "Let's try."

He said, "I'll do my best."

I looked at the rushes the next morning, and he was absolutely right. It looked like hell. A lot of this stuff I knew in my gut from all the movies I'd worked on and all the movie sets I'd been on, but it was great to have a bullshit detector like Bob Collins. I was thirty-six and he was in his late twenties.

Everybody was rooting for me, which was a great thing. R.J. was so helpful. We were friends. Stefanie was great, and they were both pros. When a crew sees that you're getting along with the actors wonderfully and they can feel that they're getting good stuff, they go right with you. If you are good to the crew and you take a special interest in them personally—when you're waiting around for five minutes you strike up a conversation not with your leading lady but with the grip, and you find out about him—there comes that time when you have to do six setups and you've only got forty-two minutes of light left, and they'll drive off a cliff for you; they will work so hard for you. Years later, when I was rewriting *Legal Eagles* in New York, I walked on the set with Ivan Reitman, the director, and not one crewmember said hello, not because they disliked him, he just had no interest in the crew. If I walked through a stage door where I was directing, I would have said hello, by name, to fifteen people and laughed with them about something by the time I got to the camera. I wasn't sucking up to the crew—it's just instinctively you're interested. It's because I started as a third assistant director in Moab, Utah, and I know what it's like.

One day Leonard Goldberg came on the set and asked me, "How's it going?"

I said, "Leonard, God help me, they're married." Stefanie on idle is like somebody else at top speed. She has fifty things to do. She's got an engine in her. R.J. can sit around and watch stew simmering in a Crock-Pot for an hour. But onscreen, they were just terrific. Everybody knew R.J. was married to Natalie Wood and Stefanie was going out with Bill Holden, but when we would go out on location, everybody thought they were married. They would just accept them as the Harts.

The tag of the *Hart to Hart* pilot was a poker game with seven jets in a private hangar. I wanted camels to show that it was an Arab country. There was an animal farm eighty miles away that had camels. I was getting ready to shoot one morning and I asked, "Where are the camels?" The camels were on a truck that broke down in Banning. I was waiting for the camels because I'd got to pan past them for a shot. I was supposed to start shooting at eight, and it was now nine o'clock.

Leonard Goldberg called and asked my assistant, John Ziffren, "So how much do we have in the can?"

John said, "Well, we don't have anything. We're waiting for the camels."

Leonard said, "What do you mean we're waiting for the camels?"

"Well, the camel truck broke down in Banning, but they're repairing it, and Mank wants to wait till the camels get here."

Leonard said, "You tell Mankiewicz that if he's not shooting within five minutes, I'm going to come down there and fire him personally."

I said, "You tell Leonard, 'Shooting now, boss. We're shooting.'" We had no camels. Stefanie comes out of the plane, she hears a camel sound and looks off. We cut to stock footage of some camels against a wall, playing the score from *Lawrence of Arabia* behind it. And it works fine.

My camera operator was Michael Chevalier, a big guy. You trust the operator so much because he's looking through the barrel of the camera and you're not. It was the last shot of the pilot. R.J. and Stefanie looked like a million dollars, he was in a dinner jacket, she was in an evening gown, and their two faces were pressed together because they were about to kiss. People from ABC, Aaron, and Leonard were waiting for the final shot with champagne and a big cake. The last shot was a slow push-in on the two of them until they filled the screen; just their mouths and their eyes. Son of a gun, the first take, they were just great. I said, "Cut it. Print it. That's a wrap." Everybody cheered.

Michael Chevalier came up to me and he said, "I don't think you're going to like it, boss."

I said, "Why?"

"When you get in that close, she's too heavily made up on the side of the eyes and you see the makeup. It's too much, and I don't think you're going to like it."

I said, "Thank you." I announced to everyone, "Ladies and gentlemen, sorry, we have to do it again. We had a flutter in the camera and we're not sure about the flutter."

Michael said, "Stay farther back. Don't go in so tight on her, and tell the makeup lady to refresh her makeup and use a little less."

So I told her that and I said, "But don't tell Stefanie."

We stayed a little farther back, and the second take was almost as good as the first, and that's the one that's in the pilot. The next day I looked at rushes, and Michael was absolutely right. You depend on your operator to do that. And a great operator does that. I've had operators say, "I think I got it. Yeah, I got it." And they didn't get it. It was the last shot of the movie, and it was going to look awful, and it would have cost a fortune to get everybody back. Peter Yates, on every picture, would write down a wardrobe lady's or an assistant prop man's name who did something wonderful. When he started a picture, he would say, "Are any of these people available? Because I want them." The Scorseses and Spielbergs of the world tend to work with the same directors of cinematography, the same editors. Every picture Marty does is edited by Thelma Schoonmaker. If she weren't available, I think he'd postpone the start of the movie to wait for her, because it's really important. By the way, there were a couple of camels present at the *Hart to Hart* wrap party.

When I was directing *Hart to Hart,* I had an office at Fox called a star dressing room that in the old days was for the big stars. It had your own private bathroom, a little outer office, a little inner office. You were out on the lot, you weren't in some office building. My dressing room connected with John Williams's dressing room. He had just done *Star Wars* for Fox. We knew each other. John had a big piano in his room. Mark Snow had written the theme for *Hart to Hart,* and he wanted to play it for me. I asked John, "When you go to lunch, can this young guy and I come in to your office? He wants to play me the theme. He's going to play it on the piano."

John said, "Absolutely, sure."

So he went to lunch, and Mark and I went in. He played me the theme, and it was terrific. On top of the piano was music for *Dracula* that John had been writing. I left John a note on top of the piano saying, "John, thanks so much. I think we found everything we need. Tom." About two hours later, John popped his head in the doorway and said, "That was a joke, wasn't it?"

The greatest joy of my life is that I had a chance to work with so many people like that; you feel like there's an elite club, whether it's a stuntman like Terry Leonard or a cinematographer like Geoffrey Unsworth or Vittorio Storaro or a composer like John Williams. These are the best of the best, and you're so fortunate to be able to work with them.

Executive Decision

They ran the pilot in New York. Leonard Goldenson, who owned ABC, was a very old man at the time, and apparently ours was the last pilot he viewed. He was sitting in the screening room. He asked, "Can I go home now?"

Brandon Stoddard, the head of production, said, "No, it's two more hours, Mr. Goldenson. It's called *Hart to Hart*."

"Oh, God." So he fell asleep during the pilot, Brandon told me later. At the end of it, the lights came up, Goldenson awoke and said, "It's *The Thin Man*. I like it."

The landscape of television in those days was all network. There was almost no cable at all in 1979. We were an instant hit, and we once got a 45 on a skiing show in Vail I directed. That meant almost half of the sets in the country were watching you. You couldn't do that today. Today, a hit share is maybe 18, because you're competing with everything on cable. ABC had a pilot with Lou Gossett Jr., whom I'd done *The Deep* with, called *The Lazarus Syndrome*. He played a doctor in those days, no black character had ever carried an hour. Brandon said, "I don't think this is going to get good ratings. It's a wonderful show, but I've got to put it on at ten o'clock Tuesday; that's our strongest night. I've got to be fair to the show." One of the executives with real class. For the first two weeks, we ran on Saturday night, and son of a bitch, they pulled the plug on *The Lazarus Syndrome*; got no ratings. So we moved to Tuesday night, where we stayed for five years. We beat some really good shows like *St. Elsewhere* that were, in their own way, at least as good as we were. But if you went up against *Hart to Hart* at ten o'clock on Tuesday night, you didn't win. That night belonged to ABC because they had *Happy Days, Laverne and Shirley, Taxi,* and *Hart to Hart*.

A series is a home, and it has a different balance than a movie. It was my script, and they were kind of my characters, and I directed the two-hour pilot. Directors in television are visiting firemen, whereas in a movie, they control the picture, or they should. What's all-important in television are the writing, the writer-producers, and the stars. Once you have a hit with R.J. and Stefanie, it is virtually impossible to replace them, because the audience knows who they like and if you suddenly said, "Starting next season, Suzanne Pleshette is Mrs. Hart," they'd go, "No, she isn't." They won the People's Choice Awards. Stefanie was unused to stardom and real recognition. She had been doing guest parts in television. Early on, we were out on location and fans would come. R.J. signed for anybody; he would always take time for people. A couple of fans asked, "Mr. Wagner, can you help us out? Ms. Powers won't come out and sign autographs."

R.J. said, "Oh, she won't, huh?" He went over to her motor home and knocked on the door. "Stefanie, it's R.J. Come on out and meet the people who pay your salary."

As an actor, Stefanie was a total pro, except for one night when she had to go someplace and we were shooting late. She had a little scene with Max at the kitchen sink, and she did it. I said, "Cut it. We'll do one more."

She said, "Why? That was great." She wanted to go.

I said, "I just want to do one more."

"You mean you have absolutely no direction to give me whatsoever. There was nothing wrong with the last take, you just want to do one more."

"That's right."

She said, "All right, let's do it."

She was about three times as good in the second take. And I said, "Cut it. Print 'em both. Stefanie, which one do you think I should use?"

She said, "The last one."

I said, "Thank you."

She called me later that night to apologize. She said, "I am so sorry. Thank you for making me stay."

Midnight Mank

I learned a lot. I started directing episodes of *Hart to Hart* like peanuts, and I had a wonderful cachet on the show since I had rewritten it and, in essence, put it on the air. I had a credit called "creative consultant" that was on all 110 episodes. I directed fourteen of them in the first couple of years. I was called "Midnight Mank" because I would keep people very late. On the wall of the stage, there was the schedule of directors, and somebody from the crew had written alongside each guy—Earl Bellamy: "No Money"; Leo Penn: "Some Money"; Tom Mankiewicz: "House Payments." You shot an episode every seven days. A lot of directors were doing three *Hart to Harts*, four *Fantasy Islands*, and a couple of *Charlie's Angels*. They would finish seven days, and there'd be one scene left to shoot. At the end of four or five episodes, you would have a "slop day," which meant all the scenes that hadn't been shot. Usually, I would come in and direct the slop day. The Directors Guild would say to Leo Penn, "You have the right to go shoot that extra scene." Normally, Leo Penn would be shooting another television series and he'd say, "No, no. Let somebody shoot it." I'd go in on slop days because it was really valuable for me. There were different guest casts and there was different stuff to do. If the whole series was, let's say, nine days over schedule, somebody would write an episode where the Harts get stuck in an elevator so you could do it in four days.

Doris DeHerdt, who was an old British script supervisor on *Hart to Hart,* would always say to me in the morning when I directed, "Good morning, Tom. You have anything for me, or will we be winging it as usual?"

And I would say, "Doris, we're winging it as usual."

Some television directors hand the script supervisor a shot list. Doris was really good at her job. We were shooting in Hawaii, and there was a scene with R.J., Stefanie, and a coast guard captain. It was a walk-and-talk scene, and I was shooting with two cameras: one was dollying alongside them, and one was a long-lens camera the three of them were walking toward. We did one take, and it was absolutely fine. I said to the dolly cameraman, "Tighten up on R.J. and the captain because they've got 90 percent of the dialogue and I've got Stefanie covered anyway. On the long lens, I just want R.J. and the captain."

Doris said, "You can't do that."

I asked, "Why, Doris?"

And she said, "Because the captain will go from the middle of the screen over to the right of the screen."

I said, "Doris, look, I'm starting with the three of them walking. Everybody knows where they are and that they're walking." She mumbled the whole time and she was a very proper British lady and so dedicated to her job. I'd hear her mumbling behind me, and I would say, "Please, don't mumble, Doris. If you think I'm an asshole, just speak up." The day we had this little contretemps about the coast guard captain going from the center of the screen to the right of the screen, I went home that night and flipped on my television set, huge Jack Daniel's in hand, and there was *Lawrence of Arabia.* Claude Rains, Peter O'Toole, and Jack Hawkins are walking together. Suddenly, David Lean cuts right in to the two-shot. So Claude Rains goes from the center to the side. I picked up the phone. "Ms. DeHerdt's room, please."

She mumbled, "Hello"; she was asleep.

I said, "Doris, I'll explain tomorrow, but if it's good enough for David Lean, it's good enough for me."

I was shooting on board a boat, and Doris, with earphones on, was in a little boat with some crew members because we couldn't all fit on the boat where I was shooting. They sprung a leak, the little boat was sinking, and Doris's script was soaked. The script supervisor's script has got all of the shots in it. After I finished shooting that night, I walked into the production office, and there was Doris in the corner, ironing her script on an ironing board, drying it out. Now that's somebody who's really dedicated. She just wanted everything to be perfect. She was of the old school.

One day, while we were shooting the pilot, I was walking down the street at Fox. I ran into Aaron Spelling, who said, "Tommy, I missed the rushes today but I hear they were good."

I said, "Aaron, they look like a million bucks."

He said, "They better look like two million–three!" Very expensive pilot.

Aaron's Broadcasting Company

Spelling-Goldberg owned their own shows; that's how they got so powerful and wealthy. They had a wonderful show called *Family*—Mike Nichols directed the pilot—and they had *Starsky and Hutch, Charlie's Angels, Fantasy Island, T.J. Hooker,* and now, *Hart to Hart.* At the time, they controlled eight sound stages at Fox out of fifteen. ABC would get an episode for two runs, and then, hello, it was a Spelling-Goldberg show; they owned it. And they owned the negatives. They were on the cover of *Time* magazine. *Charlie's Angels* was a phenomenon. R.J. and Natalie owned 50 percent of the show because they had starred together in a television movie for Spelling-Goldberg and part of the deal was co-ownership of a series. R.J. also owned half of *Hart to Hart;* he was a big star, and they gave him 50 percent. Months earlier, we were in Aaron's office—R.J., Aaron, Leonard, and Guy McElwaine, who was R.J.'s agent and had been Natalie's agent—sitting around a table, talking about *Hart to Hart* and who would play Jennifer Hart. R.J. said, "Well, as you guys know, I have costar approval."

And Aaron said, "Well, somebody who owns 50 percent of the show should have costar approval."

R.J. said, "Well, I don't know. I own 50 percent of *Charlie's Angels.* I haven't seen a dime."

There was a silence, and Leonard said, "I'll tell you what. Before you leave here, we'll write you a check for two million dollars in cash and you give up your 50 percent of *Charlie's Angels*. Fair?"

Guy McElwaine said, "Don't do it." I knew he wasn't going to do it anyway.

Aaron was so different from Leonard, and they would play good cop and bad cop. And they did it wonderfully. They would have been together forever if not that the wives didn't like each other very much. Aaron would be in the cutting room and he would turn to the editor after a rough cut and say, "What a wonderful job," even if it wasn't. Whereas Leonard might say, "Who the hell cut this? Jose Feliciano?" That was the difference in style.

I was looking for a mansion; we were always shooting in mansions and we were running out of mansions. I said, "Oh, fuck, we're really up against it next week; I can't find a mansion."

Aaron said, "My God, they should all be available. The show is so loved, and we're so careful with the crews, and we sign the guarantee, and if anything gets damaged . . ."

I said, "Aaron, I'll tell you what. You're right. Why don't we use your house?"

He said, "Are you out of your fucking mind? I'm not letting a movie crew in my house." I said, "Okay. The defense rests, Your Honor." During the time Aaron built that huge house, the writers had a long strike.

I had a big fight with the Writers Guild when I had three *Hart to Hart*s I was committed to directing, and they said, "You can't come on the lot to direct those shows," and I said, "I've got to." They said, "No, you'll be crossing the writers' picket line, and you're a member of the Writers Guild."

I said, "Yes, but I'm also a member of the Directors Guild and I have a legal contract. I've got to fulfill it."

They finally said, "Well, okay, but we know you. You're famous for rewriting. No writing on the set."

I went on to direct the show, and the very first scene, Robert Wagner said, "Aw, Jesus, there's gotta be a better line than this."

I said, "R.J., there is, but I can't tell you." Then, what I'd do is, I'd say to the grip, "Go tell Mr. Wagner your mother wears army shoes."

During the strike, which lasted a long time, I was picketing MGM with a very talented writer who's a friend of mine, David Giler, who had written a lot of wonderful scripts. It was ninety-eight degrees. There were about ten of us marching up and down, and across the street was a liquor store. I said to David, "I'll tell you what. I'll chip in, you'll chip in. Why don't you go over there and get us some ice-cold champagne?"

David did, and a couple of the people in line were just outraged. One of them said to David, "Do you realize that at any given moment, 72 percent of the Writers Guild is unemployed?"

And David said, "Do you realize that at any given moment, 85 percent of the Writers Guild is untalented?" We had our champagne.

Writers are terrible picketers. A lot of them haven't been out in the sun much in their lives. They don't know how to walk. They mill around and get caught in crosswalks and traffic. With writers, it looks like a jailbreak. They don't know what to do, and they're marching this way and that way. Writers Guild meetings are more like a socialist cell meeting in the thirties, where people get up and yell, "I was blacklisted in nineteen—" and somebody else says, "Sit down and shut up." People get up and they're booed. Thousands of writers were assembled in front of Fox. I was walking with a guy named Ben Joelson, who was one of the staff writers on *The Love Boat*, and we were stopped by KFWB and KNX Radio. A reporter said, "This is an amazing show of strength."

And Ben said, "Yeah, tomorrow we're going to be picketing Aaron Spelling's house, but we're going to need more writers."

Aaron was really hurt by that. When he built that huge mansion, which was just unbelievable, he said to me, "I grew up as the son of a Jewish tailor in Dallas, Texas. And I wasn't much to look at. And I worked my way up through all of this. I don't fly. I don't like to travel, and they make fun of me for having a big home. I earned every dollar."

After the *Hart to Hart* series was off the air, there were eight movies done of *Hart to Hart* on network and on cable. R.J., as I've mentioned, owned 50 percent. Stefanie, when she was signed, had no piece of the show because she couldn't demand it, really, with her track record in series television at the time. Later on, in her third year, when she renegotiated, she got 5 percent of the show profits, but her profit definition was worse than mine. I had 2.5 percent of the show, and my agent said to me, "Good luck ever seeing anything." We sued Spelling-Goldberg and Columbia. We all met in our lawyer's office on Sunset Boulevard: Aaron, Leonard, R.J., Stefanie, me, and the Spelling-Goldberg lawyers. Sidney Sheldon, who still got credit for creating, also had a small piece of it. Aaron's attitude was, "Listen, we all know each other. We like each other. We've had dinner at each other's homes. If we owe any money, we should be paying it."

Leonard said, "I object to the fact that this entire meeting is based on the supposition that we're crooks. If somebody wants to call me a crook, I'd like them to do it right now." He said to Stefanie, "Do you think I'm a crook?" Stefanie launched into this speech about all things socioeconomic of the world. She talked for twenty minutes and never said anything. And he said, "Mank?"

I said, "Look, Leonard, nobody's calling anybody a crook. All I can tell you is that I have a business manager and I have a lawyer and they say I'm owed money, and if I am owed money, I'd like to have the money. That's all this is about."

And Leonard said, "Okay, R.J.?"

R.J. said, "Yeah, I'll call you a crook." Right there. It was amazing. I don't think Leonard's ever forgiven him for it. When they've run into each other since, Leonard's still a little frosty.

We couldn't settle, and we went to court. Our attorney, Don Engel, negotiated the figure up to 92 percent of what we were owed, and it was a lot of money. We were playing in 125 countries, and everybody was saying, it is impossible that this is not generating income. No matter what the books say, it's got to be in profit. Of course, it's a Spelling-Goldberg show, so ABC stayed out of it entirely. While I was tense about it, for Aaron and Leonard, after having done umpty-ump series and been through so many legal fights, it was just business. When R.J. and Natalie were suing Spelling-Goldberg about their 50 percent *Charlie's Angels* ownership and then Aaron and Leonard countersued, I sent a telegram saying, "The Empire Strikes Back!"

Spelling-Goldberg was the most successful production company in television. ABC was called "Aaron's Broadcasting Company." Leonard said, "Basically, Aaron does *Charlie's Angels* and *Starsky and Hutch,* I do *Family* and *Hart to Hart,* and nobody does *Fantasy Island.*" It was a delight to work there because they ran their own shop. You didn't have to deal with levels of studio executives. Aaron's bungalow, as I've mentioned, was my father's bungalow when he was doing *All About Eve* and *A Letter to Three Wives.* They built another bungalow just like it next to it, and the two bungalows together were Spelling-Goldberg.

7

The 1970s Gallery

Paddy Chayefsky

Whiplash smart, wonderfully talented, actively plain looking, simultane-ously cynical and sentimental. Among other things, Paddy was famous for going everywhere without his wife, who apparently had no interest in show business whatsoever. I once explained to him what a great advantage that was—he could go to almost any restaurant or party with whatever woman he chose and introduce her as his wife, no one being the wiser.

Paddy was the only screenwriter I've ever heard of who had the contrac-tual power to approve or even replace a director on an original screenplay of his. He'd cut his teeth in the theater, where these powers belonged to the author of the play, and insisted on carrying them over to film as a condition of purchasing his original work. At the start of *The Hospital* (a frightening indictment of the health care system, absolutely relevant today), starring George C. Scott, he had chosen a young director, Michael Ritchie, who had made *Downhill Racer* with Robert Redford. But Paddy grew increasingly disenchanted with him. He told United Artists he wanted to replace Ritchie with Arthur Hiller. UA executives balked, explaining to Paddy that with Hiller, "All you're going to get is the script."

"Aha!" Paddy shouted. He got Arthur Hiller.

I used to play poker with Paddy in New York in the seventies. One night, the game broke up late, about 2:00 A.M. Paddy, an actor named Larry Blyden, who was on Broadway at the time, and I got into the apartment house elevator on the twentieth floor and pressed the button for the lobby. After a couple of floors, the elevator suddenly shook—then stopped dead. We were stuck, suspended some seventeen stories high. Silence. We tried the little phone on the wall—it didn't work. We pressed the red emergency button—nothing. I was stunned. Larry suddenly fell apart. He turned to me, panicked: "You write James Bond," he said in all seriousness. "How the hell would James Bond get out of here?"

"Larry, he'd take the sliding panel off the roof and climb up the cables to the next landing, except this roof's rock solid and I can't climb cables." I looked over and down. Paddy was slumped in the corner. "Paddy, are you all right?"

He looked up. "Oh, sure . . . except for the fact that I told my wife I'd be home by midnight, I lost over a thousand dollars in the game, and now I'm stuck in the middle of a goddamn Neil Simon play." Eventually, we heard someone moving in the hall above, banged on the walls, and yelled. He called the apartment house manager, and we were finally cranked up.

His brilliant screenplay for *Network* was described by critics at the time as a scathing satire of the future of television news. Paddy always insisted that actually it would become "a fucking documentary." In it, Peter Finch's newsman, Howard Beale, rants and raves as a perfect precursor of today's Glenn Beck on Fox News. Part of Beale's bizarre broadcast was a feature called Vox Populi. When Katie Couric took over the *CBS Evening News,* one of the added features (eventually dropped) was—you guessed it—Vox Populi.

Paddy and Bob Fosse

The brilliantly talented choreographer-director Bob Fosse told me this wonderfully revealing story about Paddy: Bob (the only choreographer I ever saw who always worked with a cigarette dangling out of his mouth) was in a Chicago hospital, in immediate need of a dangerous heart operation. He asked his two best friends, Paddy and playwright Herb Gardner (*A Thousand Clowns*), to fly out on the day of the procedure. In the hospital room, Bob handed them copies of his will in which he had named them coexecutors. He explained there was a real chance he wouldn't survive the operation and asked them to sign the document before he went into surgery. Herb, in tears, did so immediately. Bob then looked over at Paddy, who sat in the corner, reading. "Is something wrong, Paddy?"

"No, but I never signed anything in my life I didn't read first."

The hospital orderlies were prepping Bob to leave. Paddy finally looked up: "I'm not in your will."

"No, you're not, Paddy. You're fabulously successful. I'm leaving everything to Gwen (Verdon) and the kids."

Paddy rose and crossed to him. "I can't believe I'm not in your will." He tossed the document onto the bed. "Fuck you, then. Live."

Bob said those were the last words he heard before he was wheeled out. As he put it: "Paddy's way of saying how much he loved me."

Tony Curtis

I met Tony Curtis in Rome. He was very outgoing, very nice. I knew him when he was married to Janet Leigh. As everybody knows, his real name was Bernie Schwartz. He got so elegant. He dressed so well. He said to me, "You know, you think you're dressing well, but you're not."

I said, "I'm not?"

"No. Have you got five hundred dollars?"

"Sure I do, Tony."

"I can dress you for five hundred dollars. We'll go to Brioni's, and you're going to thank me for the rest of your life."

I said, "But, Tony, I don't want to." He kept telling me that he'd heard from so many people how bright I was.

I hadn't seen Tony in years, and I ran into him at a party in L.A. The next day, his secretary called. "Mr. Curtis is having a dinner party Sunday night and he wondered if you'd like to come." Tony had divorced Janet and was married to an Austrian actress named Christine Kaufmann. Tony bought a huge house on Sunset Boulevard that was once owned by Nelson Eddy and Jeanette MacDonald. Later, Cher had it. It looked like a property out of another country, huge rolling grounds, trees, paths, and a big house. The house was decorated like the Great Gatsby. There was a dining-room table for thirty people. He didn't know a lot of the people that he had invited. He used to invite people over who he had heard were bright. That night, Buck Henry, who was a terrific guy and a wonderful writer, was there. I asked, "So how long have you known Tony, Buck?"

He said, "I don't know him at all. I shook hands with him once, but I got an invitation. I wanted to see what was going on." We privately polled people, and a lot of them didn't know Tony Curtis very well. He just decided to collect these people.

After dinner, all the women retired to the living room, and the men took a walk through the grounds. He had a walking stick for each guy. These paths seemed to go on forever. Buck said, "Don't look now, but I think I see Jack Haley, Burt Lahr, and Ray Bolger coming the other way." We caught up with Tony in the front, and Buck said, "Quite seriously, Tony, why do you ask people over that you don't know?"

Tony said, "I'll tell you what I learned early on in life. You've got to spend your life with people who are smarter than you are, who know more than you do, who are more experienced at a lot of different things than you are. And the only people worth knowing are people who hang out with people who are smarter than they are."

We kept walking, and Buck said, "Well, in that case, Tony, what are we doing here with you?"

Tony was a terrific guy. He was married several times and he fucked a lot of women, but he acted very gay in his older age. Some actors and producers who suddenly get rich acquire an incredible thirst for elegance, for sophistication. You're Bernie Schwartz from the Bronx, but boy, you couldn't tell now. He asked me over a couple of times. The only time I ever met Desi Arnaz was there. I was shocked, and I mean this in a totally heterosexual way, at how good looking he was. He was very serious. He was in the middle of divorcing Lucille Ball. I had met her down in Palm Springs a few times. Boy, she was one tough lady. Always very nice to me, but really tough. There's a line in *Georgy!*, "tough as old boots." She had a certain charm to her. The two of them revolutionized television. I thought, Desi doesn't look at all like the one on television. "Lucy, you got some 'splaining to do." He looked like a very serious, great-looking guy. I heard he screwed everybody in the world, and I could tell why. If I was a woman, I'd have gone for him just like that.

Tony Curtis was such an underrated actor. He was great, and best when he played creeps. He played the Boston Strangler, he was fabulous; *Sweet Smell of Success,* when he played Sidney Falco, the press agent, he's brilliant. He was in a picture with Debbie Reynolds called *The Rat Race.* He was just wonderful. He was so much better than he was as romantic leads, although he could do those too.

Marlene Dietrich

I went with Natalie Wood to Garson and Ruth Kanin's house one night. The guest of honor was Marlene Dietrich. The Kanins were in the habit of inviting so-called legends to dinner, and afterward everyone would ask the "legends" a question. There was always an eclectic group of people present. In this case, it was the famous lyricist, Alan J. Lerner, one might say a legend in his own right; David Picker, who was then head of production for United Artists; Don Rickles and his wife; and myself and Natalie. The first question fell to me, unfortunately, and I was a bit flustered, not knowing what to ask. Finally, I said, "Who was the best actor you ever played with?"

Without batting an eye, Dietrich said, "I never performed with a good actor."

I said, "Really? How about Emil Jannings in *The Blue Angel*?"

She said, "He was terrible, he was dreadful. All of the actors I played with were dreadful, so I don't know how to answer your question."

The next question was for Natalie to ask. She said to Dietrich, "You and Garbo were the two great stars of the thirties. What would you say was the difference between the two of you?"

Dietrich said, "Garbo was cold, I was warm. Garbo had no friends, I had many friends. Garbo could not act, I was a wonderful actress. Garbo couldn't sing, I could sing. I had a better body than Garbo." She went on and on and on. And finally, her gaze bore in on Natalie as she said, "But even with all that, they don't make stars like they used to."

The room was deadly silent as it came time for the next question, to be asked by Don Rickles. He leaned in, stared hard at Marlene Dietrich, and said, "Who *are* you?"

Freddie Fields

Freddie Fields was the first of the new generation of agents, completely immoral. He was the first to "package" projects, and under his leadership, CMA (Creative Management Agency) became the precursor of Mike Ovitz and CAA (Creative Artists Agency), which would come along later. Freddie collected talent furiously. When I was starting to get a reputation after the first couple of Bond movies, the phone rang one day in my office and it was Freddie Fields. He said, "I want you to come to CMA. I've got a great picture for you." I believe it was going to be directed by John Frankenheimer, who was also a client, but who knows if there really was a picture.

I said to him, "Jeez, Freddie, I would love to come and all that, but I am represented very well right now by Robin French at IFA (International Famous Agency). I am working all the time, and I am doing the projects I want. I couldn't just call him up and fire him."

Freddie said, "Well, I know that you are a very moral guy, that's why we want you over here. I tell you what, you don't have to tell him anything, I'll call him and fire him for you." Freddie would do anything to get a client. When *Butch Cassidy and the Sundance Kid* was being put together, he represented Paul Newman. Everybody's choice for Sundance was Steve McQueen, who was represented by Stan Kamen at William Morris. The package was being put together. Both sides agreed there would be alternate star billing depending on which ad was being taken or which country it was in, since both Paul and Steve were big stars. As soon as this deal looked like it was coming to fruition, Freddie made sure that he kept running into Steve McQueen at parties. He would tell Steve what a bad deal Stan Kamen made for him. "You're a bigger star than Paul, you're the hottest star in the business. You should have top billing the whole way through. If you were my client, I would have gotten you that." Steve left Stan Kamen, did not play Sundance, and became a client of Freddie Fields's.

William Holden

Bill Holden was a guy I respected like crazy. He was not only a sensational actor, but he was a man of the world; spent most of the last twenty years of his life in Africa and China. We were talking one day, I was just starting to get to know him. He said, "Oh, I know everything about you."

I said, "You do? How do you know everything?"

"Well, I just spent two hours with you. You're a member of the club, aren't you?"

"What club is that?"

He said, "The world's most outgoing loners. I'm a member of that club." Stefanie Powers, whom we both knew and had gone out with—he had a long affair with her—was a member of that club. "I can recognize them a mile away. You love people, you're gregarious, people love you, and you're a loner. You'll always be a loner." Holden was, and he died alone. As many times as he was asked to appear on talk shows, he couldn't do it. He was great in the living room, but when he knew the television camera was on him and people across the country were listening to him being himself, he couldn't do it. There are a lot of actors who retreat into a character and they're wonderful.

There was a good friend of ours named Chuck Feingarten who ran the Feingarten Gallery on Melrose. Chuck died, and his wife, Gail, wanted Bill and me to be the two speakers at the memorial, which was being held at their house. Chuck was a very popular guy, and a huge number of people showed up. It was about a half hour before the ceremony was to begin. Bill and I were at the bar having a drink, and Bill asked, "What are you going to say?"

I said, "Well, I think I got it down pretty good. I've got two three-by-five cards here. I wrote down these points."

And he said, "Can I see it?"

I said, "Sure."

He looked at it. "This is great; this is great."

I said, "Thanks."

He asked, "Can I say this?"

I said, "Excuse me?"

He said, "I'm so scared of getting up there. Can I say this? This could apply to me too."

I said, "Sure." I mean, it's William Holden. I guess if it had been William Schwartz, I would have said, "Bill, you know, just do the best you can." He was that scared of speaking. I listened to my speech, which he delivered better than I could, he was such a wonderful actor—not that he didn't love Chuck, which he did. I scrambled in my head to figure out some extra things, and I got away with a speech. But Bill was really remarkable.

Stanley Kubrick

Stanley Kubrick had a housekeeping deal at Warner Brothers, but he was almost exclusively in England. Jimmy Harris, a good friend of mine, started with Stanley in New York. Jimmy had made his money in the shmata trade and provided early seed money when they did *The Killing*, their first movie together. Later, they did *Paths of Glory* and *Lolita*. Then, Jimmy went off to direct, but he was still Stanley's closest friend. At Stanley's funeral, I understand when Jimmy got up to speak, it was just heartbreaking. They were so close. At Warners, John Calley was deputized to handle Stanley Kubrick because Stanley had very little patience by then. He was getting more and more eccentric. Calley was a big executive at Warners and a producer. A smart, literate guy. Stanley loved him. So when Stanley wanted to do another picture for Warners, John Calley was the designated hitter. Stanley would talk to Calley, Calley would talk to Warners, they'd give their answer to Calley, and Calley got Stanley everything.

Stanley was an odd duck in so many ways. He was an out-and-out dyed-in-the-wool New Yorker. A *huge* baseball fan. In those days, you got the scores a day later in the *Paris Herald Tribune*. Stanley would call New York while the Yankees game was on—he'd figure out when it might be the bottom of the seventh or later—and stay on the line. He had huge phone bills. A friend would announce, "Mickey Mantle's up, Stanley. There are two men on." Later, he got a UPI ticker so he could get the scores in real time.

Stanley wouldn't fly. I saw him when he came to Los Angeles for the opening of *2001: A Space Odyssey*. He had driven to Southampton, got on the *Queen Mary*, sailed to New York, got on the train, traveled across the country, arrived in Los Angeles. It took him eight or nine days to get from London to L.A. By then, they already had polar flights. I was sitting with him and Jimmy Harris, and I said, "Boy, Stanley, if they don't like this picture, it's a long trip home."

He said, "You bet."

When Stanley directed *Barry Lyndon*, which may be the most beautiful movie ever made, he would drive all the way to the west coast of England

and get on the ferry to go across the Irish Sea to shoot in Ireland. Everybody else flew it in twenty minutes. *Full Metal Jacket* shot in England. Half of it takes place in Vietnam. They imported the palm trees.

There is the fraternity of directors, and when I talk about directors, I'm not talking about me. I'm talking about the Kubricks and the Joe Mankiewiczs. Ken Adam, who designed the Bonds, *Dr. Strangelove,* and *Barry Lyndon,* designed *Sleuth* for dad with that wonderful little house that they were in. One day, Ken said to Dad, "You know who wants to meet you, Stanley Kubrick."

Dad said, "Well, I'd like to meet Stanley Kubrick." So Ken decided to set up a dinner at his house in Montpelier Square. He had a sunken basement dining room. You could look down into the room from street level. To make it less stilted, since Kubrick was meeting Mankiewicz, Ken and his wife, Letizia, asked me and Malcolm McDowell, who had just done *Clockwork Orange* with Stanley, to the occasion. After dinner—it was about ten o'clock—Malcolm and I decided to go hit the clubs. It was great in London at that time. So we went out to Tramps. We got back to Montpelier Square, where Malcolm had his car, at two in the morning. We looked through the window, and there were Dad and Stanley Kubrick, still talking, just the two of them. We'd left them four hours earlier. Dad was puffing his pipe. They were talking. It was a heartwarming thing to see. I don't know when it broke up. They were two people who were so concerned with the quality of film; not necessarily the gross of the film, the appeal of the film, but the quality of the film.

Stanley's wife, Christiane, appears at the end of *Paths of Glory.* She is the German prisoner of war that's brought out in front of the troops to sing a song and she's terrified. As she starts to sing, all the grizzled faces start to tear up, and they sing along with her. It's an incredible ending to this movie. It wasn't the original ending. Jimmy Harris told me this: Stanley started dating her—she was a German girl—in Munich when they were shooting. It all took place in France, but it was about corruption in the French command, and the French wouldn't let them shoot there. The picture was not shown in France for ten years. Stanley said to Jimmy one day, "Got a great idea for the end of the movie. A German prisoner arrives."

And Jimmy said, "And who would that be, Stanley?"

He said, "Well, Christiane."

Jimmy said Stanley was about three days behind shooting, and when he was less than a day and a half behind, they'd shoot the ending. Jimmy said,

"You never saw anybody go up and down the trenches so fast." But it was a great ending, and she remained Mrs. Kubrick for forty years. She stayed married to him forever.

The crazy actor who was in *Paths of Glory* with the big bug eyes was Timothy Carey. He was a method actor. Huge overactor. Carey, who was nuts, doesn't show up one day. They're shooting on a tight schedule because they don't have a lot of money to do it. Kubrick and Harris are going crazy. They get a call from the police. Carey has been found bound and gagged in the woods behind a house in the outskirts of Munich. He says, "Oh, Jesus, thank God they found me. I got kidnapped and they robbed me." Jimmy thought, this is really weird. He's a huge guy. Who's going to kidnap and rob him? Carey's back working. Jimmy goes over to the house where he was found, and the residents finally confess that Carey gave them a hundred bucks to call the police and bind and gag him themselves. He'd been on a toot for two days, and he knew he'd get fired. That's why you love to work. That stuff doesn't happen in offices. It only happens on a set. That's why I love it so much.

David Merrick

In the late seventies the producer David Merrick announced his intentions to make a movie of his Broadway hit *Promises, Promises*, which was, in turn, a musical version of the famous Billy Wilder film *The Apartment*. How my name came up in connection with the project I'm not exactly sure, except that my stock as a writer was quite high at the time and I had written the book for a Broadway musical (*Georgy!*) earlier in my career. At any rate, Merrick's assistant, Alan Delinn, had mentioned to Jack Haley Jr., a close friend, that David would be interested in meeting me. Frankly, I was not particularly interested in doing *Promises, Promises*, but it was a chance to meet David Merrick, and who knows, maybe after a meeting I will talk myself into it.

The meeting started pleasantly enough. Merrick smiled at me and said, "What do you think?"

And I said, "Well, I have one concern about the project, which is, when *The Apartment* first came out, it was a little scandalous for a guy to rent out his apartment to his boss. But then, in the wake of the sexual revolution and the era of 'free love,' is it quite so shocking anymore, and is that something that should be addressed?"

Merrick looked right past me to Alan Delinn and said, "Why am I here? Who is this man? What am I doing here? Why am I talking to this person?"

Alan said, "David, you asked to see him."

Merrick said, "I don't recall." And he just got up and walked out. That was my meeting with David Merrick.

Sometime later, I was at a Tony-watching party at Leslie Bricusse's house and David Merrick was one of the guests. Merrick had produced both *Stop the World—I Want to Get Off* and *The Roar of the Greasepaint—the Smell of the Crowd* for Leslie and Tony Newley, and they were in discussion with him about a revival of one of them. Tony and David Merrick, famously, did not get along during both shows. While we were watching the Tonys, and everyone had had a few drinks, David Merrick smiled and looked over at Tony and said, "You know, we had our fights, we had our disagreements, but like a good marriage, we also had our happy times. We had a lot of happy times."

Tony looked back at Merrick and said, "Frankly, David, I can't remember one."

Robert Mitchum

I first met Robert Mitchum when I was doing the Bond movies and flying from Los Angeles to London on a regular basis. He was flying over this particular day to begin a film called *Farewell, My Lovely*. We were introduced by Tom Stout, who was the all-powerful head of public relations for TWA at the time. He later went on and founded the incredibly successful Hoffman Travel Service. Indeed, everyone in Hollywood used to joke that TWA stood for Tom's World Airlines. Mitchum and I hit it off immediately. We had a few drinks in the Ambassador Lounge, and I could see that I had to pace myself alcohol-wise, since his capacity seemed to be nearly inexhaustible.

Once aboard and up in the air, we went up to the little lounge that existed in those days on the 747. We had another drink, and Mitchum noticed two young Arab teenagers, approximately thirteen years old, playing cards. He asked them if we could all play and did they know how to play poker. "Yes," they replied and the four of us started playing poker. Within half an hour, these two kids were absolutely cleaning us out. The stewardess arrived and told us that dinner was being served downstairs, so we went back to our seats. A very well-dressed Arab gentleman came up to Mitchum and said, "Mr. Mitchum, my sons tell me they were playing poker with you. We are an observant Muslim family, and they are not allowed to gamble. And I understand they won some money from you, and I am here to give it back to you."

Mitchum looked up and said, "No, listen, the kids won it fair and square, a bet's a bet; tell them to keep the money."

The man looked back at him and said, "You don't understand, Mr. Mitchum, my children are watching me right now, and I told them I was going to give you the money back. So here it is."

Mitchum took the money, looked down, and looked back up again and said, "Well, as long as you're giving it back, it was three hundred dollars not two hundred fifty."

Mitchum had a wonderful disdain for the art of acting, which he practiced so well. "Acting can't be all that complicated," he told me, "when you consider one of the biggest stars who ever lived was Rin Tin Tin."

The last time I saw Mitchum was in Montecito, when we were shooting *Delirious*. Early in the morning, I had a cup of coffee with John Candy at a little drugstore that was opening early for us. We exited the coffee shop—it was about six in the morning—and coming down the street were Robert Mitchum and Richard Widmark. Both lived up there. Richard Widmark looked like a silver-haired devil, and Mitchum was in a caftan muumuu carrying a purse. John, Richard, and Robert were so impressed meeting one another. I said to Mitchum, "Bob, is anybody giving you any shit about the muumuu and the purse?"

He looked at me and said, "Not so far."

Mitchum had a very loyal assistant who had been with him most of his life, and her job was to take any offers that he had and count the number of pages that he was in. He wouldn't read the scripts anymore. He just wanted to know if it was going to be a good project, how many pages was he in, and how long would it take. He won the Emmy for *War and Remembrance*, playing an admiral. After the award show, breathless TV people asked him, "What was it that attracted you to the part, Mr. Mitchum?"

He said, "The director asked me to play it." That was it. He was a very simple guy.

8

The 1980s

Calling Dr. Mankiewicz

I felt the urge to direct because I couldn't stomach what was being
done with what I wrote.

—*Joseph L. Mankiewicz*

The Doctor Will See You Now

I really got to know Dad as a human being in slow stages by always stopping
by on my way to Europe, on my way back from Europe. That was seven or
eight movies. We'd already had the experience of working in the same studio when he was doing *Sleuth* and I was doing *Live and Let Die*. And I
would go back every Christmas. I wanted to find out many things, because
he could be so closed. I don't mean hostile, but closed. One night in early
1980, I was visiting, and he said, "You know, Tom, I've got all kinds of
stuff." He used to save everything, notes and pictures in file cabinets. He
had decided, I guess an elegant way to put it, to make Mother a nonperson.
He said, "I have lots of pictures of your mother if you'd like them." I realized half of it was being generous and half of it was she wasn't part of his life
anymore. He'd been with Rosemary now eighteen years. She was his wife,
they had a child. He was looking forward to many more years with Rosemary.
Mother was buried in Kensico Cemetery in Westchester.

Dad asked me to pay for the upkeep on Mother's grave. I said, "Okay,
fine." My brother Chris couldn't afford anything, so I paid for the upkeep
on her grave for fifteen years. All these years later, I said to Chris, "I'm going
to need your permission, but what if I should die? I can't keep this grave
forever, what's going to happen twenty, thirty years from now? Also,
Mother's so lonely. She's there all by herself. Dad will obviously be buried

249

with Rosemary. The Mankiewiczes are spread out all over the place. Chris, with your permission, I'd like to cremate her body and have the ashes sent to L.A., and we can scatter them at sea or do anything you want with them." So that's what we did. Chris has the remainder of Mother's ashes because he is hoping to get to Europe at some point and scatter some there.

In stages, my relationship with my father became much, much better. While we weren't equal professionally—he was the four-time Oscar winner and a legend—we became equal in the sense that I didn't need anything from him and he didn't need anything from me. We were just father and son. We could have a different kind of dialogue. Being the "son or the daughter of" is a tremendous advantage, but there are compensating disadvantages like, number one, are you ever going to measure up? Number two, when you first start, snotty reviewers will say, well, Tom Mankiewicz is clearly no Joe Mankiewicz. Also, as I've said, you have that group of people who are rooting against you in the beginning because you're Joe Mankiewicz's kid and if you were Joe Schwartz's kid, you wouldn't even be there, they think.

I concentrated heavily on writing. The most important moment in my life was when I was finished rewriting *Diamonds Are Forever* and there was no question I was writing the next one. They were making the deal already. Cubby and Harry knew who my father was, but they didn't know him socially. They were about to make another fucking James Bond film, and they figured, out of all the writers, I was the one that they wanted to have write it. That was an inner satisfaction. That's when you stopped being Joe Mankiewicz's kid and you became Tom Mankiewicz. As I've said, nobody makes your script because you're Joe Mankiewicz's kid; they make it because they want to make the film. Writing is very important in that way. Nobody is going to let you direct a film because you're somebody's son, either. When Jane Fonda first started acting, she was in a movie called *Tall Story* with Tony Perkins. Everybody said she got the part because she was Hank Fonda's daughter, and she wasn't that good in it. She learned how to act. You watch her in *Klute,* and this is a real serious actress. She's a wonderful actress. She overcame being Henry Fonda's daughter. Conversely, one of Gregory Peck's children killed himself. Ray Stark had a son who threw himself off a balcony.

Being the "son or daughter of" is an added burden, if you let it be. But on the whole, the advantages outweigh the disadvantages if you can perform. If you can do it, you do have an in. When I wrote that original called *Please,* which got optioned five times by different studios and was never made, the fact that it said Tom Mankiewicz may have caused somebody to pick it up and read it, where, if it had said Tom Schwartz, they might not have. That's how I got my rewrite on *Bob Hope Presents the Chrysler Theatre* for $500, because they said, "Get Joe's kid, he writes terrific dialogue." The original title, as I mentioned, was *Everything the Traffic Will Allow,* which is from "There's No Business Like Show Business," and it was about the last ninety minutes of a young actress's life in between the time she takes pills and the time she dies, with flashbacks. (Our family is full of flashbacks: *Citizen Kane, Letter to Three Wives, All About Eve, The Barefoot Contessa,* all flashbacks.) It was based on Bridget Hayward and later Tuesday Weld, who was one of the first people that I was crazy about after coming out to L.A., and who was in a lot of trouble. At one point, Carroll Baker, who was a big star after *The Carpetbaggers,* was going to do it. Shirley MacLaine was going to do it. People were always optioning this thing. But in the meantime, it was a wonderful exhibition of my work, or at least my dialogue.

In the early 1980s, Aaron Spelling called me one day and asked, "Tommy, what was that script, the suicide script?"

I said, "Oh, Jesus, Aaron, back then it was called *Please.*"

He said, "I remember reading that thing fifteen years ago. God, it was good. Why don't we make it?"

I said, "Aaron, let me pull it out."

So I read it, and it wasn't any good. The dialogue was very flashy. It was immature. It didn't really hold. But the part for the actress was so good. I would have had to start rewriting it, and I thought, no, I'm just gonna let a sleeping dog lie.

I told Aaron. He said, "It isn't as good as we remember from fifteen years ago?"

I said, "No, it's not."

It's the Real Thing

In 1982 Columbia and Coca-Cola were forming a new studio called TriStar, a subsidiary of Columbia. Sean Connery's lawyer and one of the producers of *Never Say Never Again,* Jack Schwartzman, was involved. The job of studio head was offered to Leonard Goldberg. Leonard had so many things going on that he suggested me. This was a no-lose proposition. TriStar had five commitments including *Places in the Heart,* which Bob Benton was going to make, *Tootsie,* which Sidney Pollack was going to make, and *The Natural,* which Barry Levinson was going to make. These things were already lined up. They needed somebody to run the studio. Bob Benton was asked, "What do you think of Tom Mankiewicz?" and Benton said, "He would be ideal. The guy's produced. He's directed. He's written. It would be such a help to have a studio head that creative. What is he famous for? Fixing pictures. He also knows people, and everybody likes him, and he's not a suit." So I got a call, would I be interested? My agent at the time was cool on it because he thought he could make more money off me if I stayed in movies than if I was an executive. He'd make one deal and that's the end of it. You sort of lost a client.

I met with Robert Goizueta, the head of Coca-Cola. We went to a dinner at the Bistro. Ray Stark was there because he was a big stockholder in Columbia. Ray had passed on me and said, "This is not such a good idea." I thought, boy, this is a complete change of life. I sat down with my assistant/associate producer/confidant Annie Stevens and said, "What do we want to do? We would have to go to Century City every morning. It's probably more like a seven-day-a-week job than a five-day-a-week job because things happen all the time. We'd probably have to get to work a little earlier because it's already nine o'clock in New York when it's six o'clock in L.A. We'll have to go to previews around the country. If I do something wonderful to fix a movie, they'll say, 'Boy, can that Barry Levinson make a good movie.' And if I do something terrible, they'll blame it on me and say, 'What a lousy studio head, he didn't make any money. How could he green-light that?'" So I was really making a negative case. I said, "On the other hand, it's awfully tough to fire a studio head for at least the first two or three years, and we can always go back to what we're doing." Annie was like a full partner. She was my alter ego and somebody who could really take the mickey out of me, as the British would say.

We decided we didn't want to do it. Most executives know nothing. There was a quote of writer-director Richard Brooks, "A fired executive trying to make a motion picture is like a turtle on his back in the sun. They all know everything except how to make one." To be with the president of Coca-Cola and Ray Stark, I mean, talk about a fish out of water. I'm fairly glib. I thought, this is not my crowd, either. The job is seven days a week and you are serving everybody else. If Barry Levinson or Bob Benton or Sidney Pollack has a problem, they pick up the phone and call you. And you've got to solve it. Son of a bitch, if Dick Donner has a problem, he picks up the phone and calls you, and if it's two in the morning, it's two in the morning. He's really pissed about something and you've got to do something about it. If you're creative, it's difficult to be on that side of the line, fixing all these problems for all these people. Whereas, when you're fixing your own movie, you're diving into an individual project with a director, and actors, and locations, and it is your project too. You're in it. You're creatively contributing to it.

But that was one brush with the executives, and it was there for the taking. No question about it. I would have gone on to produce Oscar telecasts after that. Jack Haley Jr. directed several Oscar telecasts. I helped him out. They were nightmares. But in those days, it was much more freewheeling. People were drinking. Henry Mancini, one of the great guys in the world, always led the orchestra in those days in the pit. When there was a commercial break, Hank would jump onto the stage and he and Jack and I would smoke a joint backstage. It was absolutely insane. I'm sure it's much worse today.

This Is War

In 1982 Leonard Goldberg was producing a movie called *War Games* with Matthew Broderick and Ally Sheedy. Dabney Coleman was in it, and Marty Brest was the director. He later did *Beverly Hills Cop.* This was his first movie, and they were shooting in Seattle. Leonard said to me, "You know, there are some problems with the script, but Marty thinks it's wonderful. How did I ever get into this?" Three days' rushes came in, and Leonard didn't like them at all. Marty Brest was not that adept with a camera. Even in *Beverly Hills Cop,* they had a television director, Don Medford, on the set with him at all times. Leonard said, "Marty, I think we've got to reshoot some of this. I'm flying up to Seattle tomorrow. If you think these rushes need a little work, let's sit down and see what we can redo. If you think they're great, we may have a problem."

Leonard got to Seattle, and Marty Brest said, "I think they're great."

Leonard said, "Then we have a problem."

Marty Brest said, "You can't fire me. I quit."

Leonard said, "All right, you can quit." Later on, Leonard said, "He'll learn. Never quit because, if you get fired, you get paid. That's a good lesson for him to learn."

So he hired John Badham, who had directed *Saturday Night Fever* and *Dracula.* John was an old friend of mine from Yale. As I've mentioned, when I was rewriting the *Bob Hope Presents the Chrysler Theatre* episode, John was working in the casting department at Universal, and they finally gave him a shot to direct episodic television. His very first movie was with Richard Pryor about black ballplayers called *The Bingo Long Traveling All-Stars and Motor Kings.* It was a wonderful little film. He now took over *War Games,* and Leonard and John said to me, "It just needs three or four scenes, and you'll see where they are."

We all agreed on the scenes. Nobody was supposed to know that I was on the picture. Leonard and I were walking on the MGM back lot, and here comes Ally Sheedy and Matthew Broderick on a bicycle built for two, heading to the set. They stopped to say hello to Leonard, and Leonard introduced me to them. Ally Sheedy said, "By the way, Leonard, we know who's writing those scenes; we loved those scenes." I'm just standing there. She said, "Matthew and I figured it out."

Leonard asked, "Who's writing them?"

She said, "Neil Simon."

Leonard said, "Close." And they went off.

By the way, it was a very good script. The movie came out, and it was a big hit. I was sitting at a table with Ally Sheedy at a party four months later. I said, "By the way, I didn't congratulate you on your performance in *War Games*. You were wonderful."

She said, "Oh, thank you."

And I said, "I particularly liked the scene on the beach the night before you think the world's going to end, when you say you were going to be on local television doing calisthenics the next day. It's just a lousy little show, but it really did mean something. It was so touching and sweet."

Ally said, "Yeah, it was a wonderful scene."

I said, "I wrote that scene."

She said, "You were the one."

A Tablet, a Pencil, and Thou

Dad used to write in longhand on a yellow pad. And I started that way. If you were to ask me to write a screenplay today, the first thing I'd do is get into bed with no clothes on with a yellow legal tablet and pencil and write. It's womblike. When I was doing *Superman* in London, one of the reasons I always had a suite was that I would write in the bedroom. I had so many chicken scratchings on the pages with arrows and so on, nobody could ever decipher it. Not even Annie. I would write the scene in longhand, and then I would play it to myself and I would make changes. Then I would go in and type it up. Then I'd look at it and make more changes, then I'd give it to Annie. She would type it, put it in the computer. I could never do that. I can write letters on a computer, e-mail, but I can't write a screenplay on a computer. I'm the last guy in the world to still be typing on an IBM Selectric. That's as high-tech as I got. It's still the same process. It's three times. Longhand, typing with changes, and then the clean copy.

Unfortunately, I smoke when I write. My hero was Scott Fitzgerald. I loved *Gatsby* and *Tender Is the Night*. He was a big drinker. And Hemingway. They were always drinking and writing. I can't drink and write. I write about four hours, nine to one, or eight to noon. I get up very early, around four thirty or five in the morning. I didn't always, but I do now. I read the paper, and then go write. I have to do it when my mind is relatively blank, and, hopefully, before the phone starts to ring. If you're writing, you don't answer the phone. There are some days when it just comes, and it's wonderful. And some days when it just doesn't, and it's painful to write two pages. And they're not good. Other days, six pages are easy. It just flows. One thing I notice is at night, if I have a couple of Jack Daniel's and I suddenly think of a wonderful line—I'm almost laughing out loud it's so good—and I write it down, in the morning, when I get up and look at the line, it's not so wonderful. When you've had a few drinks, everything looks fabulous. But as a writer, with a couple of drinks in me, I'm nowhere near as funny as I am stone-cold sober at nine in the morning.

When I'm really writing for four or five hours, I am exhausted at the end. I haven't gotten out of bed, except to pee. But I'm exhausted. My mind has been working and characters have been talking and things have been going on. I might as well have been on a treadmill for an hour, in terms of how tired I am. Then I get a good boozy lunch with some wine, followed by a nap. I'm a great believer in the Mediterranean lifestyle. Everybody has a big lunch and takes a nap, and they open the stores again at four. Then they're open from four to eight, and then they go out to dinner. It's such a sensible lifestyle, and they live longer than we do. Obviously, when you're shooting, you can't take naps. Any day I could take a nap, I thought was the greatest day. My old expression is, "My cats and I go paws-up for an hour and a half." They know naptime is coming when I return from the Palm. Everybody onto the bed. I love that, and I think it's a wonderful way to live.

By the way, with the European filming schedule, you get twice as much done. I'm used to the American system. In Europe, you shoot eight hours straight, like eleven to seven. There's a rolling buffet on the set. You can go get a sandwich while you're waiting for them to light. In America, the minute you go to lunch—which is supposed to last one hour—people dribble back onto the set, and some are five minutes late, ten minutes late. It's never an hour. When I was shooting, especially in television, I used to work late. I would say to Aaron and Leonard, "Let me work two hours' worth of gold time as opposed to breaking for dinner and coming back. Once you break for dinner, Jesus, it takes you forever, so let's just work straight through." I'm a great believer of if you're there, do it. It's like writing. I could not write for forty-five minutes in bed on a yellow pad, get up, and go to a dental appointment, come back, and start writing again. I can't do that.

Brandon, Leonard, and Gavilan

Next, another everything-done-for-the-wrong-reason project, though it didn't take much out of my life. In 1982 *Hart to Hart* was a big hit. NBC was being run at the time by Brandon Tartikoff. He was the nicest guy in the world and really bright. He was putting on wonderful shows. He said to me one night at a party, "Why don't you guys come over and do a series with NBC?"

I said to Leonard Goldberg, "This is too good to pass up. We've got to do this." I thought of a premise—an ex–Navy Seal who lives at the beach and works with an older guy who's a conman. I called him Gavilan because there was a fighter named Kid Gavilan and I thought it was a great name. Robert Urich, who was a big television star at the time on *Vega$*, was available. *Vega$* had run out, and that had been an Aaron Spelling show. Leonard may have had extra joy in taking him from Aaron. Anyway, I wrote a premise, we went down to Brandon Tartikoff's office, we pitched the show, and Brandon said, "Okay, you guys have thirteen on the air. You don't have to do a pilot or anything. Goldberg and Mankiewicz."

Again, this was done for all the wrong reasons. I wasn't burning to do a series about a Navy Seal. I was just trying to think of what can we do so we can get a show on the air. I met Bob Urich, who's a very nice guy, but very scared about doing a new thing because he had done *Vega$* for five or six years and just settled into it. He kept calling me day and night as I'm starting to write the script, asking, "Do you really think I should drive a Porsche? I don't know about a Porsche. You mean an old Porsche, not a new Porsche."

I said to Leonard, "Listen, I don't want to stand in the way of this, but it's getting crazy here." I realized that my heart wasn't in it. So they got some guy Urich really liked from *Vega$*, and Leonard said, "It'll say created by Tom Mankiewicz and let this guy go ahead and write the script. Bob loves him, and it won't cause you any problems."

The one joy was Fernando Lamas, who played the old conman and was an absolute hoot. I just loved him. He came from the era of MGM as the Latin lover from the forties and fifties. He was married to Esther Williams. He would say, "You know, Tom, there was Esther, so beautiful, so wonderful. And you know, in America, you have such beautiful women, but they're not fucked properly."

I had to suck it in, call Brandon, and say, "My eyes were too big for my stomach. I have a movie to do." Gavilan came out, created by Tom Mankiewicz. Single card to start the show, and was off in six episodes. I got a check for eleven dollars from the Philippines for the six episodes. I don't think anybody's heart was in it. I don't know that Bob Urich really wanted to do it. Leonard probably thought, I got thirteen on the air, Bob Urich and Fernando Lamas, maybe this is gonna be a hit.

A year later at the Golden Globes, I went to the men's room, and I found myself peeing next to Bob Urich. I said, "Hello, Bob."

And he said, "Is it too late to tell you, you were right? I should have just said, 'What do you want me to do?' and then just done it." He was very nice. I liked him very much. But he was so nervous at the time. He had his first really big hit with *Vega$*. He carried that show. Now, he thinks, what happens if that was just *Vega$* and the audience doesn't like me as anything else? I've got no place else to go. He wound up doing four or five different series. They always recycled Bob Urich. He wasn't a great actor, he wasn't a bad actor. But again, when you do things for the wrong reasons . . .

Dr. Mankiewicz Is In

Frank Wells, who's no longer with us, was the president of Warners at the time of *Superman*. He apparently said, "We wouldn't have this picture—I mean, Dick Donner did an unbelievable job—but we wouldn't have this picture without Mankiewicz; let's sign him." That's why Warners signed me. They lied a little bit, saying, "Guess what, Mank, we want you to make your own movies." In fact, they wanted me to fix everything on the lot. I had a nameplate on my desk that read Dr. Mankiewicz. The big script fixers at the time were, if you wanted a drama, especially grown men sinking to their knees and roaring, Robert Towne. If you wanted silly, sophisticated comedy, Elaine May must have fixed a dozen movies. If you wanted action/ adventure with humor, you'd go right to Dr. Mankiewicz. It gets exhausting because there's a lack of satisfaction. Most of the time, you don't get credit, and that's a condition of your employment. That's why they pay you more. So inside the industry they know, but nobody else does. The other thing is, if you rewrite it and it's not a good picture, the original screenwriters would say it was just great until Mankiewicz got on it. So it's very difficult to win. Actors get so besotted by you when you show up on location, because if you change their shoes from green to red, they say, "Isn't he great? I got red shoes now. I used to have green shoes." Almost like any change is better. Other than that, the producers give you a beautiful hotel suite, you fly first class, and the actors are always calling you saying, "You know the scene where the girl gets in bed with me? That could be a little bit better now."

Steven Spielberg, who had the bungalow next to me, was doing a picture called *Gremlins,* directed by Joe Dante. It was Dante's first movie of any consequence. Steven gave me the script, and I gave him some ideas. He said, "Can you give them to me, because Joe Dante is very sensitive and I'll tell him the ideas like they were my ideas, and then he'll take them from me."

I said, "Okay, that's fine."

Then, Dick Donner and Spielberg were shooting a picture called *The Goonies* and they needed four scenes, so off I went to work on *The Goonies.* Warners, who kept saying to me, "Oh, God, we can't wait for you to start making your own pictures," were happy as clams I was fixing all this stuff.

I wrote a script called *Rainbow* about a conman in the 1920s, and that was going to be a picture that I was hoping to direct. Bob Shapiro, who was head of production at Warners, said, "I've got good news and bad news."

I said, "Give me the good news."

He said, "Clint Eastwood loves *Rainbow.*"

"What's the bad news?"

"Clint Eastwood loves *Rainbow.*"

I had lots of meetings with Clint, and he was going to do that as his next picture. Unfortunately for Warners, Clint's *Bronco Billy* was not a big hit. It was a soft part for Clint. Then he did a wonderful little picture about the Depression, *Honkytonk Man,* with his son, but it didn't do very well either. Warners convinced him, it's time for Dirty Harry to come back. So my script kept getting postponed, but he would never give it up. When somebody wanted to direct it and take it away from him, he said, "No. If anybody ever directs this, it will be Mankiewicz or me." He wouldn't let anybody have it, and he wouldn't make it. Actually, I think Clint would have been a little miscast, because it should have been Jack Nicholson or Warren Beatty, somebody with a lot of teeth and a shit-eating grin.

In 1983 Blake Edwards was going to do a picture with Clint Eastwood and Burt Reynolds that he had written, *City Heat.* He was having real disagreements with Clint. Blake was used to getting his own way, but Clint was King of Warners. Terry Semel—again, when the mountain went down to Mohammed—came to my office and said, "Here's the script. Blake's directing it, but he and Clint are not getting along. Clint likes you and he likes you as a writer. If you could just do some writing for us."

I said, "Yeah, but Terry, it's a Blake Edwards script; he's directing it too."

He said, "Wait for Clint to call you."

So Clint called me and said, "You know the kind of stuff I do well, and I'm really thrilled that you're going to be doing this."

I asked, "Well, Clint, does Blake know about this?"

He said, "He's thrilled."

I said, "Do you mind if I call Blake, because I know him."

Clint said, "Well, what would you want to do that for?" Pause. "Do whatever you want."

I got really scared. So I called Blake because I thought, I'm not going to go on this picture with Blake Edwards, for God's sake, *Breakfast at Tiffany's*, every goddamn hit in the world—*10*. Blake said, "Oh, my God. Are they asking you to rewrite it? I thought it was a piece of shit they were going to ask. Boy, they're pulling out all the stops."

I asked, "What is the situation?"

He said, "Well, Mr. Eastwood and I don't agree. Mr. Eastwood suggested they get another writer to 'help me.'" Now, Blake was a great screenwriter. He said, "And I suggested maybe we get another actor." That was impossible at Warners if Clint wanted to do it. Blake said, "If you guys want to get another writer, that's fine with me. If I think whatever he or she is doing is better than mine, I'll shoot it." And I thought, oh, my God.

I got Terry and said, "Terry, there is a huge, immovable force named Clint Eastwood in the west, and in the east, there is a giant, unforgiving mountain named Blake Edwards. In between is something called a 'Mank Burger.' I'm not going to do this; this would be a disaster for me. Disaster." So he said okay.

I called Clint. "Clint, I'm so sorry I can't do it."

He said, "All right, send all the stuff back right now." He hung up.

Annie, my assistant, said, "Oh, my God, we're going to be killed."

A week later, Blake Edwards was off the picture. Warners paid him off. It turned out Blake was being very crafty too. He didn't mind getting paid off because he had a picture already set up at Columbia. Terry came back and said, "Here's the deal. How about if you rewrite this and you direct it?"

I said, "Terry, let me think about it." I sat down with Annie, who was the only person I could really talk to, and said, "Listen, people may think I'm fucking nuts, but I think this would be a disaster for me." Clint had directed four or five films, and Burt Reynolds had also directed a few pictures, including one about dying, *The End*. I said, "Those guys will have me for fucking lunch. I'll just stand on the set while they shoot. I've got two huge stars who are both directors and I've never directed a feature." I'd done *Hart to Hart*. I said, "And I'm supposed to come on the set with them. I think I'd slit my throat. They'll say, 'Thanks, Mank, for your opinion. Now, here's what we're going to do.'" So I wrote a couple of scenes for free. I redid the opening for them.

Burt Reynolds, as it turns out, was the last to know everything. He apparently waltzed into Terry's office and said, "This is great. Is Mankiewicz still writing?" This is way after I'd already turned down Clint. They clued Burt in last because Clint was Warners and Burt wasn't.

But that could have been my first picture. In a conversation to which I was not a party but I'm sure took place, Clint said, "Listen, Burt and I can take care of ourselves. We'll get a rewrite out of Mankiewicz and the picture will be a lot better because he'll be writing for himself as director. And don't worry about Mankiewicz on the set; we'll take care of everything." I know that conversation took place somewhere. I wrote a few scenes as my penance for not doing it. By the way, I saw Clint half a dozen times after that, and he was just wonderful to me. He's a total pro.

Ladyhawke: Million-Dollar Rewrite

Dick Donner had tried to start a picture called *Ladyhawke* twice; once in England and once in Czechoslovakia. He was always prepping and somebody was rewriting, but it never got exactly right. It was going to be a Fox/ Warners picture. Alan Ladd, who was running Fox, said to Donner, "Look, Dick, I love you to pieces"—they were very good friends, and Dick had done *The Omen* for Laddie—"but you get one more writer. I don't care if he costs one dollar or one million dollars. You get one more writer, and if the script isn't right, we're not going to do it." The producer who owned the piece was Lauren Schuler, who was a real hotshot. She had another project called *Mr. Mom.* Aaron Spelling wound up being listed as the producer. So I was on the picture now, furiously rewriting. I also got a separate credit again as creative consultant.

Ladyhawke is about a couple that's doomed; he is a knight by day with a hawk on his wrist, and at night, the hawk turns into this beautiful woman and he turns into a wolf. And they are destined never to meet until there is neither night nor day. At the end of the picture, there's an eclipse and they do meet. The casting was really difficult. Kurt Russell was originally going to play Navarre, the knight, and Kurt was a pretty big deal at the time. We were trying to find a girl for Isabeau, and Michelle Pfeiffer had just done *Scarface* with Al Pacino in which she didn't have much to do. Michelle had been Miss Orange County, and she didn't have any acting background. Dick tested a lot of people, and Michelle said she would do her own test. Because the hawk is on Navarre's wrist for most of the picture, she sent a test of herself, and it was a canary inside a cage. Every time the canary opened its mouth, Michelle said, "Oh, I'd just love to be in this picture." When we watched the video, Dick started pounding the table and laughing so hard, he said, "She's got it."

We had Kurt Russell and Michelle Pfeiffer. We needed a little pickpocket who was the spine of the piece, Phillipe. Dick said, "The guy I want is Sean Penn. I'm leaving for Italy tomorrow. Sean Penn's shooting up in northern California, and if he's interested, go up and meet with him. If he's fine with you, he's fine with me and let's just do it."

Sean Penn was at the beginning of his career; he'd done a couple of movies. I called his agent and said, "Listen, Dick Donner's sending the script of *Ladyhawke* with Kurt Russell and Michelle Pfeiffer, and this is actually a bigger part than they've got. It's the lead."

And he said, "Oh, this is going to be difficult. Sean is shooting in northern California and he doesn't have a phone because his character wouldn't have a phone and he's in character."

I asked, "Well, how do you communicate with him?"

The agent said, "Well, he goes to a payphone every Friday night and calls me."

I said, "When he calls you on Friday night from the payphone, would his character be interested in doing a medieval fantasy?"

He said, "I don't know, because he's playing a traitor."

I said, "I'm terribly sorry. I was under the impression he was an actor." That night, I called Donner. "You don't want this."

Next stop: Dustin Hoffman for the pickpocket. Dick had called a lot of people who'd worked with Dustin Hoffman, including Sydney Pollack, who did *Tootsie*. Pollack said, "Never again. I'll never work with him again." John Schlesinger did *Marathon Man* with him and said, "Never again." So Dustin met with Dick and said, "I loved the script. If I have little things to do, will Mankiewicz do them or could I get Elaine May?"

And Dick said, "No, Mankiewicz will do them."

Dustin said, "And the other thing is, I don't want to shoot in Italy because they're kidnapping people there."

Dick said, "Well, I'm sure nobody's going to kidnap you, Dustin. We'll give you a bodyguard."

Dustin said, "And I'd like to play it with a French accent."

And Dick said, "No, you can't, Dustin, because it's an international cast, and if you have a French accent, everybody's got to have a French accent otherwise you're a transplant."

Dustin said, "I know I sound picky, but you know my relationship with directors, it's like a marriage. We fight and so on, but in the end, we love each other."

Dick said, "That's not true, Dustin. I've talked to four directors and they hate you."

So that was the end of Dustin. Dick said, "If I go with this son of a bitch up in the Alps in Italy and he's scared of being kidnapped and he wants to do a French accent and Elaine May shows up in the lounge, forget that." We settled on Matthew Broderick, who was just brilliant in the film. Matthew's father, James Broderick, a wonderful actor, had just died. Matthew was in Ireland, and he leaped at the chance to do it. Dick got Vittorio Storaro to photograph it, probably the best cinematographer—he's right up there, there's two or three, he's one of them—ever in the history of film. This thing looked like it was really going to go. Dick had started this picture twice and had it aborted twice.

The rewrite was going very well, but my script was 140 pages, which was too long. Alan Ladd Jr. said, "Tell Mankiewicz he's got to take at least ten pages out of this—fifteen. I don't know how he does it, but that's his job." So I had the script retyped, cutting out the double spacing. It came in at 128 pages, so I'd dropped 12 pages. And Laddie said, "Oh, this is much better. This is really great. It's moving now." Some asshole at Fox sent out a memo saying, "This is exactly the same script. Mankiewicz just cut 12 pages." If I ever found that guy, I would have killed him. He was from the story department.

We're in rehearsals now. There's something wrong with Kurt Russell. We're going to be shooting in three weeks, and there's something really irritating him. One day he said, "I don't want to have that helmet. I don't like a helmet. I don't look good in a helmet."

Dick said, "You've got to have a helmet."

And Kurt said, "Kirk Douglas wouldn't have a helmet."

Dick said, "Kirk Douglas had a helmet in *Paths of Glory;* it looked great."

The real thing that was eating Kurt was he had just fallen in love with Goldie Hawn. She was in L.A., and he was about to spend eight months in Italy. He thought he would lose her forever. She couldn't fly over because she had pictures to do. Kurt told me one night, "Besides, I don't know if I'd go back in time anyway."

I said, "If you want my honest opinion, Kurt, you don't go back in time earlier than 1969."

He said, "Charlton Heston looks like that, other people look like that, but I'm a very modern face."

I called Dick. "We're in real trouble here because I don't think Kurt wants to do the movie. He wants to marry Goldie."

Dick said, "Oh, my God, this picture can't stop again. It can't stop again."

We ran into Cinecittà the next morning and said to Kurt, "Don't tell anybody for two days what's going on." Dick was looking through pictures of all the actors he thought of for the role, and one of them was Rutger Hauer, the great Dutch actor. He played the lead in a movie that won the Los Angeles Film Critics Association Award for Best Foreign Film called *Soldier of Orange*. He had been in the Ridley Scott futuristic movie *Blade Runner*. This is how things happen in movies at some point, like Claudette Colbert breaking her leg and Bette Davis playing *All About Eve*. We looked on the back of Rutger Hauer's glossy, and it had his apartment building in Amsterdam and his phone number. Now, what are the odds that Rutger Hauer's at home in Amsterdam? We dialed the number.

"Hello?" he said. He's at home.

Dick said, "Rutger, it's Dick Donner. How are you?"

"Oh, how are you?"

Dick said, "How'd you like to play Navarre? You always wanted to play—"

"I'd love to."

Dick asked, "Are you free?"

"Yes, I am."

"Do you ride horseback?"

Rutger said, "I was on the Dutch Equestrian Team."

Dick said, "Holy Jesus."

Rutger said, "I fight with a broadsword."

Dick said, "Oh, my God. Get your ass down here. We'll make a deal. I'll call your agent."

Rutger said, "I have a motor home. I live in a motor home."

Dick said, "Get it rolling. Come to Rome." Dick called Mike Ovitz (chairman of CAA) and said, "You've got to get on Fox and Warners and tell them that Rutger Hauer is a great idea. I can't have this picture canceled." Suddenly, Rutger Hauer's this great idea.

Kurt Russell flies off, and now we wait for Rutger. Three days later, he hasn't shown up. We can't find him. It shouldn't have taken him four days to drive from Amsterdam to Rome. There were no cell phones then. Rutger took his big motor home, and the quickest way was through Switzerland, but at that time, Switzerland didn't let motor homes into the country, they were too big for the roads. So he had to go all the way around Switzerland. We receive word that Rutger Hauer's in Florence and he's on his way. He's going to be here tomorrow morning. So Dick did the most wonderful thing. There was a terrific restaurant near Cinecittà. (Cinecittà being the Pinewood Studios of Italy, it's *the* studio. My father shot *The Barefoot Contessa* at Cinecittà in 1953. I worked there during vacations on *Cleopatra*.) Dick said, "We're going to take Rutger to lunch."

We had two trained hawks for the movie. So Rutger arrived. Dick, Lauren, Rutger, and I had lunch. Dick handed Rutger the stiff leather piece you wear around your wrist when handling a hawk. Dick said, "This is the piece you'll be wearing, Rutger. Put it on. Now, lift your hand." Rutger lifted his hand, and the trainee let the hawk go from across the street, and he went screaming into this restaurant and landed right on Rutger's wrist. It was unbelievable. We all jumped. Rutger was cool as ice. It was a wonderful introduction.

And son of a bitch, Rutger was a great rider. There are battle scenes in *Ladyhawke* where Rutger's rearing on the horse, and it's fabulous that he could ride. He was also European, and it turned out to be much better casting. The Friesian was a circus horse. They're the second biggest horse there is after Clydesdale. In the picture, the hawk is wounded with an arrow. Rutger says to little Matthew, the pickpocket, who has attached himself to Rutger, "Get on the horse. Take the hawk to Imperious," a monk. "He will know what to do." So he puts Matthew on the horse. Matthew, of course, said, "I can't ride." Rutger slaps the horse on the rear, and the horse takes off with Matthew and just disappears into a valley. We've got Jeeps chasing Matthew on this horse. Found him like half a mile away. That was Matthew's excellent adventure.

Everybody was in love with Michelle Pfeiffer. Matthew was sick in love with her, like a puppy. She's so beautiful, she was then and still is. She was at the end of a very bad marriage to a young actor who wasn't there. Everybody wanted to jump her; Rutger, Matthew, me. She carried on with an Italian soundman, a location romance. There's no question, he's not going back to L.A. and she's going to go back and sort out her life.

A town we shot in, L'Aquila, had a thirteenth-century monastery where Leo McKern, as the monk, lived. I took the L' off and made the villain the bishop of Aquila, because Aquila is the Italian word for eagle and we had hawks, so it seemed to be right. We had red-tailed hawks. They're bigger than any European hawk. We were shooting near the Alps; the male got up in the air and said, "Jeez, this looks pretty good here," and just flew away. We had the female for the rest of the picture; she stayed. But the guy was gone.

Taking the Set Back

Vittorio Storaro was almost an Italian national hero, and it was a mostly Italian crew, so that meant every grip worked through Vittorio, everyone on the camera crew worked for Vittorio, every electrician worked for Vittorio, every gaffer, even the Italian wardrobe people; 60 percent of the crew were working for Vittorio. There was a power imbalance shooting in Italy in the beginning. Dick is very much in control of his movies, but very early on, the first few days, Michelle was lying there, the arrow was in her, and Matthew was leaning over her, talking to her, when Vittorio said, "Oh, Mettu, Mettu!"

Matthew turned around and said, "Yes, Vittorio."

He said, "When you lean over Michelle and your head goes past the arrow, don't do that."

Matthew said, "Fine. Thank you, Vittorio."

Second take. "Gerrarde, speed." And before he said, "Action," Dick said, "Oh, Vittorio." Vittorio said, "Yes, Dick."

He said, "When you talk to the actors without talking to me first, don't do that." Everybody laughed, but Dick took his set back. That was so important. With that, he was saying, "It's my set."

But it was a privilege to be on the set with Vittorio. He was a very nice guy. He had 2.5 percent of the profits; no cameraman or cinematographer gets a piece of the profits. Also, the print had to be approved by him, and it had to be done in Technicolor in Rome. A great cameraman at the time would get $6,000 a week. Vittorio got $10,000 or $12,000. He had shot all of Bertolucci's films, *Apocalypse Now* for Coppola. One of the greatest jobs ever in motion picture photography is his *The Last Emperor* that he did with Bertolucci.

Dick steadfastly learned no Italian on the movie at all. He was living in Italy for eight months. I spoke Italian pretty well, having lived in Italy during *The Barefoot Contessa* and visited and worked on *Cleopatra*. Dick drives like a madman. Everybody drives like a madman in Rome. Once he took a left down a street because he wanted to see Castel St. Angelo. I said, "Dick, don't go in there."

He said, "What?" We're going the wrong way down a one-way street.

I said, "Dick, it says *senso unico*. *Senso unico* with a red bar means 'one way, don't go.'" We made a U-turn, people were screaming.

The next day, we were in a meeting with Storaro and he needed even more equipment. Dick said, "Jesus, Vittorio. I don't know. I've given you everything."

Vittorio said, "But I need this and that."

Dick said, "Boy, it's really *senso unico* around here, isn't it?" That's the only thing he ever learned. He would come on the set and say, "Oh, it's really *senso unico* this morning." He still said *gracias* as opposed to *grazie*. It was a fun picture and everybody worked hard.

Dick poured his heart and soul into *Ladyhawke*. In many ways, it's his favorite movie. When it came out, the picture was not a huge hit in the United States, but it was an enormous hit in Europe. Terry Semel said, "You know what? This thing's a keeper. People are not going to rent this a lot, they're going to buy it." *Ladyhawke* went platinum in videotape and in DVD. There are people who just love that picture. A lot of energy, a lot of passion went into that film.

An Audience with the Pope

While I was doing *Ladyhawke* in Rome, *Hart to Hart* was going to do an episode in Athens, Greece. Leonard Goldberg called me and asked, "Could you produce the show in Greece because you're right there, instead of us sending somebody over? Just go out and check on it."

I said, "Great, absolutely."

So Stefanie arrived and got us an audience with Pope John Paul at Castel Gandolfo, his summer residence. He said a little mass for fifty Polish people. Afterward, the monsignore asked, "Could you wait behind? His Holiness would like to say hello."

We said, "We'll be very happy to wait."

The pope came out, and he said to Stefanie, "I see you three times a week." He watched *Hart to Hart* on Italian television. Then he looked at me and said, "And this must be your husband."

Stefanie and I were having a thing at the time, and I wanted to say, "Well, if you say so." But I said, "I'm a colleague, Your Holiness."

And he looked at me with this sly look. He was so smart. It was like he was saying, "I know you're banging her." Then he took out a rosary and put it in my hand. He put his hand on top of mine, stared into my eyes, and said,

"May the Lord bless you and keep you. May the Lord make you safe." Suddenly, I started regressing again, like when I met Willie Mays. I was suddenly a little kid going to church. I was six years old by the time he was finished with me. I was just staring at him. He was a magnetic person. He had been an actor when he started out in life.

Into Africa

In the mid-eighties Stefanie Powers was doing a couple of *Hart to Hart* television movies a year and spending a lot of time in Africa. Bill Holden had brought her to Africa and shown her the continent. There was a ranch called the Mount Kenya Game Ranch, which was run by Bill and his partner, Don Hunt, a real old Africa hand, who lived through the Mau Mau Rebellion. Don came from an Irish-Catholic family in Detroit, and all of his family were into animals. They had a pet store. When he was fourteen, Don had a local TV show in Detroit where he would introduce animals from the pet store. Storer Broadcasting, I think it was, which produced the show, gave Don a free trip to Africa. He went to Kenya and he never came home.

So Stefanie was over there with Don, and she called one day. She always said to me, "Come to Africa, come to Africa." I'm about three parts lounge lizard. I traveled all around the world with the Bonds, but I had never been to Africa. I would say, "Sure," and I would never go. Stefanie asked, "Well, how're you doing?"

It was a particular time where a project had fallen through and I had broken up with somebody I was going with and I was feeling really shitty. And I said, "Terribly."

She said, "Well, why don't you come to Africa? You always say—"

And I said, "You know, I will."

Stefanie asked, "When?"

I said, "What's today?"

She said, "Monday."

I said, "I'll be there in one week, a week from today."

She said, "Great. We'll be at the airport in Nairobi. We'll pick you up. Boy, am I looking forward to this."

I hung up. I had three people working for me; my vast staff of three, Annie being in charge and two others. I said, "Okay, here's your job today. I just told Stefanie Powers I'd be in Africa a week from today, and your job for the rest of the day is to find me a really good excuse why I'm calling to say I can't come. I've run out of excuses."

At five o'clock, they all came into the office and said, "We think you should go."

I said, "Okay." I got my shots and went to Banana Republic.

The world's greatest airport connection was the Concorde to London—it never was late because it didn't have the fuel to circle, so it was always priority and, literally, forty five minutes to an hour later, the nonstop to Nairobi took off from the same terminal. As you're getting near Nairobi, it's dawn, and the sun is coming up over Mount Kenya, and it looks like that great flying sequence in *Out of Africa* where Redford takes Meryl Streep up in that little biplane. I just fell in love. The air smells different, the soil smells different. I stayed at the Mount Kenya Safari Club, which was surrounded by the Mount Kenya Game Ranch—eight hundred animals, a thousand acres; albino zebra, giraffes, Cape buffalo, no predators. Nanyuki Town was the nearest town to us for supplies and food. It's located in Nyeri District. From Nairobi, you could drive it. The roads in Kenya are just terrible. It would take you four hours, five hours to drive it because, God forbid, you're stuck behind a *matatu,* which is one of those little buses that has nine thousand people on it. I drove the first time—I wanted to see the country—then never again. Everybody flew. You went from Jomo Kenyatta Airport to Wilson Airport, they're right next door to each other, like having JFK and LaGuardia side by side. It was twenty minutes to the landing strip, right on the ranch.

The first night, I go to dinner at the Hunts'. We have a wonderful meal, and Don and his wife, Iris, are just great. We all retire into the living room to have some drinks, coffee, and a little brandy. Don opens the window to get some air, and a cheetah jumps through the window. If I had a bad heart, I'm done. It was their pet cheetah, Batian, and that was their way of welcoming people to Africa on their first night. Batian was named after the highest peak of Mount Kenya.

The next day, Don's going to take me out into the bush, and I feel like such a twit in my Banana Republic outfit. Don says, "Listen, I know we've just met and you're only here for a week or two, but when you leave, can I have that jacket?"

I say, "Really?"

He says, "Yeah. It's got all those zippers and pockets. They don't have anything like that in Nairobi, and when I'm out, I need stuff for ammunition, film. I wish they'd open a Banana Republic in Nairobi. We really need those clothes."

So we went out, and it was magic time. Don would go a little bit off the dirt road and stop the car. He picked up a baby ground clover, a little bird, in his hands. He said, "I'm about to get dive-bombed in a minute." There were no trees around. Suddenly, out of nowhere, these birds came—the little bird's parents—and started dive-bombing him and screaming. He put the bird back. It was so terrific going out into the bush for the first time with people who knew what they were doing. Stefanie took me around, she was so wonderful. We went to some game lodges, and she introduced me to lots of people like Richard Leakey. I met Terry Matthews, a Great White Hunter who became a wonderful sculptor. He had a pet warthog.

You Didn't Know Jack

I drink Jack Daniel's. They had Jack Daniel's in Nairobi. They didn't have it up in Nanyuki, where I was. So over the years, whenever I would come back, I would have the houseboy order Jack Daniel's from Nairobi, and everybody knew bwana Mank was coming back because Jack Daniel's was arriving. Terry was the preeminent hunter in the early fifties. People would go out to get the "big five"—elephant, lion, rhino, leopard, and buffalo. Bing Crosby was coming over with a bunch of people. He was, in 1950, the biggest star going. He wanted Terry to take him around. Terry said, "This was the biggest thing." If he had Bing Crosby, he could have everybody. Terry said, "About two days before he arrived, I get a telegram from Bing. It says, 'Phil Harris wants to know is Jack Daniels available.' Now, in 1950, we never heard of Jack Daniel's. Nobody knew what it was. I thought it was a person. So I looked in the Nairobi phonebook and there's John Daniels listed, and I call him up. I said, 'Do people call you Jack?' He said, 'Yes, they do.' I said, 'Well, what do you do?' And he said, 'I'm a wildlife photographer.' And I said, 'Well, for some reason, Bing Crosby wants you to come on his safari.' He said, 'He does? I've never met Bing Crosby.' The next day, I picked up Bing with all his people. We got to the house and I said, 'And this is Jack Daniels.' Phil Harris looked at him and said, 'Uh, this is not Jack Daniel's.'"

Terry had a limp and a patch over one eye; he looked like the quintessential Great White Hunter. He got the patch during that safari, when they were hunting the African equivalent of sage hen. They scattered up in the sky, and somebody wheeled around, fired a shotgun, and took his eye out. Terry would never say who. I would ask, "Was it Phil Harris? Was he drunk?"

He said, "I will not tell you who."

I asked, "All right, how'd you get the limp?"

He said, "That also came from Hollywood." There was a very famous attorney, Greg Bautzer, whom I knew some. I knew his wife, Dana Wynter, better. Bautzer was a huge show business attorney and a big, tough guy. He wanted to go to Terry Matthews's. He had his own special-built rifle, a .458, made by Purdey's. Terry said, "I always tested people to see their marksmanship before we went out. These people want to get the big five. So I put a cardboard box with a little red circle in it about 150 to 180 yards away, and son of a gun, Bautzer drilled it four times out of five. He was an amazing shot. So we go out, and the first thing we run across is a herd of Cape buffalo. Buffalo are the most dangerous animals in Africa. They charge completely unprovoked. They're mean bastards. There was one old bull that had been thrown out of the herd. He was to the side, and I thought, those are the horns that Bautzer would want, and we could pick him off without pissing off the whole herd.

"The buffalo sees us. Greg cocks his rifle. I'm behind him and I've cocked my rifle. Bautzer turned around and looked at me like he was really pissed off. He said, 'You don't think I can drop this animal?' I said, 'I know you can. I've seen you shoot.' I slid the bolt back, and son of a gun, the buffalo charged right for us. Bautzer's first shot went off his flank, second shot missed him completely. I'm whipping my rifle up, and I hit him twice in the heart. But the momentum was such that he was on top of me, blood flying out of him in every direction. He was trying to hook me. Bautzer had a side arm. He pulled it out to shoot the buffalo in the head, to kill him, but he missed and shot me in the foot. And the buffalo collapsed on top of me, dead. Tom, I've been at this forty years. Animals have done nothing to me, but people? Especially people from Hollywood."

Terry had stories about taking people out, guys who were supposedly tough guys, to get the big five, and they would be faced with a buffalo or a lion and start crying. They would say, "You kill everything and just tell my wife I did it." When hunters were really in charge out there, there was almost no poaching, because poachers would be shot on sight by them and it was fine with the government. The minute the World Wildlife Fund outlawed hunting in Kenya, that's when all the poachers moved in.

You didn't have any problems like you did in South Africa with apartheid. Whites were a little richer, but every member of Parliament was black, every member of the government was black, every policeman was black. Whites were called "the forty-third tribe"; there are forty-two tribes. Don taught me all the things you needed to know in Africa. If you're white, you're going to get stopped all the time; the reverse of racial profiling in the United States. I had a little Isuzu Trooper. Don said, "They assume you have some money, so they'll stop you for speeding even if you're not. Here's what you do: You have a thousand shillings on you"—which wasn't much money then; a hundred bucks or less—"Keep most of it in your inside jacket pocket, so when the cop stops you, you reach into your pants pocket, pull out your money. If you've only got forty shillings, that's what it is; he's not going to ask you for more." It got to be such a wonderful joke. I'd get stopped by the cops and I would ask, "How much was I going?" They would just grin.

There was a guy named Alec Wildenstein, of the famous Wildenstein Galleries, a French-Jewish family similar to the Rothschilds that was heavily into finance and art galleries. Alec owned a big ranch, seventy-five thousand acres, down the road on the Laikipia Plateau. He had a former game warden named Mike Webley, a terrific British guy. Mike asked me if I wanted to come down and do some hunting. I didn't particularly like to hunt, although I'd shot some antelope that we had eaten on safari; I had never hunted big game at all. Mike said, "We'll get an old impala that's been thrown out of the herd—lion food."

So I go down there, and this is when a city dude who is three parts lounge lizard is really being Mr. Africa. I have the only rifle, a .270. Mike and I and a Masai tracker go out. We see the old impala, who keeps going uphill. I'm a smoker. I keep saying, "God, why does he go uphill? Why doesn't he go downhill?" We're a mile and a half away from the car, in the middle of nowhere. We round a stand of acacia trees and almost walk into a pride of lions; there are at least a dozen. Two big males get up. I whisper, "Oh, my God." They're half a football field away, which they can cover in two and a half seconds. I whimper, "Mike?"

He says, "Just keep walking and talking. Keep looking at me. We're not on their menu. It's the middle of the day. They want to go to sleep. For God's sake, don't look at them. We're fine."

I notice the Masai tracker is not that upset either. I ask, "If one of them comes for us, should I take a shot at him?"

Mike says, "Oh, my goodness, no. Don't irritate them." With a little antelope gun, I'm not going to drop a lion; not that I could have. I could feel them running at me from behind, even though they didn't. Mike was absolutely right. As long as you don't cause them any trouble, we really aren't on their menu. They're not used to eating people.

I start to feel the adrenaline pumping, like when you almost have an accident on the freeway. I'm feeling great, and I say, "Boy, that's the most exciting thing that's ever happened to me in my life. That's just incredible." We get back to the car. I have these big tacky pants on, and as I swing up to get in the car, I look down and I've urinated all over my pants. The stains are all the way down. Mike and the Masai must have seen them all the way while I'm talking. Suddenly, I'm Frank Buck. I have just urinated all over myself, and I know when it happened: when the two big males stood up. Thank God I hadn't had a big breakfast. By the way, Mike and Don Hunt said the most dangerous lions in Africa are in the game parks. Why? Because they're used to people. They've seen people their whole lives, trams with people. They have no fear of people.

One of the times I was in Kenya, *Out of Africa* was shooting there. Sydney Pollack, whom I knew quite well, was directing. People don't think of him as one of the great directors, but he could do everything; a social drama like *Absence of Malice*, a comedy like *Tootsie*, a romantic adventure like *Out of Africa*. Sydney signed agreements with the Masai to clear a landing strip. There were fifty boulders, and the Masai would remove one every three days. Everybody in Kenya's on their own time, Kenyan time. He was getting really disillusioned trying to prep there. Sydney said, "We were down in the Masai Mara. We each had a tent, and there was a common loo tent where you went to the bathroom. It was the middle of the night. Should I get up at two thirty in the morning? I have to go. Every tent had a Masai guard. So I open my flap, I look at the loo tent, and there's a Cape buffalo grazing in front of the tent. I said to my guard, 'Get rid of him.' And he said, 'No, bwana. He will be moving on.' I sat down on my little step in front of my tent, and I thought, what is this New York Jew doing in the middle of Africa? I'm doomed. I looked up and I saw all the stars. More stars than you ever saw in your life. I never really looked at them before. I heard the sounds of the night: lions roaring, birds, hyenas. I got lost, and I suddenly realized that if there was a Garden of Eden, this must have been it. Suddenly, the guard taps me on the shoulder and says, 'Bwana, he's gone; the buffalo's gone.' I looked at my watch and I'd been there forty minutes. I thought it was more like four minutes, but I had completely tripped out. I got up the next morning with a new drive." You can feel a lot of Africa in that movie.

How This Place Works

You think of Robert Halmi as a big-time producer, but Robert Halmi was an African correspondent and a photographer for *Life* magazine in the late 1940s and was based in Kenya. So Halmi had a house there. Stefanie built what we thought was the African equivalent of Tara, and she's still there four or five months a year; she loves it. There was a house in between that was about to be finished. And after a few trips, I said, "Okay, that's going to be my house." There was a phone in my living room—the Kenyan phone company was just so great. You would want to call the United States, they would say, "How long will you be talking?" You'd say, "Oh, fifteen minutes." And they'd say, "Thank you." I learned this the first night. You'd call, and if you were still talking after about fifteen minutes, they'd just pull the plug. They didn't have that many facilities. Next time, they'd ask, "How long will you be talking?" Now, I'd say, "Half an hour." I knew that was enough time. So you'd have a ten-minute conversation or you got somebody's answering service and they'd still charge you for half an hour.

I had to have a little road built to my house from the main dirt road. Don Hunt said to me, "It's going to cost you." The road people from Nanyuki, our little town, came up and said, "It's two hundred dollars."

I said, "Two hundred, fine." They were just going to clear a little road so I could drive my Trooper into the garage.

Don said, "It's going to cost you two thousand dollars."

I said, "No, Don, they said two hundred."

"Two thousand," he said.

I said, "Two hundred, Don, and these are nice guys."

Next day, I get a phone call, "This is the head of Land Management in Nanyuki."

I say, "Yes."

"I understand my men were out there. They quoted you two hundred dollars."

"That's right."

He says, "Well, yes, and I get the same. I'm the head of Land Management." So I lay $200 on him.

Then I get a call from the head of Land of Nyeri District; districts are like states here. He gets $500. Then somebody from Nairobi calls and says, "The district manager in Nyeri had no right to do this without clearing with me first." He gets $1,000, plus the $500, plus the $200, plus $200. And yeah, it was $2,000. Don said, "What, do you think I'm crazy? I know how this place works."

John Hurt is an incredibly talented British actor who was the villain in *A Man for All Seasons* and who played *The Elephant Man*. He had huge drinking problems. He'd gotten married to an American girl. John had heard about this place and decided to build a house there. He announced in the *Kenya Times* that he had come to Africa to stop drinking, among other things. Everybody read this and said, "You picked the wrong place." They have what are called "sundowners" every night. That's the wrong place to stop drinking. But he was a remarkably intelligent, bright guy, and I drove around with him a few times. So it was really Halmi, Stefanie, John Hurt, and me for quite a while. Then Julian McKeon, who was an ex–professional hunter, and his wife, Jane, moved up to the ranch. I met photographer Peter Beard, and Adnan Khashoggi, international wheeler-dealer and financier. Kenya had a lot of those people then. David Lean got married for the sixth time and he headed right for Kenya, Don Hunt's house, to show his wife Africa. Producer John Calley was there. Alan Ladd Jr. was in Kenya staying overnight at the Safari Club. He said to the manager, "Doesn't Tom Mankiewicz have a house around here?"

The hotel man said, "Yes, Mr. Mankiewicz has a house out on the ranch. You go out the gate and up the dirt road about two miles."

I had a guy named Henry, a Masai, who was the guard at the house. The Masai don't like to live indoors if they can help it. So Henry had a little lean-to, which he preferred. Locals told you to mix up the tribes for your household because they always keep an eye on each other; Kenya's very tribal. If you get them all from the same tribe, they may take your whole home. So Laddie pulls up and says, "Hi," and Henry just stares at him. "Is this Mr. Mankiewicz's house?" and Henry nods. "Mr. Mankiewicz isn't here, is he?" and Henry shakes his head no. Laddie says, "Well, we're just going to go in and take a look around," and Henry says, "No," shakes his head. Laddie says, "It's okay because we're great friends. It's just a quick look; we're not going inside the house."

Henry says, "No." Laddie looks at him, and Henry pulls out his machete.

Laddie says, "We're leaving right now."

I sent Henry a bonus. I told him, "Good for you, Henry. Don't let those fuckers in that house."

I would start to feel guilty because Mina, my houseboy, would ask, "When are you coming back, boss?" He spoke three languages. He was so smart, and he really nailed nationalities. He said, "Africans like the British and Americans for different reasons. The Brits hold you in a certain amount of contempt, but they let you know that. You know exactly where you stand with British people all the time. The French pretend to love you, but they hate you. They really think less of you than the Brits do. They're terrible people. When the French left their colonies, they took everything with them. The British left roads and a telegraph and a post office. Nobody has any use for the Germans. And Americans are so much like Africans. They're always bubbling around, 'Can I take a picture? Can your wife take a picture with me?' Americans will hug you the second time they see you, you know? It would take a Brit ten years to shake your hand."

Bob Rafelson, who directed *Five Easy Pieces,* was directing a movie in Kenya called *Mountains of the Moon* about an explorer, Sir Richard Burton. He called me. "I understand you've got a great house in Kenya, and I'm going to be shooting there. Can I stay in it? Can we make a swap? I have a condo in Aspen."

I said, "We don't have to swap, because I hate skiing, but if you want to stay in the house, sure, if you'll just pay the expenses of the house and my staff. Mina gets a hundred dollars a month, the *shamba* boy gets seventy-five, and Henry gets fifty."

He said, "No problem."

So Rafelson arrived, moved in. I thought I'd call and find out how things were going. Mina answered. I said, "It's the bwana, Mina."

He said, "Bwana Mank. How are you?"

I asked, "So how is bwana Rafelson doing?"

"Bwana Rafelson doing well, bwana, but he take much *dawa.*" *Dawa* is medicine.

I thought it through and, on a hunch, sent Rafelson a cautionary telegram. You didn't do drugs in Kenya. The American ambassador can't do much for you if you're caught.

I'm flying from London to Nairobi on that nonstop, and sitting next to me is Bishop Desmond Tutu. He was just becoming world famous. I think, This is great. I start talking to him. When he extends his seat, the big lounge seat with the little blanket, he disappears. He's a very short guy. The flight lands in Nairobi and then goes on to Johannesburg, which is almost as long a flight as it is from London to Nairobi. In Nairobi there was a ninety-minute carryover to refuel the plane. The Kenyan government would not let South Africans off the plane because of apartheid. The Kenyans would say, "Fuck you. No South Africans allowed on Kenyan land." So they had to sit on the plane.

It's six in the morning and I say to Bishop Tutu, "You know, it's an hour-and-a-half wait, and the Norfolk Hotel isn't far. I've got a car picking me up and I'd love to take you for a little breakfast at the Norfolk, and I'll get you back here before the plane leaves."

He says, "Oh, but I'm South African; I'm not allowed off the plane."

I say, "Well, I think they'd make an exception for you."

God bless him, Bishop Tutu says, "You know, there are only four black people who have South African passports right now. I think I should stay with my fellow countrymen. But I thank you very much. I'd dearly love to have breakfast." He chose to stay on the plane for ninety minutes with his fellow countrymen who were all white. South Africa, the white apartheid government, was so embarrassed by him, as well as impressed by him, that they let him fly to conferences in Europe because they thought it was good public relations for them.

I was never afraid living in Kenya. When you're in a place with people who aren't afraid like Don Hunt, Iris, Stefanie—everybody was having such a good time there—you're not afraid either. William Holden had died, and Stefanie was learning a lot from Don because she was going to start the William Holden Wildlife Foundation, which still exists. I'm on the Board of Directors. Every year, we teach upward of ten thousand Kenyan schoolchildren about their ecology and wildlife. There are camp-overs and lectures. So Don was saying to her, "You have to slide into this carefully because the African male does not want to be told what to do by a woman. That's why Joy Adamson was killed," *Born Free*. "That's why Diane Fossey was killed. I'm not saying there weren't other circumstances as well. But they became arrogant to the African male. They were ordering people around. You've got to be very careful about this; this isn't Beverly Hills. Once they get to know you, it's easier. But in the beginning, don't start ordering men around, they'll really, really resent you." Don got her a special-made, sawed-off shotgun, which she kept in her bedroom. He said, "If anything ever happens to you at night, just aim in the direction of the door, pull the trigger, and it will wipe out everything in its path." She's never used it, and it's never been a problem.

I owned the house for three or four years. I realized something big was starting to happen inside me. I thought, God, there's so much wonderful life out there, so many wonderful things. It was Christmas Eve and we were at the Safari Club dining room, and I got a call from Mike Ovitz. The host said, "Mr. Mankiewicz, Mr. Ovitz is calling, and you can take it in the kitchen."

I said, "Please tell Mr. Ovitz I've just left here and you can't find me; you don't know where I am." I thought, oh fuck, it's Christmas Eve. As much as you love show business and it's part of you, it starts intruding when you're in Africa. Who the fuck wants to talk about a deal at that time? It was a wonderful tonic at that point in my life to remind me that there were other things in the world, other places, and there were wonderful people that had nothing to do with show business. They couldn't care less whether a Bond movie opened big or small; their lives were about something else.

Kenya is an amazing country, and it opened my eyes. Even though I'd been traveling a lot and living in Europe, it was a great burst of fresh air coming through a window. I made friends there that I still have. In the eighties, Kenya was such a fun place to live, like Italy. In Italy, you cannot speed things up. You either get into the rhythm or leave. If you say, "I've got to have the following nineteen things done and I've got thirteen seconds," they'll just throw up their hands; it's not going to happen. One day you get sick, but the doctors are on strike, you just have to wait. Kenya, the same way. It reminded me a lot of Italy.

I sold my house, finally, because though I'd go there for weeks at a time, I'd only been there four or five times. I'd been all over the country and I'd been on safari, but I was also working. It's not like having a house in Lake Arrowhead. It's a big schlep, and you don't go unless you can spend a lot of time there. You can't go for three days; it takes you two days to get there. I have not been back in years, and I don't want to go back because it's not going to be the same. I'm not the same person, and it's not going to be like when I was bopping around the country with Stefanie and Don and Iris. Iris is sick now, and Stefanie might not be there, and I'm older, and it's just not the same.

Mank One

Warners treated me very well, even though they really only wanted to use me for rewrites. They wanted their money's worth. They were giving me a huge bungalow with four or five different rooms, and I had a development person. Frank Price at Universal said to CAA, "I'd really like to get Mankiewicz over here. He can make a picture. I'm not sure which picture, but he can make a picture here."

I had left Jeff Berg, my agent at ICM, because Mike Ovitz had romanced me. He said, "You know, every project that my clients are involved with all have something to do with you. There's Dick Donner and Steven Spielberg—Mankiewicz is doing this, Mankiewicz is doing that. And I thought, why doesn't he join us?" At the time, it was clear Ovitz was the most powerful agent. Donner said to me, "You're a fool if you don't come to CAA." They also happened to represent Frank Price, and Ovitz said, "You know what? Frank would like you to come to Universal." Ovitz was the latter-day Freddie Fields. Freddie, when he had Sue Mengers with him, was the first guy who really started to cock around with producers and became as big as the movie and the actors and the actresses were. Ovitz couldn't have been more charming and more humble. He could be really seductive, and at the time, there was no question that CAA was the place to be. I called Jeff Berg and said, "I'm going with Mike Ovitz." I've never fired anybody without cause. Jeff Berg was head of ICM, which was a big agency. But I really felt like I was better off going to CAA. I really wanted to make pictures. And here was Frank Price dangling this deal at Universal. I had fulfilled my obligation to Warners on so many different projects, and I couldn't get my own picture off the ground there.

So Annie Stevens and I moved to Universal, where we got a really nice bungalow, "Mank One Productions." And the first thing Universal did was to ask me to fix a movie for Colin Higgins, who had done *9 to 5* with Jane Fonda, Dolly Parton, and Lily Tomlin. Higgins was having trouble with a script for a sequel to *9 to 5*. Frank Price said, "Listen, while you're settling in, will you work with Colin? Colin would be delighted. He wants to work with you."

Colin was at a loss. Jane Fonda didn't really want to do a sequel. Dolly Parton did. She had done *Best Little Whorehouse* at Universal. We had meetings with her. She was the brightest person. I mean, she plays "Dolly" real great. I'm not surprised at her huge musical or acting success. She's real smart. Look at Dollywood. But the sequel was never going to happen. I helped Colin as much as I could. We had lunch three times a week, and I'd go through pages with him and say, "How about blah-blah-blah?" I don't know if his heart was in it. So I said to Frank, "I don't know if this is happening."

He said, "Okay, now listen. I swear to God you'll make a picture here, but there's one more script . . ."

I said, "Oh, boy, here we go again."

Legal Eagles: The Package

In the Ovitz era, what was happening to Hollywood was "the package." *Legal Eagles* started as a project for Bill Murray. It was a buddy movie. Bill Murray was represented by Ovitz. But he backed out. Jim Cash and Jack Epps, who'd written the script, were represented by CAA. Robert Redford mentioned to Ovitz that he'd love to do a romantic comedy. In a CAA meeting, the agents said, "You know what? We can retool this buddy movie as a romantic comedy. They're both lawyers. This would be like Spencer Tracy and Katharine Hepburn." So it was Redford, then Debra Winger, whom CAA represented. It was being done at Universal, where Mike Ovitz represented Frank Price; and Ivan Reitman, whom they represented, was directing it. It needed a rewrite. Neither Reitman nor Redford nor Winger thought that the script was good enough. So, who're you going to call? I was on the lot; Mank One Productions. Frank said, "Look, we're going to get a picture for you to make, but in the meantime, you've got to do this. It's Redford and Debra Winger."

Ovitz called me. I said, "Mike, this is a television movie. I know what's special is Robert Redford and Debra Winger, but this is a TV movie."

"No, no, no, it's going to be great. When you get home tonight, Ivan is coming over to see you." Now, if the director of *Ghostbusters* is coming to my house, it's like the old days at Warners, if Terry Semel's coming down to see me, then they really want something. I agreed because I was under a lot of pressure. I was CAA, the actors and director were CAA, and the studio head was CAA. I thought, I certainly can make it better.

We scheduled a meeting with Ivan, Redford, and me. Debra Winger was in New York. Redford was the guy you had to please, he was the huge star. Bob was an hour late for the meeting; Ivan and I were just sitting there. There were all these phone calls, "Redford's on his way. Redford's on his way." I gather this is something that he had really gotten into in his life; he always was late, inexcusably late. Melanie Griffith, on a movie that Redford directed called *The Milagro Beanfield War,* said, "I remember it was so hot in New Mexico, where we were shooting. It was the first day, and we all sat and waited in the heat, made up, for Redford. He finally showed up at nine thirty. We were ready to go at eight. He was meeting with the cameraman, Robbie Greenberg. Redford said, 'We're shooting here?' And Greenberg said, 'Yes, Bob, you picked it.' He said, 'No, we can find a better place than this.' Then Redford took off looking for places." He was maddeningly late all the time, and I don't know when he got into that habit.

But we had a meeting. It was pleasant. He remembered me very well through Natalie Wood and Alan Pakula. I hadn't seen him in years. I was at the wedding of David Lange, Hope Lange's brother, Alan Pakula's brother-in-law, in Toronto, where David's wife's family came from. I was one of the two best men at the wedding. Me and Bob Redford. He was a young actor. Alan had worked with him on *Inside Daisy Clover.* It was a Sunday night, and you couldn't get a drink in Toronto on Sundays except in the hotel. We were in the hotel bar, and Redford got a phone call from whatever charlatan was running the Foreign Press Association. The Golden Globes were the next night. And he said, "Congratulations, you've just won the Star of Tomorrow Award. You have to be here to accept it." It was so clear that they had given it to somebody else who wasn't going to be there so they decided to give it to Redford.

He said, "Unfortunately, I'm leaving for Europe tomorrow from New

York with my wife, Lola, so I can't be there." Then they clearly said he had to be there in person to receive it or they wouldn't give him the award. Redford said, "Listen, I don't care about the award so much, but since you guys offered it to me, if I don't get it, I'm going to reprint this phone conversation on the back of both trade papers." He got it. The Golden Globes were quite a different thing then.

We all agreed on what had to be done. The picture had to start because everybody had a window. Redford said to me, "Listen, when you're writing, I don't say funny lines very well."

I said, "Gee, I'm sorry to hear that, Bob, because it's a comedy. That's really devastating."

He said, "But I react great. So give her the funny lines and then cut to me. I'm great reacting."

So I started writing. I got to New York. I met Debra, crazy about her. She was kooky, talented, had a husky little voice, and she was obviously emotionally troubled in some ways. In our first meeting, she stood on her head. She asked, "Does this make you nervous?"

And I said, "No, I went with Tuesday Weld for three years," and she laughed and fell down.

She called me in the middle of the night as pages were flying out of my suite at the Helmsley Palace. She said, "Do you know what's wrong with this picture?"

And I said, "No, Debra, what's wrong with this picture?"

She said, "This is a Tracy-Hepburn comedy and I'm playing Spencer Tracy. When did I get all the funny lines? When did I become Henny Youngman?"

I said, "Ms. Winger, meet Mr. Redford. Mr. Redford doesn't like to say funny lines." She and Redford didn't get along. I mean, they didn't hate each other.

She said, "Redford is always the love object; he's never the leading man. In *The Way We Were*, Barbra Streisand played the man, he was the love object. In *Out of Africa*, Meryl Streep was the man, he was the love object. In *The Electric Horseman*, Jane Fonda was the man, he was the love object on the horse. Jesus, even in *Butch Cassidy*, Paul Newman was the guy and Redford was the love object. So this is what he wants to be." Years later, *Indecent Proposal* presented the same scenario—Redford as the love object in the sense that there was a million dollars offered to spend the night with him. There was a scene in *Legal Eagles* where Redford had to sleep with Daryl Hannah. He was really upset about it. Originally, he took her to bed, and then he thought that was really bad because he realized she was half his age. Also, he didn't do that as Robert Redford. I had to twist the thing around so that he falls asleep in bed, he wakes up, and she's just lying there next to him saying, "I couldn't sleep either." So it was like she forces herself on him. Again, he was the love object.

Debra Winger was going with Governor Bob Kerrey of Nebraska at the time, and he was in New York. She had a limousine and a driver at her call twenty-four hours a day. She had her German shepherd with her named Petey. Once, I was in a rush to do something and I asked, "Is your car down there? Can I borrow your car?"

She said, "Oh, damn, I wish I'd known. He's out with Petey."

And I said, "What?"

She said, "I never know what to do with the car, so I say to the driver, 'Why don't you show Petey New York?'" So he's driving the fucking dog around New York. Show him Central Park. She felt guilty about being in New York with this dog. You didn't want to keep him in a room all day. So it was the only car and driver that was showing a German shepherd New York.

Terence Stamp was in the cast as a villain. We had a great reunion because he was General Zod in *Superman*. What a terrific man. Redford was a handful. The problem was that Ivan Reitman was not in control of the movie. Nobody was in control of the movie. Ivan Reitman's wife wanted to be a director. She was onset always standing in Debra Winger's eye line. And Debra would say, "I don't want to work if your wife's on the set."

Ivan had scenes written by art experts, which he would hand me. His dentist had ideas. I'm not exaggerating by much. I would get forty pages from different people, and Ivan would say, "See what you can do with this."

Laszlo Kovacs was the cameraman. I knew Laszlo very well, and I'd known him for years. My assistant, Annie, was married to Bobby Stevens, who had been his operator on all the famous pictures. Outside of Laszlo, I don't know that Ivan knew anybody's name on the set. You can get a buzz off a set. Many times they would wait for Redford. I said to Ivan, "Can you talk to him?"

Ivan said, "What am I going to do, fire Bob Redford? I can't fire Bob Redford. I've talked to him. He says, 'I'm sorry.'"

Now it's Christmastime. I've finished my rewrite, and I'm going to my house in Kenya. I call Mike Ovitz. "Mike, I just want you to be aware, I'm going to Kenya on the fifteenth. I've done my draft."

He says, "Bob doesn't want you to leave."

I say, "Well, I'm really sorry about that, but I have gone through it. I've done a whole draft, and I've talked to him. Bob has been in movies for thirty years. Surely he knows somebody who he would want to work on it."

Mike calls me back and says, "He does, and it's you."

I say, "I can't do it. I'm going to Kenya."

Ovitz calls again later. "Bob wants to know, can you come through New York on your way to Kenya? Oh, and Bob has a message: 'It's not a lot of fun in Kenya.'"

I say, "No, it is a lot of fun there."

I liked Redford a lot when I knew him earlier, and I'm sure he's done a lot of wonderful things as a person. So I take the red-eye to New York so that I can be down in SoHo where they're shooting by eight in the morning so I can meet with Redford. Then I can get on a plane in the afternoon to go through London on to Kenya. I get there, downtown, eight o'clock. Everybody's shooting, but Redford's not there; he didn't show. Nine o'clock, he's not there. Ten o'clock, he's not there. Now Ivan's run out of other stuff to shoot. Finally, at eleven thirty, Redford shows up. He gets out of the car and says, "Oh, hi, Tom. I'll be just a minute." He goes into his motor home and shuts the door. A few minutes later, he says, "Come on in." So, I oblige.

I'm sitting there. Bob says, "So, I think the script's looking pretty good."

I say, "Well, I did my best, Bob. Are there any particular scenes that you think still need some work, because I can be doing them on the plane and send them."

He says, "No, I think we're in pretty good shape."

I say, "Well, thanks. That's it?" And that was it. I thought, no way to prove it, but it's just his ego. He felt fucked if I was just going to take the next flight to Kenya. So instead, I stopped in New York to see him. There was no reason for the meeting.

It was a lesson in how not to make a movie, because it started all wrong. If this had been a Bill Murray–Dan Aykroyd buddy movie about two lawyers, it would have been completely different than what it turned out to be. Nobody was in it for the right reasons; Redford thought he wanted to do a romantic comedy, which he hadn't done in a while; Debra Winger needed that kind of part; this was a property Universal owned anyway, and they had the guy to rewrite it. But there's no reason to make the movie. And you saw so many movies like that in that time. CAA was involved with a lot of them. The reason to make the movie was the package.

"Why the Fuck Are We Here?"

Sometimes projects just happen. An example is a picture called *Hot Pursuit,* produced in 1986, of which I was one of the executive producers. There was a French-Canadian producer named Pierre David, with whom we almost got a film off the ground called *The Practice* about doctors owning a certain drug and masking the fact that it was actually killing people. David got a little project together with a director named Steve Lisberger, who directed *Tron,* which was a big flop when it came out and is now regarded as a great science fiction piece. Steve had written a script, a coming-of-age story about a kid who falls in love in Mexico. I read it and liked it and tried to help Steve Lisberger with some ideas. They couldn't get the budget down below $4 million. Nobody was interested in making it except RKO, which had some money to invest, but they only had $2.8 million.

Ned Tanen was one of the greatest guys who was ever an executive. If he had been an executive my whole life, I would have only done pictures with him. I never did. He started at Universal and was a real iconoclast. You could come in with the biggest stars in the world and he'd say, "No fucking way, I just hate this script," or, "I love it, I don't care who's in it, let's make it." He was funny and smart. He was then head of production at Paramount. I said, "Maybe, we could get a million-two from Paramount."

Ned and I saw each other socially. So they set up a meeting with Ned. He'd just had a big hit with *48 Hrs.,* and they'd announced a sequel. Paramount was doing great. David said, "If we can get this money, Tom, you'll be executive producer." They wanted to use my name because I was hot at the time.

So we all assembled at Ned Tanen's office, and the RKO guys were dressed to the nines. They'd got three-piece suits. Pierre David looked like he'd just come from a wedding. They'd rehearsed their speeches. I was in a shirt and pants. I wasn't in a jacket. We waited ten or fifteen minutes in the outer office, and I could hear them mumbling and going through their notes. An assistant appeared. "Come in, Mr. Tanen will see you now." So we all walked in. "Hey, Ned, how are you?" "Great, Mank." Everybody sat down. It was one of those nervous Hollywood beginnings with "How 'bout those Dodgers? Thought they were going to lose last night." "It sure is hot today."

Ned cut right through it. "So, why the fuck are we here?"

I said, "Ned, we sent a script to you guys. We're asking for a million-two, or slightly less than you're going to spend on the wrap party for *48 Hrs. II.*"

Ned said, "Yeah, you got it." There was a big silence. He said, "So, do we have anything else to do?"

I said, "No." All these guys have their speeches. Never said a word. "That's it, Ned. Thank you."

"Okay." So off we went. We looked at young actors. There was a wonderful young actor named Anthony Michael Hall who almost got the part. We settled on a young actor who had never played a lead but had played a couple of small parts, John Cusack. And the villain kid, in his first lead, Ben Stiller. Robert Loggia played the old sea captain. And son of a bitch, they had a $4 million budget; shot it for $3.999 million. Paramount owned the cable rights. Everybody came out fine, especially Cusack and Ben Stiller, who went on to bigger and better things.

Dum, Da, Dum, Dum

In 1986 Frank Price called and said, "Dan Aykroyd's here, and he's going to do *Dragnet*. He's written an original screenplay. Ted Kotcheff is supposed to direct it. He's a Canadian director who's done a lot of things—a good football movie, *North Dallas Forty*; the Mordecai Richler thing, *Apprenticeship of Duddy Kravitz*."

I said to Frank, "It's inspired to have Dan Aykroyd play Jack Webb. He'll be great."

Danny was bouncing off *Ghostbusters* and he was a huge star. He was getting $2 million for the picture, which was a huge amount of money. His screenplay was hysterical, but it didn't make any sense, didn't hang together; insane stuff like kidney thieves who would sit down on a bus bench and knife you in the back and take your kidney and leave you. Danny had a friend involved named Alan Zweibel, a good writer who was working on *It's Garry Shandling's Show* and had written *Saturday Night Live*. Frank said, "Try and meet with Danny. He was great with Ted Kotcheff. But I've got to warn you, Danny can be very prickly. He's not the easiest guy in the world to work with. He's an acquired taste like mushrooms, and very smart."

So I went over to Danny's bungalow, and I just fell in love with him. We got along like a house afire from the beginning, the same kind of humor. I said, "Okay, you can never get away with this stuff in the script."

He said, "I know, I know, but I like to make them suffer up there."

We started to work, and it was the most complete collaboration I've ever done. Danny did a script with Alan Zweibel. Then I did the rewrite with Alan. Then Danny and I wrote the final script. So we worked with each other, never the three of us in the same room at the same time. Ted Kotcheff was in Europe. We sent him the script, and he sent back a long memo. I told Frank, "The things he likes the best about the draft are the things I think are the weakest. And the things he really thinks have to be fixed, I think are its strong points. We're the wrong chemistry for this script, because everything I think is gangbusters is what he thinks has to be worked on."

And Frank, out of the clear, blue sky, said, "How about if you directed it?"

A shudder went through me. I said, "Well, I wouldn't let you down."

He said, "If I thought you'd let me down, I wouldn't have asked you in the first place." This obviously had been arranged. Danny had approved me in advance, because he never would have asked me.

The Best Reasons to Do a Movie

The next thing was Tom Hanks, who was on the verge of becoming a huge star. He had done *Splash* and *Bosom Buddies* on television. Tom was, and still is, somebody who tries all kinds of material. He had just done a love story in Israel that no one had seen. He'd done a picture with Jackie Gleason called *Nothing in Common*. It was not a big hit, but Tom was just wonderful. Danny had originally wanted Jim Belushi to play his sidekick. I mean this with great respect to Jim, he's a nice man and talented, but thank goodness he was busy and Tom Hanks was hired. Hanks came in to see me. I asked, "Why do you want to do this picture, anyway?"

A lot of times, actors make up stuff, saying, "I think I can get to the root of this guy." Hanks said, "I think the script is very funny, it's going to be a big hit, and I'm going to love the company I'm keeping."

I said, "These are the best reasons to do a movie."

When you talk to actors, always talk to them privately. Meet with them privately. Dabney Coleman, who was going to play the Bob Guccione/ Hugh Hefner character, came up to the house. We sat in the bar and talked for a long time. Dabney said, "I think he should be talking like this," and he started talking with a southern accent and lisping. I asked, why? He said, "In school, he had this lisp, and the girls wouldn't go out with him. And he comes from the south." He started this whole back story, and as he did it in that lisp, it was so funny.

I said, "Okay, I'll buy it." It was hysterical in the movie.

I thought Chris Plummer would be great for the phony preacher. We'd sent him the script. I called him up in New York. He said, "This looks like it could be a lot of fun. I'd love to work with you."

I said, "Chris, it would be, believe me." Danny loved it because Chris was Canadian.

Chris said, "I've got a thing I'd like to play with this minister because I've been watching ministers on television now for two weeks since I got the script. There's this curious man named Pat Robertson, who's the only man in the history of the world with a totally unmotivated laugh. He'll say, 'Yesterday, my wife and I went down to the store,' and he really laughs for no reason, and I'd like to make that part of my character." He's hysterical doing that at times in the movie.

It is total joy working with people who have that kind of talent. But always meet with them privately, and meet with them as soon as you possibly can so that you have a personal relationship with them. Have lunch with them, have drinks with them, have dinner with them. You've been through the script with them, just the two of you, so that you don't have an actor suddenly say, "You know, I never liked this line." Now you have to deal with that, and what happens is it gets contagious with actors. Then another actor feels he or she has to object to something to show that they're contributing too, and now you've got anarchy. A movie set is not a democracy. The director is in charge on a movie set, and he or she is the ringmaster at the circus. No matter how much fun you're having, you've got to be able to pull people back and say, "Wait a minute, guys, this is our next shot, and this is what we're going to do."

We were looking for the Virgin Connie Swail, and I wanted a fresh face. Lots of people came in, including Danny's wife, and I said, "No, you can't, Donna, you can't do that." Lots of people wanted to play the Virgin Connie Swail because, again in the words of Tom Hanks, they wanted to be "keeping good company." I saw this beautiful girl in a picture called *American Flyer*, directed by John Badham, reminiscent of Jackie Bisset in *Two for the Road* when we hired her for *The Sweet Ride*. It was Alexandra Paul, and she played a small part. I called John Badham and asked, "Do you think she's a good actress?"

Just like Stanley Donen, he said, "I have no idea. I asked her to do a few things and she did them well. But I have no idea whether she can act or not."

She came in to see me, and she was so charming, I said, "Okay, this is the Virgin Connie Swail." She was nervous about it. Actors have to feel comfortable with each other, and in the first couple of days, I saw her sitting off to the side. I said to Danny and Tom, because they liked her instantly, "Any time you guys are sitting and talking, ask Alexandra to come over and sit with you. Make her feel part of this, because I think she's a little intimidated." Pretty soon, she was just one of the gang. We called her our lucky penny.

Triple Jack and a Joint

At the beginning of the picture, Danny and I made a pact, which was that he was not to smoke marijuana while we were working and I wouldn't drink while we were working. Now, it was easier for me to keep that because, although I loved Jack Daniel's, I didn't drink when I worked anyway. So every night after we wrapped, I would go into Danny's motor home or he'd come into mine. He'd have a joint, and I'd have a triple Jack Daniel's. We were driven home by teamsters. On our first day, Danny said, "May I address the police officers?" and I said, "Oh, shit." There were about a dozen of them on their motorcycles. He said in his Jack Webb voice, "We are about to embark on a great adventure. We will be all over the City of Los Angeles; the City of Angels. I would like to announce to all of you right now that, in the months to come, you will notice that I smoke a lot of weed." I've never seen the blood drain out of a dozen police officers.

There was a silence, and the head sergeant said, "Well, Mr. Aykroyd, I'm sure whatever you do in the privacy of your motor home is none of our concern," meaning, don't you dare walk around with a joint because we'll have to bust you. That was Danny's way of getting it straight, letting them know and finding out from them so he didn't have to ask anybody. We'd be filming around L.A. and I'd have my Jack Daniel's, and Danny would have his joint.

Sometimes, when we were downtown, I drove myself. At the end of the day, I'd come out of the motor home and the sergeant would say, "Ready to go home, boss?" I'd say, "Yup." Two or three of them, with lights flashing, would go out into the middle of Hoover, stop traffic, and escort me onto the freeway. It was the greatest sense of power I've ever had in my life. I said to the sergeant, "Yeah, but will you do that once the picture's over?"

And he said, "Not a chance." People would see my car go by and ask, "Who's that prick that's holding everything up?"

Sketch Artist and Actors

Sixty percent of the movie is Danny and Tom. So I'm going to have many over-the-shoulders and many close-ups. I saw right away that Danny, in spite of a lovely performance later in *Driving Miss Daisy*, was not really an actor. He's a sketch artist, and he is always best on the first take, or the first two takes. He's still good on the fourth take, but that kind of explosion that Danny has is in the first couple of takes. Tom is really an actor, and he's almost always best on the third take, the fourth take. I could see that the first couple of days, so I went up to them and said, "Now listen, because we're going to be doing this for months, I'm always going to shoot Danny first so that he can get that off. And Tom, you've got at least two or three takes of Danny's to wind up on. They both said, "Thank you so much," because they'd seen it right away as actors.

Chris Plummer had his performance down. So you tuned him in like a radio station that you're not quite getting perfectly. After a take, I'd just gesture a little bigger or a little smaller. He'd nod. You're not going to put your arm around Chris Plummer and take him for a walk and explain to him the intricacies of the line he's saying. He knows what he's doing. Dabney, the same way. I don't think I ever directed Dabney once because he was locked. Elizabeth Ashley had a few nights when she couldn't remember. We had to shoot line by line. That was kind of a tragedy. She comes out fine in the picture; she's a pro. But she had some problems at the time.

Danny had Jack Webb down pat. It wasn't an imitation, it was an incarnation. He had his speaking patterns, like the fact that you don't say, "Yes, sir," you say, "Ya' sir." We hired Harry Morgan, who had done the series with Jack the second time around as his partner, as Captain Gannon, Danny's boss. Harry used to say, "I close my eyes, and son of a bitch, it's Jack. I can't believe it. The syncopation with the speech pattern." Harry Morgan had played in *M*A*S*H*, the television series, and was very funny. Harry said, "You know, for the first fifteen years of my acting life, I only played creeps and petty crooks and stoolies in every drama possible. I got that part in *M*A*S*H*, and now all they want me for is comedy. I could always do comedy, but they never hired me to do comedy." Suddenly, he was a comic actor.

He told me Jack Webb would read off a teleprompter a lot. He had those long speeches. It was the most economically done television show in the world. Harry was with Jack six years on the show. He said, "I had the same fucking suit, every episode. The only place where you're on for six years and you don't want any of the wardrobe. It's that one suit." They would do scenes from several shows at the same time where Jack's standing on the left and Harry's standing on the right and they interview the hotel manager behind the desk. It's three shots; Jack, Harry, and the hotel manager. When they're finished, they wheel the hotel desk out and put in a fireplace and the girl is sitting there. They're interviewing her, and the lighting is exactly the same, the same three-setup. Harry said, "The efficiency of it was just unbelievable. Nobody moved a fucking light." Jack became huge; Mark VII Productions, Marty Milner and Ken McCord, *Adam-12; Emergency!* with Julie London and Bobby Troup.

A Master and a Disaster

Our production manager, Don Zepfel, called me. "You know who's available? Bob Boyle."

I said, "Bob Boyle. I know the name."

He said, "How about the guy who built the Bates Motel for *Psycho*? He did all of Hitchcock."

I said, "Oh, jeez, let's get him on." Boyle was seventy then.

One of the things that was most gratifying to me was when he got the honorary Oscar years later. They did a montage of all of Bob Boyle's work, and the last shot was Danny and the Virgin Connie Swail pulling in to park under the Hollywood sign. I wanted to have them kiss for the first time under the sign in the parking lot. The problem is there is no parking lot. The Hollywood sign is stuck in the middle of a mountain. Bob Boyle said to me, "No problem. We're going to have a beautiful parking lot and the Hollywood sign." It's such a staggering shot, the Hollywood sign and the glow over the parking lot as they pull in. The picture came out in the summer, and the people who lived on the streets above the sign had to call the police because there were so many teenagers who wanted to park underneath it that they were creating traffic jams. There's no parking lot there; it looked so realistic. Bob Boyle was one of those people you meet in your life and you say, "My God, I worked with John Williams, who wrote a score, or Vittorio Storaro, who shot a picture." There was nothing he couldn't do, and do quickly and do well and do better than you thought.

I don't like to fire people. We had a Universal special effects guy named Whitey Krumm, and it took him three tries to blow up a car in Venice. It was just pitiful. Six cameras were rolling, and nothing. Then the trunk flew open. We finally blew it up. Bob Weiss was the producer. He worked on the *Naked Gun* movies. I said, "Bob, listen, here's where the producer comes in. Whitey's fired." I don't like to throw tantrums on the set. It's not in my nature. I said to Bob, "As of tomorrow morning, I've got to have somebody else. Can you call Universal now?"

My bungalow at Universal was next to director Joe Sargent's bungalow.

He was, for his sins, doing *Jaws: The Revenge,* starring Michael Caine. Apparently, Michael had three months free. I was walking out of my bungalow one morning, shooting on the lot, and I heard Joe Sargent's voice. "Mank?"

I said, "What."

"Did you fire a guy named Whitey on your picture a couple of days ago?"

"Yeah."

"Oh, I'm sorry to hear that."

"Why?"

"They just put him in charge of the shark on my movie."

I said, "Joe, maybe he's good at sharks. You don't have any cars blowing up in your movie, do you, because he's not good at that." I never saw *Jaws: The Revenge,* but I read a not-so-good review. "And the shark moving across the water looks like a copy of the *New York Sunday Times.*" I thought, There he is. Whitey strikes again.

"We're Shooting a Movie Here!"

We are shooting on the 405 Freeway, which you're really not supposed to do, but we have so much police help. It's a car shot with mounts involving Danny and Tom. We keep shooting and shooting, and now it's getting to be rush hour on the 405. Of course, we have our own cars behind Danny and Tom's car, so we're slowing everything down. People are honking, and there's lots of obscenities being yelled. The motorcycle sergeant comes over and says, "Boss, I think we better call it a day here. There's going to be a revolution."

So we pull Danny and Tom's car over, and I say to Danny, "That's it for today. We're causing a lot of trouble."

Danny gets out of the car in his Jack Webb garb, looks at all the people driving by, and says, "Sure, maybe they've been waiting two years to go to Hawaii and this is the only flight they can take and if they miss it, they can't get on another. And sure, maybe somebody's fiancée is arriving from Europe and now he's not going to meet her and she's going to be all upset and go home. And sure, maybe a guy back there is having heart palpitations and he can read 'Emergency Hospital' a mile away but he can't get there. But don't they realize, we're shooting a movie here!" His mind was like a steel trap. Half of Danny is this wild guy on the Harley, John Belushi's best friend, and a habitual pot smoker. The other half of him just loves the police, has impressionist paintings, has been married to the same woman, Donna Dixon, for

290

twenty-five years, and has got a farm. Lorne Michaels once said about him, "Dan Aykroyd's ultimate fantasy would be to commit the perfect crime and then arrest himself."

In the movie, he's introducing his grandmother to Connie Swail. He says, "And Granny, this is the Virgin Connie Swail." She says, "You're kidding?" We got a big laugh with, "Granny, this is the Virgin Connie Swail"—he always called her the Virgin. Dan said to me, "Do you think that's going to offend people, that I say the Virgin Connie Swail?"

I said, "No, Danny, believe me, it will get a laugh."

He said, "Okay, I just don't want to offend anybody with that." So Danny, who could be this absolute wild man, also had a conservative side.

Daryl Gates was very concerned in the beginning because Danny wanted to go on robbery/homicide calls out of Parker Center. We did some ride-alongs, and it was easier then than it is now. Daryl Gates was a very straight-arrow guy. He asked me, "You're not making fun of the police, the LAPD, in this movie, are you?"

I said, "Well, Chief, it is a comedy with Dan Aykroyd and Tom Hanks, but it's affectionate. We're laughing with the LAPD, not at the LAPD."

He said, "Good."

He was so nervous about this picture that when we started previewing it, he would send assistant chiefs down to sneak into the previews to tell him. We were in Long Beach and an assistant chief of police introduced himself to me and said, "I'm going to go back and tell Daryl I laughed like hell. There's been one of us at every preview."

The Picture Comes Together

We previewed the picture very long. I asked Frank Price if I could have a free preview without opinion cards. I said, "Then I'll see where I want to cut. I don't want anybody from the studio there. I just want to run it once and take a look."

He said, "Absolutely."

Well, the son of Sid Sheinberg (president and COO of Universal Pictures) sneaked in and the next day said, "This thing's so long. Oh, God. We've got a disaster on our hands." I'm having lunch in the commissary, and Lew Wasserman, king of all he surveyed, comes over to the booth and says to me, "It's supposed to be a comedy." And I thought, oh, fuck, it was Sheinberg's kid. So we decided to go back and reshoot a couple of scenes and connect and cut, but the picture never was in trouble.

Tom Hanks loved the movie so much, loved the experience so much, he was pissed off that we were shooting two new scenes. It's hard getting actors back into their parts, because they haven't played them in four or five months. Getting them back into that mood that they were in, recreating the atmosphere in which people can do their best work, is tough to do. It was very rare in the thirties, forties, and even into the fifties that people reshot unless there was something glaring. Then it became a matter of course. *Fatal Attraction*—the Michael Douglas, Glenn Close movie—shot three endings because one ending didn't work in a preview. It suddenly was not abnormal to hear that a movie was reshooting. Let's say you have a bumpy twenty minutes inside your movie where it just isn't hanging together right, slows down, and you realize that you can do a one- or two-minute scene, bridge the gap, and keep the movie going. You watch the rushes every day and you say, "Boy, we nailed that. We nailed that." Everybody's laughing. Then you put the whole thing together and you say, "Oh, boy, are we in trouble here." Then the work starts. It's really the second making of the movie. That's why it's good to get a movie on its feet as quickly as possible and show it to an audience.

We reshot a couple of scenes, and suddenly, the picture came together. Danny, doing his Webb, goes to see Tom in his apartment in Venice. One of the extras passing Danny was Japanese. Danny said, "It would be funny if I talked to him in Japanese." Well, it was so funny that I ruined the first take because I started roaring with laughter. I said to the assistant director, "I'm leaving. Just let them do the second take and print it, all right? If it's fine with Danny, it's fine with me."

The next day in rushes, people were pounding the seats during this scene. We previewed the movie, and out of three hundred people, maybe ten people laughed. I thought, it's because the picture's too long. We short-ened the picture, but we still had the Japanese guy in. Seven people laughed. I said, "Okay, we're doing this wrong. When Danny meets him, give me a Japanese gong." We do that; nothing. I called Danny and said, "I really hate to break your heart, but say sayonara to the Japanese guy. So far, I would say fifteen hundred people have seen this movie, and twenty-one have laughed. I can't explain it." The last thing you did at Universal was to send the answer print up to Lew Wasserman's house. We got two thumbs up from Lew, thank God.

Opening night, the premiere was a benefit for DARE, the police drug education program, and everybody arrived in old cars. We had the normal complement of half a dozen or so motorcycle cops. All the cops wanted to be on *Dragnet*. Sometimes we had as many as sixteen. When we broke for lunch, motorcycle cops would appear from everywhere, and we gave them all lunch and invited their families down. And I've never met a better bunch of people in my life. They were terrific.

Dragnet Redux?

We were the number four grosser of the year, and it was a big hit. It's never stopped running on cable. Universal was going to do a sequel, but it was really difficult because Tom had done *Big*, then this picture's a hit, and he was impossible to get back to play Danny's sidekick. He was already eclipsing Danny. At one point, it was going to be Danny and John Candy. They were thinking about it. But I didn't want to write the script and neither did Danny. The Farrelly Brothers wrote a draft. It was early in their career. It didn't hang together, but there was hysterical stuff in there. Danny and Tom are driving along and they see a Mexican guy about to jump from a roof. They scream to a stop, Danny runs out. You cut to the roof, and you see that he's working there as part of a group, but he's the only one they can see. Danny looks up at him and says, "Sure, maybe you're living twenty in two rooms and you have no health insurance. And sure, maybe you don't speak English and you can't understand a word I say. And sure, maybe nothing's ever going to happen to you in your life." The guy's staring at him. Danny keeps going, "And sure, your wife is probably ill, and your children don't like—" and he depresses this guy so much, the guy jumps.

Movie Stars and Actors

The kind of stardom that Tom Hanks finally attained is very difficult to predict. I knew he was a wonderful actor. But everybody was the next comedy star. I was the next John Landis. Danny called Tom the white Eddie Murphy. I said to Danny, "I think he's a lot more than that." I don't think the world had seen Tom do drama until *Forrest Gump* and *Philadelphia*, although *Nothing in Common*, the picture he did with Jackie Gleason, had some dramatic scenes in it.

There are so many wonderful actors that the audience never accepts as a star; case in point, Jeff Bridges. You can go all the way back to *Star Man*, or you can watch him in *Seabiscuit*; just a wonderful actor. He had the lead in a lot of pictures, but the audience said, "No, you are not a movie star. You're a wonderful actor, but you're not a movie star because we say so." And Tom Hanks is a movie star because they say so. One day I was working at my desk at Warner Brothers. Outside, I heard clink, clink, clink. I looked up, and it was Clint Eastwood dressed in a western outfit walking to a stage.

He was doing a picture called *Pale Rider.* I said to my assistant, Annie, "Come in here. That's a movie star." When the audience accepted him, it was on a whim. He was on *Rawhide* on television, and then he couldn't get a job. He went over to Italy, and Sergio Leone rediscovered him, and he became the Man with No Name in *A Fist Full of Dollars.* And *bang,* he was a movie star. Demi Moore, very good actor and, for a time, the highest paid actress going. She was in lots of pictures. But the audience never said, "Yes, you're a movie star." Julia Roberts, for at least ten years, was a movie star, and she still could be, given the right part. Audiences would go because Julia Roberts was in it.

The best movie stars are wonderful actors. Jimmy Stewart is the perfect example of Tom Hanks. Jimmy Stewart could play farce comedy in *Harvey* with an imaginary eight-foot white rabbit, he could make you cry in *It's a Wonderful Life,* he could play a hard-boiled guy in a western, he did five pictures for Hitchcock, he could play sophisticated comedy like *The Philadelphia Story.* The audience trusted him. Audiences are used to paying, in those days, two bucks or five bucks, or today, ten bucks, to see a movie star. In public, they tend to stare at Robert Redford. "That's Robert Redford, that's Robert Redford." They don't go up to him. Sean Connery, when I was with him on location, was very intimidating to people; their jaw would drop. He was very difficult to approach. You walk down the street with Robert Wagner, everybody goes up to him because he's a television star. My theory is people are used to watching him while they're lying in bed, or they're on the can, or they're getting laid, or the kids are running around the house. They feel like those people are part of their family. They watch them for free. So television stars are very approachable. Robert Wagner is the perfect example of a guy who's been a star in various ways on television and in movies for fifty years. Everybody feels like they know him, and he spans so many generations. Women in their fifties and sixties are looking at him from *Hart to Hart* or *It Takes a Thief,* older people are looking at him from the movies in the fifties, and little kids know him as Number Two in the Austin Powers movies with Mike Myers. He's just part of the furniture in a wonderful way.

I would have told you, conventionally, that after *Rawhide,* Clint Eastwood would not be a star. I never thought Tom Hanks would be as big a star as he is. I mean this in the nicest way possible, Danny Aykroyd was so lucky to be a movie star, because he wasn't really a good actor. But he was billed above the title for a long time. Chevy Chase, the same way; not a really talented person that way to be a movie star. I thought Bill Cosby was going to be a bigger movie star, but I think a lot of that had to do with what he wanted to do. If Bill had decided, "I'm going to be Sidney Poitier, I'm going to take some heavy roles," he could have been a big star, because he is a really talented actor.

George Segal was headlining in all these movies, *King Rat, A Touch of Class* with Glenda Jackson. George was riding high. Then the audience suddenly said, "No, we've had enough of him." He made a very big mistake. George Segal was cast by Blake Edwards as the lead in *10*. George was doing a few drugs at the time; he was never an addict, but he was riding high. George's then-wife, Marion, wanted to be an editor. He said, "I'll do the picture, but I need my wife to be signed on as an assistant editor. She wants to learn how to edit. That's a condition of employment."

And Blake said, "Okay, then, see ya." Blake went with Dudley Moore, who became a star off that movie, albeit an unlikely movie star. You count your pictures if you're Dudley because you're a wonderful specialty act. You can make people cry and laugh, but basically, Dudley was a little guy who was married to two beautiful women, Suzy Kendall and Tuesday Weld.

Monkey Points

Today, if you're going for a star of Tom Hanks's stature, you're talking $20 million, $30 million, or they might take less, but a big piece of the pure gross. For *The Da Vinci Code*, Hanks got a big piece of the gross along with the director, Ron Howard. The theater's take is about 30 percent, at least the first week, sometimes it goes down after that. Seventy percent of what you read was grossed comes back to the studio, then you're giving away pure gross to these people. Whereas, if you make a film like *X-Men*, which did hundreds of millions of dollars, there was no actor big enough to get a piece of the gross, and the director didn't get a piece of the gross. So Fox keeps everything.

The net profits are what Eddie Murphy once called "monkey points." I just got a check from *Mother, Jugs & Speed* the other day; I have a piece of the net. Also, *The Eagle Has Landed* is in profit. All the Bonds, which I didn't have a piece of, and practically everything I've ever had a piece of, are in profit. *Dragnet* is the one picture that I got stiffed on. I have 5 percent of the profits of *Dragnet*, and it was a big hit. But Universal has loaded up the red column. In fact, they stopped sending me statements. Hanks has a smaller piece than I do, but he's rolling in money. He hasn't had to sue to pick up a million bucks. Danny, because he had done *Ghostbusters*, had a piece of the gross. The whole cost of a suit would be on me. Then what you do is spend hundreds of thousands of dollars going to court, the studio lawyers make life difficult for you, and if you win, they'll appeal or they'll low-ball you.

The Best of Both Worlds

Right after *Dragnet,* Danny Aykroyd wanted to direct a movie. So he rewrote his script *Valkenvania.* Got Warner Brothers to finance it. Forty-million-dollar budget. Great cast—Danny, Chevy Chase, Demi Moore, who was a big star at the time, and John Candy. There wasn't a first-rate comic actor that wasn't in this movie, but it just died. It was appropriately called *Nothing but Trouble.* I walked on the set about two weeks in. Danny said to me, "I'm having some problems." Immediately, I saw what one of the problems was. All the actors had their own video screen. So they would look at their own takes and decide whether they wanted to do another one. Please! You can't do that. Danny said, "This is crazy. If I could quit, I would. Everybody wants to know everything. Two hundred questions a day: Is this okay? Do you like her hair that way?"

I said, "Danny, here's the solution. The answer to every question is either six or green. Just keep saying six or green."

He called me about midnight that night and said, "You know what? It works!"

But again, it takes a certain emotional makeup to be a director. To like it. Writers write alone, or if you write with somebody, it's the two of you alone. It's an antisocial experience. Directing is a very social experience. Everybody comes to you with their problems. Everybody asks, "Where are we going next? What's the next shot? Do you like her wardrobe? We can't get to that location tomorrow; what do we do now?" You're socializing. You're the ringmaster at the circus. A lot of writers have directed once. David Giler directed a movie called *The Black Bird,* which was very funny. It was a takeoff on *The Maltese Falcon.* Never wanted to direct again. A guy like Paddy Chayefsky wasn't even interested in it. Lots of actors tried it once. Marlon Brando, *One-Eyed Jacks.* Anne Bancroft, a picture called *Fatso* with Dom DeLuise. She said, "I realized halfway through the movie that, when I act, everybody takes care of me. When I'm directing, I'm supposed to be taking care of everybody else, and I don't like to do that."

Almost every director admires every other director just for the job that he or she has. So you won't find directors saying that even crappy directors are crappy. Writers, on the other hand, are very jealous people. The reason that more editors have made good directors than any other occupation is that they are, in effect, the director of the second half of the movie. They're working under the director, but their profession is trying to cut that scene together so that it plays great; so that you get the most out of the dialogue, the location, the camera shots. David Lean was an editor. Cameramen are very much like actors. Most of them try it once and they don't ever want to do it again. Gordon Willis tried it once. When you have a love scene in bed, the cameraman is more interested in how the light is streaming through the window, whether he can see through her negligee, how the breeze is wafting. He couldn't give less of a shit what they're saying to each other; he's interested in how it looks.

My father always used to say, "If you can direct what you write, then you've got the best of both worlds because when you have written a script, it has already been directed. As you wrote it, you saw it. My definition of a good actor is someone who says a line better than I heard it when I wrote it." Moss Hart used to turn to actors who tried to change dialogue and say, "Where were you when the pages were blank?" Redford is a good director. *Quiz Show* and *Ordinary People* are wonderful films. Olivier, of course, with *Henry V* and *Hamlet*. He was in them, but they're well directed. My father always said about Orson Welles, his first two films were his best two films; *Citizen Kane* and *The Magnificent Ambersons*. He said, "If Orson had been smart enough to just direct and keep himself out of the movies—even though he was a wonderful Kane. He never made a truly good movie after those two."

When you can write and direct, then that's a filmmaker. I love being a writer-director. The two-hour pilot of *Hart to Hart*. *Dragnet*. I did a lot of work on the script of *Delirious,* but I didn't take any credit. Dad always used to say, "If you've written it and directed it, when you run into a problem, the writer's on the set." What's always shocking to me is how many talented directors who are really intelligent people cannot write their way out of a paper bag. They haven't got the slightest idea what the line should be, and they're wonderful directors. But they're not writers. If you're in trouble on a Billy Wilder movie, son of a bitch, the director's a pretty good writer.

I asked Wilder once, "Who's the most difficult actor you ever worked with?"

He said, "There were lots of them, but the most puzzling was Marilyn Monroe in *Some Like It Hot*. She would arrive late. Jack Lemmon and Tony Curtis were really pissed at her. There was a scene where Tony Curtis is doing his Cary Grant imitation. He's on his yacht and he's wooing her. Tony had thirty-five or forty lines, and she had three. She kept blowing her lines. We tried writing them out on a card. Tony was getting very frustrated and a little pissed. It went take twenty. I said finally, 'Everybody take ten minutes. We'll start fresh.' I walked up to Marilyn and I said, 'We'll just take ten minutes and don't worry about it.' She looked at me very genuinely and said, 'Worry about what?' There was not the slightest recognition that we were on take twenty because of her. She was being totally sincere. I thought, boy, this is a whole other realm that I can't get into."

X-Man

You didn't split with CAA. There was a famous writer at the time who left and almost never worked again—Joe Eszterhas. Rand Holston, my agent, was a terrific guy. But Joe Eszterhas kept saying in interviews, "Rand Holston said to me, 'We're going to beat you down—make sure you never work again.'" Ovitz had completely infiltrated every studio, and they were dependent on CAA. CAA represented just about everybody.

It's the late eighties. I'm reading lots of scripts now. I'm a director of a hit movie, *Dragnet,* and I read a script I really want to do called *Sleeping with the Enemy.* I thought it was a terrific script. It turns out Leonard Goldberg, my friend at Fox, who's now head of production, owns the property. So I call Leonard and say, "I would love to do *Sleeping with the Enemy.*" There's a strange silence, and I don't know where the silence is coming from.

Leonard says, "Oh, Rand gave that to you, did he?" This is not Leonard, it's other people at CAA.

I get a message through CAA, "If you get one of the following three people to play the girl, you can do it: Kim Basinger," who was very hot at the time, "Demi Moore, or Debra Winger." What I didn't know at the time was Debra Winger and Demi Moore had already read it and passed on it, and CAA was saying to Kim Basinger, "You don't want to do this movie."

I meet with Kim at the Bel Air Hotel for an hour and a half. At the end of the meeting, she says, "Great, let's do it." I'm driving out of the Bel Air gate, and I call Leonard Goldberg and say, "I got Kim Basinger." Total silence. I thought, what the fuck is wrong here? It turned out Leonard had already decided to leave as head of production of Fox, which he didn't want anybody to know about. This was going to be his first movie. I felt as though there was a conspiracy for me not to do this movie. I said, "Guys, somebody's lying to me here." CAA kept saying, "The next big picture's yours." I got an offer from Fox that they would pay me $250,000, as if I had done the picture. I said, "Listen, I'm not a whore; I don't take money for pictures I don't do. I want to do the picture."

Nobody was fucking telling me the truth about anything. It got to be so crazy that I started to hate these people. When you're on the inside and you watch them maneuvering somebody else, like putting *Legal Eagles* together, it's fun. But it's a different story when you are the maneuveree. So I took my life in my hands and I called Jeff Berg, who had been my agent before. Apparently, he announced that I'd called him at an ICM meeting, and they burst into applause because CAA was taking everybody. I said to Jeff, "I might want to come back." Jeff Berg came over to my house like a shot, and we sat down. Now, Jeff is very dry. He once said to me, "I may be a prick, but I'm your prick"; that's Jeff's philosophy. He's not a romancer and a charmer. This is how this town works, and I suddenly started to get so exhausted.

Jeff goes home and puts an item in Army Archerd's column saying, "Tom Mankiewicz Thinking of Leaving CAA." CAA calls me and I say, "No, I'm not, guys. I'll be very honest with you, I'm talking to people. I haven't left CAA."

CAA says, "Well, we want to keep you, obviously. But you have to call Army Archerd and tell him that's not true."

I say, "I don't have to call Army Archerd. I didn't call Army Archerd in the first place. I'm not calling Army Archerd."

Dick Donner, who is a CAA client, was deputized to take me on his boat and talk to me about staying with CAA. Coincidentally, we're going to be driving his boat right by CAA honcho Ronny Meyer's house. Ronny Meyer is going to be out there waving. It just got crazy. I thought, fuck, I just want privacy. I want peace and quiet. I don't want to be part of this whole fucking circus. So I went with Jeff.

Suddenly, Frank Price and Universal weren't so sure that they wanted me on the lot, even though I had two years left on my contract. I would hear from people that CAA agents were knocking me to every executive: "You don't want him. Drinks too much." That kind of stuff. I couldn't get work. Nobody wanted to fuck with the CAA. Jeff Berg wasn't powerful enough to get a package going.

Dick Donner was such a great friend. I got *Delirious* because Dick said, "I read the funniest fucking thing. You'd be so great for it." I read it and I thought it was hysterical. Nobody from CAA would touch it. Donner said, "Fuck you guys. I'm the executive producer. Tom's going to make a picture. He's going to direct it." CAA wouldn't mess with Donner. Dick was Mr. Lethal Weapon, Superman, and so on. He was a great friend of Ovitz's. Not one actor in the picture came from CAA. The casting directors knew they couldn't get any CAA actors.

One day I got a phone call from Ron Meyer, who was second in command to Ovitz. Ronny said to me, "Listen, can you do us a favor? Can you see Loni Anderson?" She was with Burt Reynolds, who was a big CAA client.

I said, "Yeah, but she's all wrong for it."

Ronny said, "I know she's wrong for it, but would you see her anyway?"

I said, "Sure." Loni came in. She was very nice. "Burt says hi." I knew Burt.

I got a call the next day from Ron Meyer saying, "What's the matter? Why didn't you hire Loni?"

I said, "I told you she was wrong. You said you knew she was wrong."

"Burt's really upset."

You just can't fucking win. My career had, apparently, peaked with *Dragnet*. Now I was the exile from CAA with the *X* on his chest.

9

The 1980s Gallery

Uncle Hume

Hume Cronyn, one of Dad's closest friends, would say to me, "He brags on you all the time. Just not to you. That's just him."

In 1981, Hume is doing *Honky Tonk Freeway* with his wife, Jessica Tandy. They're staying at a hotel two blocks up from Fox because it's easy for them to walk to Fox, where they're shooting. John Schlesinger is directing it. One night Hume is up in their suite with Jessie, and she's doing a crossword puzzle. He says, "I want to go down to the dining room. I'm feeling antsy. Do you want to come down?"

She says, "No, honey, you go down and get something to eat. I'll just do the crossword puzzle."

So he goes down into the dining room, and there's William Holden having dinner with Sterling Hayden. So memorable in *Dr. Strangelove*, Sterling was a druggie in a wonderful way. He smoked marijuana. He lived on a houseboat on the Seine River in Paris. But he was in L.A., working. Hume walks into the dining room, and Bill and Sterling both go, "Hume!" because they had worked with him. Hume sits down, and they have the most wonderful dinner. Everybody is drinking way too much, Hume said. It's a long dinner. They finally wrap up. Bill is staying at the hotel, and Sterling has a car outside. Hume turns to Sterling and says, "So, Sterling, when do we see each other again?"

Sterling says, "Well, how long has it been since the last time?"

Hume says, "About thirty years."

Sterling says, "Well, then I guess never." Sterling hugs him with a bear hug and walks off.

Hume gets in the elevator. He walks back into his room with Jessie, and he is crying. She says, "What's wrong?"

He says, "I'm never going to see Sterling Hayden again."

She says, "What are you, crazy? I'm going to call a doctor."

Skitch Seitz

When I was at Yale, one of my roommates was Skitch Seitz. His real name was Raymond G. H. Seitz. His father was Major General J. F. R. Seitz, who was married to, of all people, Jessie Royce Landis, a wonderful actress who played Grace Kelly's mother in *To Catch a Thief* and Cary Grant's mother in *North by Northwest*. Skitch and I were close friends. He always wanted to be a diplomat. When we were shooting *Man with the Golden Gun* in Thailand, he was head of the CIA in Southeast Asia. He was instrumental in getting us helicopters from Air America to fly down to Phuket. Skitch had been head of the CIA in Africa, based in Lagos, Nigeria. Then he became under-secretary of state under James Baker during the Reagan administration. He and a couple of other guys that Secretary Baker co-opted were called the fabulous Baker boys. Skitch used to tell me stories. They would go and negotiate with Hafez al-Assad of Syria. Assad would start by having twenty or thirty toasts to this and that. You had to take some of his booze, a little sip on each toast, so he's hoping to get you a little whacked. He wasn't actually drinking his. It was water. As you got into negotiations, which are supposed to be very long, you would have to pee. But you couldn't leave the president of Syria. So Baker would artificially have these blow-ups where he would get so angry, "I am so outraged," and he would walk out. Everybody would walk out with him, but of course, they ran to the men's room.

Skitch became undersecretary of state for Europe. During a brief period, I was going to do a movie about the Loch Ness Monster. It was a charming script. The producers didn't have a lot of money. George Bush Sr. was president. Skitch was named ambassador to England. He was ambassador to the Court of St. James. I couldn't believe it. So I would go over on location scouts, then go to Winthrop House. He was the only ambassador that didn't have a penny to his name. He lived on the government allowance in this huge house. I would hang out, and the marines would drive me home. He would give parties because it was all on the government nickel. Everybody was so impressed I was the roommate of the ambassador. When Clinton was elected, they replaced him, but he was so loved in England, Lehman Brothers hired him as a partner for Europe because he knew everybody in government in every country. For the first time in his life, he was earning a buck. He's gone through my life and I think about him all the time. Every time I see Jessie Royce Landis, I think of Skitch's father, the major general. At the time of Vietnam, I was terrified of being drafted. I remember General Seitz saying to me one night, "You don't think too much of the army, do you, Manky?"

I said, "Well, General, it certainly wouldn't be my profession."

He said, "Well, let me tell you something, I don't think the army's going to think too much of you, either. So if you're ever called up, get in touch with me and I'll help you get out."

This man was Patton's lead tank commander in World War II. Seitz's tank battalion arrived first on some cliffs that overlook Aachen, a German city that was the first city taken. They were almost out of fuel. They sent a message back to Patton saying, "We're here, but if we take the tanks into town, we're going to run out of fuel. We're going to be sitting ducks. We have no fuel left to negotiate a battle with." They had plenty of ammunition. When they started lobbing shells into this town, which was a fairly big city, the Germans left. Retreated. And they captured Aachen. General Seitz said to me, "If the Germans had only known if they just came up the hill to get us, we couldn't go anywhere. If they had bazookas or antitank weapons of any kind, they could have just crippled us. We had nothing to fight with." When he was made chief of staff of the Allied Forces in southern Europe, the first meeting between the British, French, Germans, and Americans was at Aachen. He said, "I checked into the hotel. I couldn't believe this city that I had destroyed was completely rebuilt and spanking new and wonderful. I remember walking into the Four Seasons, signing in, and thinking, God, if they knew who I was, they'd take me out and hang me in the public square."

Lew Wasserman

Lew was a wonderful man to me. I used to see him and his wife, Edie, socially at their house, later on, after I, sort of, became somebody. We would run into each other at a couple of places. I'd see him at Natalie Wood's. He was the most powerful man in Hollywood by far at the time. He ran Universal, had run MCA (Music Corporation of America). Lew was second to Jule Styne when the company started in Chicago. It was very mob connected because to play in clubs in those days, you had to be mob connected. If you were representing musical acts, you had to play ball.

If you asked Lew to your house for dinner, you had better ask him for the time you were sitting down. In other words, if you're going to eat at eight, but you say, "Please come at seven," he expects to eat at seven. He didn't have a lot of small talk. He'd talk at the dinner table. Natalie Wood knew if she was going to eat at eight, she asked Lew for eight, and he would come at five minutes to eight and we'd sit down. Sometimes he'd stay late. But he hated that hour of chit-chat before because people were always hitting on him for something. I got to know him better when I was doing *Diamonds Are Forever* at Universal, where we had rented stages. I got my first really snazzy car that I was leasing, a twelve-cylinder Jaguar. I drove up to Universal one day, and Lew was in front of me at the guard gate talking to the guard. He was in his twelve-cylinder Jag. It was about ten in the morning. I yelled out, "Hey, Lew, nice car!" He looked back at me and he lifted his sleeve and tapped his watch. He was usually there at six in the morning because it was nine o'clock in New York and he was doing business.

I had lunch at only two restaurants for twelve years. When I was at Warners, it was the Café Francais. I had the same table every day in the corner. Writer Frank Pierson had his table nearby. It was French country food, and I had the same thing every day, coq au vin. One day I was sitting there with some people. They were looking at the menus, and I said to the waitress, "And you know what I want."

She said, "Monsieur, there is no coq au vin today."

You might as well have told me Santa Claus was dead. I said, "There's no coq au vin?"

And she said, "Monsieur, be brave." Annie, my assistant, was there. Ever since then, whenever we were in a pickle, Annie would say, "Monsieur, be brave."

When I moved to Universal, which is not that far away, a new restaurant had opened on Lankershim Boulevard called Café Barzac. It was packed. I knew how to worm my way into a restaurant, and I had the corner table every day. I was in my office in my bungalow. It was about 11:00 A.M. Lew Wasserman's secretary called. She said, "Mr. Mankiewicz, Mr. Wasserman is having a very important business lunch today, and he wanted to go to Barzac and they're completely booked. But we understand you have a table in the corner."

I said, "Yes."

She said, "Can Mr. Wasserman have your table today?"

I said, "I will never let him forget this. Yes, he can have my table."

So Lew sat there with people from Matsushita and did a lot of negotiating in my booth. He called me to thank me. He said, "That's a nice table. Food's not bad, either." He'd never eaten there.

When word came out that Lew had cancer, MCA stock shot up to like 55. Everybody thought, he's gonna die, and then they're going to take it apart and the pieces will be sold. The pieces are worth a fortune. Then came the word that he'd been successfully treated, and the stock sank again. Lew said to me, "Do you have any idea what it's like when people think you're going to die and the value of your company goes up, and then they find out you're getting better and it goes down? It's the most humiliating thing. I may not have that long. This is the kind of cancer that comes back. So I decided if anybody's going to sell MCA, I'm going to sell it. I don't want the stock price to go up or down based on whether or not there's an ambulance in my driveway."

There was going to be yet another Writers Guild strike in 2002. One night shortly before he died, Lew said, "Are you guys going to strike? You shouldn't, you know. It's all different now. You have a twelve-month-a-year launching pad for new series. There's no fall season you can threaten them with anymore. Four companies own everything now. We used to have eight studios. Today, Time Warner owns TNN, CNN, TNT. Viacom owns Paramount, CBS, Nickelodeon, the Discovery Channel. Disney owns ESPN, ABC, ESPN1, and ESPN2. Fox owns Fox Sports Net 2 and 3 and Fox News. These four companies own everything. If I had to solve this strike today, I don't even know where I'd start." One of the reasons it was so difficult to solve was that you didn't have that structure anymore. He was one of the people who built that negotiating structure. Now it's so nebulous. It's how much do you get of streaming off the Internet? The writers can say, "Well, we were out for another two or three weeks so that, on the streaming of original content, you're going to make $5.23." They're going to steal from you anyway. But Lew was a titan.

Natalie Wood

Jack Haley Jr.'s house was where I met so many people who were so seminal in my life. One of them was Alan Pakula. We became friends, and he was so kind to me. I would spend a lot of holidays at his house, because I didn't have any family in L.A. He did a couple of pictures with Natalie Wood. I met Natalie through Alan, and we became really fast friends. And really close. She was divorced from R.J. Wagner at the time. He was the guest star of the *Bob Hope Presents the Chrysler Theatre* episode I rewrote. R.J. and I had become friends independently, and he actually hired me to write a screenplay for him, which never worked out.

Natalie was fiercely loyal to her friends. I was so desperate to keep her as a friend. Natalie was the one woman whom I swore to God, under no circumstances was I ever going to have an affair with. She knew it. She was so valuable to me and such a great friend. We would take sauna baths together, and we necked a couple of times. But all I knew was that everybody who'd ever had an affair with Natalie had lost her, meaning was no longer around, with the exception of Arthur Loew. It was instant simpatico. Right away, we just took to each other. Gavin Lambert wrote a book about her, and in it he described our friendship as a "fierce friendship." Every time I'd been with somebody, I'd lost them. I didn't want it to happen with her.

Natalie was doing a movie called *The Great Race* with Tony Curtis and Jack Lemmon. Dorothy Provine was also in the movie, and I was having a short, happy thing with Dorothy. Apparently, Natalie was cruel to her, and she wasn't a cruel person at all. Dorothy said, "I think she's jealous. I think she's saying, 'I'm better looking than she is. What the fuck is he doing with her?'" Natalie was a fierce she-bear with her friends.

I really hung on to that friendship; it was amazing to have a friend who was that beautiful, smart as a penny, and really quick. I didn't have anybody like that in my life, and I thought, I'm just going to fuck this up. We're going to have an affair; it's not going to work out. She was four years older than I was. She had just done *Bob & Carol & Ted & Alice,* which would be a huge hit, and she was the only actor that had a piece of it, too, so she was doing very well. She couldn't not work. She'd been working since she was four years old, since *Miracle on 34th Street.* We used to go to the movies. She got so excited when the movie was starting. She was a great movie fan. She would say, "Let's go see Claude Lelouch's film," and I'd say, "Okay." We'd bring our Academy cards because you could get in free in those days. She'd say, "Badges? We don't need no stinkin' badges," the famous line from *Treasure of the Sierra Madre.* She would just show up at the theater, and the manager would come running out, "Oh, Ms. Wood, please come in."

In 1969 she married a British talent agent named Richard Gregson, who was a wonderful guy; I liked Richard. They had a tumultuous marriage and they had Natasha, who's now an actress. Everything that Natalie wanted in life was to have a child. She quit acting to have that child. I saw her in the hospital. She used to love Mel Brooks' *2000 Year Old Man.* She'd memorized the whole album. There's a piece in there where Carl Reiner says to him, "When you were back in prehistoric times, two thousand years ago—" and Mel says, "We lived in caves." "So, you didn't have countries with a national anthem." Mel says, "No, every cave had a national anthem." And Carl Reiner says, "Do you remember the national anthem of your cave?" Mel says, "Yeah. Let 'em all go to hell except Cave Seventy-Six." I walked into Natalie's hospital room, and there she was with the baby. She looked at me and sang, "Let 'em all go to hell except Cave Seventy-Six."

Richard, in an act of pure self-destruction, had an affair with Natalie's secretary when Natalie was out of town a couple of times. Natalie found out about it, and one night Richard came back from being out of town to find all of his belongings in the driveway. The door was locked and there was a security guard. And that was that. Richard was devastated. I was appointed an ambassador to come over to see if she would see him. I rang the doorbell, "It's Mank." Natalie was sitting on a couch in the living room. She looked up at me and said, "If this is about Richard, you can turn around and walk right out the fucking door. If it's not, please come in."

I was in London a lot because of the Bonds, and Richard was in London and I used to see him. When Natalie was in London on a movie, she called me and we had lunch. She said, "If you're going to continue to see Richard, you can't see me anymore."

I said, "Natalie, listen, whatever happened between you guys—I love you; you're my friend, but you can't start ordering me as to who to see and who I can't have lunch with or have dinner with."

She burst into tears. She said, "You're right. I'm sorry. I'm sorry." She was very complicated.

Natalie is having some construction done on her house. This is before she remarried R.J. She is going to spend a month in Leslie Bricusse's house, which is in Beverly Hills, some five or six miles away from her home. Natalie has two Australian shepherds, Penny and Cricket. Two days after arriving at Leslie Bricusse's, Cricket runs away. Natalie is beside herself. She puts ads in the newspaper and has a service out looking for the dog. Nobody can find Cricket. Natalie is miserable. A couple of nights later, Natalie and I are going to dinner at some friend's house. We will be driving by Natalie's house. On the way home, she says to me, "Let's stop by my house if you don't mind. I just have a feeling . . ."

I say, "Natalie, Cricket would have no way of knowing how to get to your house. It's six, seven miles away through Bel Air and Sunset Boulevard. She's never been out of the house before."

Natalie insists. I think she is just going to get her heart broken again. We drive up to the house where the construction is going on. It is the middle of the night. We get out of the car. There is silence. Natalie yells, "Cricket, Cricket!" More silence. She hangs her head. I open the car door for her to get back in, when suddenly, bursting through the hedge by the side of the driveway, is Cricket! Neither of us can believe it. Cricket is jumping up and down, we are in tears. It is a scene out of *Lassie Come Home*. I still cannot understand how that dog could walk seven miles through territories she had never been through before and wind up at her own house.

Natalie had an interior decorator's card. When I bought my home in the early seventies, she said to me, "Listen, don't pay retail for anything. I've got a decorator's card." She beat her little buns up and down Robertson

Boulevard for me. We would go in a store and she would say, "No, don't take those towels. Here are the towels." This was the essence of Natalie. She said, "We're going to have a big housewarming party for you." I had a lot of friends; I thought it was a nice idea. She showed me the guest list, and there were people like Laurence Olivier and Henry Fonda. Natalie said, "Oh, they're not going to come. But when I invite them, they're going to send a gift." I got a set of twelve crystal glasses from Laurence Olivier! She invited studio heads that I'd never worked for. She said, "They'll send something, believe me," because it was signed "Natalie Wood" and everybody wanted her. That's how her little mind worked. Son of a bitch, a gift showed up from Lew Wasserman. They were all really good gifts. She said, "That's how you get the loot."

One night we were sitting in her living room, talking. She turned around and started to cry. I asked, "What the hell is it?"

She said, "I met him again, and I'm in love again." It was R.J. They had been divorced years ago. She saw him at John Foreman's party, he took her home, and she just dissolved into tears, she loved him so much. And they remarried.

What supposedly happened did happen, and this is what it was. If you knew Natalie Wood, you would understand it. Christopher Walken was doing a movie with Natalie, *Brainstorm*, and Natalie and R.J. invited Walken out on their boat. In those days, R.J. would drink a little, Walken (as Mel Brooks calls it) smoked different barks from different trees, and Natalie would imbibe. Walken and R.J. got into an argument about acting. The radio was playing music. When there was anything uncomfortable or at a certain time of the evening, even if there was a big party, you'd suddenly turn around and Natalie would be gone. You wouldn't see her again. R.J. and Chris Walken were keeping up this argument. Natalie went to their stateroom and disappeared, which, for R.J., would be totally normal. She was just going to sleep. The Zodiac boat was banging against the side of the big boat, the *Splendor*, named for *Splendor in the Grass*. I spent many a trip on the *Splendor*. Natalie put on a navy pea jacket to go outside and pull the Zodiac up to tie it. She was scared of dark water—when she was doing *Splendor in the Grass* and had to swim, Charlie Maguire was holding her up. She slipped, and the minute the pea jacket hit the water, she went right under. She couldn't swim very well. Natalie was 105 pounds, fighting weight. They would not have heard anything because the radio was going, and as I said, it was not unlike Natalie to disappear. That was really common with her. She might not have had time to yell if she went into the water that fast. It was at night, the water was cold, and that pea jacket just filled up, and suddenly, it weighed as much as she did. Apparently, she had had quite a few drinks. Didn't take much to fill her up. I'm sure she was under the influence of alcohol when she slipped. She was, we would say, drunk. I know for a fact that it wasn't suicide. Two things: number one, she had been drinking; number two, she was going to play Anastasia at the Music Center heading for New York, and she was looking forward to it like crazy. It was going to be her debut on the stage; she was so excited about it. Bobby Fryer was producing it. That was all she was looking forward to.

Natalie dies at night, and I don't hear about it until six o'clock in the morning when Margot Kidder, who had been up early and heard the news on the radio, calls. I am devastated. I get a call from Roddy McDowall, a very close friend of Natalie's, saying that R.J. Wagner will be returning home in a couple of hours. He thinks it would be a good idea if I was there along with him, Paul Ziffren, their friend and attorney, and Guy McElwaine, her agent and longtime friend, to provide some comfort. I get over to the house and join the others, and we wait for R.J., who finally arrives. They have tried to keep the news from the two little girls—Natasha, who is six, and Courtney, who is two—but they already know somehow. R.J. walks in, ashen, moving like a zombie. He recognizes the four of us standing there, nods, walks into the living room, and looks up at the staircase, where the two little girls are staring back at him. There is an endless silence, and then Natasha says, "I guess you'll have to be both the mommy and the daddy from now on."

I was one of the guards at R.J.'s door, along with Mart Crowley and Roddy McDowall. Everybody wanted to rush over to R.J.'s. He didn't want to see a lot of people. So we were screening at the door. Army Archerd came up to the house—everybody knew Army Archerd—but we said, "Sorry, Army. No columnists allowed," because nobody from the press was allowed in.

Army said, "But guys, my God, I'm not going to say anything. I've known R.J. since 1949."

We said, "Okay, come on in." It was Army Archerd. Next day, that prick put everything in his column, everybody who was there. Chris Walken was there sitting at the bar, drinking. He was devastated.

R.J. takes to bed, totally drained. I am talking to him as Willie-Mae comes in. Willie-Mae is the housekeeper, surrogate mother to the children, one of the strongest women I have ever known. She looks down at R.J. and says, "I'll tell you one thing, come Monday morning, my children are going back to school."

R.J. looks up at her, nods, and says, "I'd like an English muffin if I could, Willie-Mae."

She says, "Sure, and I'll cut it up for you just like I do for Courtney. Why don't you come on down if you want an English muffin and have one in the kitchen?" Slowly but surely, Willie-Mae is getting this household back on its feet again.

Gene Kelly was very close to R.J., as was Fred Astaire, who played his father in *It Takes a Thief.* Gene was on the bed talking to R.J., and I was sitting in a chair nearby. All of a sudden, standing in the doorway was Fred Astaire with his wife, Robyn. Fred said, "Hi, Gene."

It was very dark, and Gene said, "Who's there?"

He said, "It's Fred." Fred Astaire and Gene Kelly. Fred walked around to Gene and talked to R.J.

Later, as Fred Astaire was leaving, Gene said, "I'll call you, Fred."

And Fred said, "You always say that, but you never do."

The next day was Natalie's funeral. A car pulled up just before the funeral started, and out stepped Fred Astaire and Gene Kelly, together. They must have talked that night. It was such a sad occasion, but it was a historic moment to see Fred Astaire and Gene Kelly exiting the same car together. It was unbelievable.

Natalie's funeral is held in a small cemetery right in the middle of Westwood. It is attended by, it seems to me, about every notable person in all of show business. The press is not allowed. However, they fill the windows of the surrounding buildings, which look down on the cemetery. Helicopters fly overhead. I am one of six pallbearers who are to carry the casket some fifty yards from the funeral home to the burial site, where a couple of hundred people are waiting. The casket is enormous and extremely heavy. I don't see how the six of us are going to carry it. We take a deep breath and pick up the casket. I can't believe how much it weighs. I think of tiny Natalie inside there somewhere; someone who had a fighting weight of 103 or 105 pounds. I don't know how we carry it, but somehow we manage, staggering to make the fifty yards to the burial site. At a moment like that, I suppose everybody has a little bit of superhuman strength.

I had sustained a series of losses among women in my life. I was thinking about that as I was carrying the coffin; my mother, Bridget, could have been Tuesday, now Natalie. I had a tremendous fear of abandonment, that if I really fell in love and took the plunge, I was going to lose that person. It even affected my relationship with animals. I had a cat for nine years. A female. She was indoor/outdoor, and a raccoon got her one day. There she was on the lawn, and I cried so hard. It was reminiscent of my mother dying, oddly enough, because there was so much bottled up inside me for so long. The cat and I were glued together for nine years. We woke up together and went to sleep together. Losing her was like being abandoned again; you and the animal are the only two beings in the house, always together, interacting all the time.

10

The 1990s

What a Fucking Business

I think it can be said fairly that I've been in on the beginning, rise, peak, collapse, and end of the talking picture.

—*Joseph L. Mankiewicz*

Delirious **Director**

I used to bound out of bed to get on the set. *Delirious* was the single happiest experience I ever had. I loved everybody in it. I loved everybody on the crew. I loved everybody around it. John Candy was such a wonderful leader, and I felt I was a leader as well. We were smart and funny and good. My biggest disappointment was that MGM went belly-up. If that picture had been pushed correctly, I'm not saying it would have done $150 million or won any Oscars, but it would have been known as the different kind of picture that it is. It should have been really exploited. John should have been on a nationwide tour with Mariel Hemingway. All the talented people in there: Charlie Rocket, who killed himself; David Rasche, who was so funny; Emma Samms was terrific, wonderful in it; Dylan Baker's working all the time; Robert Wagner, wow! I do things with R.J. all the time.

I was so delighted Raymond Burr was in *Delirious*, but I originally wanted Jason Robards. I thought, God, it would be great if he would do something like this. A soap opera heavy. The word comes back from Jason's agent, "Mr. Robards would love to do it." He got $75,000 a week. The way the schedule worked, it was going to be ten weeks. I said, "We cannot pay Jason Robards $750,000." We didn't have it in the budget. There was no way to squeeze all his work into a few weeks. So the answer was no. But he was just for hire. Wasn't really interested in reading the script. He knew I was doing it and John was doing it and it was supposed to be funny. He makes a living as an actor, and he knows he's in good company.

Then I thought of Richard Widmark. The silver fox. He had done *No Way Out* for my father. He said, "I am so flattered. I think it's very funny. I don't want to act anymore particularly. I'm a good actor, but I don't think I'm really good at this kind of comedy, with the kind of people you're going to be hiring." It was amazing.

I said, "Well, thank you for reading it." I was just so thrilled.

Then I was fixated on Raymond Burr. I watched him play Perry Mason as a kid, and he was larger than life. He was huge. He lived in Sonoma, where he had a vineyard. He was living with the same guy he lived with for years. We were told by his agent, "Mr. Burr is not interested in doing films. He does his six *Perry Mason* movies a year and that's all. He doesn't want to do anything. So forget it." I called somebody at CBS that I knew and I asked, "Can you get me his address?" I got it and sent him the script with a note saying, "I understand you don't want to do movies, but it would be so much fun if you would do this."

About five days later, I was in my office. Annie was at lunch, and I was working on the script. The phone rang, I said, "Hello?" And this voice says, "Well, this could be a great deal of fun, couldn't it?"

I said, "You're Raymond Burr." You could not miss that voice.

He said, "Yes, I am. Listen, when are you starting?"

I said, "Well, here's the thing, we would work you for two weeks then leave you for a month."

He said, "That's fine with me because I'm flying back and forth to the vineyard and we shoot the *Perry Mason*s in three weeks."

I'm the guy who's worked with Marlon Brando and Sean Connery and, oddly enough, I was very nervous about meeting Raymond Burr. He was part of my childhood. I said to John Candy, "Tomorrow, Raymond Burr is coming at eleven. Can you drop by and say hi to him?"

John said, "Absolutely."

The next day, Ray came into the bungalow. He was walking with a cane, and I was amazed that he was bigger than John, heavier than John. Wardrobe told me he was one size bigger than John. Ray started talking, "You did that wonderful series with R.J., he's an old friend." And Ray seemed to be getting a crush on John. He was getting so cozy with him. He said to John, "When this film is over, you'll have to come up to Sonoma one day. Just the two of us, no phones." I don't know whether Ray meant anything or whether he was trying to see what kind of people he was working with, because it was clear that he lived with a guy. He had an island in Fiji as well.

Ray worked off teleprompters. So we had a teleprompter for him in every scene. It was like a security blanket. Some actors can't do it. Dan Aykroyd had to give long speeches in *Dragnet,* and sometimes Danny would trip all over them, and he had a mind like a steel trap, as I've said. I would say, "We'll put it on a teleprompter," and Danny would say, "No, I can't read it. I lose all the performance." Some actors can actually do it. Ray was a wonderful actor—the villain in *Rear Window,* the district attorney in *A Place in the Sun.* A very cultured man. Nobody mentioned that any actor was gay in the days of Montgomery Clift, James Dean, Raymond Burr, Rock Hudson, even though the press all knew. Now, you wouldn't last two seconds; not that it's a big deal, because a lot of people come out. But then, they were terrified. If the audience knew that Rock Hudson was gay and he kissed a woman onscreen, they would burst out laughing.

On *Dragnet,* Chris Plummer arrived three weeks into the shoot, and it was important to me that everybody was getting along. In my experience, sometimes, when an actor joins a picture a couple of weeks in, he or she makes a lot of noise. The actor is establishing his or her own territory. We were shooting *Delirious* in New York, and Mariel Hemingway had been on the picture a couple of weeks. It was Emma Samms's first shot; at night, a scene where John Candy gets hit on the chin by the car. She had done *Dynasty* and other things. She missed her mark on the very first take, and she said, "Oh, I'm terribly sorry."

I said, "That's okay, do you want to go again?" Then, she missed it again.

John Kretchmer, the first assistant, said, "Can you imagine that? She's missed her mark twice. This woman shoots six, eight pages a day on *Dynasty.*"

And I said, "John, she's establishing her own territory. She's saying, 'I'm here.' She's joining the picture a couple of weeks in, and she feels like the odd lady out. And she's just saying, 'No, it's my time. Pay a little attention to me.'" And boy, the third take, she hit the mark. She never missed marks for the rest of the picture. She was a pro. When an actor joins a film that's already started, he or she feels like the bus has already left for camp. So you always have to be very careful with actors when they join after the shoot has begun.

When we were filming in New York, Jerry Orbach told us about an Italian restaurant we must visit. He said, "Tell the maître d' Jerry Orbach suggested I call you."

So I called the restaurant and spoke with the maître d', who said, "Oh, great. How many are you going to be?"

I said, "Well, we're going to be three." It was John, Mariel, and me. We got to the restaurant, walked in, and all of the guys there looked like they were in *The Godfather.* They were all sitting against the wall in booths. The table that was open was in the middle of the room. I said to John, "If a car comes by with some guys with machine guns, these guys are all ducking and we're going to get it."

John said, "You sit with your back to the street. I'll let you know if anything goes by." It was amazing because there was no menu. You told the waiter what you wanted, veal, any kind of pasta, just say what you want to eat. It was a great Italian meal. We called Jerry the next day and said, "Thank you so much." He was a terrific guy.

Mank's Mirror Period

I do a whole hour for my film students on mirror shots. One of the examples I use is a spoof film we made on *Delirious.* Doug Claybourne, the producer, says to Bill Gordean, the editor, "What is this with Mankiewicz and mirrors? We have so many mirror shots in this movie." Gordean says, "Well, Picasso had his blue period, and—" Doug says, "Oh, and this is Mankiewicz's mirror period." Then Bobby Stevens, the cinematographer, comes on and says, "I think mirror shots, when used sparingly, are very effective." There's a whole montage of all the mirror shots I did in the movie, which is an unbelievable number. That has to do with looking at myself in the mirror. I've always been fascinated by mirrors and, as a director, I don't think I've ever done anything without mirror shots. It's a wonderful dramatic device because a character's allowed to talk to himself if you've got a mirror there. If you don't have a mirror there, it looks crazy. But if you're looking at yourself in the mirror, and you're Bobby De Niro saying, "Are you talking to me?" you can do a lot with that. Whereas, if he's just walking down the street saying, "Are you talking to me?" you'd say, "Boy, this guy has got to be institutionalized."

In *Delirious,* Mariel is in a phone booth talking to her mother. In her compact mirror is a reflection of Mariel. Margot Kidder with Mariel in the women's room, there's four of them, the two of them with their backs to us, but the faces are visible in the mirror. I love mirrors, Doctor. *Reflections in a Golden Eye.* I'm gonna lie down now. Oddly enough, I stay away from looking at myself in the mirror now. Once in the morning, comb the hair, a little spray on, and that's it. I don't want to look at myself anymore.

I run *Delirious* for my students, really talking about little things they can do in their films like making a guy disappear, exactly how you do a camera lock-off or the blood stain going backward. It's very simple, but they're ideas that they don't have for their ten- or twelve-minute film. It's not that complicated. They see those sequences from *Delirious,* and they laugh like hell.

The Candy Man in Vegas

John Candy and I drove to Las Vegas to make an appearance at ShoWest, the film exhibitors' convention. John wanted to stay at the Desert Inn because it had the best golf course. I actually played nine holes with him. And John isn't bad. He liked it a lot. We were gambling one night, and John took the dice and started making passes. He must have held the dice for ten minutes. John didn't know how to bet at craps. I was betting along with John. I was winning more than he was. The stickmen were so happy that it was John Candy. They were saying, "Mr. Candy, you should take the odds back on the floor." He would say, "Okay, whatever."

So we won really big. Among my winnings was a thousand-dollar chip. We all decided to have a drink in the bar and cool off. The cocktail waitress came by, and we each had a couple of drinks, so the bill was thirty bucks. I thought I was being Mr. Big, and I gave her a hundred-dollar chip, keep the change. Big-timer. Without realizing it, I gave her the thousand-dollar chip. And she took it. We left the lounge, and midway through the casino, I checked my chips and said, "Oh, my God, I gave her the thousand-dollar chip." Now we couldn't find her. I called the manager over and said, "I was going to give her a hundred dollars but I gave her a thousand by mistake. I'm not going to give her a thousand dollars for two rum and Cokes and two Jack Daniel's." The manager checked, and the waitress had already packed her bags and was gone. She had a thousand bucks, she was outta there. But the hotel made good on it. They gave me the thousand-dollar chip back, and I said, "Well, if she comes back, here's a hundred for her." That's what I was going to give her. But she was gone like a shot.

MGM couldn't afford the one-sheets. John Candy and I were in a meeting in Vegas with Joe Westerman and Laddie, and John offered to loan the studio money because they said they didn't have enough money for one-sheets. John said, "How about if I loan you guys a few million dollars for this picture?"

And Laddie said, "No, you can't do that, John, because we're in bankruptcy and I don't know where that money's going to go." I thought, boy, what a fucking business.

We were driving back from Vegas, and John was playing his agent character, which he did from time to time. I called him Irving when he was the agent. Irving was a loser. He always lost a client. But he always felt that he was right. He'd say, "You know who fucking left me yesterday?"

"No, who was that, Irving?"

"Vic Damone. I said to him, 'Vic, sweetheart, after all we've been through together. Never should have gone out with a black woman. You never should have married.' What pipes this man had."

I asked Irving, "You represented Frank Sinatra?"

"Represented him? I fuckin' made him! And he comes out with he's gonna do this thing 'Wee Small Hours of the Morning.' I say, 'Frank, you're depressing people. Don't do it. Stay up, stay bright!'"

I said, "Well, the tune was a big hit."

Irving said, "What do people know?"

But it was always somebody. We were driving past a sign that said, "You're now leaving Nevada." And John said to me as Irving, "You see that sign? I was fucking Keely Smith under that sign fifteen years ago. And a rattlesnake comes along and bites me right in the cock." I was pounding the dashboard. If I had been driving the car, it would have gone out of control.

As we drove, we saw a huge sign with Trigger and Roy Rogers sitting on him. It was the Roy Rogers Museum. We said, "We have to go." We pulled off the freeway. There was a big parking lot mostly filled with RVs. We got out of the car and walked into the ticket office, where they recognized John. Somebody called for Roy Jr., who was running the place, and he came out and shook hands with us. "I'll tell Dad you're here."

The one thing I remember about the Roy Rogers Museum; if it moved or it lived, Roy shot it. There were more dead animals; from polar bears to raccoons, opossum to a lion, anything that moved, Roy shot and stuffed. I walked into one little room and there was a stuffed Trigger, a stuffed Buttermilk, Dale's horse, and Bullet the dog. John said to Roy Jr., "Well, Roy, I guess one day you'll be in here."

Suddenly, one of the sweetest moments of all time—here comes old Roy Rogers. He's gotten into his boots and hat. The place is getting very excited. Roy is very old and shrunk. He was never a big guy anyway but the big hat is on and the boots and those little Chinese eyes that he had. "Hello, John." We all say hi to Roy. People are all around us with cameras. Roy says, "You can take pictures, but no autographs, right, John?"

And John says, "Right, Roy. Pictures only, no autographs." Everyone is taking pictures with John and Roy. It's the middle of the day. Dale's probably half in the bag somewhere, because she didn't come out.

Roy finally left, and I asked John, "What was all that stuff about no autographs?"

John was signing some autographs at that point. He said, "Didn't you see his hand? It was trembling. He can't sign."

I said, "No shit, I didn't notice." John picked up on it right away. He was such a sensitive guy that way. John said he didn't think Roy could hold a pen. I said to him, "Good on you." Who would notice that? John Candy would. When we left, they gave us drinking glasses of Roy and Trigger. We insisted on paying for them. It was quintessential John Candy because, first of all, the idea, yes, of course, you're going to go to the Roy Rogers Museum, you couldn't miss it for the world; and second, that little moment in there that he would pick up on immediately.

Delirious sneaked out; no publicity. I just hated everything about the business. What I loved was working. I loved it when the bell rang at seven in the morning. I loved the grips and the gaffers and the stuntmen and the actors. But all of the people who were in the offices absolutely sickened me.

From Delirium to a *Crypt*

I directed a *Tales from the Crypt* around the time of *Delirious.* Donner was one of the executive producers. I got Mariel to do it. She was thrilled, and the episode was terrific. It starred Andrew McCarthy, Mariel, and Kathleen Freeman, whom I'd used in *Dragnet,* and David Hemmings, my great friend, who played the evil landlord in the basement. That was a lot of fun. It was five days' work and you shot fourteen hours a day. The crew loved it because they were all young and athletic and they got into platinum time every fucking day. The episode was the season's opener. Arnold Schwarzenegger directed the one before me, and Bob Zemeckis was directing the one after me. Everybody worked for scale. I just got a big check from the show the other day, actually. It's the first time *Tales from the Crypt* went out on DVD. They packaged three episodes on each DVD and put mine on the first DVD because Mariel was bare chested in it; saw her tits. It was a fun show.

Miami House of Horrors

I wanted to do a picture called *Skin Tight* based on a novel by that wonderful columnist in Miami, Carl Hiaasen. I was down in Miami, I even prepped it. That was an MGM picture, and I had already written a screenplay under the people, including John Goldwyn, who were at MGM when we started

Delirious. Now, Laddie took over and Tom Selleck was going to do it, but Selleck wasn't box office enough because he'd done too many bad movies. Then Burt Reynolds wanted to do it. Even though he was CAA, he didn't give a shit. Craig Baumgarten was going to produce it. He and Burt Reynolds and I met in the bar at the Bel Air Hotel, that big oak-paneled bar. Burt, who was just nuts by this point, said to me, "This is going to be great, and I know Miami. Working with you is going to be fabulous, you know? We'll hire a good cameraman." He was grabbing my wrist all the time and cutting off my blood supply.

He had just done a film in Vegas, *Heat,* with a director named Dick Richards, whom he really hated. I said, "I heard you punched him out."

Burt said, "Well, yes. We got in an argument in the casino, and *pop.* The punch only went about four inches, I cold-cocked him onto a crap table."

I thought, oh, fuck, I'm going to Miami with this guy. It was like a house of horrors. It was unbelievable. Then there was a rumor that Burt Reynolds had AIDS. He didn't have AIDS. But something was wrong. I thought, I'm trapped in the fucking funhouse here. I'm going crazy. I said to Laddie, "Tom Selleck would be perfect for this."

Laddie said, "I don't know. It can be expensive in Miami." And I thought, oh, fuck it all.

Hiaasen took me around Miami and showed me where all the drug lords lived and the business they'd done. They'd laundered so much money through Florida banks, and the banks really wanted them there. The deal they'd made with the State of Florida and the City of Miami was, as long as they didn't kill each other there, they were welcome. As long as there wasn't crime. Hiaasen would say, "Now, here's a guy from the Cali cartel." You'd see guys with machine guns patrolling his house behind the wall. It was a strange place, Miami. But *Skin Tight* was a really good script. Annie and I loved that script. But it never got made. Another abandoned project. It seems like my career had been one wonderful picture followed by an awful experience, followed by a *Hart to Hart*—a wonderful time—then a *Legal Eagles;* then a *Dragnet*—wonderful—and so on.

Joe Calls It a Wrap

My father, at a certain point, just stopped working. He never developed any interests in life. He was a giant intellectual who would still toy with movies. He would figure out how not to do a movie. After *Sleuth,* which was his last picture, there was only one project he really liked, *Jane.* It was a wonderful novel about a girl who is sleeping with three guys and gets pregnant, and nobody knows who the father is. It provided him with a huge capacity to comment on modern society. He was writing it, he had a draft, but then he got in fights with the producers and the studio and he said, "Oh, fuck it." It was the one real regret he had. He wanted to do *Jane*. Columbia owned it. But he stopped.

Redford came to him with *All the President's Men*. He found a reason not to make it. Paul Newman, who was his neighbor, was over all the time. They were going to do a movie in which Paul was going to play a gay track coach. But Dad figured out how not to do it. Universal asked him to remake *Front Page*, which Billy Wilder eventually did, and he figured out a reason not to do it. But he was always figuring out a reason not to make the picture. I never realized it until I was getting real hot at Warners and I got the studio to buy *Jane* away from Columbia for him. It was a deal. It wasn't terribly expensive. I surprised Dad on his birthday. I said, "Dad, I got you *Jane*. And you can do it."

There was a silence, and he asked, "You're producing it?"

I said, "No, no, Dad, you make it. Go ahead and work on it. My company owns it, but you have 100 percent creative control." There was a silence, and I thought, boy, he doesn't want to make another movie. I had seen him turn down all these things, but he always found an excuse. In his life, he never had an interest—gardening, horses, collecting art, running for public office. Anything. It was like he'd shot his bolt pleasing Pop, his father. If he hadn't been married to Rosemary, he probably would have died ten years earlier. I was determined not to have that happen to me. I started getting interested in the zoo and teaching a film course. Then I bought a couple of racehorses and got into racing. I got on the Board of the Thoroughbred Owners. And I found out how much life there was other than in show business. Show business is still my first love. Ninety percent of my friends are in the business. All my happy memories are of working. The work. But the rest of it, you can have.

I worked in the sixties, seventies, eighties, and nineties. At a certain point, you just say, "God, it's enough now." There are some people who can't stop. Billy Wilder couldn't stop. Wilder's one of the greatest talents that ever lived in the history of film. Yet if you look at his last four or five films—films like *Avanti!*—he was too old. The opposite is true of William Wyler, who goes back to *The Best Years of Our Lives* and *Roman Holiday* and all these great movies. After he did *Funny Girl*, he said, "I quit. That's it. Thank you." My dad's life pre-*Cleopatra* and post-*Cleopatra* were two completely different lives, professionally. He got into numerous fights and arguments with Daryl Zanuck, who fired and then rehired him. Dad did a couple of films after that. *There Was a Crooked Man* with Henry Fonda and Kirk Douglas is a fun movie. He fell in love with Robert Benton and David Newman. He loved them as writers. *Sleuth* was nominated for a Golden Globe for Best Picture. Dad was nominated for an Oscar for Best Director. Both Laurence Olivier and Michael Caine were Oscar nominated for Best Actor, the entire cast. He thought, all right, I'm going off on a high note. I don't want another thing to happen.

Dad passed away February 5, 1993, in Bedford, New York. Heart failure. The Academy held a posthumous tribute to my father. There was a new print of *Suddenly, Last Summer* out. Almost every Mankiewicz was there at the tribute, including many cousins. Ben Mankiewicz, who's a Turner Classic Movies host, was the moderator of the panel. I had a piece of a minor league ball club, Class A, the Reno Silver Sox. I barely knew Ben because he'd been working in Atlanta so long, but he could tell me everybody who played on the Reno Silver Sox. He knew more about sports than anybody I'd ever known. Has a lifetime love of films. TCM got him to be the host on the weekend. It's the greatest gig in the world. He tapes one day a month and gets paid a lot of money. He's very popular. My father once said, "My life was over, Tom, when I met Tuesday Weld and she said, 'Oh, you must be Tom's father'"; I said to Ben, "My life was over the minute people asked, 'Are you any relation to Ben?'"

Ben married the only African American member of our family, Contessa, who was the press secretary to Rocky Delgadillo, L.A.'s district attorney, and she's now with the Poverty Law Center. Ben's brother, Josh, got up at this huge dinner and said, "Contessa, look around the room and mark every Mankiewicz that's here, because you may never see this many Mankiewiczes in one room again for the rest of your life." There were that many Mankiewiczes at Dad's tribute. Josh, a correspondent on *Dateline,* has been with NBC for a long time. He's a godfather to Brian Williams's kid. Josh has been a lifelong bachelor, though always with a girl. A little bit like me in the sense that Josh has been with lots of women but he is never going to get married.

John, who used to be all screwed up, was there that night. He's Don's son. Don was a dreadful father. Compulsive gambler. As I've mentioned, Don wrote a Harper Prize Novel called *See How They Run* about horse racing. He wrote the pilots for *Marcus Welby* and *Ironside,* got very successful, and lost almost everything at the track. John, when I really got to know him in L.A., was bulimic. He'd throw up after every meal. He was skinny, doing drugs, but he was a talented writer. I signed him to write a script for my company. He wrote a beautiful one about a blind guitar player in the south. We could never get the money for it, but it got him going. He was one of the writers on the staff of *Miami Vice,* the Don Johnson series, and one of the original writer-producers of *House.* He resuscitated a USA Network series, *In Plain Sight.* Now he's one of the writer-producers on *The Mentalist,* which is one of the biggest hits on television. He's the only Mankiewicz, wounded though he is, who doesn't drink or do drugs. He really is a success story, with a wife and children who are functioning. In the Mankiewicz family, they're the Ozzie and Harriet, even though Mankiewiczes are usually peculiar.

My stepmother, Rosemary, was there. My dad was married to her for thirty-one years. I'll bet you he never fooled around on Rosemary. Never. She kept him alive. She loved him. They moved to the country—first, Pound Ridge, then Bedford, New York. They loved that area so much. Alex Mankiewicz, my half sister, Rosemary and Dad's daughter, was in Australia and couldn't come to the dinner. Chris didn't show. He was the only Mankiewicz who wasn't there but could have been. He doesn't like Rosemary. I love Chris because he's my brother, but at the same time, we've had so many difficulties. There were also some honorary Mankiewiczes like Ann and Bobby Stevens in attendance: Annie, my assistant for twenty-five years; Bobby, my DP on a couple of pictures. Dad loved them both.

Richard Meryman, who used to be the entertainment editor of *Life* magazine, wrote a book about Uncle Herman called *Mank.* Although I didn't really know my uncle that well because I was eight years old when we moved to New York and Herman was living in Los Angeles, I did offer to Meryman that we Mankiewiczes don't seem to have the same outward affection of some families, but we caress each other with one-liners. The hardest meals I've ever worked were Mankiewicz Thanksgivings. I mean, you've got all those people around the table, you'd better be good. If you're going to say, "A funny thing happened to me yesterday," it better be a funny thing.

Who Are These People?

The thing that finally did it was a Showtime script, *Taking the Heat,* which wasn't in good shape at all. Would I direct it? The producer was Gary Hoffman, a really smooth guy. I had a meeting with him, and I said, "I'd have to rewrite this script." It was written by Dan Gordon, not a bad writer, but it just didn't work.

Hoffman said, "Okay, sure. You can rewrite it, but I started this with Dan. So even if it's totally your script, will you agree to let Dan have sole credit?"

I thought, okay, I have so many good credits. I said, "Fine, I just want to get it written the way I want it," which I never should have done.

We started to assemble a really good cast: Alan Arkin, Peter Boyle, George Segal, Tony Goldwyn, Lynn Whitfield, who'd just won the Emmy for *The Josephine Baker Story*. Hoffman, who later became the head of television movies for Fox, nickel-and-dimed our production to the point where he would say, "Shoot these eleven pages on Thursday." I'd say, "Wait a minute, wait a minute." He was trying to shorten the shooting schedule. We were going to New York for action sequences with helicopters, and Hoffman wanted to arrive on a Saturday and shoot on a Monday. I said, "Wait a minute. We've got to rehearse here. Have you guys heard of John Landis? There's all kinds of action. There's thousands of squibs, there's helicopters. Fuck you. I'm going to write a letter to the Directors Guild and I'm going to say, 'I'm not responsible for anything that happens on Monday and that these were exactly your instructions.'"

He said, "You can't do that."

I said, "Yes, I can, and I will." The unit production manager, Fred Blankfein, was there. I said, "You're a member of the Directors Guild. You're going to put up with this?" He had made a deal with Gary, and they had told Showtime they could make it for less money than it actually was going to cost. We didn't know we were going to have Alan Arkin. The experience was just like Chinese fucking water torture. I said, "Who are these people?"

I knew and accepted the fact that my career was not anywhere near as stellar as my dad's, loaded with Oscars and accolades. But now, I also had to face the fact that I was just tired, and I was tired of the people that I had to deal with. In retrospect, I never should have left CAA. I never should have been outraged that they lied to me, that they set me up. I got one of the actresses they wanted, and then they decided five different ways I'm not going to make this picture without ever telling me. I should have just said, "Okay, guys, you don't want me to make the picture? What do I get next?" But I have a sense of morality and I don't like to be lied to. So I dug my heels in. Maybe I thought I was a little bigger than I was and I could get away with it. It was like reading your biorhythms, you just know there's something wrong.

Even though I liked Frank Price, Bob Daly, and Terry Semel, I probably would not mention an executive or an agent among the highlights. I would mention actors and composers and other writers and cameramen, but nobody who sat in an office. I couldn't think of one. There were other writer-directors who became disillusioned with people in offices who don't make the movies. John Hughes disappeared for the last ten years of his life; my guess is for much the same reason. He was very disillusioned. He disappeared at the height of his powers. He'd done those wonderful kids' movies, which were the soul of that generation, and pictures like *Planes, Trains and Automobiles,* where Hughes and Candy as writer-director and actor, respectively, could break your heart and make you cry. In every obituary of Hughes, it said he grew disillusioned. I think it's with all the suits. They wanted different kinds of pictures from him than he wanted to make. He did go ahead and make *Miracle on 34th Street.* When Fox offered me that picture, I was smarter than John Hughes because I said, "If I can't get Sean Connery or Jack Nicholson for Kris Kringle, I ain't doing it." It had a cute girl, it would have been foolproof. I can't imagine that a guy whose screenplays were so original would want to remake *Miracle on 34th Street.* It's a classic. It was a strange career choice for him, and, maybe, disillusioning, because the picture was not a big critical or financial success. Even Hughes's moderate successes like *Weird Science* were big successes with smart people and kids. Nobody over thirty went to see *Weird Science,* but everybody under thirty got it.

11

The Tag
Out of Film

High concept is the enemy of the writer. The friend of the writer is
the human being, the full-blooded character interacting with another
character.

—*Joseph L. Mankiewicz*

Team Players

When I was at Warners, it was almost a privilege harking back to the forties
and fifties when everybody was under contract to a studio. It was like major
league baseball before free agency and Curt Flood. You were on a team. You
were with Fox, MGM, Warners, Paramount, or Universal. Then, all of a
sudden, there was free agency. Kirk Douglas had his own company. My
father was one of the first independent companies, Figaro. They made *The
Barefoot Contessa* and *I Want to Live,* which Robert Wise directed. Burt
Lancaster had his own company. The Mirisch brothers became very famous
because they said to filmmakers like Billy Wilder, "You do your film through
us. We'll handle all the bullshit. You're not working for a studio. We're
working together. You write and direct the film, and we'll get you the stage
space and so on." United Artists was the studio everybody wanted to work
for when I was first starting in the sixties. United Artists didn't have a studio
lot, per se, but they made the Beatles films, the James Bond films, *Tom Jones*
with Albert Finney, the Woody Allen pictures. They would get the right deal
for you in the right place, and they would leave you alone and let you make
the picture. Studios always charged 10 or 15 percent overhead just to run
the studio, and it was added on to every budget. United Artists had much
less overhead because they didn't have a physical plant. So on *Diamonds Are*

Forever, we shot mostly at Universal when we were in Los Angeles. They had the bungalows, the stages, and the back lots that we could use at the right price.

After that big burst of independent fervor, studios started to make housekeeping deals so that Dick Donner would have his company at Warners, I would have my company at Warners. You were not exclusive to Warners like the old days, but they had first call on you. You had to tell Warners if you wanted to do something somewhere else. They could suspend you, pick you up again, or talk you out of it.

Warner Brothers was at its best when Steve Ross was running the company from New York. He said, "Let's get the best people and treat them in the best way." So at its height, Warners had Richard Donner, Steven Spielberg with Amblin Productions, Clint Eastwood with Malpaso, Goldie Hawn, when she was a huge star, and Billy Friedkin for a while. Bob Daly and Terry Semel were the chairman and president, respectively. They treated everybody really wonderfully. There was a nominal head of production, Mark Canton. They all worked together so well. Bob and Terry sometimes would share a car to the studio together.

Warners was famous for having eight private jets. One night, Stefanie Powers and I were shooting at Columbia because Spelling-Goldberg had sold *Hart to Hart* to Columbia. Columbia shared the same lot with Warners in those days. For a few years, Stefanie and I bred Arabian horses. We wanted to go to the Arabian Nationals, which started at nine o'clock in the morning on a Saturday in Albuquerque. We were shooting late Friday night until midnight and couldn't get out. There were no flights to Albuquerque. I called Terry Semel's office and asked, "Can I get a little plane just to take us to Albuquerque?"

"Absolutely." They would treat you so wonderfully. You were a member of the Warners family. Steve Ross would insist on that. Clint had first call on the big plane. I didn't take advantage. I only took a plane twice. They would fly you everywhere if you were a talent with them.

The exact opposite of that was when I was at Universal. Lew Wasserman ran the whole joint. And Lew was amazing. He knew everything that was going on, and this was his kingdom. Johnny Carson used to joke about the big black office building—"If you ran a studio, would you stick this in the middle of the San Fernando Valley?" But then again, it only takes one man. So this was Lew's place. Sid Sheinberg was his second in command. Universal was not making moneymaking movies at the time. It had hit bottom, financially speaking, with a movie called *Howard the Duck*, which cost a fortune and grossed nothing. *Dragnet* was its first moneymaker in a long time.

There was an opening for a new head of production. Frank Price had been head of production at Columbia during *Ghostbusters* and *Gandhi*. Lew wanted him. Sid Sheinberg didn't want him, because Sid thought he was number two and Frank was going to take over at the studio. Lew won. Frank came.

Immediately, there was a big unspoken fight involving two movies. Frank brought *Out of Africa* with him, and it was made. Lew had *Back to the Future*. They came out the same year. At Universal, the question was who you were with. Sid Sheinberg was very close to Steven Spielberg, whose company produced *Back to the Future*. Oscar time came; *Out of Africa* won Best Picture, Best Screenplay, Best Director, Best Score, Best Photography. It won seven Oscars. Things were very uncomfortable at Universal. Not everybody was rowing in the same direction.

The housekeeping deals disappeared because studios found them too expensive like everything else. You'd make a housekeeping deal with John Travolta, who becomes a star again. Now he's got his own chef and martial arts expert and everybody goes on salary, and all of a sudden, it's costing you a fortune. Maybe that year he does one picture that doesn't gross a lot of money, and the studio is saying, "Jesus, I'd rather hire him on a picture-by-picture basis." On the other hand, Dick Donner makes *Superman* for Warners. Then he makes all four *Lethal Weapon* movies for Warners. He makes *Conspiracy Theory* for Warners. He makes *Ladyhawke* for Warners and Fox. *Free Willie* and all those movies he produced with Lauren Shuler. He had twelve people on salary. But Warners was happy because, my God, it's making so much money off him. The *Lethal Weapon* movies alone made billions—not millions, billions.

A Vast Wasteland

It's so expensive now to open movies that you would rather give somebody a piece of the gross than to give them $20 million or $30 million up front. The salaries got so high: Hanks was getting $25 million; Mel Gibson got $25 million when he was really big as an actor. So now studios say, "Look, if we give away 5 or even 10 percent of the gross, at least we're giving away a piece of what we're getting. Whereas, if this picture turns out to be a big flop and it was made for $140 million and $40 million of that is two actors' salaries, then we can't get that money back." Everything is just so bleeping expensive now. That's why reality television is on. It's too expensive, on a steady diet, to do *NCIS*, because you've got actors in the fourth or fifth year of their contract, they're making a lot of money, you've got writers, you're paying directors, special effects, scoring. That costs you a lot more than if you do "The World's Tallest Nun," or "Fat People Fall in Love." H. L. Mencken had the classic quote, "No one ever went broke underestimating the taste of the American public." And son of a bitch, there is an audience out there for *The Bachelorette*. I see five minutes of it and I want to throw up. It's so stupid. But it gets the ratings, so somebody's watching it.

Most studios agree Will Smith is worth $20 million, but his last couple of pictures were not hits. Years ago, if it was a Jerry Lewis comedy, you could predict X. Clint Eastwood was the biggest star in the world, but when he did *Bronco Billy* and that little movie about the Depression with his son, they didn't make any money. It wasn't the Clint Eastwood the audience wanted to see. Paul Newman probably delivered more than anybody, but I could run you a festival of *The Drowning Pool* and *Winning*, and you don't hear about those movies. So I don't think anybody's infallible, even the biggest names—Paul Newman or Tom Hanks or, back then, Jimmy Stewart. Steven Spielberg made *Always*, which didn't make any money. But if I could have the rest from *Jaws* to *E.T.* to *Close Encounters* to *Schindler's List* to *Private Ryan*, I would be rolling in it. They're all different kinds of films, and they're all wonderful films. He had a certain eye for it. I love Steven Spielberg, he's one of the three or four best directors that ever directed. Any kind of film is his kind of film, except what Robert Shaw said, a love story between a man and a woman or a comedy. After *Jaws*, everybody got sequel-itis. I'll bet you when Spielberg was making *1941*, somebody was already drawing up the plans for *1942*. Then the picture came out.

Francis Coppola said recently that the major studios are almost out of the quality filmmaking business. Just like the *World's Biggest Loser*, world's greatest blah-blah-blah, they know if they do *Transformers VI*, they can just keep going until finally one of them doesn't make it. *Iron Man III. Spider-Man IV.* There will be an audience out there that's going to run to it. I give credit to J. K. Rowling. She said, "There are seven *Harry Potter* books and it's over. It's finished. You can make seven movies out of it." I'm sure the studio will try and make a deal with her, since she owns the character. "Can we make new ones?" I don't know what she'll say. Harry and the Magic Bachelorette. The only guy who really stayed true to it was J. D. Salinger; never let any of his books be made as a movie. Somebody made a movie that steals from *Catcher in the Rye*, and it's done as an homage, but Salinger's estate is suing him.

What terrifies me (and I'll probably sound like a snob for saying it) is the Internet has made everybody so ubiquitous and so omnipresent; Facebook,

Craigslist—almost nothing is special anymore. It's the dumbing down of America in terms of entertainment. Not that great films aren't made every year, but not as many great films. The films I'm talking about, the *Shane*s and the *High Noon*s and *From Here to Eternity*s and *On the Waterfront*s, those were mainstream major studio films. And the people who made them were fucking proud of them. Also, somehow, adults were in those films. Look at *Roman Holiday*. Audrey Hepburn's twenty-three and Gregory Peck's thirty-four, but they look like a man and a woman. Today, everybody looks like a kid, even at fifty-five. Judd Apatow makes a semiserious film, *Funny People,* and it's not serious and it's not funny, and the problem is, he should have made me cry. But everybody in it is a big kid, even Adam Sandler. They're just all big kids. You wouldn't call anybody a man in that film. Even now, when they're in their forties or fifties, they're big, shaggy kids. Maybe George Clooney is a man. He looks like a guy. But there are damn few. He's had a wonderful career. He's made a fortune and he directed a movie, *Good Night, and Good Luck,* the Edward R. Murrow movie. One of the reasons that no great operas were written after the twentieth century was that Mozart or Rossini were sitting in their house and they had nothing the fuck to do except this opera. Today, you've got radio, television, the Internet, you're Twittering, you're texting. How does anybody have the time to concentrate on a great piece of work? You have to have such will-power to sit down and work on it.

Everybody feels as if they could be, in fact, famous for fifteen minutes. All they have to do is put the right thing on their blog. Newton Minow, the famous head of the Federal Communications Commission in the late fifties, called television a "vast wasteland." A reporter said, "You know, Mr. Minow, one day there are going to be three or four hundred channels." And, he said, "Good God, what on earth are they going to put on it?" Well, we're getting the answer right now. I've got *Project Runway*. You don't like that? *America's Next Top Model*. I got three other model shows and cooking shows. Make sure it's show business. The chef gets angry, and I want to see him throw a cleaver because you've got to have a little drama. My chef show's angrier than your chef show. Horse racing is dying, but there are two racing channels. We've got Santa Anita and Hollywood Park.

One of the reasons that politics has gotten so hostile is that if I'm Sean Hannity, or I'm Keith Olbermann, take the left or the right, or I'm Glenn Beck—who I think needs professional help, he's a psycho—I have to fill an hour every night. How do I do that? That's why Larry King did eighteen straight hours of Michael Jackson coverage. There aren't that many interesting people. So now you have, "Tonight, for the whole hour, Barbara Eden." And, you say, "No, please!" Jermaine Jackson has been seen more on the Larry King show in the last year than he has been seen in the last ten years anywhere. It's just insane. And that's what worries me. There are fewer and fewer truly fine films every year. There used to be many, many more. When I was growing up, if you lived in Los Angeles, New York, Chicago, Saint Louis—any big city—every year you would see an Ingmar Bergman film, a Claude Chabrol film, a Truffaut film, a Fellini film, a Visconti film, an Antonioni film. There was a whole world of cinema out there. Today, you can't even find a film from any other part of the world except if you go to Little Tokyo, where they have films in Japanese. They were all fine films by wonderful artists. That just doesn't exist anymore, because "Fat People Make Love" gets a 45 share.

A studio will make a picture like *G.I. Joe,* which gets derisive reviews and, apparently, hoots from the audience, but it still does $59 million the opening weekend. So they have private-label studios—Fox Searchlight—that make the films that literate people would want to see. An amazing statistic is, of the last fifteen films nominated for Best Picture, fourteen of them were not made by a major studio. Now the Academy is doubling the number of nominees. You can say they used to have ten in the thirties, but there was no television. Now *Transformers* can be one of the ten even though it's not going to win to generate more TV ratings. What happens now, with these mass entertainments, is somebody like Marion Cotillard wins for *La Vie en Rose* and there's a collective "Who?" sucked in around the country. Nobody's seen the fucking movie and she wins the Oscar. The public says, "These are specialty awards now." But she did the best work. She should have won it.

The Coen brothers make wonderful films that no one sees. *Raising Arizona, The Big Lebowski. No Country for Old Men.* That was such a great movie. I was hypnotized by it. It was well written, wonderfully played, so perverse, and brave. They have the courage to make these idiosyncratic movies that they know in advance are not going to be huge grossers. But they go ahead and make them anyway. *Fargo* was a wonderful picture. You knew everybody in that movie: Bill Macy, Frances McDormand, Steve Buscemi. These were real people. They were all just great. I admire work like that so much.

A major disappointment to me is Quentin Tarantino. After his first two pictures, I thought he was going to be a wonderful director. They're still the best two he ever made, *Pulp Fiction* and *Reservoir Dogs*. He just has never grown up. He's never made a movie about a human being. I thought, here's somebody who, as he gets older and more experienced, is going to make some real movies. I look at the trailer for *Inglourious Basterds*—oh, Jesus, I don't want to see that. It's just fooling around. He should be making some real movies.

Brokeback Mountain was an exceptional piece of work. Ang Lee is one of my favorite directors, even when he goes to wretched excess like the Chinese exotic film he did. But why I think he's so good—George Stevens was like this, and Sydney Pollack was like this—is if I cut the main titles off and showed you *Sense and Sensibility, Crouching Tiger, Hidden Dragon, Brokeback Mountain,* you would swear on your life they were not directed by the same person, but they were all directed by him. He threw himself into the project, into the style, the way George Stevens could direct *Swing Time* with Fred Astaire and Ginger Rogers, a musical, then *Gunga Din,* a huge adventure picture, then *Woman of the Year,* a sophisticated romantic comedy with Tracy and Hepburn, then *A Place in the Sun,* a moving melodrama, then *Shane,* a great western. You look at those and say the same guy could not possibly have done that. Sydney Pollack, the most underrated director, could do a social picture like *Absence of Malice,* then do a hysterical comedy like *Tootsie,* then do a lyrical love story like *Out of Africa* because he threw himself into it. I miss those people. As they start to drop, it's the last generation for me of really good filmmakers.

I got to know Jack Lemmon at Irving Lazar's parties. I really liked Jack. He was a wonderful guy, wonderful actor. He liked to drink and play the piano. One night, during a party, Jack and I were lying on chaises by the pool. He asked, "What are you doing next?"

I said, "I'm doing another comedy." Beat. I asked, "What are you doing next?"

Jack said, "Doing another film with Walter Matthau." Silence. He said, "You went to Yale, didn't you?"

I said, "Yeah. You went to Harvard."

Jack said, "That's right." Pause. He said, "What a waste of a great fucking education."

Suffer the Pain Alone

When George Peppard said to me, "I told my agent, 'I didn't know Tom was a great writer; all I know is he's fucking my wife,'" I said to him, "George, what can I tell you? Your agent's right and you're right." That was so unlike me because I am not a conflict person. I do not dare the person I'm saying things to to take a swing at me. I heard so much screaming and yelling when I was growing up, doors slamming, and I spent so many nights on the bathroom floor wheezing, that I will avoid conflict if I can. I wouldn't call myself a coward. I have a very dexterous personality; I can figure out how to get out of the situation, and then come home and direct all the pain on me. Suffer the pain alone. I'm running from conflict and anxiety that, as a kid, I experienced with my mother and father. What I'm running to is some kind of peace. It's never going to be realized in the sense that you can't ever have perfect peace. If you had perfect peace, you'd be a vegetable. A certain amount of stress keeps you alive. In all the relationships I had, I was having the same relationship with my mother in various ways, where I was hopelessly attracted to women who were troubled. They could recognize in me the perfect foil, the perfect person to get involved with, because it made me even more solicitous, more eager to help. You feed off each other that way. The opposite reaction was the screenplay I wrote where there was a guy on the beach who was an ex-detective and a young, cute girl in a bikini who had a crush on him. She asked, "What is your ambition in life, Nick?" He said—I said—"To be left alone." Even though I never did a movie about it, I always liked characters like Jim Rockford or Harry O living on the beach. There was this thing about leave me alone. Let me be. One of the reasons I may have had a talent for adventure and comedy is that it was so distracting from having to sit down and write serious things.

I'll never find peace. On one hand, I've led a very successful life. I have lots of friends. But on the other hand, I'm sixty-eight years old, I live alone with two cats, I have no children, and I've never been married. I don't know anybody who has it all. Rich people would never commit suicide if the solution was to have money. Although, to be able to live a comfortable life is a tremendous advantage. I've successfully sat on the demons that I have inside me. I don't take tranquilizers, maybe one five-milligram Xanax every three weeks. My cousin John, who used to take a lot of drugs, calls them training wheels. He said, "Five milligrams of Xanax, I wouldn't even know what that is." I've been in analysis a couple of times in my life. One of the things that has always driven me crazy about analysis, if I can use that reference, is when am I through? I've heard about Woody Allen going to the analyst for forty years. I didn't want to. You have a problem? Now fix it. The two times I went into analysis, both were as a result of my getting involved over and over again with the same woman. I thought, okay, when you get cured . . . in other words, it's like having a rash and it goes away, or you have a cold, then you don't have a cold. There seemed to be no end. I'd go into a session, and I felt as a human being, much less as a writer, that I was losing my spontaneity. Everything I was going through during the day, I knew I was going to report on tomorrow. I was censoring myself, saying, "Here, I'm doing this again."

Fred Hacker, who had been my mother's analyst, was personally taught by Freud. He was a family friend. In the beginning, when I was late for an appointment by three minutes, I said, "I'm sorry I'm late."

Fred said, "There is no correct time to arrive at the analyst. If you're early, you're anxious. If you're late, you're hostile. And if you're on time, you're compulsive. So, don't worry about it."

He was totally bizarre, as most great analysts are, and he never paid a parking ticket. But he was finally arrested. One hundred thirty-four parking tickets. The judge said to him, "Dr. Hacker, you are an embarrassment. Here you are, one of the eminent psychoanalysts in the world, and you have 134 parking tickets. I can't even explain it."

Fred said to him, "Your Honor, it is possible to cure cancer and die of the disease." So, Fred was sentenced to fifteen weekends in the Beverly Hills jail. He shared a cell with a kleptomaniac who took his pen.

Tuesday Weld was really in trouble, freaking out one night, and I called Fred and asked him if he'd go out and meet her. I think he saved her life. Tuesday had the attention span of a hamster. She saw him once and she called him the Wizard. This is why I love Fred so much. In the early seventies, when Elizabeth Ashley and I were going together, she gave a dinner party at her house. The buffet table was outside. In the center of the table in a jar were joints. There were lots of people from the music business. Tuesday was there. I asked Fred to come. I said to Tuesday, "We're going to ask the Wizard." Fred came by for a drink. He stood there, looked at Elizabeth, who he thought was clearly nuts, looked at me, then looked at Tuesday. He asked Tuesday and me to go into the corner with him. He said, "Do either one of you ever talk about me, that I'm your analyst or I'm helping you?"

I said, "No," and Tuesday said, "No."

Fred said, "Good. Keep it that way. I have a reputation to uphold. I would hate to have people think that you were my patients." Then he left. That kind of analyst I really enjoyed.

The other analyst that I had was more serious. I would ask, "When is this over?"

He would say, "Well, when do you think it should be over?"

"When I'm cured."

"What do you think a cure is?"

"When I'm coping."

"Are you coping?"

"If you answer one of my questions with a question again, I'm going to come over and wring your neck."

"You see, you are crazy!" I had been through so many bad relationships and I was really depressed that I started to go five days a week. Then, thank God, *Superman* came along. I had to go to England. I was there for a long time and I never went back. By the way, I felt a lot better not going back, because part of my experience with the second round of analysis was like self-flagellation. I was punishing myself every day by saying what I wasn't doing right. And son of a gun, I had a romance with maybe the loopiest, in the most wonderful way, person I was ever with, Margot Kidder, and I could handle it just fine. It wasn't destroying my life. Nobody knew Margot was bipolar. She had many eccentricities. I said to Dick Donner, who always joked with me about crazy people, "Margot is the only person I know where all the craziness is directed against herself. She's a kind person. There's nothing about her that intentionally tries to hurt anybody else. Although she makes so many missteps, they're all directed against herself." I could understand a person like that.

There was one relationship—I don't want to name her specifically—in which the woman wound up being one of the few that's not a friend anymore. She was nuts. One day I came home, and I had a problem. She was so uninterested in it because she was so narcissistic. I turned to her and said, "You know what? For the past ten months, I have been a combination lover, father, brother, psychiatrist to you. I've poured myself into you, and I come home with a problem one day and you're off in the corner putting chewing gum on the cat's face." I meant that figuratively speaking.

She said, "Oh, no, Mank." But, I knew.

I just said, "Okay." It wasn't so much anger as disappointment that she wasn't interested in my problem and I didn't have what I thought I had, which is somebody who was going to reciprocate when I had a problem.

There's no question that abandonment is a huge deal for me. In my relationships, I would leave first because I was sensing that they were going to. I live alone, and I feel guilty leaving a dog in my house if I'm gone all day. But I've grown to love cats, and cats have personalities that are so matched with mine. I decided to get two cats. I went to the Amanda Foundation and found a cat named Margot—that was the name from the shelter. She was two or three years old. They said, "She's a touch nuts, Margot, and you're probably best off with a kitten. If you get another cat the same age, they'll probably fight." I found a little orange tabby, a kitten. Brought them back home. I had the litter box and the food set up. Margot just terrorized this kitten for two or three days. Margot would live behind the television set. I would never see her, but I could clearly see she ate in the middle of the night. She used the litter box. But she would terrorize the kitten. After three days, I called the Amanda Foundation and said, "I'm afraid I'm going to have to give one back."

The girl said, "No, no, we were waiting for the call. Poor Margot, she doesn't get on with anybody."

I said, "No, I want to keep the crazy one. I'm going to have to give the kitten back because the kitten is going to find a wonderful home. She's great." Abandonment. I couldn't even drive the kitten back. Three days! There was no relationship. Annie, my assistant, had to drive the kitten back to the Amanda Foundation.

Then Margot sat behind the television for another two days. One day she was walking through the living room on her way to eat, and I was watching television. There was no contact between us. I said, "Hey!" She turned and looked at me, and I said, "It's just you and me, kid. Just the two of us in the house. Better get used to it." She walked on, and about ten minutes later, I'm watching television and I feel Margot rubbing against my knee. Then we were so close. She was with me nine years. A raccoon got her one day. I felt a sense of abandonment that I hadn't felt since my mother died, like I'd lost mother again. Margot had left me. It wasn't that she had been killed by a raccoon, but she left me. Here I was, fucking alone again. Yes, it was a cat, but I had poured so much affection. We were inseparable. I said, "Okay, I'm gonna get cats again." I was not going to be dependent on one animal. So I got a mother and son: Colors is a calico and Mr. Squirt is an orange tabby. The three of us are like a traveling act around the house. The two keep each other company, but it also has to do with I'm never going to rely on one animal, because if that animal leaves me, I am alone again.

Almost every woman I've ever had a relationship with of any import is a friend today. Always made sure that they were still friends. I tend to make friends for life. Margot Kidder and I just talked the other day. Stefanie Powers and I are very close. So many women that I've slept with and had relationships with, I still know. Not Elizabeth Ashley, I don't see her. She got to be a theatrical impersonation of herself. But she was very smart and bright when I was going out with her. I'm friends with almost all the women.

Time Out of Life

I lived a charmed life working with Cubby Broccoli on the Bonds, Donner on *Superman,* and Jack Haley Jr. with the musical specials. But the business side just got uglier and uglier and uglier. I was getting older, I'd sold the house in Kenya, and I'd gotten on the Board of the L.A. Zoo. They elected me chairman, and I started to meet all these wonderful people who were in different walks of life. I thought, you know, unless a project is really good, I don't give a shit now. I was with Ron Mardigian at William Morris through *Superman*. Then I moved to Jeff Berg and ICM. Jeff sought me out. Then Ovitz and CAA. Ron is a very good friend of mine right now. If you look me up, my representation is Ron Mardigian, because we have a perfect relationship—I have no intention of working, and he has no intention of getting me work. Working was a release to a lot of people. I'm sure John Candy felt that way when he was working. It was almost time out of life. Of course, you're privileged if you're good at what you do, you have an assistant like Annie and another assistant back at the bungalow, and they'll pick this up for you and a teamster will drive you home, and you don't really have time to think about what isn't going well in your life because you're shooting again tomorrow. You've got problems there, but they're wonderful problems. We're all rowing in the same direction. So for me, working was easier than living a lot of the time.

This was the perfect time for me to have lived, both as a writer and director, aesthetically and politically. The talking movie is eighty years old. And I knew people from every generation in its history. Billy Wilder and George Stevens were directing in the thirties. My father was producing in the thirties. I saw television come into being, then cable and DVDs. I saw the biggest revolution in American history, the sixties and the seventies, when people started free love and "Hell, no, we're not going to fucking Vietnam"; unbelievable tragedies with Martin Luther King and others saying, "No, we're not going to put up with this racial shit anymore." The whole country was in revolt. My generation changed this entire country, the landscape of movies, of social mores. I saw rock 'n' roll come in. People smoking grass. People saying thank-you by screwing each other after a date. It was a whole different mentality. Films became very different. There were wonderful filmmakers like the Hal Ashbys, the Sydney Pollacks, and Mike Nichols in his way. They were so observant about what was happening to the country and what was happening to the world.

I think now everything has been debased a little, communication's been cheapened a little. You think about when you were driving and you didn't have a cell phone on which to tweet or text, and you actually had to think about things. I would not want to be twelve years old today. Even if there's never another world war, I don't envy what's going to be happening to the world. There's too much communication now. When Antonioni was making all of his films, there was a wonderful comedian named Tom Lehrer who was a mathematics professor at MIT and played little, wonderful, satirical songs. At one point, he said, "This man keeps making films about how there's such a lack of communication in the world. I feel if you're obsessed with that, the least you could do is shut up once in a while." There's too much communication. Stop communicating!

The best advice I ever received, life-wise, was what Cubby Broccoli said to me: "First, you've got to be a gent." The people I dislike the most are people who are rude, who put people down to their face, who humiliate or marginalize people. There's plenty of time to do that when you're alone or with your friend in another room. But first, you've got to be a gent. The best professional advice was Dick Donner saying to me, "If you're over budget and over length and it's a good picture, all they'll remember is it's a good picture. And if you're under budget, under schedule, and it stinks, they'll never remember you were under budget; they'll just remember the film stinks. So don't worry about that. It's really difficult to fire a director unless he's making a fool of himself or spending money like water. So figure out the movies that you want to make, and if you're a few days over, you're a few days over."

Leonard Goldberg said the same thing, having done thousands of hours of television. Most hour-long series, in those days, were on a seven-day shoot. He said, "If a guy comes in in five days and it's a lousy show but we saved a lot of money, I don't mind. If a guy comes in at eight and a half days and it's the best episode of the season, I don't mind. The only thing I mind is somebody comes in at eight and a half days and it's a lousy show." If you throw yourself into the project and you're true to the project, that's all they remember. Nobody remembers the dramas and crises in *Superman* that Dick and I went through. They only see what's on the screen.

We were shooting *Hart to Hart* and it was about to rain. I said, "Let's just do this all in one because it's going to rain."

R.J. Wagner said, "It's not going to look very good, is it?"

I said, "No."

He said, "See, it won't say on the bottom of the screen the reason this looks so shitty is it was about to rain. They don't get to see that. So why don't we shoot it properly and hope the rain holds off?"

Good advice very early on. All the audience knows is what they see.

Acknowledgments

Pat McGilligan, Anne Dean Watkins, Liz Smith (copyeditor), Bailey Johnson, David Cobb, Mack McCormick, the staff of the University Press of Kentucky, Grace Kono-Wells and Vernon Wells of Keystrokes, Ashley Zastrow, Dan Leonard, Andy Erish, Chapman University.

Bob Stevens, Ann Moss, Russell J. Frackman and Abe Somer of Mitchell, Silberberg & Knupp, Gail and Jerry Oppenheimer, Stefanie Powers, Jill and R.J. Wagner, Richard and Lauren Donner, Alex Mankiewicz, Sandra Moss, Cedric Castro, the Palm West Hollywood, Connie Morgan, Genie Vasels.

Desly Movius, David Arnoff, Kathy Holt, D.J. Hall, Toby Watson, Judy Diamond, Deborah Hildebrand, Richard Harris, Barbara Margulies, Leslie Bockian, Jerry Henderson, Istvan and Rosa Toth, John Cerney, Bret Gallagher, Jane and Doug Poole, Kel O'Connell, Marilyn Bagley, Dr. Joe and Liz Ruiz, Susan and Joe Coyle, Jonne-Marie and Paul, Steve and Pete.

Leslie Bertram Crane, Meagan Hufnail, Chloe Crane, Anne and Charles Sloan, Deborah Agar, Eric Agar, Ian and Kim Agar, Steve and Karen Wilson, Bill and Marlene Bertram, Michael Bertram, David Bertram, Bob Page.

Christopher Fryer, David Diamond, Suzy Friendly, Niki Dantine, Drs. Tom and Jeri Munn.

Filmography

Writer

Superman II: aka The Richard Donner Cut (2006; Video; Warner Brothers)

Richard Lester, Richard Donner (uncredited)—director
Jerry Siegel, Joe Shuster—creators
Mario Puzo—story
Mario Puzo, David Newman, Leslie Newman, Tom Mankiewicz (uncredited)—screenplay
Tom Mankiewicz—creative consultant
Ilya Salkind, Pierre Spengler—producers
Gene Hackman, Christopher Reeve, Margot Kidder, Valerie Perrine, Marlon Brando, Jackie Cooper, Terence Stamp, Susannah York, Ned Beatty—cast

Dragnet (1987; Universal Pictures)

Tom Mankiewicz—director
Dan Aykroyd, Alan Zweibel, Tom Mankiewicz—screenplay
Bernie Brillstein, David Permut, Robert K. Weiss—producers
Dan Aykroyd, Tom Hanks, Christopher Plummer, Harry Morgan, Elizabeth Ashley, Dabney Coleman—cast

Ladyhawke (1985; 20th Century Fox/Warner Brothers)

Richard Donner—director
Edward Khmara—story
Edward Khmara, Michael Thomas, Tom Mankiewicz, David Peoples —screenplay
Tom Mankiewicz—creative consultant
Harvey Bernhard, Richard Donner, Lauren Shuler Donner—producers
Matthew Broderick, Rutger Hauer, Michelle Pfeiffer, Leo McKern, Alfred Molina—cast

Filmography

Gavilan (1982; MGM Television/NBC)

Tom Mankiewicz—creator
Leonard Goldberg—executive producer
Robert Urich, Patrick Macnee, Kate Reid—cast

Superman II (1980; Warner Brothers)

(credits—see *Superman II: aka The Richard Donner Cut*, above.)

Hart to Hart, "Hit Jennifer Hart" (1979; ABC/Columbia Pictures Television, Rona II, Spelling-Goldberg)

Tom Mankiewicz—director
Tom Mankiewicz—teleplay, creative consultant
Rogers Turrentine—story, teleplay
Sidney Sheldon—creator
Leonard Goldberg, Aaron Spelling, David Levinson—producers
Robert Wagner, Stefanie Powers, Lionel Stander—cast

Hart to Hart, "Pilot" (1979; ABC/Columbia Pictures Television, Rona II, Spelling-Goldberg)

Tom Mankiewicz—director
Tom Mankiewicz—teleplay, creative consultant
Sidney Sheldon—creator
Leonard Goldberg, Aaron Spelling—producers
Robert Wagner, Stefanie Powers, Lionel Stander—cast

Superman (1978; Warner Brothers)

Richard Donner—director
Jerry Siegel, Joe Shuster—creators
Mario Puzo—story
Mario Puzo, David Newman, Leslie Newman, Robert Benton, Tom Mankiewicz (uncredited)—screenplay
Tom Mankiewicz—creative consultant
Alexander Salkind, Ilya Salkind, Pierre Spengler—producers
Marlon Brando, Gene Hackman, Christopher Reeve, Margot Kidder, Jackie Cooper, Susannah York, Terence Stamp—cast

Mother, Jugs & Speed (1978; 20th Century Fox Television)

John Rich—director
Tom Mankiewicz—teleplay

Filmography

Bruce Geller—producer
Ray Vitte, Joanne Nail, Joe Penny—cast

The Eagle Has Landed (1976; Columbia Pictures)

John Sturges—director
Tom Mankiewicz—screenplay
Jack Higgins—novel
David Niven Jr., Jack Wiener—producers
Michael Caine, Donald Sutherland, Robert Duvall, Jenny Agutter, Donald
    Pleasence—cast

The Cassandra Crossing (1976; Avco Embassy Pictures)

George P. Cosmatos—director
Robert Katz, George P. Cosmatos—story
Tom Mankiewicz, Robert Katz, George P. Cosmatos—screenplay
Giancarlo Pettini, Carlo Ponti—producers
Sophia Loren, Richard Harris, Martin Sheen, O.J. Simpson, Lionel
    Stander, Ava Gardner, Burt Lancaster—cast

Mother, Jugs & Speed (1976; 20th Century Fox)

Peter Yates—director
Stephen Manes, Tom Mankiewicz—story
Tom Mankiewicz—screenplay
Joseph Barbera, Tom Mankiewicz, Peter Yates—producers
Bill Cosby, Raquel Welch, Harvey Keitel, Allen Garfield, Larry Hagman,
    Bruce Davison—cast

The Man with the Golden Gun (1974; United Artists)

Guy Hamilton—director
Richard Maibaum, Tom Mankiewicz—screenplay
Ian Fleming—novel
Albert R. Broccoli, Harry Saltzman—producers
Roger Moore, Christopher Lee, Britt Ekland, Maud Adams, Herve
    Villechaize, Clifton James, Bernard Lee—cast

Live and Let Die (1973; United Artists)

Guy Hamilton—director
Tom Mankiewicz—screenplay
Ian Fleming—novel

Filmography

Cubby R. Broccoli, Harry Saltzman—producers

Roger Moore, Yaphet Kotto, Jane Seymour, Clifton James, Bernard
Lee—cast

Diamonds Are Forever (1971; United Artists)

Guy Hamilton—director

Richard Maibaum, Tom Mankiewicz—screenplay

Ian Fleming—novel

Cubby R. Broccoli, Harry Saltzman—producers

Sean Connery, Jill St. John, Charles Gray, Lana Wood, Jimmy Dean,
Bernard Lee—cast

Georgy! (1970; Broadway)

Peter H. Hunt—director

Tom Mankiewicz—book

Carole Bayer—lyrics

George Fischoff—music

Dilys Watling, John Castle, Melissa Hart, Stephen Elliott—cast

The Sweet Ride (1968; 20th Century Fox)

Harvey Hart—director

Tom Mankiewicz—screenplay

William Murray—novel

Joe Pasternak—producer

Michael Sarrazin, Jacqueline Bisset, Anthony Franciosa, Bob Denver—cast

The Beat of the Brass (1968; CBS)

Jack Haley Jr.—director

Tom Mankiewicz—teleplay

Jack Haley Jr.—producer

Herb Alpert and the Tijuana Brass—cast

Movin' with Nancy (1967; NBC)

Jack Haley Jr.—director

Tom Mankiewicz—teleplay

Jack Haley Jr., Nancy Sinatra—producers

Nancy Sinatra, Dean Martin, Sammy Davis Jr., Frank Sinatra—cast

Filmography

Bob Hope Presents the Chrysler Theatre, "Runaway Boy" (1966; NBC)

Ben Masselink—story
Ben Masselink, Tom Mankiewicz—teleplay
Dick Berg—producer
Lola Albright, Carol Lynley, Robert Wagner—cast

Director

Hart to Hart: Till Death Do Us Hart (1996; Columbia TriStar Television)

Tom Mankiewicz—director
Bill Froehlich, Mark Lisson—teleplay
Sidney Sheldon—creator
Stefanie Powers, Robert Wagner, James Veres, Uwe Schott—producers
Robert Wagner, Stefanie Powers, George Hamilton—cast

Taking the Heat (1993; Showtime)

Tom Mankiewicz—director
Gary Hoffman—story
Dan Gordon—teleplay
Gary Hoffman, Neal Israel—producers
Tony Goldwyn, Lynn Whitfield, George Segal, Peter Boyle, Alan
    Arkin—cast

Delirious (1991; MGM)

Tom Mankiewicz—director
Lawrence J. Cohen, Fred Freeman—screenplay
Doug Claybourne, Richard Donner—producers
John Candy, Mariel Hemingway, Emma Samms, Raymond Burr, Dylan
    Baker, Charles Rocket, Jerry Orbach, Robert Wagner—cast

Tales from the Crypt, "Loved to Death" (1991; HBO)

Tom Mankiewicz—director
Joe Minion, John Mankiewicz—teleplay
Richard Donner, David Giler, Walter Hill, Joel Silver, Robert
    Zemeckis—producers
Andrew McCarthy, Mariel Hemingway, David Hemmings, Kathleen
    Freeman—cast

Filmography

Dragnet (1987; Universal Pictures)

Tom Mankiewicz—director
(additional credits—see Writer section)

Hart to Hart (1979–1982; ABC)

"Harts and Palms" (1982)
"From the Depths of my Hart" (1982)
"Murder Up Their Sleeves" (1981)
"The Latest in High Fashion Murder" (1981)
"Homemade Murder" (1981)
"Murder in Paradise" (1981)
"Murder Is a Man's Best Friend" (1980)
"Murder, Murder on the Wall" (1980)
"Death Set" (1980)
"Downhill to Death" (1980)
"The Man with the Jade Eyes" (1979)
"Hit Jennifer Hart" (1979)
"Pilot" (1979)
Tom Mankiewicz—director
(additional credits—see Writer section)

Producer

Hot Pursuit (1987; Paramount Pictures)

Steven Lisberger—director
Steven Lisberger—story
Steven Lisberger, Steven Carabatsos—screenplay
Pierre David, Tom Mankiewicz, Jerry Offsay—producers
John Cusack, Robert Loggia, Jerry Stiller, Ben Stiller—cast

Mother, Jugs & Speed (1976; 20th Century Fox)

Joseph Barbera, Tom Mankiewicz, Peter Yates—producers
(additional credits—see Writer section)

Index

Across 110th Street (movie), 158
Act, The (Broadway musical), 92–94
actors: as movie stars, 293–95; production companies of, 188, 327–28. *See also* movie stars
Adam, Ken, 143, 145, 151, 163, 244
Adams, Edie, 71
Africa, 32, 267–77
Agutter, Jenny, 181
Alamo, The (movie), 55
Albert, Eddie, 222
Algonquin Round Table, 4
All About Eve (movie), 21, 22–23, 135
Allen, Fred, 25
Allen, Irwin, 208
Allen, Woody, 150, 334
Allenberg, Burt, 22
All the President's Men (movie), 152, 197, 321
Alonzo, John, 119, 120
Alpert, Herb, 14, 87–89, 174
Alston, Walter, 115
Always (movie), 330
Amblin Productions, 328
ambulances, 170–71
A&M Records, 14, 87–88, 89, 174
American Flyer (movie), 286
American in Paris, An (movie), 116, 118
analysts, 334–36
Anchors Aweigh (movie), 116
Anderson, Loni, 300
Andress, Ursula, 163
Andrews, Julie, 118, 176
Ann-Margret, 192–93
Antonioni, Michelangelo, 111

Apartment, The (movie), 245
Apatow, Judd, 331
Apocalypse Now (movie), 265
Applause (Broadway musical), 23
Archer, Anne, 195
Archerd, Army, 299, 309
Arkin, Alan, 324
Arnaz, Desi, 187–88, 240
Arness, Jim, 188
Ashby, Hal, 71–72
Ashley, Elizabeth, 160–61, 335, 337
Assad, Hafez al-, 302
Astaire, Fred, 116, 310
Aubrey, Skye, 195
Aykroyd, Dan: *Dragnet,* 284, 285, 286 88, 290–91, 292, 293, 315; as a movie star, 294; net profits from movies and, 295; *Valkenvania* project, 296

Bacall, Lauren, 23, 31, 216
Bach, Barbara, 163, 164
Bacharach, Burt, 89, 97
backgammon, 140
Back to the Future (movie), 329
Badham, John, 58, 73, 253, 286
Baker, Carroll, 251
Baker, Dylan, 313
Baker, James, 302
Balin, Ina, 53
Ball, Lucille, 187
Bancroft, Anne, 296
Bangkok, 161, 162
Bannen, Ian, 140
Barbera, Joe, 170
Barefoot Contessa, The (movie), 5, 27–28, 34–35, 61

Barefoot in the Park (play), 160
Barnes, Clive, 99
Barry, John, 143, 192, 199
Barry Lyndon (movie), 243–44
Barrymore, John, 32
Basil, Toni, 172, 175
Basinger, Kim, 298
Batman (movie), 213
"Battle for Hollywood," 15–17
Battle of Britain, The (movie), 165
Baumgarten, Craig, 320
Bautzer, Greg, 269–70
Bayer, Carole, 97
Beard, Peter, 274
Beat of the Brass (album), 88
Beat of the Brass, The (television musical special), 87–89
Beatty, Ned, 197
Beck, Glenn, 238, 331
Begelman, David, 107, 187
Belafonte, Harry, 130
Belushi, Jim, 285
Benchley, Peter, 38, 183
Benchley, Robert, 4
Benedict Canyon, 13
Bennett, Joan, 63
Benton, Robert, 189, 199–200, 212, 216, 220, 251–52, 322
Berg, Dick, 72
Berg, Jeff, 277, 278, 298, 338
Bergen, Candice, 129, 195
Berle, Milton, 101–2, 111
Berle, Ruth, 101
Berman, Shelley, 71
Berne, Jack, 49, 53, 54
Best Man, The (movie), 71–72, 105, 107, 130
Best Man, The (Vidal), 37–38
Beverly Hills, 13
Beverly Hills Cop (movie), 253
Bingo Long Traveling All-Stars and Motor Kings, The (movie), 253
Binion, Benny, 139–40
Binion's Horseshoe casino, 139–40
Bisset, Jacqueline, 95–96, 97, 183, 186, 208

Black Bird, The (movie), 296
Blaine, Vivian, 44
Blair, Bob, 225
Blake, Yvonne, 199
Blakely, Colin, 65
Blakely, Susie, 195
Blankfein, Fred, 324
Blow-Up (movie), 111
Blyden, Larry, 237
Bo (dog), 74
Bob & Carol & Ted & Alice (movie), 306
Bob Hope Presents the Chrysler Theatre (television show), 72, 222, 251, 305
Bogart, Humphrey, 27, 29, 31, 35
Bolger, Ray, 110, 111
Bolt, Robert, 32
Bound for Glory (movie), 71–72
Bourguignon, Serge, 127
Boyd, Stephen, 60, 61
Boyle, Bob, 289
Brando, Marlon, 61; director of *One-Eyed Jacks,* 205–6, 296; *Guys and Dolls,* 44; *Julius Caesar,* 42–43; Joseph Mankiewicz and, 205–6; Tom Mankiewicz on the talent and craft of, 135; practical jokes and, 202; the *Superman* movies, 189, 193–94, 202–9; *Superman II: The Donner Cut,* 214–16
Brazzi, Rossano, 28
Breakfast at Tiffany's (movie), 160
Breslin, Jimmy, 200
Brest, Marty, 253
Brice, Fanny, 13
Bricusse, Evie, 45, 115, 122
Bricusse, Leslie, 45, 115, 122, 123, 124, 307
Bridges, Jeff, 293
Bringing Out the Dead (movie), 175
British Virgin Islands, 184
Broccoli, Albert "Cubby": backgammon and, 140; the "Bond club" and, 162–63;

Diamonds Are Forever, 133, 134, 135, 136–37, 144, 145, 146–47; gains control of the Bond films, 165; gambling and, 137–38, 139; importance of behavior to, 138; *Live and Let Die,* 147, 148, 153, 154, 158–59; Tom Mankiewicz and, 339; *The Man with the Golden Gun,* 161, 162; *Moonraker,* 186; *Never Say Never Again* and, 151; *On Her Majesty's Secret Service,* 164; other films of, 165; rights to the Bond movies and, 150; success of, 165–66

Broccoli, Barbara, 140, 165, 166

Broccoli, Dana, 137, 165

Broderick, James, 262

Broderick, Matthew, 253, 262, 264, 265

Brokeback Mountain (movie), 333

Bronco Billy (movie), 258, 330

Brooks, Mel, 306

Brooks, Richard, 16, 44–45, 126–27, 252

Brosnan, Pierce, 167

Brothers Johnson, 174

Buchwald, Art, 63

Bujold, Geneviève, 218

Bullitt (movie), 96

Burns, George, 111

Burr, Raymond, 313, 314–15

Burton, Phillip, 64–65

Burton, Richard, 184; *Cleopatra,* 61, 64–65, 69–70; relationship with Elizabeth Taylor, 62–63, 65, 66–67

Burton, Sybil, 65, 67

Bush, George, Sr., 302

Butch Cassidy and the Sundance Kid (movie), 241, 280

Butkus, Dick, 172, 173

By Myself (Bacall), 31

Café Barzac, 304

Café Francais, 304

Caine, Michael, 45, 141; *The Eagle Has Landed,* 179, 180–81; *Jaws: The Revenge,* 290; marriage to Shakira Caine, 152–53; Harry Saltzman and, 136; *Sleuth,* 151, 152, 322; Jill St. John and, 145

Caine, Shakira, 152–53

Calcutta, 162

Calhern, Louis, 43

Calley, John, 243, 274

Camelot (movie), 111

Camelot (play), 65

cameramen, 198–99, 228–29, 297

Canby, Vincent, 157–58

Candida (Shaw), 124

Candy, John, 247, 293, 296, 313, 314, 318–19, 325

Can Heironymus Merkin Ever Forget Mercy Humppe and Find True Happiness? (movie), 124

Cansino, Rita, 118

Canton, Mark, 328

Cantor, Jay, 193

Capra, Frank, 17

Captain Newman, M.D. (movie), 103

Cardinal, The (movie), 75

Cardinale, Claudia, 108, 109

Carey, Timothy, 245

Carolco production company, 121

Carpenters (music group), 89

Carpetbaggers, The (movie), 160

Carsey, Marcy, 223–24

Carson, Johnny, 70, 328

Carter, Jack, 90

Caruso, Bruna, 70–71

Cash, Jim, 278

Casino Royale (movie), 150, 166

Cassandra at the Wedding (movie), 127

Cassandra Crossing, The (movie), 121, 177–79

Castle, John, 97

Catholic Church: Sophia Loren and, 119–20; the Mankiewiczes and, 11–12

Cavett, Dick, 58
CBS Evening News, 238
Central Intelligence Agency (CIA),
302
Century City, 19
Cerf, Bennett, 38, 40
Cerf, Chris, 38
Cerf, Phyllis, 38
Champion, Gower, 94
Channing, Stockard, 195
Charade (movie), 108
charades, 126–27
Charlie (dog), 225
Charlie Chaplin Studios, 89
Charlie's Angels (television series),
233–34, 236
Charisse, Cyd, 118
Chase, Chevy, 294, 296
Chasen, Dave, 8
Chasen, Maude, 8
Chasen's restaurant, 8, 16
Chayefsky, Paddy, 237–38
Chevalier, Michael, 228–29
Chinatown (movie), 119
Chitty Chitty Bang Bang (movie), 165
Chitwood, Joie, 142–43
Chrysler Corporation, 73
Church of the Good Shepherd, 11
Cilento, Diane, 145
Cincinnati Kid, The (movie), 76
Cinecittà studios, 264
Citizen Kane (movie), 135
City Heat (movie), 258–59
Clark, Petula, 123
Claybourne, Doug, 316
Cleopatra (movie): Richard Burton,
61, 64–65, 69–70; effect on
Joseph Mankiewicz's health,
152; impact on the Mankiewicz
family, 70–71; Joseph
Mankiewicz becomes director of,
60–62; postproduction and
release, 69–70; production,
62–64; shooting in Egypt,
67–68; Elizabeth Taylor, 60–61,
63–64, 65–67, 140; Taylor–

Burton relationship during,
62–63, 65, 66–67
Clift, Montgomery, 46
Clooney, George, 331
"Close to You" (song), 89
Clothier, Bill, 52
Coates, Anne V., 180
cocaine, 92
Coe, Fred, 97, 98
Coen brothers, 332
Cohn, Art, 47
Cohn, Harry, 7–8, 82
Coleman, Dabney, 253, 285, 288
Collector, The (movie), 75
Collins, Bob, 227
Collins, Joan, 45, 123, 124
Color Purple, The (movie), 34
Columbia Studios, 71, 97, 328
Columbo (television series), 168–70
Comancheros, The (movie), 40, 49–55
Comeaux, Jerry, 156–57
Company (Broadway musical), 130
Connaught hotel, 182–83
Connery, Sean: advice to Christopher
Reeve, 217; Sammy Davis Jr.
and, 82–83; *Diamonds Are
Forever,* 133, 134, 136, 140 44,
145; *Dr. No,* 150; Guy Hamilton
and, 158; Roger Moore
compared to, 159–60; as a movie
star, 294; *Never Say Never
Again,* 150–51; portrayal of
James Bond, 166–67; Scotland
and, 141; Robert Shaw and, 184,
185; turns down *Live and Let
Die,* 147–48
Cooper, Jackie, 4, 198
Coppola, Francis, 180, 330
Corey, Jeff, 195
Cosby, Bill, 172, 174, 175, 294–95
Cosby Show, The (television series),
223
Cosmatos, George, 177, 178
Costa, Don, 86
Couric, Katie, 238
Court Jester, The (movie), 115

Cover Girl (movie), 116
Coward, Noel, 154
Cracknell, Derek, 184
Craig, Daniel, 150, 166, 167
Crain, Jeanne, 41
Crawford, Joan, 18
Creative Artists Agency (CAA), 241,
    277–78, 298–300, 324
creative consultants, 218–19, 231
Creative Management Agency
    (CMA), 241
Creech, Everett, 142
Cricket (dog), 307
crocodiles, 156
Cronyn, Hume, 301
Crosby, Bing, 84, 85, 130, 269
Crowley, Mart, 127, 309
Crowther, Bosley, 70
Cry, the Beloved Country (movie), 42
Culp, Robert, 172
Curtis, Howard, 185–86
Curtis, Tony, 144, 239–40, 297–98,
    306
Curtiz, Michael, 40, 51–52, 55

Daily News, 98
Daily News building, 200
Dalton, Timothy, 167
Daly, Bob, 151, 328
Damone, Vic, 85
Danjaq company, 137, 165
Dante, Joe, 258
Darin, Bobby, 102–5
Dateline (television news show), 11
Da Vinci Code, The (movie), 295
Davis, Bette, 23
Davis, Josie. *See* Mankiewicz,
    Johanna (cousin Josie)
Davis, Nick and Tim, 10
Davis, Ossie, 42
Davis, Peter, 10
Davis, Sammy, Jr., 80, 81–83, 91
Davison, Bruce, 172, 175
Dee, Ruby, 42
Deep, The (Benchley), 38
Deep, The (movie), 183–88

DeHerdt, Doris, 232–33
Deighton, Len, 168
Delgadillo, Rocky, 322
Delinn, Alan, 245–46
Delirious (movie), 247, 297,
    299–300, 313–19
Deliverance (movie), 197
DeLuise, Dom, 296
DeMille, Cecil B., 15, 16, 17
Denby, David, 213
Deneuve, Catherine, 163
De Niro, Robert, 92
De Sica, Vittorio, 120, 121
Detective, The (movie), 96
Diamonds Are Forever (Fleming),
    138
Diamonds Are Forever (movie):
    Albert Broccoli and, 133, 134,
    135, 136–37, 144, 145, 146–47;
    Sean Connery and, 133, 134,
    136, 140–44, 145; Las Vegas car
    chase scene, 142–43; Tom
    Mankiewicz's rewriting of,
    133–36, 146–47; plot, 138;
    Harry Saltzman and, 136–37;
    score and production design,
    143; sex and violence in, 164;
    shooting in Las Vegas, 137;
    shooting in London, 144–46
Dickinson, Angie, 222
Dietrich, Marlene, 111, 240–41
Dietz, Howard, 36
Dillinger, John, 18
directors and directing: Richard
    Donner on, 225–26, 339;
    fraternity of, 244; John Huston's
    advice to, 114–15; importance of
    controlling the set, 43; Tom
    Mankiewicz on, 296–97; Robert
    Wagner on, 339; Billy Wilder on,
    297–98
Directors' View Film Festival,
    216–17
Disneyland, 113
Dixon, Donna, 290
Doctor Dolittle (movie), 123

Dominguin, Luis Miguel, 30
Donen, Stanley, 96, 171
Donner, Lauren Shuler, 215
Donner, Richard, 183; advice to Tom
    Mankiewicz about directing,
    225–26, 339; Marlon Brando
    and, 204; brings Tom
    Mankiewicz into the *Superman*
    movies, 188–89; casting the
    Superman movies, 189, 190,
    191–97, 198; Creative Artists
    Agency and, 299; *Delirious* and,
    299; directing the *Superman*
    movies, 198–99, 200, 201–2,
    203, 204–5, 208–9, 210, 211;
    first meets Tom Mankiewicz, 79;
    The Goonies, 258; Jack Haley Jr.
    and, 94; invents "creative
    consultant" credit for Tom
    Mankiewicz, 218–19; Joseph L.
    Mankiewicz Award for
    Excellence, 216–17; *Ladyhawke,*
    260–66; movies produced at
    Warners, 329; *The Omen,* 175,
    204; practical jokes and, 202;
    production company, 328; the
    Salkinds and, 206–8, 209–10,
    212; *Superman II: The Donner
    Cut,* 214–16; *The Toy,* 154
Douglas, Kirk, 322
Douglas, Sarah, 215
Dragnet (movie), 12, 21, 284–93,
    295, 315
Dragonwyck (movie), 20–21
Dr. No (movie), 136, 150
Dr. Strangelove (movie), 198
Durocher, Leo, 26
Duvall, Robert, 179, 181
Dynasty (television series), 123

Eady Plan, 163
Eagle Has Landed, The (movie),
    179–83, 295
Eastwood, Clint, 187, 258–60,
    293–94, 328, 330
Easy Rider (movie), 57, 113

Ebb, Fred, 91
Ebony magazine, 42
Ebsen, Buddy, 110
editors, film, 296–97
Edku (Egypt), 68
Edwards, Blake, 176, 258–60, 295
Eggar, Samantha, 75
Egypt, 67–68
Egyptian Camel Corps, 68
Elam, Jack, 54
Electric Horseman, The (movie), 280
Engel, Don, 236
Entratter, Jack, 88–89
Epps, Jack, 278
Equus (play), 65
Erede, Alberto, 36
Erickson, C. O. "Doc," 63
Espy, Freddy, 38
Eszterhas, Joe, 298
Excelsior Hotel (Rome), 31
Exner, Judith, 87

Factory (art studio), 125
Falk, Peter, 168–70
Fame Is the Name of the Game
    (television series), 95
Farewell, My Lovely (movie), 246
Farewell to Arms, A (movie), 129
Fargo (movie), 332
Farmer's Daughter, The (television
    series), 130
Farrelly Brothers, 293
Farrow, Mia, 96
Fatal Attraction (movie), 292
Father Goose (movie), 108
Fatso (movie), 296
Feingarten, Chuck and Gail, 242
Feldman, Charlie, 150
Feldman, Milton, 134, 140
Fellini, Federico, 120, 121
Ferber, Edna, 6, 25
Fiametta theater, 30
Fields, Freddie, 107, 241–42
Figaro company, 27, 61, 327
film industry: Desi Arnaz's impact
    on, 187–88; "hello partner"

deals, 187; housekeeping deals, 328–29; loyalty oath controversy, 15–17; Tom Mankiewicz on studios, 327–29; Tom Mankiewicz on the costs of making movies, 329–30; Tom Mankiewicz on the dumbing down of entertainment, 330–33; Tom Mankiewicz's disillusionment with, 323–25, 337–39; negative pickup, 189; net profits and "monkey points," 295–96; racism and, 41; "the package," 278
Finch, Peter, 60, 61, 238
Fine, Sylvia, 116
Finney, Albert, 96, 145, 196–97
Fiondella, Jay, 81
Firth, Peter, 65
Fischoff, George, 97
Fisher, Eddie, 66–67, 139
Fitzgerald, F. Scott, 128, 254–55
Fleming, Ian, 143, 150, 155, 164
Fleming, Victor, 110
Fonda, Henry, 51, 57, 71, 105–6, 182, 322
Fonda, Jane, 105–6, 250, 278, 280
Fonda, Peter, 57, 113
Ford, Cecil, 33
Ford, John, 16–17, 50, 51
Foreman, John, 105, 106
Forest Hills Country Club, 83
Fosse, Bob, 90, 238
Four Musketeers (movie), 191
Fox Searchlight studios, 332
Frampton, Peter, 174
Franciosa, Anthony, 95
Francisco, Bill, 57
Frankenheimer, John, 128, 241
Freeman, Kathleen, 319
French, Robin, 148, 241
French Connection, The (movie), 190
Friedkin, Billy, 328
Friesian horses, 264
Frings, Kurt, 120
From Russia with Love (movie), 136, 185

Frost, David, 98
Fryer, Bobby, 309
Full Metal Jacket (movie), 244
Funny People (movie), 331
Furth, George, 130

gambling: Benny Binion and, 139–40; Albert Broccoli and, 137–38, 139; Allen Garfield and, 173; Herman Mankiewicz and, 9; Robert Mitchum and, 246–47
Garbo, Greta, 241
Gardner, Ava, 27, 29–30, 34, 121, 177, 178
Gardner, Herb, 238
Garfield, Allen, 172, 173
Garland, Judy, 18, 106–8, 118
Garner, James, 220–21
Garner, Peggy Ann, 131
Garson, Greer, 43
Gates, Daryl, 291
Gavilan (television series), 256–57
Gavin, John, 134
Geeson, Judy, 179
Gentleman's Agreement (movie), 41
Georgy! (Broadway musical), 97–99
Ghost and Mrs. Muir, The (movie), 21–22
Giancana, Sam, 85
Gibson, Mel, 144, 216, 329
Giddings, Al, 186
Gielgud, John, 43
G.I. Joe (movie), 332
Gilbert, Lewis, 163, 186
Giler, David, 234–35, 296
Gleason, Jackie, 111, 167–68, 285
Glover, Danny, 216
Goizueta, Robert, 252
Goldberg, Leonard: *Charlie's Angels,* dispute over co-ownership of, 233–34; *Gavilan* television series, 256, 257; *Hart to Hart* television series, 14, 19, 221, 222, 223, 227–28, 233–36, 266; on producing for television, 339;

Goldberg, Leonard *(cont.)*
  Sleeping with the Enemy script
    and, 298; TriStar studios and,
    251; *War Games*, 253–54
Golden Globe awards, 279–80
Goldenson, Leonard, 230
Goldfinger (movie), 136, 155
Goldwyn, John, 319
Goldwyn, Samuel, 128
Gone with the Wind (movie), 41
Good Night and Good Luck (movie),
  331
Goonies, The (movie), 258
Gordean, Bill, 316
Gordon, Dan, 323–24
Gormé, Eydie, 101
Gossett, Louis, Jr., 230
Grable, Betty, 13
Grade, Lew, 179
Grand Dolder Hotel, 210
Granger, Stewart, 44
Grant, Cary, 108–10
Gray, Charles, 146
Great Race, The (movie), 306
Greenberg, Robbie, 279
Gregson, Richard, 306–7
Gremlins (movie), 258
Griffith, Melanie, 279
Groleau, Pierre, 116, 117
Groves, Regina, 118
Gruenwald, Henry, 9–10
Guber, Peter, 177, 184, 186
Gunfight in Abilene (movie), 103
Gunsmoke (television series), 188
Gustav, Bill, 182
Guys and Dolls (movie), 43–45

Hacker, Fred, 335
Hackman, Gene, 171–72, 189–90,
  213
Hagen, Uta, 106
Haggis, Paul, 159, 186
Hagman, Larry, 74, 172, 173, 179,
  181
Haley, Flo, 110
Haley, Jack, Jr.: *The Beat of the Brass*

television special, 87, 88;
  direction of Oscar telecasts, 253;
  Tom Mankiewicz and, 79–80;
  Liza Minnelli and, 18, 90,
  91–92, 93, 94; *Movin' with
  Nancy* television special, 80, 81,
  84, 85, 86, 87; television
  documentary on Sophia Loren,
  119
Haley, Jack, Sr., 80, 110–11
Halmi, Robert, 272
Hamburg, 90
Hamilton, George, 222
Hamilton, Guy: in the "Bond club,"
  163; Sean Connery and, 158;
  Diamonds Are Forever, 133, 136,
  139, 143, 145, 146; *Live and Let
  Die*, 153, 154–55, 157, 158;
  Tom Mankiewicz and, 162, 166;
  turns down the *Superman*
  movies, 190–91
Hanks, Tom: *Dragnet*, 285, 286–87,
  288, 291–92, 293; as a movie
  star, 294; net profits from movies
  and, 295; salary of, 329
Hannah, Daryl, 280–81
Hanson, Jack and Sally, 111
Harriman, Averill, 39
Harris, Jimmy, 243, 244–45
Harris, Phil, 269
Harris, Richard, 121, 177, 178
Harrison, Rex, 21, 61, 64
Hart, Harvey, 94, 96
Hart, Melissa, 97
Hart, Moss, 36–37, 58, 297
Hartford, Diane, 103
Hartford, Huntington, 103
Hart to Hart (television series):
  camera operator, 228–29;
  casting, 222–25; episode in
  Greece, 266; Tom Mankiewicz's
  credit as "creative consultant,"
  231; Tom Mankiewicz's
  directing of, 225–33; Tom
  Mankiewicz's dispute with the
  Writers Guild, 234–35; Tom

Mankiewicz's rewriting of, 14, 19, 221–22; script supervisor, 232–33; Spelling-Goldberg ownership, 233–36; theme song, 229
Harz, Claude, 76
Hauer, Rutger, 263–64
Hawn, Goldie, 192, 262, 328
Hayden, Sterling, 301
Hayes, Helen, 8
Hayward, Bill, 56–57
Hayward, Bridget, 56–57, 251
Hayward, Brooke, 56, 57, 112–13
Hayward, Leland, 51, 56, 57, 112
Hayward, Susan, 61
Haywire (Hayward), 56
Hayworth, Rita, 118
Hazard, Tom "Hap," 170–71
Hazelwood, Lee, 80
Hearst newspapers, 15–16
Hearts and Minds (documentary), 10
Heaven Knows, Mr. Allison (movie), 114–15
Hecht, Ben, 8
"hello partner" deals, 187
Hemingway, Mariel, 112, 313, 315, 316, 319
Hemmings, David, 86, 111–12, 319
Henry, Buck, 239–40
Henry the Bootblack, 19
Hepburn, Audrey, 96, 118, 160, 331
Hepburn, Katharine, 20, 32, 34, 46–47, 97
Herald Tribune, 98
Herb Alpert and the Tijuana Brass, 87, 88
Hiaasen, Carl, 319, 320
Higgins, Colin, 278
Higgins, Jack, 179
Hill, Arthur, 106
Hill, The (movie), 140
Hill & Knowlton, 10–11
Hiller, Arthur, 237
Hitchcock, Alfred, 109
Hoffman, Dustin, 261–62
Hoffman, Gary, 323, 324

Holden, William, 32, 128, 129, 208, 242–43, 267, 301
Holston, Rand, 298
Homer (dog), 74
Hong Kong, 161
Honky Tonk Freeway (movie), 301
Honkytonk Man (movie), 258
Hope, Bob, 78
Hopper, Dennis, 57, 112–14
Hopper, Marin, 113
Hornblow, Arthur, Jr., 8
Hospital, The (movie), 237
House (television series), 11, 135, 323
House Committee on Un-American Activities, 15
housekeeping deals, 328–29
Howard, Ron, 295
Howard, Trevor, 205
Howard the Duck (movie), 328
Hudson, Claude, 162
Hudson, Rock, 129, 315
Hughes, Howard, 34–35, 138–39
Hughes, John, 325
Hunnicutt, Gayle, 111
Hunt, Don, 32, 267, 268–69, 270–71, 272, 273, 276
Hunt, Iris, 32, 268, 277
Hunt, Peter, 58, 97, 164
Hurt, Donna, 32
Hurt, John, 32, 33, 273–74
Huston, John, 16, 114–15, 129, 170
Huston, Walter, 21
Huxley, Aldous, 127

I'll Take Sweden (movie), 78
I Love Lucy (television series), 187–88
Indecent Proposal (movie), 280
In Plain Sight (television series), 170, 323
International Creative Management (ICM), 72, 277, 278, 299, 338
Internet, 330–31
Ipcress File, The (movie), 136
Ironside (television series), 10, 135

Index

I Spy (television series), 172
I Want to Live (movie), 11, 61

Jack Daniel's whiskey, 92, 125, 194, 232, 255, 269, 287
Jackson, Jermaine, 332
Jackson, Kate, 31, 219
Jackson, Michael, 82, 83
Jamaica, 153, 154
James, Clifton, 157
James, Harry, 13
James Bond films: actors wanting to play James Bond, 143–44; the "Bond club," 162–63; *Casino Royale,* 150, 166; Sammy Davis Jr.'s love of, 82; *Diamonds Are Forever,* 133–47, 164; *Dr. No,* 136, 150; *From Russia with Love,* 136, 185; *Goldfinger,* 136, 155; *Live and Let Die,* 144, 147–60; Richard Maibaum and, 147; Tom Mankiewicz on the actors portraying bond, 166–67; Tom Mankiewicz stops writing for, 162; Tom Mankiewicz writes for, 99; *The Man with the Golden Gun,* 147, 161–62; *Moonraker,* 167, 186; *On Her Majesty's Secret Service,* 164; *Quantum of Solace,* 166; rights issues pertaining to, 150–51; sex and violence in, 164–65; *The Spy Who Loved Me,* 163, 164–65; *Thunderball,* 150; *You Only Live Twice,* 144
James Bond stage, 152
Jane (script), 320–21
Jannings, Emil, 240
Jaws (movie), 185
Jaws: The Revenge (movie), 290
J.B. (MacLeish), 12
Jewison, Norman, 107
John Paul (Pope), 266–67
Johnston, Johnny, 63
Jomar (schooner), 20
Jones, Ike, 130

Jones, Jennifer, 126, 127–28
Jones, Quincy, 174
Jones, Tom, 141–42
Joseph L. Mankiewicz Award for Excellence, 216–17
Jourdan, Louis, 38, 126
Julius Caesar (movie), 42–43

Kamen, Stan, 241, 242
Kanin, Garson and Ruth, 240
Kassar, Mario, 121, 177, 179
Kaufman, George S., 6, 37
Kaufmann, Christine, 239
Kaye, Danny, 115–16
Kaye, Stubby, 44
Kazan, Elia, 16
Keitel, Harvey, 172
Kelly, Gene, 44, 45, 116–18, 310
Kendall, Suzy, 79, 182–83, 295
Kennedy, John F., 59, 85, 150
Kennedy, Robert, 10, 85, 103–4
Kenya, 32, 267–77
Kerr, Deborah, 43, 114, 115
Kerrey, Bob, 281
Keys of the Kingdom, The (movie), 6
Khashoggi, Adnan, 274
Kidd, Michael, 44
Kidder, Margot: *Delirious,* 316; Tom Mankiewicz and, 200–201, 219, 220, 309, 336, 337; *Superman* movies, 195, 200–201, 214, 215, 216, 219
Killing, The (movie), 243
King, Henry, 128
King, Larry, 331, 332
King, Martin Luther, Jr., 83
Klute (movie), 250
Korda, Zoltan, 42
Korshak, Sidney, 81–82
Kotcheff, Ted, 284–85
Kotto, Yaphet, 158
Kovacs, Laszlo, 281
Kramer, Stanley, 72
Kretchmer, John, 315
Krishna Menon, V. K., 25
Kroll, Jack, 199, 205

Krumm, Whitey, 289–90
Kubie, Lawrence, 39
Kubrick, Christiane, 244–45
Kubrick, Stanley, 206, 243–45

La Bohème, 36
Ladd, Alan, 13
Ladd, Alan, Jr.: *Delirious,* 317; in
  Kenya, 274; *Ladyhawke,* 260,
  262; Tom Mankiewicz and, 14;
  Mother, Jugs & Speed, 171, 173,
  174, 175; *Skin Tight* script, 320
Ladyhawke (movie), 176, 260–67
Lahr, Bert, 110
Lake, Sol, 88
Lamas, Fernando, 256
Lambert, Gavin, 306
Lancaster, Burt, 121, 177–78, 327
Lancer (television series), 87
Landau, Martin, 70, 109
Landis, Jessie Royce, 302
Lang, Jennings, 63
Lang, Otto, 15
Lange, David, 279
Lange, Hope, 22, 126
Lange, Jessica, 195
Last Emperor, The (movie), 265
Last Gangster, The (movie), 6
L.A. Times, 216
Lawrence, Steve, 101–2
Lawrence of Arabia (movie), 32, 180,
  232
Lazarus Syndrome, The (television
  pilot), 230
Lazenby, George, 138, 164
Leakey, Richard, 269
Lean, David, 32–34, 123, 180, 232,
  274, 297
Lear, Norman, 167, 168
Lee, Ang, 333
Lee, Bruce, 161
Legal Eagles (movie), 109, 227,
  278–82
Lehrer, Tom, 339
Leigh, Janet, 239
Leighton, Margaret, 71

Lemmon, Jack, 297, 306, 333
Lenya, Lotte, 136
Leonard, Sheldon, 3
Leone, Sergio, 294
Lerner, Alan J., 240
Lester, Dick, 191, 212–13, 215
Lethal Weapon movies, 329
Letter to Three Wives, A (movie), 15
Levinson, Barry, 251
Levinson, Richard, 168, 169
Life Signs (Josie Mankiewicz), 10
lighting cameraman, 198–99
Link, William, 168, 169
Live and Let Die (movie): Albert
  Broccoli and, 147, 148, 153,
  154, 158–59; locations shot at,
  153–54, 156; Tom Mankiewicz's
  screenwriting for, 147–48, 159;
  Roger Moore and, 144, 148,
  152, 154–55, 156; race issues
  and, 155–56, 157–58; Harry
  Saltzman and, 147, 148, 153,
  154, 156; Sheriff J. W. Pepper
  character, 157; Solitaire character,
  155–56; stage sets, 152; stunts in,
  156–57; theme song, 158–59
"Live and Let Die" (song), 158–59
Liza with a Z (nightclub show), 90,
  91
Loeb, John, 25
Loew, Arthur, Jr., 118–19, 127, 306
Loew, Marcus, 118
Logan, Joshua, 51, 57, 75
Lollobrigida, Gina, 34
London, 144–46
"Lonely Bull, The" (song), 88
Look Back in Anger (movie), 184
Loren, Sophia, 119–21, 177, 178
Los Angeles Zoo, 338
Louisiana, 153–54
Love Is a Many-Splendored Thing
  (movie), 128–29
loyalty oath controversy, 15–17
Lubitsch, Ernst, 20–21
Lucchese, Tommy, 85
Lucky Lady (movie), 171

Lucky Liz (plane), 47
Lumet, Sidney, 140
Lupino, Ida, 16
Luther (dog), 75, 77
Lynley, Carol, 73, 75, 98
Lyons, Cliff, 55

MacArthur, Charles, 8
MacDonald, Peter, 198, 199
MacLaine, Shirley, 118, 251
Magnani, Anna, 95
Maguire, Charlie, 172, 173, 308
Mahoney, Jim, 107
Maibaum, Richard, 147, 162
Malibu Colony, 73–75, 76, 131
Malpaso company, 328
Maltin, Leonard, 175, 179
Mamoulian, Rouben, 16, 60
Mancini, Henry, 253
Manhattan Melodrama (movie), 18
Mank (Meryman), 323
Mankiewicz, Alexandra, 5
Mankiewicz, Ben, 11, 181, 322
Mankiewicz, Chris: absence at
    father's tribute, 323; birth, 6; at
    Columbia University, 56;
    cremation of mother, 249–50;
    growing up in the 1940s, 13–15;
    life in New York City in the
    1950s, 25–26; marriage to Bruna
    Caruso, 70–71; mother, 5
Mankiewicz, Contessa, 322
Mankiewicz, Don, 4, 11, 135, 322
Mankiewicz, Eric, 5
Mankiewicz, Erna, 10
Mankiewicz, Frank, 3–4, 10–11, 104
Mankiewicz, Herman: abrasiveness
    with studio executives, 7–8;
    biography of, 323; Chasen's
    restaurant and, 8; *Citizen Kane,*
    135; death of, 4, 9; gambling
    and, 9; pre-Hollywoood career,
    3–4; wife Sara, 8, 9
Mankiewicz, Jason, 71
Mankiewicz, Johanna (cousin Josie),
    7, 9–10, 37, 39, 57

Mankiewicz, Johanna (grandmother),
    4–5
Mankiewicz, John, 11, 135, 170,
    322–23, 334
Mankiewicz, Joseph L.: Academy
    tribute to, 322–23; *All About
    Eve,* 22–23, 135; assistance to
    cousin Josie, 9–10; Lauren Bacall
    and, 23; *The Barefoot Contessa,*
    27–32, 34–35; Marlon Brando
    and, 205–6; burial, 12; Chasen's
    restaurant and, 8; as a child
    prodigy, 3; *Cleopatra,* 60–62,
    63–64, 68–70, 152; control of
    the set, 43; death of, 322; end of
    film career, 151–52; extramarital
    affairs, 18; as a film producer, 18;
    Judy Garland and, 106–7; *The
    Ghost and Mrs. Muir,* 21–22;
    Guys and Dolls, 43–45; Katherine
    Hepburn and, 46–47; home in
    Westchester County, 149–50;
    Howard Hughes and, 34–35;
    Julius Caesar, 42–43; Danny
    Kaye and, 115; Stanley Kubrick
    and, 244; *La Bohème,* 36; last
    years of, 320–22; the loyalty oath
    controversy and, 15–17; Ernst
    Lubitsch and, 20–21; marriages,
    5, 6; married life with Rosa,
    17–18, 26, 27, 28, 35; Rosemary
    Matthews and, 63, 70, 323;
    Marilyn Monroe and, 22–23; *No
    Way Out,* 41–42; religion and,
    11, 12; Rosa's suicide, 39–40;
    Jean Simmons and, 44; Frank
    Sinatra and, 84; *Sleuth,* 151, 152,
    322; *Suddenly, Last Summer,*
    45–47; Elizabeth Taylor and, 46;
    Timber the dog and, 14–15; on
    Tom's acting, 58–59; Tom's
    entry into the film industry and,
    40; Tom's fake birth certificate,
    14; Spencer Tracy and, 20; at
    20th Century Fox, 19; *Woman of
    the Year,* 20; Natalie Wood and,

22; Prince Felix Yusupov and, 31–32

Mankiewicz, Josh, 11, 322

Mankiewicz, Rosemary, 4, 5, 11, 249, 323. *See also* Matthews, Rosemary

Mankiewicz, Sara, 7, 8, 9

Mankiewicz, Thomas Frank "Tom": Elizabeth Ashley and, 160–61, 335, 337; asthma of, 26; *Batman,* 213; *The Beat of the Brass,* 87–89; *The Best Man,* 71–72, 105, 107, 130; birth, 6; *The Cassandra Crossing,* 177–79; cats and, 149; cocaine and, 92; *Columbo,* 168–70; *The Comancheros,* 40, 49–55; on conflict, relationships, and suffering, 333–37; on the costs of making movies, 329–30; Creative Artists Agency and, 298–300, 324; cremation of mother, 249–50; Sammy Davis Jr. and, 82; *The Deep,* 183–88; *Delirious,* 297, 299–300, 313–19; *Diamonds Are Forever,* 133–47; on directing, 296–97; disillusionment with the film business, 323–25, 337–39; *Dragnet,* 284–93; on the dumbing down of American entertainment, 330–33; *The Eagle Has Landed,* 179–83; entry into the film industry, 40; fake birth certificate, 14; on film studios and housekeeping deals, 327–29; *Gavilan* television series, 256–57; *Georgy!,* 97–99; Jackie Gleason and, 167–68; growing up in the 1940s, 13–15; Jack Haley Jr. and, 79–80; Guy Hamilton and, 162, 166; *Hart to Hart,* 14, 19, 221–33; Bridget Hayward and, 56–57; William Holden and, 242–43; house in Malibu, 148–49; interests outside of film, 321; Jack Daniel's whiskey, 92, 125, 194, 232, 255, 269, 287; on James Bond actors, 166–67; James Bond films and, 99; Suzy Kendall and, 79, 182–83; Pope John Paul and, 266–67; in Kenya, 267–77; Margot Kidder and, 200–201, 219, 220, 309, 336, 337; *Ladyhawke,* 176, 260–67; David Lean and, 32–34; *Legal Eagles,* 278–82; life in Malibu in the 1960s, 73–75; life in New York City in the 1950s, 25–26, 27; life in Rome in 1953, 28–30; life in Westchester, 38–40; *Live and Let Die,* 147–60; Carol Lynley and, 73; *The Man with the Golden Gun,* 161–62; Willie Mays and, 26–27; Liza Minnelli and, 89–94; mirror shots, 316; Robert Mitchum and, 246–47; *Moonraker,* 186; Jerry Moss and, 87–88, 89; *Mother, Jugs & Speed,* 170–77; mother's suicide, 38–40; move to Universal studios, 277–78; on movie stars and actors, 293–95; *Movin' with Nancy,* 80, 81–87; nanny, 6; net profits from movies and, 295–96; *Never Say Never Again* and, 151; Joan O'Brien and, 55; Mike Ovitz and, 277–78; at Phillips Exeter Academy, 37–38; *Please* script, 250–51; poker and, 53–54; Stefanie Powers and, 32, 220, 337; *Rainbow* script, 258; on relationships with actresses, 30–31; relationships with women, 219–20, 336, 337; relationship with father, 29–30, 149–50, 249–50; relationship with mother, 6–7, 29, 38; religion and, 11–12; screenwriting and, 72–73, 94–97; script fixing for Warner

Mankiewicz, Thomas Frank *(cont.)*
Brothers, 257–60; David O.
Selznick and, 129–30; Jean
Simmons and, 44–45; *Skin Tight*
script, 319–29; *The Spy Who Loved
Me*, 163; Inger Stevens and, 130;
stops making Bond films, 162;
the *Superman* movies, 188–219;
The Sweet Ride, 94–97; *Taking the
Heat* script, 323–25; *Tales from
the Crypt*, 319; tarot and,
152–53; Elizabeth Taylor and,
66–67; television documentary
on Sophia Loren, 119–21; turns
down the TriStar studios offer,
251–53; Gore Vidal and, 37–38;
War Games, 253–54; Tuesday
Weld and, 75–79, 335; at the
Williamstown Summer Theater,
57, 58–59; Natalie Wood and, 6,
7, 22, 99, 171, 219, 220, 240,
305–6, 307, 309–11; on
writer-directors, 297; on writing
for Roger Moore, 159–60;
writing habits, 254–56; at Yale
University, 40, 56, 58–59
Mankiewicz family: character of, 3;
the making of *Cleopatra* and,
70–71; religion and, 11–12;
writing and, 135
Man Who Would Be King, The
(movie), 153
Man with the Golden Gun, The
(Fleming), 143
Man with the Golden Gun, The
(movie), 147, 161–62
Marathon Man (movie), 261
Marcus Welby, M.D. (television
series), 10, 135
Mardigian, Ron, 168–69, 338
Margaret, Princess of England, 45
Margot (cat), 336–37
"mariachi" music, 88
Mark VII Productions, 289
Marsh, Jean, 179
Marshall, E. G., 121–22

Martin, Dean, 80, 81
Martin, Nan, 121
Martin, Ross, 3
Martin, Tony, 176
Marvin, Lee, 52
Mason, James, 43
Matter of Gravity, A (movie), 194
Matthews, Rosemary: Joseph
Mankiewicz and, 5, 63, 70; Tom
Mankiewicz and, 28; on the set
of *Cleopatra*, 63. *See also*
Mankiewicz, Rosemary
Matthews, Terry, 269–70
Maverick (television series), 221
Mayer, Louis B., 18
Mays, Willie, 26–27
McCarthy, Andrew, 112, 319
McCarthy, Joseph, 15
McCarthy, Kevin, 71
McCartney, Paul, 158
McClory, Kevin, 150–51
McCord, Ken, 289
McDaniel, Hattie, 41
McDowall, Roddy, 66, 70, 73–74, 309
McDowell, Malcolm, 244
McElwaine, Guy, 107, 233, 234, 309
McGoohan, Patrick, 173–74
McGuane, Tom, 201
McKeon, Julian and Jane, 274
McKern, Leo, 264
McQueen, Steve, 72, 241–42
Mechanic, Bill, 70
Meddings, Derek, 199
Medford, Don, 253
Mencken, H. L., 330
Mentalist, The (television series), 11,
135, 323
Merman, Doc, 40, 49
Merrick, David, 245–46
Merrill, Robert, 36
Meryman, Richard, 323
Meston, John, 188
Metropolitan Opera, 36
Meyer, Ron, 299, 300
Miami Vice (television series), 11,
135, 323

Index

Michaels, Lorne, 291

Milagro Beanfield War, The (movie), 279

Mielziner, Jo, 98

Millar, Stuart, 71, 105

Miller, Artie, 21

Million Dollar Legs (movie), 18

Mills, Juliet, 182

Milner, Marty, 289

Mimieux, Yvette, 122

Minnelli, Liza, 18, 80, 87, 89–94, 171

Minnelli, Vincente, 18

Minow, Newton, 331

Miracle on 34th Street (movie), 325

Mirisch brothers, 327

Mirror, 98

mirror shots, 316

Mister Roberts (movie), 51

Mitchell, Elvis, 174

Mitchum, Robert, 114–15, 246–47

Mix, Tom, 13

"monkey points," 295–96

Monroe, Marilyn, 22–23, 297–98

Monsignor (movie), 218

Montecito Hotel, 71

Moonraker (movie), 167, 186

Moore, Demi, 294, 296, 298

Moore, Dudley, 79, 183, 295

Moore, Roger, 141; *Diamonds Are Forever* offered to, 143–44; *Live and Let Die*, 144, 148, 152, 154–55, 156; Tom Mankiewicz on writing for, 159–60; portrayal of James Bond, 167; *The Spy Who Loved Me*, 163, 164–65

Morgan, Harry, 21, 288–89

Moss, Jerry, 14, 87–88, 89, 158–59, 174, 216

Mother, Jugs & Speed (movie), 170–77, 295

Mountains of the Moon (movie), 275

Mount Kenya Game Ranch, 32, 267, 268

Mount Kenya Safari Club, 268

Mount Kisco, 38–40

movie stars: Tom Mankiewicz on,

293–95; salaries, 329. *See also* actors

Movin' with Nancy (television musical special): conception of, 80; Sammy Davis Jr. and, 81–83; Dean Martin and, 81; shooting of, 81; Frank Sinatra and, 84–87

Mulligan, Bob, 72

Munsel, Patrice, 36

Murphy, Eddie, 295

Murray, Bill, 278

Murray, William, 94

My Fair Lady (musical), 37

"My Way" (song), 86

Natural, The (movie), 251

Navajo Indians, 52–53

negative pickup, 189

Negulesco, Jean, 126

Neill, Noel, 200

net profits, 295–96

Network (movie), 197, 238

Never Say Never Again (movie), 150–51

Newley, Anthony, 45, 122–24, 246

Newley, Leslie, 246

Newman, David, 189, 199, 212, 322

Newman, Leslie, 189, 212

Newman, Paul: *Butch Cassidy and the Sundance Kid*, 241, 280; Connaught Hotel and, 182; Freddie Fields and, 241; flop films of, 330; interest in playing James Bond, 144; Joseph Mankiewicz and, 152, 321; *When Time Runs Out*, 208

New Orleans, 153–54

Newsweek, 181, 199

New York, New York (movie), 92

New York City: shooting the *Superman* movies in, 200–201

New York Giants (baseball team), 26–27

New York magazine, 213

New York Times, 70, 98–99, 174, 212

Index

New York World, 4
Nicholson, Jack, 135
Niven, David, 143, 182
Niven, David, Jr., 179
Nixon, Richard, 83
Nizer, Louis, 120
No Country for Old Men (movie), 332
Nolte, Nick, 183, 184–85
North by Northwest (movie), 109, 302
Nothing in Common (movie), 285
Novak, Kim, 82
No Way Out (movie), 41–42
Nye, Carrie, 58

Oberon, Merle, 124
O'Brien, Edmond, 27–28, 34, 43
O'Brien, Joan, 55
O'Connor, Donald, 118
Offence, The (movie), 140
O'Halloran, Jack, 209, 215
O'Hara, Maureen, 50
Oliver Twist (movie), 123
Olivier, Laurence, 151, 152, 297, 308, 322
Olmedo, Alex, 102
Omen, The (movie), 175, 191, 204
One-Eyed Jacks (movie), 205–6, 296
On Her Majesty's Secret Service (movie), 164
opera, 36
Oppenheimer, Jerry and Gail, 175–76
Orbach, Jerry, 315–16
Oriental Hotel (Bangkok), 162
Out of Africa (movie), 272, 280, 329
Ovitz, Mike, 276; Creative Artists Agency and, 241, 298; *Ladyhawke*, 263; *Legal Eagles*, 278, 281–82; Tom Mankiewicz's move to Universal and, 277–78

Pakula, Alan, 72, 305
Palance, Holly, 196
Paley, Bill, 188

Paris, 31–32
Parker, Dorothy, 4
Parker, Sue, 148
Parks, Bert, 70
Parsons, Louella, 15–16
Parton, Dolly, 278
Passage to India, A (movie), 34
Pasternak, Joe, 94–95, 116
Paths of Glory (movie), 244–45
Patton, Gen. George, 303
Paul, Alexandra, 286–87
Peace Corps, 10
Pean, The (school yearbook), 38
Pearl (television miniseries), 222
Peck, Gregory, 6, 250, 331
Penn, Leo, 232
Penn, Sean, 261
Penny (dog), 307
"People" (song), 85–86
Peppard, Christian, 160
Peppard, George, 160, 333
Perkins, Anthony, 65, 250
Perrine, Valerie, 172, 193, 197, 216
Persuaders, The (television series), 144
Peter Island, 184
Petey (dog), 281
Pfeiffer, Michelle, 260–61, 264, 265
Philadelphia Story, The (movie), 18, 34
Phillips Exeter Academy, 37–38
Picker, David, 133, 135, 145, 155–56, 157, 240
Pierce, Fred, 221–22
Pierson, Frank, 304
Pinky (movie), 41
Places in the Heart (movie), 251
Planes, Trains and Automobiles (movie), 325
Please (script), 250–51
Pleasence, Donald, 180
Pleshette, Suzanne, 58, 222
Plimpton, George, Jr., 38
Plummer, Christopher, 12, 183, 197, 285–86, 288, 315
Poitier, Sidney, 41, 42, 83

poker, 53–54, 246–47
Pollack, Sydney, 251, 261, 272, 333
Polygram, 87
Ponti, Carlo, 119–20, 121, 177, 178
Poseidon Adventure, The (movie), 190
Poston, Tom, 58
Powers, Debbie, 118
Powers, Stefanie: Columbia studios
    and, 328; *Hart to Hart* television
    series, 222–23, 224, 225, 226–27,
    228, 231, 235, 236; William
    Holden on, 242; and Pope John
    Paul, 266–67; in Kenya, 32, 267,
    269, 272, 276; Tom Mankiewicz
    and, 32, 220, 337
Preminger, Otto, 16
prep school, 37–38
Pressure Point (movie), 103
Previn, André, 98
Price, Frank, 277, 278, 284, 285,
    291, 299, 329
Price, Vincent, 21
production companies, 188, 327–28
Profiles in Courage (Kennedy), 150
Promises, Promises (Broadway
    musical), 245
Provine, Dorothy, 306
Pryor, Richard, 154, 213, 253
psychoanalysts, 334–36
Pulp Fiction (movie), 332
Puzo, Mario, 183, 189

Quantum of Solace (movie), 166
Quiet American, The (movie), 63

race issues: *Live and Let Die* and,
    155–56, 157–58
racism: film industry and, 41; in
    Louisiana, 153–54
Rafelson, Bob, 275
Raffin, Deborah, 195
Raging Bull (movie), 175
Rainbow (script), 258
Ransohoff, Martin, 76
Rapf, Harry, 7
Rasche, David, 313

Rasputin, 32
Rat Race, The (movie), 240
Redford, Robert, 109, 152, 279–82,
    294, 297, 321
Redgrave, Vanessa, 167
red scare, 15
Reeve, Christopher: Sean Connery's
    advice to, 217; *Monsignor,* 218;
    paralysis, 216–17; the *Superman*
    movies, 194–96, 201–2, 208,
    213, 217–18
Reeve, Dana, 216, 217
Reiner, Carl, 306
Reitman, Ivan, 227, 278, 279, 281
Remick, Lee, 72
Reno Silver Sox (baseball team), 322
Reservoir Dogs (movie), 332
Reynal, Elizabeth, 5
Reynal, Eugene, 5
Reynolds, Burt, 144, 171, 188, 260,
    300, 320
Reynolds, Debbie, 118, 240
Richards, Dick, 320
Rickles, Don, 88, 95, 240, 241
Rigg, Diana, 164
Ritchie, Michael, 237
Riviera Hotel, 90
*Roar of the Greasepaint—and the
    Smell of the Crowd, The*
    (Broadway musical), 123
Robards, Jason, Jr., 129, 197,
    313–14
Roberts, Julia, 294
Roberts, Tanya, 212
Robertson, Cliff, 71
Robin and Marian (movie), 184
Robinson, Edward G., 6
Robinson, Frank, 27
Robinson, Sugar Ray, 224
Rocket, Charlie, 313
Rodgers, Richard, 25, 26
Rogers, Roy, 318–19
Roman Holiday (movie), 118, 331
Rome, 28–30, 62
Roquebrune, Micheline, 145
Rosemary's Baby (movie), 96

Rosenberg, Stuart, 72–73
Ross, Diana, 155
Ross, Steve, 328
Roth, Ron, 72, 73
Routh, Brandon, 215
Rowling, J. K., 330
Roy Rogers Museum, 318–19
Rubenstein, Arthur, 58
Runaway Boy (teleplay), 73
Russell, Kurt, 260, 262–63

Sager, Carole Bayer, 97
Saint, The (television series), 143–44
Salinger, J. D., 125, 330
Salkind, Alexander, 189, 191, 192,
    206–8, 209–10, 211
Salkind, Bertha, 192, 206–8
Salkind, Ilya, 189, 191, 192, 206,
    209, 213, 215
Saltzman, Harry: *Diamonds Are
    Forever,* 136–37, 144; *Live and
    Let Die,* 147, 148, 153, 154,
    156; *The Man with the Golden
    Gun,* 161–62; other films of,
    165; rights to the Bond movies
    and, 150; sells control of the
    Bond films to Broccoli, 165
Saltzman, Jackie, 137, 165
Samms, Emma, 313, 315
Samuels, Lesser, 41
Sands Hotel, 88–89
Santa Anita racetrack, 9
Sardi, Vincent, 99
Sargent, Joe, 289–90
Sartosha (schooner), 20
Saturday Night Live (television
    show), 176
Saturn Award, 219
Savalas, Telly, 170
Schaefer Ambulance Company,
    170–71
Schaffner, Franklin, 71
Schickel, Richard, 181
Schlatter, George, 80
Schlesinger, John, 261
Schoonmaker, Thelma, 229

Schubert Theater, 98
Schuler, Lauren, 260
Schwartz, Bernie. *See* Curtis, Tony
Schwartzman, Jack, 251
Schwarzenegger, Arnold, 319
Scorsese, Martin, 92, 93, 94, 175,
    229
Scotland, 141
Scott, George C., 237
Screen Directors Guild, 15–17
script supervisors, 232–33
Secret Life of Walter Mitty, The
    (movie), 115
Sedgwick, Edie, 125
See How They Run (D. Mankiewicz),
    11
Segal, George, 295
Segal, Marion, 295
Seitz, Maj. Gen. J. F. R., 302–3
Seitz, Raymond G. H., 302–3
Selleck, Tom, 320
Selznick, David O., 126–30
Semel, Terry, 151, 196, 212, 213,
    258–59, 266, 328
Seymour, Jane, 156
Shapiro, Bob, 258
Shaw, Robert, 136, 183–86
Shaw, Run Run, 161
Shaw Studios, 161
Sheedy, Ally, 253
Sheena, Queen of the Jungle (movie),
    212
Sheinberg, Sid, 328, 329
Sheldon, Sidney, 221, 235
Ship of Fools (movie), 160
Shiva, Gil and Susan, 125
Shriver, Sergeant, 10
Shuler, Lauren, 329
Simmons, Bob, 156
Simmons, Jean, 44–45
Simpson, Freddy, 63–64
Simpson, O. J., 178
Sinatra, Frank: birthday gift to Nancy,
    101; Jacqueline Bisset and, 96;
    on Sammy Davis Jr., 81; Ava
    Gardner and, 29, 30; on Judy

Garland, 108; *Guys and Dolls,* 44; Howard Hughes and, 138–39; Tom Mankiewicz and, 8, 84–87; *Movin' with Nancy,* 80; Jill St. John and, 145

Sinatra, Nancy, 80, 81, 86, 91, 94, 101

Singer, Bryan, 215, 219

Singin' in the Rain (movie), 116, 118

Skin Tight (script), 319–29

Skippy (movie), 4

Skouras, Spyro, 69

Sleeping with the Enemy (script), 298

Sleuth (movie), 151, 152, 322

Smith, Jeannie, 6

Snow, Mark, 229

Some Like It Hot (movie), 297–98

Somewhere in Time (movie), 217

Sopranos, The (television series), 170

Sorrentino's restaurant, 86

Spelling, Aaron: *Hart to Hart* television series, 14, 19, 221, 222, 224, 233–36; *Ladyhawke,* 260; Tom Mankiewicz's script *Please,* 251; *Vega$* television series, 256

Spengler, Pierre, 189, 193, 206, 209

Spiegel, Sam, 46

Spielberg, Steven, 33–34, 185, 258, 328, 329, 330

Splendor (boat), 308

Splendor in the Grass (movie), 308

Spy Who Loved Me, The (movie), 163, 164–65

Stacy, James, 87

Stamp, Terence, 197, 281

Stander, Lionel, 178, 224–25

Standing, John, 180–81, 191

Stark, Ray, 250, 252

Stealers Wheel, 89

Steinem, Gloria, 129

Stevens, Annie, 33, 252, 254, 259, 267, 278, 281, 304, 323

Stevens, Bobby, 281, 316, 323

Stevens, George, 16, 20, 60, 333

Stevens, Inger, 130

Stevens, Stella, 223, 224

Stewart, Jimmy, 6, 294

St. John, Jill, 136, 141, 142, 143, 145, 223, 224

Stoddard, Brandon, 230

Stone, Peter, 98, 102, 108, 122, 125

Stop the World (Broadway musical), 123

Storaro, Vittorio, 262, 265, 266

Stout, Tom, 246

Stradner, Rosa: children of, 5; cremation of, 249–50; family history of, 5–6; films of, 6; Louis Jourdan and, 38; life in the 1940s, 17–18; Joseph Mankiewicz and, 5, 6, 17–18, 26, 27, 28, 35; mental health, 5, 35, 38; opera and, 36; relationship with Tom, 6–7, 29, 38; religion and, 11; suicide, 38–40

Stravinsky, Igor, 127

Streep, Meryl, 280

Streisand, Barbra, 280

Stuart, Malcolm, 99

"Stuck in the Middle with You" (song), 89

stunts: in *Live and Let Die,* 156–57

Sturges, John, 179, 180

Styne, Jule, 175, 303

Suddenly, Last Summer (movie), 45–47, 322

Suddenly, Last Summer (Williams), 37

Sullavan, Margaret, 56

Summertime (movie), 32

Sundays and Cybele (movie), 127

Superman (movie): Marlon Brando, 202–9; the capsule speech, 202–4; casting, 189–98; cinematography and design, 198–99; cost of, 210–11; costumes, 199; Council of Elders, 204–5; making Superman

Superman (movie) *(cont.)*
fly, 201–2; Tom Mankiewicz's
credit as "creative consultant,"
218; Tom Mankiewicz's rewrite,
188–89, 199–200; opening,
211; practical jokes during, 202;
the Salkinds and, 189, 191, 192,
206–8, 209–10, 211; score, 211;
shooting of, 200–201, 211;
styles shot in, 199
Superman II (movie): cost of,
210–11; Dick Lester finishes
shooting, 212–13; Tom
Mankiewicz's credit as "creative
consultant," 218; E. G. Marshall
and, 122; the Salkinds cut
Brando out of, 214–15; shooting
of, 198, 211
Superman II: The Donner Cut
(DVD), 214–16, 218–19
Superman III (movie), 213
Superman IV: The Quest for Peace
(movie), 213
Superman Returns (movie), 219
Sutherland, Donald, 179, 181
Sweet Ride, The (movie), 94–97
Sweet Smell of Success (movie), 240
Swink, Bob, 71

Taking the Heat (Showtime movie),
323–25
Tales from the Crypt (HBO series),
112, 319
Tall Story (movie), 250
Tandy, Jessica, 301
Tarantino, Quentin, 332–33
tarot, 152–53
Tartikoff, Brandon, 256, 257
Taylor, Elizabeth: Chasen's chili and,
8; *Cleopatra*, 8, 60–61, 63–64,
65–67, 140; relationship with
Richard Burton, 62–63, 65,
66–67; *Suddenly, Last Summer*,
46, 47
Technicolor, 137
television industry: actors' production

companies and, 188; impact of
Desi Arnaz on, 187–88
10 (movie), 295
Tender Is the Night (Fitzgerald), 128
Thailand, 161–62
Thatcher, Margaret, 191
That's Entertainment (movie), 94
There Was a Crooked Man (movie),
322
"This Guy's in Love with You"
(song), 89
Thomopoulos, Tony, 223
Three Days of the Condor (movie), 170
Three Musketeers (movie), 191
Thulin, Ingrid, 178
Thunderball (movie), 150
Tierney, Gene, 21
Tijuana Brass, 14
Timber (dog), 14–15
Time magazine, 9–10, 181
To Catch a Thief (movie), 302
Todd, Mike, 47
Tom Jones (movie), 145
Tonight Show, The (television show),
70
Too Late Blues (movie), 103
Tootsie (movie), 261
Tormé, Mel, 107
Torres, Eddie, 139
Toy, The (movie), 154
Tracy, Lee, 71
Tracy, Spencer, 20, 51
TriStar studios, 251–53
Truman, Harry, 130–31
Tucker, Richard, 36
Turman, Larry, 71, 105
Tutu, Desmond, 275–76
20th Century Fox studios: *Cleopatra*
and, 60–61, 69–70; in the
1940s, 19
21 Club, 59–60
Two for the Road (movie), 96–97
2000 Year Old Man (album), 306

United Artists, 327–28
Universal Studios, 277–78, 328–29

Unsworth, Geoffrey, 196, 198–99, 200, 227
Ure, Mary, 184
Urich, Robert, 256, 257

Vajna, Andy, 121, 177, 179
Valkenvania (script), 296
Veevers, Wally, 199
Vega$ (television series), 256, 257
Vidal, Gore, 37–38, 45, 72, 76
Visit, The (play), 121
Visit to a Small Planet (Vidal), 37
Voight, Jon, 195

Wagner, Robert "R. J.": advice to Tom Mankiewicz about directing, 339; co-ownership of *Charlie's Angels,* 233–34, 236; *Delirious,* 313; *Hart to Hart* television series, 222, 224, 226–27, 228, 231, 233–34, 235, 236; Gene Kelly and, 116–17; Tom Mankiewicz and, 20; as a movie star, 294; *Runaway Boy,* 73; *What Price Glory,* 51; Natalie Wood and, 220, 305, 308–10
Walden Robert Cassotto (album), 104
Walken, Christopher, 308, 309
Wallace, Adelaide, 56
Wanger, Walter, 63, 69
War and Remembrance (movie), 247
Warden, Jack, 131
War Games (movie), 253–54
Warhol, Andy, 125
Warner Brothers: Clint Eastwood and, 187; housekeeping deals, 328, 329; Tom Mankiewicz on, 327, 328, 329; Tom Mankiewicz's script fixing, 257–60; the *Superman* movies and, 211
Warren, Lesley Ann, 195
Wasserman, Edie, 303
Wasserman, Lew, 291, 292, 303–5, 308, 328, 329
Watling, Dilys, 97

Wayne, John, 40, 50–51, 52, 53, 54, 55
Way We Were, The (movie), 280
Weaver, Dennis, 169, 170
Webb, Jack, 288–89
Webley, Mike, 271–72
Weird Science (movie), 325
Weiss, Bob, 289
Welch, Raquel, 172–73
Weld, Tuesday, 75–79, 129, 183, 251, 295, 335
Welles, Orson, 204–5, 297
Wells, Frank, 257
Werner, Tom, 223
Westchester, 38–40
Westerman, Joe, 317
Wexler, Haskell, 71–72
What Price Glory (movie), 51
When Time Runs Out (movie), 208
Whitman, Stuart, 52, 54
Who's Afraid of Virginia Woolf? (play), 106
Widmark, Richard, 41, 42, 247, 314
Wiener, Jack, 179
Wildenstein, Alec, 271
Wilder, Billy, 16, 297–98, 321
William Holden Wildlife Foundation, 276
Williams, Esther, 256
Williams, John, 211, 229–30
Williams, Tennessee, 45
Williams, Treat, 181
Williamstown Summer Theater, 57, 58–59
Willis, Gordon, 297
Wilson, Michael, 165
Winger, Debra, 278, 280, 281, 282, 298
Winter Garden Theater, 98
Winters, Shelley, 95
Wise, Robert, 61, 327
Wizard of Oz, The (movie), 110
Wolders, Rob, 124
Wolfe, Thomas, 14
Wolper, David L., 79, 119
Woman of the Year (movie), 20

Wood, Lana, 164

Wood, Natalie: *Cassandra at the Wedding*, 127; co-ownership of *Charlie's Angels*, 233–34, 236; death and funeral of, 308–10; Marlene Dietrich and, 241; John Frankenheimer and, 128; Richard Gregson and, 306–7; *Hart to Hart* television series, 222, 223; Arthur Loew Jr. and, 119; Tom Mankiewicz and, 6, 7, 22, 99, 171, 219, 220, 240, 305–6, 307, 309–11; Robert Wagner and, 220, 305, 308–10; Lew Wasserman and, 303

Woodward, Joanne, 128, 204

World, the Flesh, and the Devil, The (movie), 130

writer-directors, 297

Writers Guild, 218, 234–35

Wyler, William, 16, 23, 69, 75, 118, 321

Wynn, Tracy Keenan, 186, 198

Wynter, Dana, 269

Xanax, 334

X-Men (movie), 295

Yale University, 40, 56, 59, 130–31

Yates, Peter: *Bullitt*, 96; *The Deep*, 183, 184, 185, 186, 187; as a director, 229; *Mother, Jugs & Speed*, 171, 173–74, 175, 176

York, Susannah, 205, 214, 215–16

Yorkin, Bud, 167

Young, Loretta, 18

Young, Terence, 163

"Younger Than Springtime" (song), 84

You Only Live Twice (movie), 144

Yusupov, Prince Felix, 31–32

Zanuck, Darryl F., 7, 18–19, 41, 42, 69

Zareen (jaguar), 122

Zemeckis, Robert, 319

Zepfel, Don, 289

Ziffren, John, 228

Ziffren, Paul, 74, 104, 309

Zinnemann, Fred, 16

Zukerman, Pinchas, 79

Zukor, Adolph, 118–19

Zweibel, Alan, 284

SCREEN CLASSICS

Screen Classics is a series of critical biographies, film histories, and analytical studies focusing on neglected filmmakers and important screen artists and subjects, from the era of silent cinema to the golden age of Hollywood to the international generation of today. Books in the Screen Classics series are intended for scholars and general readers alike. The contributing authors are established figures in their respective fields. This series also serves the purpose of advancing scholarship on film personalities and themes with ties to Kentucky.

SERIES EDITOR
Patrick McGilligan

BOOKS IN THE SERIES
Hedy Lamarr: The Most Beautiful Woman in Film
  Ruth Barton
Von Sternberg
  John Baxter
The Marxist and the Movies: A Biography of Paul Jarrico
  Larry Ceplair
Warren Oates: A Wild Life
  Susan Compo
Being Hal Ashby: Life of a Hollywood Rebel
  Nick Dawson
Raoul Walsh: The True Adventures of Hollywood's Legendary Director
  Marilyn Ann Moss
Some Like It Wilder: The Life and Controversial Films of Billy Wilder
  Gene D. Phillips
Arthur Penn: American Director
  Nat Segaloff
Claude Rains: An Actor's Voice
  David J. Skal with Jessica Rains
Buzz: The Life and Art of Busby Berkeley
  Jeffrey Spivak
Thomas Ince: Hollywood's Independent Pioneer
  Brian Taves
Carl Theodor Dreyer and Ordet: *My Summer with the Danish Filmmaker*
  Jan Wahl